CLOSE TO THE EDGE
THE STORY OF

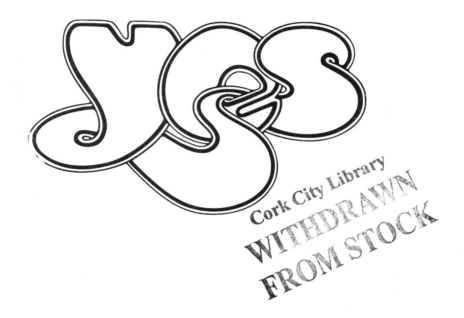

CHRIS WELCH

OMNIBUS PRESS
London / New York / Sydney

Copyright © 2000 Omnibus Press
(A Division of Book Sales Limited)

Edited by Chris Charlesworth
Cover design by Martyn Dean
Yes logo Roger Dean © 1973, 1999
Picture research by Nikki Russell and Chris Welch

ISBN: 0.7119.8041.1
Order No: OP 48180

Exclusive Distributors
Book Sales Limited,
8/9 Frith Street,
London W1V 5TZ, UK.

Music Sales Corporation,
257 Park Avenue South,
New York, NY 10010, USA.

The Five Mile Press,
22 Summit Road,
Noble Park,
Victoria 3174, Australia.

To the Music Trade only:
Music Sales Limited,
8/9 Frith Street,
London W1V 5TZ, UK.

Photo credits:
Every effort has been made to trace the copyright holders of the photographs in this book but one or two were unreachable. We would be grateful if the photographers concerned would contact us.

Printed by MPG Books, Bodmin, Cornwall
Typeset by Galleon Typesetting, Ipswich

A catalogue record for this book is available from the British Library.

Visit Omnibus Press on the web at www.omnibuspress.com

For Marilyne & Steven

Contents

Acknowledgements

During the many months spent doing interviews, researching and writing *Close To The Edge* I was given generous help and assistance by a large number of Yes people, including members of the band both past and present, friends and associates. Particular thanks are due to Jim Halley, the band's tireless co-ordinator and personal assistant to Steve Howe, who spent many hours on the telephone helping to locate scattered interviewees around the globe, from Switzerland to Kauai, from Seattle to Boston and from Florida to Los Angeles. He also provided encouragement with what proved an increasingly massive task and offered many examples of Yes memorabilia as well as insight into the life of a touring band.

Special thanks go to Peter Banks for his stories of the formative years, told with his customary humour and perspicacity. Jack Barrie, once the manager of the Marquee and La Chasse clubs, was happy to talk about his crucial role in bringing Chris and Jon together and the support he gave when Yes was just an idea. Roy Flynn spoke for the first time about his role as the band's first manager and once again proved to be a generous host. Bill Bruford gave freely of his time to reminisce about the good and the bad times of the band he still loves. Jon Anderson, Steve Howe, Chris Squire, Alan White, Billy Sherwood and their newest member Igor Khoroshev all spent many hours helping me understand the important changes in the band's career and the meaning and progression of their music. Steve in particular was most helpful, as he has been since his earliest days in the band, and Chris gave me perhaps our best interview since we flew to Berlin on a Comet! Patrick Moraz enthusiastically described his tenure with the band during the important *Relayer* era. Trevor Horn and Geoff Downes spoke incisively about their dramatic intervention during the early Eighties. Trevor Rabin was most helpful in assessing his crucial contribution when Yes enjoyed some of their greatest hits. Many thanks also to Rick Wakeman who spent an afternoon sharing Yes stories while he was in the throes of putting together *Return To The Centre Of The Earth*. Not long after our interview Rick was taken seriously ill and hospitalised.

This time he couldn't blame the curry — we only had a cup of tea and a cheese sandwich! And thanks to Adam Wakeman for tales of his close encounter with dad's old band, and to Candy Atcheson, Rick's assistant.

Thanks are also due to all the Yes associates and friends who proved so helpful, notably Brian Lane, Phil Carson, Roger Dean, Michael Tait, Roy Clair, Tony Dimitriades, and Lewis Kovak of Left Bank management; also Sally Gavaghan at Atlantic Records. Much appreciation goes to Clifford Loeslin, long time fan and expert on all matters Yes who boosted the discography to encyclopaedic proportions. Tanya Coad, co-founder of *Relayer*, the world's first Yes fanzine, kindly gave permission to quote from her proposed book on Jon Anderson while singer/researcher Dan Duggan became a Yes fan after spending hours trawling the archives. Thanks also to David Watkinson of Yesterdays Collectables (e-mail: david@yes.k2net.co.uk) for his help with the discography, and to Reinhard and Renate Sauer and their son Arne for their assistance while I was staying in Reinbek in Germany.

Special thanks go to Chris Charlesworth and Andrew King at Omnibus Press for their help and patience with a project they initially conceived as a 'single' that grew into a concept album — if you see what I mean. Well, that's progressive rock for you!

Finally the author would like to offer special thanks to Jon Anderson for his encouragement, good vibes and much valued friendship over so many years and to thank all the 14 members of Yes who played in the band from 1968 to 1998 for so much wonderful music and so many wondrous stories.

Chris Welch, West Wickham, Kent, England 1999

1

BEYOND AND BEFORE

OVERTURE

"I don't believe it – he's eating a curry!" Jon Anderson's jaw drops. Clad in brilliant white robes, bathed in laser beams and facing a vast audience, the singer pauses in mid song to glare across the stage. Yes are in the throes of a thunderous performance, their music cascading around them from dozens of speaker cabinets, a great swirl of amplified guitars, keyboards and drums. But instead of concentrating on the depths and intricacies of their masterwork *Tales From Topographic Oceans*, Rick Wakeman, their berobed keyboard wizard, is cheerfully chomping on a chicken Byriani.

While Jon is singing his Lancashire heart out to admiring crowds, his star sideman is once again staging a private rebellion. Handily placed on top of the banks of keyboards before him, where you might normally expect to find a pile of sheet music or at least the racing results, is Rick's supper. And he's tucking in. Is this a simple prank, or a calculated act of defiance?

Of course, it could be dismissed as a carnivore's protest at the vegetarian food served back stage. Jon and his guitarist Steve Howe are both high profile veggies while Rick is a steak, chips and six pints of beer man – or was before his first heart attack. Only later does it emerge that Wakeman was undergoing the kind of pressure that many members of this extraordinary band have endured over the years. The pressure caused by the constant struggle for perfection. The pressure caused by his leader's constant cry of "Get it right!"

No band in the history of rock has dedicated itself to creating original music with quite the same intensity as Yes. In the process they have produced some of the most richly satisfying, exciting and challenging work of their era. The cost has been the shredding of nerves and battering of personalities. Yet amid the rows and upsets, the strife and torment, that have beset their thirty extraordinary years together, there have been wondrous songs, spectacular stage shows and chart topping records, all of

1

which has endeared them to a vast following of loyal fans throughout the world.

And in this band that is so often and somewhat mistakenly regarded as the epitome of earnest intent, there has also been a good deal of comradeship and laughter. Indeed, it was frequent outbreaks of mirth that kept them sane as they hit the road to fame. Whether it was crazed exploits in Ireland, an aborted gig next to a pork abattoir, setting up cardboard cows in their recording studio or erecting Red Indian tepees in the dressing rooms, there was always more cause for hysterical fun than gloomy despair.

There is also a dark fascination concerning the moments of crisis that have faced Yes, the details of which have until now invariably been concealed from public scrutiny. Such matters are investigated herein, and revelations of turmoil exposed for the first time might place the individuals in the group in a new and not always flattering light. But for most of their career they have enjoyed tremendous success and experienced the good times and euphoric happiness that only a transcendingly brilliant stage performance, a stunning hit single or a blockbuster album can bring.

It can never be said that Yes have been a party to the violence, drug busts, arrests and the general lawlessness that are *de rigeur* in most rock band sagas. Theirs is truly no disgrace. Well, there was the time when the drummer hit the bass player – but then you would expect a little tension in a band that has been going strong since 1968 and was still busy winning new audiences in 1998.

The story of Yes sometimes appears as complex as much of their music. Behind it all lies a simple truth, as Jon Anderson is wont to explain, "Yes – life is worth living. Yes – life is exciting and wondrous. Don't let go of your dreams and your ideology. That is what Yes is really all about."

FIRST MOVEMENT

Yes were born and nurtured in the fertile soil of the British rock scene of the psychedelic Sixties. It was a time when idealism and increased playing skills combined to produce some of the most exciting and intensely creative music devised beyond the realms of jazz and the classics.

Dubbed leaders of 'progressive rock', Yes were at the forefront of this new musical movement. Although hailed as pioneers of the genre, they didn't really sound or play like any other band. An intense drive for perfection amongst its members actually turned an ordinary, albeit prodigiously talented, pop covers group into something quite extraordinary. Their fairly rapid progress from the tiny clubs and bars of London's West End to huge stadium rock venues around the world would see a whole procession of eager, ambitious and gifted musicians drawn into the Yes environment. Each would make a vital contribution and themselves become part of Yes lore.

Many would find their stay a mixed blessing. Some who came and went were shattered by the experience and have yet to fully recover. Yet all regard their stay in the band as the most important years of their musical lives. Yes would also mean a lifetime's work and experience to various non-musicians who became part of the team. Former and current managers, technicians, graphic artists and road crew all regard Yes with a mixture of affection, respect, awe and occasionally anger. The anger stems from what they see as misjudgements and missed opportunities. But then they wouldn't be angry unless they really cared. And people associated with Yes do care. Their affection and loyalty towards the band was invariably rewarded when the group somehow managed to pluck victory from the jaws of disaster, and come back in triumph when their house of cards seemed certain to collapse.

To Jon Anderson and Chris Squire, who created the band, Yes is not just a group. It is an entity, a kind of living being. For them above all the others, the battle to keep its heart pulsing would become a crusade. Even when Jon was physically absent from the band on at least two occasions, his presence was the glue that held it all together. When Jon first quit the band in 1980 his manager Brian Lane told the remaining members of Yes, "You should get down on your knees and kiss Jon Anderson's feet and beg him to come back."

Yes is a band that has constantly rebuilt itself from within. Such a process inevitably fuels arguments which lead to resentments, some lasting for years. Yet the end result has nearly always been music of such quality it has inspired tremendous love and loyalty from its fans and continuing respect from fellow musicians. There was a time when every aspiring young musician with the ability to contribute wanted nothing more than to be a part of Yes – but once on board the roundabout the centrifugal force could fling off all but the most tenacious.

Says Jon Anderson, "One of the reasons the band has survived this crazy music business more or less intact is because there has been this guiding force. When you start making music that is neither sex, drugs and rock'n'roll nor politically correct but is more spiritual, then it becomes like a crusade. The aim has been to create very good music and at the same time create a good message that the word 'yes' implies. We have had to do battle all the way through even though it's been a good fight. It still is a good fight. There have been times when people have said, 'Why don't you sell more records, why don't you make a pop hit?' And I've actually tried to and it never worked. So I've just continued on the path that has been set out for me and at least I've been true to that ideal. At many times during the course of our career there have been very sobering moments . . . especially when we got to the Cork pork abattoir!"

Yes at their peak epitomised the sound and fury of the Great Age of Rock Excess. Yet they started out as a penniless covers band, scuffling for gigs and living in squalor. It was the vision of Anderson and Squire that led them to create what they saw as the ultimate supergroup. Says the more pragmatic Chris Squire, "If ever there was a blueprint for the band it was to be able to have good instrumentals and vocal harmonies as well." It was a simple enough policy that would lead to magical perform-ances of semi-mystical songs and extended works. 'Heart Of The Sun-rise', 'I've Seen All Good People', 'Yours Is No Disgrace', 'Siberian Khatru' . . . these are themes that once performed stay in people's con-sciousness, to emerge like bursts of sunshine evaporating the fog of mediocrity.

During their glory years they sold albums by the ton. *Fragile*, *Close To The Edge* and *Tales From Topographic Oceans* caused a sensation during the Seventies. The band packed out concert halls and stadiums on tours that broke all attendance records. And then, during their unexpected renais-sance in the mid-Eighties, new recruit Trevor Rabin ensured Yes had even greater success with the smash hit single 'Owner Of A Lonely Heart' and their dance influenced *90125* album.

Yes was always more than just another 'stadium rock' battle wagon. They constantly changed and absorbed new influences while retaining their basic beliefs. Particularly important to their fans was the way Yes exuded a seductive, mystical image in which brute strength was countered by frailty, melody by discord, innocence by aggression. This ebbing and flowing of musical moods was notably complemented by the wondrous fantasy world created by artist Roger Dean, whose work graced many of their most important album covers. The famed swirling, almost Dali-esque, Yes logo and graphics he devised became an instantly recognisable symbol for their band and their music, so much so that whenever Dean worked for other artists their albums invariably looked like Yes albums.

Jon Anderson's enigmatic lyrics also set the band apart. Eschewing more common rock themes like romantic love or the angst of adolescent confu-sion, he wrote virtual sound poems, awash with words rich in imagery that defied logical interpretation and contained the sort of fabulous motifs that the receptive could appreciate and the rest could absorb as simply a part of the band's overall sound. *Yes − but what does it mean?* The answer was − whatever you wanted it to mean.

According to the founding fathers, the stated aim of Yes was to be a 'selfless' band in which the music was put above the aspirations of the individuals. This noble but demanding ideal resulted in the many dramatic changes of direction and personnel that have enlivened their career. It was amazing. Here foregathered were the most charming and civilised of English gentlemen, yet there was hardly another bunch like them for upsets and disturbances. To the best of my knowledge, every single member, including the lead singer, has stomped off, quit or been fired at least once and in some cases twice or even three times!

There have been no less than 14 full time Yes men since the group first assembled in 1968, and a scattering of shadowy figures in the background that have undergone periodic reshuffles. Although there have only been two significant Yes drummers powering the engine room, there have been at least three lead guitarists, a brace of singers and innumerable keyboard players. By 1998, the year that marked their 30th anniversary, only bass player, singer, composer and founder member Chris Squire had remained continuously on board the roundabout.

Squire, the tall, friendly giant is usually regarded as the quietest, most equable Yes person. Jon Anderson is perceived as the leader, the spokesman and the keeper of the flame. However even Jon, gentle poet, mystic and lover of mushy peas, has twice quit the band in high dudgeon. When it comes to rows it seems none are more prone to bust-ups than the old firm of Anderson and Squire. During one extraordinary period of infighting, Jon even fronted an alternative, rebel outfit which assembled in Europe under the name of ABWH – Anderson, Bruford, Wakeman & Howe.

Although they sounded like a firm of lawyers, in fact they held out a promise of rekindling the flames of creativity, until rock biz politics intervened. Meanwhile Chris Squire retained the Yes name and led another version of the band in California with 'new' guitarist Trevor Rabin. And so for a while there was a Yes in the West and a Yes in Europe. Rabin had actually been the power base of a revitalised Yes for some nine years at this point, though his very presence in Yes was enough to cause apoplexy in Steve Howe, a man whose sole *raison d'être* would seem to be the furthering of his extraordinary dexterity on fretted instruments. Still, when you probe deeply enough, you find even mild mannered Steve has trodden on a few toes in his time. Yet, somehow, against all odds, the two factions came together again to smoke a pipe of peace and a Yes that once more featured both Anderson and Squire finally came together for their *Union* tour in the early Nineties.

When the smoke had cleared, Chris Squire emerged as the real power behind the throne. Unless, of course, you talked to Jon Anderson first. So it seems odd, given the air of love and peace always mooted to be at the heart of Yes music and expressed in the lyrics so endlessly debated by eager fans, that there should be a prevailing atmosphere of feuding and dissent. The ascerbic Bill Bruford, bruised by his experiences in ABWH, has his own explanation.

"There are seething undercurrents in Yes," says Bruford. "Only very few people surely can have failed to see behind the love and peace? If you took the group only at that level, then you'd have to wonder where all that aggressive playing came from for a start. There has been some severely aggressive playing in Yes. It is an interesting irony that there is all this love and peace and hippiedom, whereas in fact Yes is a very tight, highly structured, nerve-wracking organisation always short of money and always spending too much and always in trouble, which is eventually reflected in the music. If they had better inter-personal skills and better management things might have been different. Yes has always been dogged by this short term vision and crippled by extremely bad management in the past. That has had its effects on the music which is why in 1998 they are still playing *Close To The Edge* from 1972."

SECOND MOVEMENT

On April 22, 1998, Jon Anderson sits in a communal rest area back stage at Croydon's Fairfield Halls during the band's *Open Your Eyes* tour of England. He is tired and suffering from a cold. He and the revitalised band, complete with new Russian keyboard player Igor Khoroshev and additional guitarist Billy Sherwood, have been on the road for weeks. It is good to see him for the first time in ages. As Jon enters the room, which is filled with rather glum roadies mulling over egg and chips, the darkness fades and the place lights up with his smile. I suddenly remember Jon and his first wife Jenny struggling to get past a pram in the hall of their tiny flat in London's Cromwell Road. That was in the summer of 1970 and we were off to find a restaurant. There we sat for one of many far reaching conversations laced with wine and laughter. Jon was smoking Benson & Hedges and mulling over the prospects for the band. The tape recorder was whirling while he talked excitedly about some new piece of music he'd discovered or written. I remember him once asking me, "Chris . . . what does Topographic mean?"

It's amazing how much can flash through your mind in the time it takes to shake hands and sit down. "Make it funny," was Jon's only injunction when I told him about my plans to write a book about the band.

"There was a time when I was thinking of giving music up completely and going to live in China," he blurts out. I am shocked. Such has been the stress and strain of trying to keep the Yes dream alive for all these years. It seems that Jon, the incurable optimist, the romantic dreamer, has been close to the edge of despair. But he met a new lady friend who urged him, "You are a musician. This is what you do. You've got to carry on."

It was all the encouragement Jon needed. He forgot about carving a new life in the Far East and returned to singing. Old mates and some new faces helped him recreate the magical, timeless sound of Yes. Jon gets up from the table. He's got to forget the past for a moment and try to forget his cold. His audience awaits. "Why don't you come on the road with us?" he asks as he heads for the stage. Where were they going? "South America!" Alas Croydon would be the extent of my 1998 tour with Yes.

But what had caused Jon to even consider giving up? The answers came in dribs and drabs, as I spoke to band members both past and present over the coming months. It proved to be far more than just a story of a big rock band buffeted by the winds of change.

Of course they'd had their share of knocks. Once punk rock overturned prog rock they had to abandon the big, epic productions of the Seventies that had once seemed so . . . progressive. The mid Eighties saw Yes streamlined, modernised and relevant to a new world order. During their Indian summer, Yes were hip again. Come the Nineties there was a general unwillingness by the media to even acknowledge their existence. Jon tells how his management phoned a major music company on Yes business and were greeted with the reply, "Yes? Who are Yes?"

A band that has been making records, touring and shaping the course of rock music for thirty years expects a few snubs and humiliations along the way but they don't deserve to be ignored and forgotten, not when the music they have made is so special and worth all the pain that has so often accompanied its creation.

So we are not talking about any old English rock band from the Sixties here. This is Yes – creator of 'And You And I', 'Heart Of The Sunrise' and 'Long Distance Runaround' – soaring, dynamic and very special music. Sometimes they overreached themselves. Sometimes studio perfection came at the price of spontaneity. But there isn't one track on any of their albums or singles that does not have something to say and that does not bear the Yes stamp of originality.

THIRD MOVEMENT

Yes mesmerised me when I first saw them play, on the night of November 26, 1968. They were booked to support Cream at their farewell concert at London's Royal Albert Hall and they blew the audience away with an astonishingly mature and confident performance. I became a fan and was determined to trumpet their cause to all who would listen – or read.

I wasn't the only Yes fan in the media. There were plenty of other rock critics who recognised the potential of a group who sang in near perfect harmony (when they finally got some monitor speakers) and played with all the dynamic power and subtlety of a big band. Tony Wilson, my colleague on *Melody Maker,* was also an enthusiastic and perspicacious Yes man. He was invited to write the sleeve notes for the band's début album. It's worth quoting his comments to emphasise the impact Yes made on the scene.

'At the beginning of 1969 I was asked to pick two groups who I thought would make it in the following year. One of my choices was Led Zeppelin. A bit obvious perhaps, but then we all like to back a winner occasionally. The other was YES. I'd just heard them in a London discotheque where all too often the groups tend to be over amplified and under talented. Yes were not. They had much more than the usual wallpaper music sound. There was life, virility and musicianship in their approach. They had a superior vocal sound — assured, clear and harmonic. They knew what they were doing and did it with style. It showed in their own songs and imaginative arrangements. It all shows on this, their first album. So Yes became my other choice. My second runner in the Great Group Most Likely To Make It Stakes. And my money is on them! Naturally I've watched them with special interest — the Marquee, the Speakeasy, in concert with Janis Joplin and Cream. Totally convinced after these events, my choice is confirmed.' Tony Wilson.

Tony was quick to pinpoint the special qualities of the band that everyone was talking about. One of the first non-American acts to be signed to Atlantic Records, they were clearly destined to be huge. At least that's the way it seemed to everybody except the band themselves, who knew the reality of living on handouts, helpful girlfriends and a few grubby pound notes doled out by grudging promoters.

What seemed so fresh about Yes to Tony Wilson was the way they brought together such a broad and unexpected range of influences, from folk to jazz and rock and made it all sound new, fresh and attractive. They were already playing advanced arrangements. Here were songs that stopped and started with nerve shattering suddenness, paused for reflection and then stormed back again with all guns blazing.

Songs like The Byrds' 'I See You', Paul Simon's 'America' and Lennon and McCartney's 'Every Little Thing' were given the Yes treatment. They re-arranged songs by taking them apart, dissecting the verses and choruses and rebuilding them as pieces with several layers, extending instrumental bridges, adding harmonies to a hitherto familiar single voice, and placing a sudden, unexpected emphasis where before there was none. It was an approach that contrasted sharply to the kind of one dimensional, locomotive rumbling of the average 'beat group'.

Of course it wasn't all original thinking, and — like the ensembles that followed — the original Yes quintet brought together a wide variety of disparate influences. The Who under the aegis of Pete Townshend, especially their extended works, inspired original guitarist Peter Banks. The free-flowing Jimi Hendrix Experience was an influence, as were The Nice with Keith Emerson. Jon Anderson loved classy performers like Frank Sinatra and Paul McCartney. Chris Squire liked The Fifth Dimension, The Byrds and The Beatles. Drummer Bill Bruford was into Miles Davis. Yes were cool. They could dig it. They were also very together. They were ready to take ideas and push them someplace else.

And they had the musical firepower to make their ideas work. The earliest Yes line-up became the articulate voice of the post-Flower Power generation. They appealed to the intelligence of their audience, considered a dangerous move in rock'n'roll. It was all done with infectious enthusiasm and zeal. When Yes took a piece of music and reshaped it into a concert piece, Yes weren't being 'pretentious'. They were being true to themselves.

Rare colour film of the band during this period shows a shockingly young looking bunch of 20 year olds acting more like The Monkees than serious prog-rockers. A clip of Bill Bruford in a studio, cigarette between his lips, blond hair flying and roaring over his drum kit during a storming performance of 'No Opportunity Necessary, No Experience Needed' is the epitome of pop cool!

Peter Banks' guitar style was at the core of early Yes music and set standards that have been adhered to ever since. His playing, rich in improvisational skill and tonal ingenuity, shone through the first two albums *Yes* (1969) and *Time And A Word* (1970). Steve Howe, who replaced Peter, would become the guitar star most readily associated with Yes. His output was astonishing on a huge mass of work from *The Yes Album, Fragile* and *Close To The Edge* to *Tales From Topographic Oceans, Relayer, Going For The One* and more. Trevor Rabin, who took over the Banks/Howe tradition in the Eighties, would spearhead the Yes revival and help create some of their best selling music.

Tony Kaye, the band's ebullient first keyboard player, was a master of the funky organ sound. His swirling crescendos and classical flourishes established what became the pattern for keyboard playing in Yes. Even the more technically capable Rick Wakeman who joined later would pay tribute to Tony's contribution, while Geoffrey Downes continued in the tradition with his own richly rhapsodic playing.

Bill Bruford was something special. He wasn't just a great young percussionist with a sharp and intelligent mind, he was a vibrant, sometimes even abrasive personality; practical where others were scatty, eminently sensible when others weren't. His background, education and instincts meant that he tended to be amused by rather than hung up on the rock

9

and roll lifestyle. A jazz fan for whom Philly Jo Jones and Max Roach meant more than Keith Moon, Bill was enthusiastic about the opportunities Yes offered. Alas, he quickly tired of the regimented discipline that lay behind the laissez faire, hippie idealism. It was a great shock when he decided to quit the band to join King Crimson in August, 1972. His replacement, Alan White, came just in time to power up the band in readiness for its onslaught on American touring. His powerhouse playing and rock steady beat were all that Yes needed to enter their second phase.

The old firm of Anderson and Squire has reigned over Yes since the days when they were called Mabel Greer's Toyshop. Jon, from Accrington in Lancashire, is a soft spoken man for whom Yes became a medium through which to express his own pent up love of emotional, joyous music. Stravinsky, Sibelius, Frank Sinatra and The Beatles are all sources of inspiration for Jon. Warm and gentle in character, Jon has long aspired to different religions and varieties of mysticism, and he was a natural convert to the hippie idealism of the Sixties which sought to unify all religious beliefs into a kind of single Earth spirit. Yet Jon is also a hustler, a hardened music business pro, fully aware that if he doesn't exert his authority others might try to use or abuse him. As a bandleader he has been called 'a little Napoleon' but he could bring together warring factions and instil order – most of the time. Although he was unable to write or read scores or even play an instrument with any great skill, he could sing like a bird, and exhort his players to turn personal flights of fancy into playable form, into magnificent reality.

If his determination to succeed and create would earn him a reputation for being a stickler and a disciplinarian, then it was no worse a reputation than any other truly successful bandleader before him. What some found shocking was his ability to make sudden, abrupt decisions that directly affected their lives. Invariably they were for the best reasons. During innumerable conversations with Jon over the years, the message has clearly emerged that it was never his intention to hurt anybody. Ever. He still regrets some of his actions. But he always knew that if Yes was to survive and have a future, then firm decisions would have to be taken. And Jon, with the ready laugh and angelic voice, had the power to decide.

Chris Squire, Jon's long term vocal partner, is perhaps the most enigmatic Yes man. Slower than most to show his feelings or reveal his inner thoughts, he can nevertheless sometimes appear impatient and agitated. Eager for a laugh as much as the next muso, there is a more calculating air about the man who has actually held Yes together since it started. While others chatter and scamper around at his feet in a frenzy of emotional activity, Chris remains laid back and impassive. There are probably very good reasons for his gentle giant demeanour. Tall people quickly learn that unless they are very careful they can knock people and things over very easily. Better to approach life at a slower pace. Less risk of damage. But this apparent slow down of the body clock can be infuriating to others.

Quite early in the band's formative years Chris gained the nickname Fish, simply because he spent too long luxuriating in the bath. Okay when you are living alone, but when you are living with an entire band and various girlfriends, who have to get ready for the next gig, and there is only one bathroom in a shared flat, then tempers get frayed. Doubtless Mr. Squire got called worse names than Fish when the group were packed together in their flat in Munster Road, Fulham. Some complained at the way he consumed the band's precious resources. But then it was Chris and Jon who had put the band together. They were entitled to reap the rewards of their labours, and to take their time in the bath.

What Chris brought to Yes, apart from his unshakeable power as one of the three great British rock bass guitarists (along with Jack Bruce and John Entwistle), was his dogged determination to keep the whole thing going. And yet, you could never quite pinpoint a decision making moment. "Things just happened – behind the scenes," says one band member. Whatever happened to Yes, you could be sure that Chris, above all others, would keep his eye on the ball.

Sometimes the ball seemed in danger of going out of touch. Peter Banks and Tony Kaye were early victims of Yes purges. When Bill Bruford left of his own accord, just as the band were enjoying major success, it was a big shock. Yet replacements arrived in a steady stream and the group continued to prosper. All became accepted as part of the Yes family from the moment they joined but as we shall see, it was a family frequently at war. When Rick Wakeman left to concentrate on his solo career, it was an even greater blow than Bill's departure. The group hastily recruited Patrick Moraz who stayed for three productive years. But when Rick came home again he brought his own very special charisma as well as his keyboard talents. Patrick would find a more comfortable home with The Moody Blues.

More dramatic still was the moment at the end of the Seventies when Jon Anderson quit and Rick left for the second time. How was it possible that the voice of Yes, surely the key element in their unique sound, could leave the group? And how could they carry on as if nothing had happened? And yet that's just what happened. This bust-up, the most controversial of their career, was precipitated by the failure of the band to record a new album to succeed their unsatisfactory 1978 effort *Tormato* and might well have brought down the final curtain. Yet only two months later, in May 1980, Chris Squire recruited two new members whose pedigree caused even the most die-hard Yes fan to gasp. Enter producer, singer and bassist Trevor Horn, and keyboard player Geoff Downes, better known as The Buggles.

The Buggles!!!? In Yes!!!? This latest twist to the tale seemed like the final nail in the band's coffin. But it wasn't. In the event, it actually ensured their survival. The Buggles version of Yes lasted until April, 1981. Then Steve Howe left to form Asia with Geoff Downes which led to a Yes renaissance with guitarist Trevor Rabin writing the songs and Jon Anderson back at the microphone. The comeback was sealed with the number one US single, 'Owner Of A Lonely Heart', and their astonishing album *90125*.

In many ways this album represented the end of their quest for technical perfection. Ironically, this was a needless quest by the Nineties. There was no excuse for *imperfection* when studios and stages were equipped with the latest in digital, computer technology. Sampling had replaced the need for 'live' orchestras and drum machines could provide that metronomic beat and crisp sound all producers craved and audiences now took for granted. Pop music technology had advanced rapidly.

Human skills, the skills that had made Yes so precious, were less important. It was now possible for a recording star to sell millions of CDs without ever venturing out of the studio, and certainly never having to battle up and down motorways in the search for gigs. The whole concept of Yes seemed out of date and redundant. Except . . . it was Yes that conceived many of the innovations now taken for granted. And there was a new generation of fans for whom a living, breathing band of top performing musicians was a rare treat.

In 1998 a low budget CD appeared on the market. It wasn't given much space in the music press reviews pages, if it was noted at all. The origins of the CD were somewhat dubious but it served an important purpose in that it brought back to light the original sound of Yes. Titled *Something's Coming* it comprised broadcast recordings of Yes from 1969 to 1970. Would it shatter long cherished beliefs and illusions? Would the sound of the band first heard in London all those years ago now seem too primitive?

The opening bars of *Something's Coming* with its triumphant organ and guitar chords and the unexpectedly violent drums, recalled all the magic. Jon Anderson sang 'Who knows?' in his husky Lancastrian burr, answered by witty musical ripostes from the ensemble. All the charm and excitement of their original performances came surging back. This was the song and arrangement that knocked me out when I saw the band for the first time. The echoing radio sound quality, so different from the muffled albums of the period, itself had a nostalgic ring. The record transported this listener back to people, places and memories once thought lost in space and time. 'Something's Coming' and companion pieces like 'Every-days', with their rapidly shifting moods and exciting solos, seemed like a revelation, a restoration of faith and values.

Strangely enough, this CD of ancient recordings gave me even more pleasure than the very latest high quality Yes release *Open Your Eyes*. This was a daring young band, rough at the edges and taking risks. These BBC tapes culled from the archives, done with barely time for a sound check, let alone a rehearsal, capture Yes at a crucial moment, on the verge of greatness, still full of naïve hopes and dreams.

Which is more important – yesterday or Yes today? The answer is that Yes continues to grip the imagination in all its forms, past and present. There are fanzines and websites throughout America and Europe devoted entirely to their doings, and for whose subscribers Yes is a ruling passion. They are the people who gathered for a special 'Yestival' held in America on June 27 and 28, 1998, one of a series of annual events held to celebrate the band's life and times.

Aficionados gathered at Cherry Hill, New Jersey, from all over the States to greet their heroes and other guests from Britain. Ambassadors from Yes past and present came to receive homage. Chris Squire was there – keeping the fans on tenterhooks as the large audience waited for a special interview session. There were 'new boys' like Billy Sherwood while veterans Alan White and Steve Howe were happy to meet, greet and even perform. Peter Banks, a hero from 1968, flew in from his home in Barnet and jammed while Geoff Downes played a special concert described as 'awesome' by delegates and visitors alike.

But what had drawn them all together in celebration? Yes is much more than a joke about curry on the organ, or a series of internal rows about money, or the reasons behind its shifting personnel. It is about the power to create music that moves the heart and mind.

The musicians themselves have grown up over these past thirty years and many of the old problems have been solved or simply faded into insignificance. Says Steve Howe, "As you get older you are more able to talk and deal with the psychological and physiological things that go on and the business problems that always plague a group. There's an awful lot more to being in Yes than just playing the music! I wish there wasn't. Some members of the band have said quite regularly, 'That's it. I'm not having bugger all to do with the business. I'm just going to sing, or play and let everything else go.' And then they don't know what to do.

"They just dissipate or become phased out. You *can't* leave any part of your life just to destiny. Jon has said to me many times that he'd sooner live for two months up a mountain. He has that ability to go off into the unknown. I just like to create a space for myself and get lost in my music. I

13

can't force music to happen. You can't turn it on like a tap. But if you can create the right environment then it will flow. In Yes the guys want you to use self control, to be very organised and together, happy and positive. It's a big demand. You can't be in Yes and take a back seat. There's no room for someone to take a back seat. They'll be out! But if there was any time when I've thought what a good band Yes was – it's right now."

And right now we go back to the beginning, to beyond and before.

2

SOMETHING'S COMING

If any single member truly embodies the spirit of Yes, at least in the eyes of their fans, it is Jon Anderson. A dreamer with a passion for alternative life styles and what used to be called hippie philosophy, he is also a practical man. As a touring rock singer he quickly learned how to cope with the harsh realities of life. He was once described as, 'An incurable romantic with a deceptive iron streak, a babbler of dreams with a firm grip on reality.'

There is no doubt that his beliefs run deep. The quest for wider arcane knowledge is as important to him as the creation of good music. Jon Anderson comes from an ordinary, hardworking background and left school at an early age. As a musician he is very much self taught. He can play the guitar and dabbles with percussion. As a singer he learnt from everyone from The Beatles and Otis Redding to Frank Sinatra and Simon & Garfunkel. All his general knowledge and accumulated wisdom has been gleaned from reading, listening, observing and, above all, conversing with other people. His working-class roots were no impediment to his gaining a heartfelt appreciation for art, literature, religion, philosophy and classical music.

The inspiration he gets from great music and grand ideas is genuine and something that has never left him, even during his darkest moments of self doubt. Yes became Jon's orchestra of the imagination. Chris Squire, his kindred spirit, helped turn the vision into a reality but from their first enthusiastic beginnings Yes was a means to surf the cosmic waves of possibilities. All he and Chris had to do was find the right people to share their vision. It was only when that quest was thwarted, either by personal intrigue or financial pressure, that battle ensued.

From his stage and public persona, Jon Anderson might seem a gentle, inquisitive character, a soft touch perhaps, someone who can be taken for a ride. Jon is indeed charming and approachable and gifted with a sparkling sense of humour, and he is not so precious that he can't laugh at himself or others. But at the same time his steely determination to communicate his ideas induces a kind of iron resolve that brooks no argument. He is stubborn. Proud. Determined. A wave of the hand and an intense look are the warning signals all but the most insensitive must surely recognise. He is no sucker. Having travelled the world and dealt with many a threatening situation, he is more aware of life's perils than most.

But where does the little guy with a velvet voice and big ideas find such strength of personality? How did he beat his way to the top of a business notoriously unsentimental and oft steeped in treachery, devious machinations and downright skulduggery? How could a spiritual soul, who has on occasion been known to set up a portable tepee in his dressing room and sport Red Indian feathers and face paint, come to be harshly spoken of as 'Napoleon' and even 'Hitler' by some of his more fearful confreres? To find the answers we must explore his background.

★　★　★

John Roy Anderson was born in Accrington, Lancashire, on October 25, 1944. His father Albert was a salesman, while his mother Kathleen worked in a cotton mill, then the staple industry of Lancashire. John grew up in a small house in Norfolk Street and was the second youngest of four siblings, Stuart, Tony and Joy.

"They named me John Roy after a music hall singer who was billed as 'John Roy the Melody Boy'," he says. "You can find his name on some of the old variety show posters from the Forties and Fifties. In my dreams my name was always 'Jonathan' but it was actually John. When I came to London I decided to drop my 'aitch' and become the Jonathan that I always wanted to be. Roy comes from 'Royston' which is a classic Scottish name."

Jon's father was Scottish and his mother was second generation Irish with French ancestry. "I never had any problem about relating to people from different countries and that came out later in my life when I was working with Vangelis Papathanassiou. I've always been adventurous about who I work with. You don't have to be an English person in order to make good music. Sometimes that became the criteria in Yes. It always had to be done with English musicians in England. Towards the end of the Seventies I rebelled against that idea and said there was no reason why we couldn't write music abroad."

Although Jon's parents were not musicians they had a keen interest in the world of entertainment. They were both accomplished ballroom dancers and county champions. "It's only in the last two or three years that I've realised how much influence my father had on me as a performer," says Jon. "I can remember seeing him on stage in Accrington when I was two or three years old, working as a comedian. He was from Glasgow and he had a kilt on. When he was in the Army he was in ENSA (the troop's entertainment service, alternatively known as 'Every Night Something Awful') and he would go on stage, tell jokes and sing a couple of songs. My mother and my father were ballroom dancing champions of East Lancashire. They had cups on display and photographs of my mother in her beautiful ballroom gown and my father in his bow tie. Basically they were a couple of show offs!"

Jon went to St. John's Infants School in Accrington and his teachers remembered him as a strong class leader. One of his teachers, Mrs. Irene Smith, says, "He was a lovely looking little boy with a happy disposition. He always seemed to have a smile on his face and loved singing." Mrs. Ada Thurman remembers Jon as a, "very happy little boy who thought a lot about his classmates and school, and in particular his sister". Another teacher, Clifford Collinson, recalls that he was "a good leader in the class, with a particular expertise in geometric drawing, but Jon did not wish to go to Grammar school".

Times were harsh and money was tight in the Anderson household. Says Jon, "I lived on a farm when I was eight years old and worked as a labourer from the age of 15. My father used to be very ill and I had to work hard." Anderson was very keen on football and dreamed of playing for the famous local side Accrington Stanley. But when his father became ill, he had to leave school at 15 to go to work. He toiled as a farm hand with his older brother Tony and later got a job driving a lorry delivering bricks. He also worked on a milk round for a while. It all seemed a far cry from the artistic life he dreamed about. There was no chance now of going to a Grammar school, let alone a university. Instead of giving in to circumstances Jon was determined that one day he would succeed – at something. For the moment he had to earn a living to help support his family.

Said Jon later, "Being in a working-class area of Accrington, you work for a living. You don't become an artist. You don't paint. For me it was a fight to get away from that kind of situation. I didn't want to end up all my life driving long distance lorries or delivering milk."

Jon would rarely talk about these early days when he became successful with Yes. It was not that he wanted to deny his roots. In the excitement of becoming a successful rock musician, it simply didn't seem relevant. He needed to move on in a process of self discovery that remains at the core of his personality. The realisation that Jon Anderson, mystic and superstar, once had to deliver piles of bricks and slog at menial tasks from dawn to dusk, certainly explains his drive, his urgency, the ruthless need to hustle as well as dream and fantasise. It's a combination that produces extraordinary practical results and makes him a singularly magnetic personality. People find themselves drawn to him. Would-be fellow mystics appear at his side at airports and stage doors, seeking an audience. But he subtly lets them know that he needs his personal space.

While driving his lorry or resting at home Jon listened to a wide variety of music. His favourite rock'n'roll artists were Elvis Presley, Eddie Cochran and The Everly Brothers. Later came the British rock and blues and groups like The Who, The Spencer Davis Group and The Nice. Says Jon, "I was brought up on The Everly Brothers. Then I tried singing like Stevie Winwood for a couple of weeks – and failed!"

He also liked the smooth melodic sophistication of Dionne Warwick, Nina Simone, and Frank Sinatra and Bing Crosby, the stars of *High Society*. The Beatles were the ultimate voices of expression for his generation and he grew to admire and appreciate the great vocal groups like The Fifth Dimension and soul singers Otis Redding, Wilson Pickett and Joe Tex. He especially appreciated strong vocal harmonies and also dug the clear and precise enunciation of jazz singer Jon Hendricks. All these elements would later combine and inform his own unique vocal style and even his speaking voice, with its pleasant mixture of Lancashire burr and American drawl.

Although Jon was fascinated by pop records and admired great singers, he had no special desire to become a musician himself and in any case there was little time off work to learn to play an instrument. His older brother Tony, however, had taken up singing and joined a local group called The Warriors. One day the group's back-up vocalist left to work full time as a hairdresser and Jon stepped into the breech. At the age of 18, Jon Anderson found he could make a better living and have more fun singing and gigging with The Warriors than doing anything else. The band's line-up included Tony and Jon on vocals, Michael Brereton on lead guitar, Rodney Hill on rhythm guitar, David Foster on bass and vocals, and drummer Ian Wallace who was also destined for a rock career of no little distinction.

Clad in their smart suits and natty pullovers, they were a well rehearsed band who played mainly cover versions, earning £25 a gig playing nearly every night of the week in the Lancashire towns of Bolton, Bury, Blackburn, Rochdale, Accrington and Manchester. One of the first numbers Jon sang with the band was a spirited version of The Beatles' 'I'm Down' with Jon doing a fair approximation of his hero Paul McCartney. "I used to do a great McCartney," he says. "But I once heard somebody say I sounded more like Cilla Black!"

The Warriors recorded two singles for Decca: 'You Came Along' (written by Barry Mason and Les Reed) and 'Don't Make Me Blue' written by the group's bass player David Foster who would later co-write 'Sweet

Dreams' and 'Time And A Word' with Jon for Yes. The recordings, made under the aegis of producer Ivor Raymonde, were quite an experience for the young musicians. Recalls Ian Wallace, "I was really nervous and spent most of the session locked in the toilet." The Warrior's first single was released in 1964 amidst great local excitement but failed to receive sufficient air play to get into the charts. 'You Came Along' found its way onto a double compilation album *Hard Up Heroes* (Decca DPA 3009/10) released in 1974. The B-side 'Don't Make Me Blue' was later used in a film called *Just For You.*

After long exposure to the complexities of Yes music, the innocence of 'You Came Along' is mind boggling. You can hear Tony and Jon singing merrily as if entertaining a holiday camp full of mums, dads and screaming kids. There is a snatch of Neil Innes style de-tuned guitar work before Ian Wallace's drum coda – so hurried you can almost visualise him dashing to the loo 'for a nervous', as Phil Collins would say. But it's very sweet and full of energy.

Jon later told *New Musical Express*, "The main factor with The Warriors was being able to just about live off the music. Our situation was like that of most bands of that era. We were copying the more successful bands. In the five years The Warriors were together we only ever wrote two songs for the simple reason that there was all this incredible mass of good material around coming from The Beatles and those fabulous American songwriting teams. We used to look up to these people because they were so great at what they were doing. Though you didn't ever stop to think about it at the time, being in a band like The Warriors was great schooling. All those chords and notes that you hit really came in handy later on, because you'd learned your trade by practising on the very best material available."

The Warriors spent many years playing Northern working men's clubs, then left England for Germany where they worked hard following in the footsteps of the pioneering Merseybeat groups. Then, in 1967, Jon Anderson quit. He'd had enough of singing cover versions and needed a break to see more of the world. Although this abrupt decision failed to make headline news, word got back to London. And so began the chain of events and the crossing of paths that resulted in the birth of Yes.

Without Jon, The Warriors returned somewhat chastened to England and began to hang out at a newly established music business drinking haunt in London's Soho called La Chasse. The club was situated at number 100 Wardour Street and was run by Jack Barrie, assistant manager of The Marquee Club, just a few doors along the street at number 90. The bar, a tiny affair with minimal decor and primitive furnishings, was on the first floor above a betting shop. Its walls were decorated with caricatures of figures from the pop music industry and its juke box was filled with an eccentric selection of top quality pop singles, the sort of music that musicians admired. It was informal, cosy and often very crowded, and it became a vital meeting place for musicians working at The Marquee. The betting shop was quite useful as well.

As the Marquee didn't have a drinks licence and nearby pub The Ship was often overflowing with fans, La Chasse became a kind of sanctuary. It was the ideal place for guitarists, drummers, keyboard players and singers to meet, tank up and exchange phone numbers and girlfriends. As a result it became the launch pad for some of the biggest and most influential rock bands of all time. Much of the credit for the formation of Yes goes to Jack Barrie. From his position, polishing glasses behind the bar, he could observe which of his customers could benefit from some friendly advice. Certain visitors like Vivian Stanshall of The Bonzo Dog Band might not take kindly to any advice and would abuse anyone who offered it. But not all the customers were as cantankerous as Viv.

On a busy night the tiny bar might accommodate Peter Frampton in full satin stage gear, taking a break from his gigs with The Herd, Peter Banks of The Syn in search of sustenance, or hairy young Phil Collins hoping to blag a way into The Marquee to see The Who for free. Keith Moon once arrived at La Chasse via the fire escape, having climbed over the rooftops from The Who's offices in Old Compton Street. Rubbing shoulders with these musicians was a newly arrived and unemployed young singer from Accrington via Hamburg, looking for a gig and a floor to park his overnight bag. And so it was that mine host Jack Barrie called the singer over, made his fateful introduction and encouraged him to talk to a very tall bass guitarist called Chris Squire, hot foot from Mabel Greer's Toyshop via The Syn.

★ ★ ★

Jack Barrie, a caterer by trade, was never the manager of Yes, not even in these early days. It might have been a good thing if he had been. After all he went on to run The Marquee with great success for the next thirty years and would encourage and assist the formation and growth of legions of groups. His favourite was undoubtedly Yes, but for all his enthusiasm for the project, he lacked the killer instinct and the resources needed for successful rock group management.

Jack opened La Chasse in May, 1967. "It had been open as a member's bar two or three years before I first went into the business. It was an old West End style club. I discovered it because the couple Bill and Jessie who used to run The Ship took me up there for a drink one night. I thought it was fantastic and took all my music biz friends there. After making it a roaring success I then foolishly put in a bid for the place. It probably cost me three times what I would have paid, had I been more discreet. It had been a failing business. I made it a success and then bought it!"

Jack was busy at The Marquee and involved with the annual National Jazz Federation festivals (which evolved into the Reading Rock Festival), but still found time to run his new bar. He had started at The Marquee in 1964 as assistant to the club's manager John Gee. "I was still doing things for The Marquee Organisation like festival catering and I was also running La Chasse," he says. John Gee would run The Marquee until 1970 when Jack took over the management of the club.

Yet Barrie did not actually meet Anderson at his newly established drinking club. The fateful encounter took place on the platform of Victoria Station. "Jon's old group The Warriors had split up in Germany and came back home while Jon stayed on for some reason. The Warriors came to London in October 1967 looking for work and ended up at La Chasse club. I got to know Brian Chatton who was their keyboard player at the time and in March 1968 he told me that the old singer with the band was coming back to London. They had kept in contact and he had to go down to Victoria Station to meet him. So I went with Brian to meet Jon coming off the boat train from the Continent. My first vision of Jon Anderson was seeing him playing the alto saxophone. He saw Brian coming towards him, dropped his luggage, got out his sax and pretended to be busking. That was my first visual sighting of Jon Anderson – playing the sax on Victoria Station!"

Says Jon, "I had been with The Warriors for five years and in fact it was a very good band. When I got back to London, having left them in Germany, I realised what a really good band it was. We had Ian Wallace on drums who is now one of the top session men in LA. Brian Chatton is still writing songs. My brother Tony was in the band in the early days but that's a long story."

Brian and Jon shared accommodation courtesy of Jack Barrie, who temporarily put them up at his flat as they were both broke and homeless. "The story goes that to pay his rent Jon used to come and sweep up the Chasse club. But he never slept there," says Jack. "He may have used the sofa when he had a girlfriend visiting. After all the flat was full of people. It's an exaggeration to say he used to sleep on the sofa but it makes a good story! He certainly used to sweep up. He felt he was doing something useful to help pay for his accommodation. We used to have long conversations about music and I would look after his interests through contacts in the business."

Among those who used to drink in La Chasse was EMI producer Paul Korda, a relative of film producer Sir Alexander Korda. He was impressed with Jon and decided to record a couple of demo tracks with him. Jack Barrie tried to find his protégé some suitable songs. "We were looking for material for Jon and I knew a couple of budding songwriters. Mainly I knew the keyboard player who used to play at the Marquee. I took Jon to meet these struggling young songwriters at Dick James Music. They were Elton John and Bernie Taupin. They played Jon some music and he took a few things away to hear. But he didn't find anything much he liked. I suppose I was sort of managing Jon at this point, but not on a professional basis. I was taking an interest in his future. I thought he had a lot of talent and I loved his voice. Jon was very interested in using vocal harmonies and he already had a strong idea of how he imagined his ideal group. I was trying to help him achieve his dream."

With plans afoot to promote Jon as a solo artist, the Paul Korda demos were turned into two singles released under a new name. Jon Anderson became Hans Christian. Although nobody was supposed to know his pseudonym, the habitués of La Chasse couldn't fail to recognise him, mainly because Hans Christian's records were regularly played on the club's juke box — by the singer himself. "That was during the period when we were trying to get a group for him," says Jack Barrie. "We wanted a band to help promote his solo singles."

The first was called 'Never My Love', released on Parlophone and reviewed by the author in *Melody Maker* in March, 1968. The song was a re-make of a hit by The Association which got to Number 2 in the American *Billboard* chart in September, 1967. Dropping heavy hints about the identity of the singer I wrote: "Leap into your Anderson shelters, here comes a blockbuster of a hit from a hip young fairy tale teller with an emotion packed voice. The orchestral accompaniment builds up into a veritable frenzy with a gibbering vocal chorus and battering drums. It's pretty exciting and no doubt we shall all be seeing Mr. Christian bringing mutiny to the good ship Top Of The Pops 'ere long."

Peter Banks, the first lead guitarist with Yes, recalls, " 'Never My Love' was very appropriate. Never put that record on! In fact it came out when I first met Jon. He was cleaning up the glasses in La Chasse and kept putting this bloody record on and going, 'Ee, that's my record that is!' 'Yes we know Jon . . . we've heard it!' He certainly wasn't backward about coming forward."

A few months later in May came his second attempt at cracking the charts, this time with a ditty called 'The Autobiography Of Mississippi Hobo' (Parlophone). Once again I waxed fulsome in a vain attempt to boost Mr. Christian's career. "Remarkable rhythmic effects distinguish this bright performance from the miserable dross that frequently finds its way on disc these depressed days. Hans sings with youthful enthusiasm and the production has all the brightness that made Manfred Mann's early records so popular. Gawd knows what the words are all about but there are flutes aplenty and a fidgety beat that will set the nation's toes tapping. A hit." Despite this display of enthusiasm – it wasn't.

Hans Christian sank into obscurity, his name just a memory as, indeed, is that of The Warriors. But Jon wasn't about to give up. Meanwhile, he continued to hang out at La Chasse and visit The Marquee where such bands as The Syn and later Mabel Greer's Toyshop were nightly blasting away on the sweat soaked stage and fighting for space to park their guitar cases and hair dryers in the tiny, cramped, graffiti covered dressing room. Among the graffiti at this time, a drawing of The Who's lead guitarist bore the legend 'Pete Townshend is a nose on legs'.

"I used to see Syn and Mabel Greer," recalls Jack Barrie. "There was nothing outstanding about them. You wouldn't stand and watch them and get a shiver of excitement down the spine. There were a lot of very good quality bands like them in those days. I'd see them at the club and in order to play at The Marquee you had to have a certain quality. The musicianship in a band like Mabel Greer's Toyshop was very good but it was obvious they weren't going anywhere."

Meanwhile Jack Barrie was trying to find a backing group for his protégé. Paul Korda tipped him off about an unknown band rehearsing at EMI called The Gun. Jack and Paul took Jon down to meet the group and they started rehearsing together. The plan was to showcase The Gun with Jon Anderson at a Marquee gig in order to gain them some work and put them on the road. "We felt it was a good marriage at the time," says Jack. However The Gun was the province of two feisty brothers, Paul and Adrian Gurvitz, who did not take kindly to the idea of either putting on a free gig or acting as a backing group for some unknown singer.

Jack: "We got them a support spot at The Marquee one night and an agent came down to see them. He thought they were fantastic and the following morning the phone didn't stop ringing. We had six gigs offered right away. I couldn't wait for Jon to come home. He had gone off to rehearsals and I wanted to tell him the good news. He came back to tell me that the only news of the day as far as he was concerned was that his 'backing group' had sacked him! They were so pleased at the reaction to The Marquee gig they felt they didn't need a singer. They wanted to go out on their own, which was shattering for Jon."

However once the agents found out that Jon Anderson was no longer with The Gun the offer of future gigs was withdrawn. In the event The Gun enjoyed a hit with 'Race With The Devil' and became a moderately successful band under their own steam. Their first album sported a remarkable cover depicting hairy monsters. Coincidentally, it was the first project by a rising young artist called Roger Dean. Jon Anderson, meanwhile, had endured his first real setback.

Jack Barrie: "We then decided that the only thing to do was find individual musicians who were not part of a group. And that's why I introduced him to Chris Squire. I knew his groups from The Marquee like Syn and Mabel Greer's Toyshop. So I introduced Jon to Chris, gave them a drink each and suggested they go in a corner and talk. They obviously found they had a lot of musical ideas in common."

As a direct result of this conversation the concept of Yes was born. Chris and Jon discovered they were both fans of Simon & Garfunkel and were especially keen on the idea of harmony singing in a group. Jon went to Chris' home that same night to jam and by the next day they had written their first song together, 'Sweetness', which would appear on the first Yes album.

For a brief period Jon became an unofficial member of Chris Squire's latest group, Mabel Greer's Toyshop, although he made it clear he didn't like the name and wanted something simpler and more positive – like Yes. At the time Clive Bailey was on guitar as their original guitarist Peter Banks had left to join Neat Change. When the new band was formed, Chris recommended bringing Peter back into the fold.

★ ★ ★

Chris Squire, Jon Anderson's new partner was born on March 4, 1948 in Queensbury, a suburb of north west London near Wembley. Tall, deceptively slow to speak and react, his sudden bursts of laughter show Chris knows exactly what is going on in people's minds. He has the ability to adapt to each new situation, once he's figured it out. Chris was able to interpret Jon's ideas and help bring in the right people to make it all happen. It's a role he's been doing for the full thirty years of the band's turbulent existence.

Unusual among rock musicians Chris was a trained choir boy. He was educated at Haberdashers' Aske's public school, Elstree, and sang in the choir. He also sang in the choir of St. Andrew's Church, Kingsbury, famous for its standards and quality. It was here that he learned to understand and appreciate harmony. Fellow chorister Andrew Pryce Jackman became a close friend and they played together in Chris' first rock group Syn.

Barry Rose, who taught Chris to sing at school, later became choir master at Guildford Cathedral. Recalls Chris, "When I was 12, I went there for a bit. It was England's newest cathedral and they had to start a choir from scratch. Barry took me from Kingsbury with five other guys to be the nucleus of the choir there and he later got the job at St. Paul's Cathedral and so I also sang there. Barry Rose came from Cambridge University to be our local choirmaster when he was about 23 and he ended up in charge of the music at Charles and Diana's wedding, so he had a meteoric career and rise to fame in church music. He dragged me along with him and I learned everything I know from him.

"Kingsbury is where I grew up and that's where I got into my first amateur group called The Selfs. All we really did was learn to play. We played at the local church hall on a Friday evening. We organised our own little dance and sold the Cokes and made about £15. I had just left school and was about 17 years old."

Chris' time at Haberdashers came to an abrupt halt. "I was actually expelled for having my hair too long! We did all the 'O' levels and then me and this friend of mine John Wheatley, who also had long hair, got into trouble on the day before the very last day of school. The headmaster called us into the study. We had only grown our hair long for the summer, but he was very smug about it. He handed us two shillings and sixpence each and told us to go to the local barber's and get a haircut, on the day before we broke up. We kind of looked at him and said, 'Uh huh, okay.' We walked out of his office and the front door of the building. We then looked at each other and the two and sixpence in our hands and said, 'Let's just *go!*' That was our last day at school. We kept his money and left!"

This didn't impress the headmaster and he wrote to Mrs. Squire saying that until the matter was resolved her son was suspended. Chris talked it over with his mother and decided that he might as well leave during the summer holidays and find a job. He ended up working at Boosey & Hawkes, the instrument dealers in London's West End, earning £8 a week. "I never went back to school, so I suppose I was *suspended* rather than expelled."

Chris' parents weren't particularly musical. "My father liked to listen to music and he built his own hi-fi system from a kit and played records by Lena Horn and Ella Fitzgerald, so I learnt a lot from listening to my dad's records. My mother liked music too but really I got all my musical interest from the choir when I began singing at the age of six. Being in a really good choir made it more fun. I sang at St. Paul's because every time the choir there went on holiday in the summer, then St. Andrew's, Kingsbury, used to dep for them. So I had a whole career as a child, singing in cathedrals. I got a great understanding of music from that and this was a time in my life when rock 'n' roll didn't play any part in it at all. In fact whenever I heard an Elvis Presley record on the radio I used to think it was crap! It's only when I turned 15 in 1963 that I was the right age to be a Beatles fan. They sort of changed my musical tastes from church to secular music."

Chris was strictly a singer and hadn't picked up any musical instruments. His friend John Wheatley, however, played guitar. "He played

25

Spanish and classical stuff and then of course he too became interested in rock'n'roll. The last I ever heard of John was he'd become a travel agent. One day he said, 'Chris, you're tall and you've got quite big hands. You should play bass.' "

Chris thought this was a fine idea, so he asked his mother to buy him a Futurama bass guitar at Macari's Musical Exchange in Wembley. Now he was equipped to form his own rock'n'roll group. "I never seriously learned anything until I was about 16," he says. "Then I started on the bass and carried on from there. I just felt that it was the instrument I wanted to play. I appreciated right from the start the importance of the bass." Later he would buy his first Rickenbacker bass on hire purchase from Boosey & Hawkes, replacing the trusty Futurama with the make of instrument he would continue to play throughout his days with Yes.

Apart from his mate John, another important early influence was Andrew Jackman. "He was in the church choir with me and lived six houses away from my house in Kingsbury. Andrew became the keyboard player in The Selfs and later The Syn. I grew up with him in the choir and his father was actually in the London Symphony Orchestra and played clarinet and oboe. That family had an influence on my life too, because they were very musical." Andrew would later play and help with the arrangements on Chris's 1974 solo album *Fish Out Of Water*, and arrange songs for Yes on their 1978 *Tormato* album.

The Selfs enjoyed playing at youth clubs and church events but it didn't take Chris long to realise that one of the guitarists wasn't good enough and the drummer couldn't keep time. "So that's why it fizzled out." In the meantime he had befriended Steve Nardelli, a teenager of English/Italian parentage who would become The Syn's lead vocalist. "He was a pretty good singer who sounded rather like Rod Stewart. I started hanging out with him because he was another local North London lad and that's how The Syn got formed in around 1965. The Syn was Andrew Jackman, Steve Nardelli, myself and of course Peter Banks. We got a Tuesday night residency at the Marquee supporting the main feature band. We got on really well with the management. For some reason they really liked us. We never made an album but we made a couple of singles for Decca Records. The first one was a piece of pop architecture called 'Created By Clive' which was a ditty about a fashion photographer. The B-side was called 'Grounded' which was a pretty good song. Then we did '14 Hour Technicolour Dream' and they sold quite well and got us noticed and enabled us to play in such exotic places as Stoke-on-Trent. We did vocal harmonies and The Syn were very similar to Yes in fact. It was very much a precursor of Yes – a five piece with drums, bass, guitar and keyboards and a vocalist. And we used to do similar stuff with three and even four part vocal harmonies. That was because Andrew Jackman, my keyboard playing friend, had been a chorister too and we had been doing that for years."

Like so many bands that lacked that indefinable ingredient to go the whole way, Syn dissolved without tears as each member realised the band was going nowhere, though in the band's final days strange things had begun to happen. Says Chris, "Eventually we got to a certain plateau and couldn't go any higher. It got a bit boring and it was time to move on. In fact our singer Steve was a very fashionable kind of guy and he got interested in opening clothes boutiques. That became his passion and he was getting married and stuff, so the band broke up. I was enjoying being a musician but it was still a rocky road. I had a rather nasty experience with some LSD and was in a bit of a haze for a few months. Somebody gave me some bad acid. Yet the experience kind of had a positive effect on me."

Chris became a recluse and for a long time just didn't go out. Still coming down from the trip, he was literally afraid to go out into the street. "I stayed in my girlfriend's apartment while she went out to work. I was there all day for quite a few months recovering from this bad trip. I was practising my guitar all day. So after eight months of doing that I was pretty good on the instrument and built a relationship with my bass guitar. I didn't take acid again after that, funnily enough! Having seen the end of the world I thought I'd gone far enough. I had taken it so many times during nights at UFO (the hippie club in London's Tottenham Court Road), when it was all fun and great and colourful. But then I guess I had the 'flu and this guy had made his own acid. 'Oh, man you gotta try some of this — I just made it!' So somehow or other I ended up in a Fulham hospital for a couple of days, being interviewed by the cops. 'Where did you get the drugs from kid?' I didn't know where I was. I was just smiling at them thinking they weren't even there."

Once out of hospital Chris concentrated on his studies. He used to play without plugging in the bass and he grew to understand the natural timbre of the instrument. "I learned to do a few tricks that other people hadn't done before, which enabled me to go on and win awards and stuff. By then I'd bought my first Rickenbacker, which I got when I was 16 from Boosey & Hawkes in Regent Street. They were the importers and I managed to get one of the first three imported into England. The Kinks had one and John Entwistle had another."

Squire practised on his Rickenbacker for months while in recovery. "That side of it was good, but at the end of the day I'm glad the trip didn't kill me. It was after this period I ran into Jon Anderson and we started putting Yes together. When we met in La Chasse Club I was very broke and living off various girlfriends, which used to be *de rigeur* at that time."

Chris was undoubtedly inspired by Paul McCartney's melodic violin bass style but he was also influenced by the mighty John Entwistle of The Who. Recalls Chris, "I developed that trebly bass thing a little further. I spent a lot of time alone in the proverbial garret, playing and hoping it would all lead somewhere." His twangy, treble-toned Rickenbacker bass sound would eventually become one of the crucial components of the rapidly developing Yes sound. Another was the vocal lines he blended with Jon Anderson's plaintive lead to produce a choral effect rarely heard amid the coarse bedlam of contemporary R&B.

While he was in Syn the band paid themselves six pounds a week each and they could just about survive on that. Once he was out of the band, the gig money dried up and loyal girlfriends came to the rescue providing food and accommodation. "I had one girlfriend I was with for a year or two. I don't know where she is now, but God bless her soul," says Chris fervently.

When Chris first met Jon in La Chasse he was intrigued. "He was very Northern when I first met him, ha, ha! He had a pretty thick Accrington accent which I found kind of amusing, but charming as well. Having been a southern English public school boy I hadn't really encountered many people like Jon. So I found him fascinating. That was part of the reason we decided to work together, because I could see we had quite different backgrounds. Putting the two together would seem to be a good thing. We sat down at the Chasse at our first meeting and decided that we both liked Simon & Garfunkel and The Association and that vocal group The Fifth Dimension who made an album called *The Magic Garden*.

"We had a lot of similar tastes, mainly vocal stuff and that's when we decided to form a band. The very next day Jon came round to my flat and we sat down and attempted to write a song together and we actually came up with 'Sweetness' which is on the first Yes album. The funny thing is there was a very hip movie which I saw in 1998 called *Buffalo '66*[1] about a guy growing up in Buffalo, NY. There's lots of Yes influence in there. 'Sweetness' is the closing title theme for the whole movie. The film is full of early Yes music and I thought, 'My God – we're hip again!' "

★　★　★

---

[1] *Buffalo 66* is the work of director and actor Vincent Gallo who in the movie plays the part of an ex-convict who is tormented by the defeat of his home town baseball team and goes on to kidnap a girl he tries to pass off as his wife. The soundtrack of the movie uses both King Crimson and Yes tracks, and Gallo told the British Q Magazine in October, 1998: "The single most exciting day of my life was when Chris Squire, the bass player from Yes, invited me to dinner. The second most exciting day was when I met Jon Anderson of Yes."

The group's guitarist, Peter Banks, was born Peter Brockbanks in Barnet, North London, on July 15, 1947. Though The Syn offered Peter his first real taste of professional touring, he had been playing guitar in bands since the age of 16 and listening to music from the age of eight. His first brush with pop was the stream of skiffle hits unleashed by the energetic Lonnie Donegan, the catalyst and inspiration for many British school kids. Peter was among them.

"I listened to all of Lonnie's records on 78s. I got an acoustic guitar as a present from my parents and tried to figure out what an A and G were. But the guitar only cost £5 which was a month's wages in those days and it was practically unplayable. I also had a ukulele which I still possess."

Peter's first real guitar was a Gretsch and he got it because George Harrison played one. He rapidly progressed from Donegan's records to The Beatles whose success made him feel he too had a chance to succeed as a musician. He also listened to jazz and liked the Dave Brubeck Quartet, Wes Montgomery, Miles Davis and John Coltrane. Peter also played the drums from the age of ten, practising on a cousin's rudimentary kit. He used to play along to The Shadows and The John Barry Seven. But he found the co-ordination difficult and concentrated on guitar.

Banks went on an art course but he always intended to be a professional musician. There was one alternative he briefly considered. "I went through a stage of wanting to be a zoo keeper. Then I found out what the hours were! You had to start at 5 a.m. Either that or I wanted to be a TV camera man, but you had to pass exams in mathematics. That put paid to that, because I was lousy at maths. I think I really knew I wanted to be a musician from the age of ten."

At school Peter was quiet and shy. He went to Barnet Secondary Modern, sat at the back of the class and rarely spoke to anybody. He didn't have many friends, so he would go home and practise the guitar. The thought passed through his mind, 'One day when I've learned to play, they'll all love me.' It was his main motivation, as well as the even more rewarding prospect that he'd get to meet girls.

He left school at 16 and later joined a Borehamwood band called The Devil's Disciples. He made his first record with them in 1964. It was a demo still circulating among collectors on rare acetates. "It was never released but it has appeared on a couple of bootlegs," says Peter. He had previously been with local Barnet band The Nighthawks on rhythm guitar and they played what proved to be Banks' first ever gig, at the New Barnet Pop Festival. They played rock'n'roll at weddings 'and all social occasions' according to their neatly printed business cards.

"I can't remember what they sounded like, but The Devil's Disciples, which came later, used to play the whole of The Rolling Stones' first

album, in the same order that the tunes were on the record. We were doing covers of Howlin' Wolf and Muddy Waters and we didn't even know who the hell these people were. We were just copying the Stones! Another guy who was in the Disciples was Dennis Cowan who later joined the Bonzo Dog Doo Dah Band as their bass player. Dennis was a big blues fan and he actually had records of black blues musicians from America. He was a rhythm guitar player but ended up as bass player with the Bonzos. He died of cancer about fifteen years ago."

The Disciples lasted for a year but found it hard to make any progress beyond a few gigs abroad. Peter's first important band was undoubtedly The Syn. "They had no connection with another band called The Syndicats whatsoever," says Peter, dispelling myths about their origins. "The only slight connection with The Syndicats was that both myself and Steve Howe were at one time in the Syndicats. But there is no Syn connection."

When Syn started around 1965 they were playing strictly Motown 'covers' with a few soul tunes thrown in. Peter replaced their original guitar player John Paynter and was on the two Deram singles, 'Created By Clive' and 'Flower Man', which can now be heard on a compilation CD. Peter says he first met Chris Squire in Denmark Street, off Charing Cross Road, known as London's Tin Pan Alley. A short stretch of road, used mostly as a short cut by taxi drivers, it was the home of many music publishers and publicists. Many aspiring bands including The Who and The Small Faces gravitated towards the street's Gioconda coffee bar. Today it remains a music business centre, lined with instrument and book shops.

Peter remembers the Gioconda well. "Somebody introduced me to Chris near there. I just remember seeing this very tall guy appear." Drummer Martin Ableman, who had just joined the group, introduced Banks to Squire, who promptly said The Syn were looking for a guitar player. They wanted him to replace their current guitarist John Paynter and Peter started surreptitious rehearsals.

"It was all rather brutal. I came to see them play a few times knowing that I had the gig. I watched what the guy would play. I even inherited his Rickenbacker, so he lost his gig and he lost his Rickenbacker. He was a nice chap and I still feel kind of bad about it – even now."

The Syn were managed by Peter Huggett who was Lonnie Donegan's old bass player. Banks went into their office in Denmark Street and bumped straight into his old hero Lonnie, an encounter which strangely enough didn't impress him at all. "I was a teenager now – I'd grown out of Lonnie Donegan! But years later I played on a Donegan album, when I was doing sessions in LA."

The fateful meeting of Peter Banks and Chris Squire actually took place in the street outside the coffee bar. "It was an event that affected the rest of my life. If I hadn't been walking down Denmark Street – what would have happened?" The immediate effect was that Peter joined The Syn as their lead guitarist. With Steve Nardelli up front, keyboard player Andrew Jackman in place and a succession of drummers, Syn became quite busy. While playing all the usual out of town gigs they also played regularly at The Marquee.

"That was my dream, to play at The Marquee. I never thought any further than that. Everybody wanted to play there. In the end The Syn got bored with it because we were there every week. We supported Jimi Hendrix there on its busiest night ever, in 1967. It was a very peculiar gig. All the Beatles were there and the Rolling Stones. Eric Clapton and Jeff Beck and every other guitar player in town came along and we had to play one set to all these people! They were waiting for Jimi Hendrix, but we had to play once, come off and then play *another* set. So people were going, 'Well thank God they've gone.' Then we came back on again! It wasn't very nice for us but it was great meeting Hendrix."

However The Syn had their own following who loyally turned up to see them on their Tuesday night spots when they acted as the regular support band for a year. The music scene underwent drastic changes during the Summer Of Love in 1967 and Syn responded quickly to the new fashions. "We became psychedelic and dropped most of the Motown stuff," recalls Peter. "We started writing rock operas! Andrew did the writing and we played these set pieces of six or seven songs. It's painful to remember this – excruciatingly embarrassing – but we did one called 'Flower Man' where we all dressed up as different flowers. Of course Chris loved all this because he was well into flower power."

The crucial question. Which flower was Peter? "I was a buttercup."

The Syn also did a rock opera about gangsters, well ahead of Genesis' 'Battle Of Epping Forest' on 1973's *Selling England By The Pound*, but it was another Sixties' band which influenced Syn's gangsterish designs. "We were always ones to jump on a bandwagon. The Move played at The Marquee dressed in a uniform of gangster suits. So we thought we'd do a rock opera – or at least a musical – about gangsters. Incidentally The Flower Man thing ended in a mock fight – with the singer attacking members of the band with a garden hoe. I swear it's true. I remember Chris got rather badly injured. He has very large feet, size 13 and he stepped on this hoe and the handle kind of hit him in the face and caught him between the eyes. So there were a few flesh wounds. Somebody got stabbed in the arm with a rake as well during these mock fights. It was very dangerous. The rule is – never take garden tools on stage."

Peter remembers it as a growing period in many different ways. "It was kind of peace, love and flowers and we started taking drugs at this time too. Especially Chris and I. Acid was around. I only took it once. I never inhaled. Allegedly. So we had these operatic things about peace and love which would end up in fights! Chris and I were both into The Who, so there was a little bit of mock equipment smashing and I broke at least two Rickenbackers through overenthusiasm. It was an odd mixture. Here were these idiots dressed like hippies with a gangster theme as well."

Unfortunately none of this has survived on tape or film as they never recorded any of these wild outbursts. They did a lot of TV in Holland, France and Germany, yet none of that has been seen on video. At least the band toured abroad, which was a major coup for a struggling London band. Most of their work was confined to the UK. Syn would find themselves playing in Glasgow one day and Penzance the next, travelling up and down the country in a Transit van supplied by their new manager Kenny Bell.

"Off we would go, very enthusiastically, sitting in the Transit with all the equipment, trundling up and down the country for £25 a gig. I never kept a track of the money, unlike Bill Bruford who knows the price of every gig he's ever done. I think the most we ever made was £100, which was big money. We had a minor hit in France with 'Flower Man'. We also wrote a song about the '14 Hour Technicolour Dream' at London's Alexandra Palace which we played at. The song was a B-side and it's the best Syn track there is. I still quite like the song which is a nice Sixties period piece. I remember the 'Technicolour Dream' was a bit of a shambles because they had two bands playing at the same time at either end of this cavernous hall which had very bad acoustics. I remember seeing John Lennon there and it was a lot of fun and a lot of drugs were consumed by just about everybody."

Peter Banks' main role was to provide lead guitar and backing vocals with Chris Squire. "Which is how the Yes sound started," affirms Peter. "We were very big on backing vocals and Andrew Jackman also sang, so we had pretty good three part harmonies. We used to spend as much time rehearsing the vocals as we did playing. In a way you could say the roots of what became Yes were apparent in Syn. Chris and I got used to each other's styles and we were both playing Rickenbackers."

In due course the band split, but Peter cannot remember how it all came to an end. "I think we died due to lack of interest. There was a bit of arguing and I remember being very crushed when the band broke up. We had been together for two or three years which in those days was a long time. We were consistently gigging but in the end we just died a slow death."

In January 1968 Chris Squire put together a new band called Mabel

Greer's Toyshop. Says Peter, "I think he was going to call the band Yes instead of Mabel Greer's Toyshop. And I said he couldn't do that because it was my idea. I had thought of this name Yes a couple of years beforehand. Everybody kept saying, 'What a *silly* name.' My answer was that it would get printed big on posters because there were only three letters like The Who. And it wasn't going to be The Yes – it was going to be Yes. Just like it wasn't meant to be The Syn. It was always Syn."

Peter Banks joined Mabel Greer's Toyshop for a while before working with another Marquee band called Neat Change, looked after by Billy Gaff who later managed The Faces. The Toyshop included Peter, Chris, and Clive Bailey (guitar) with a drummer called Bob whose surname everyone seems to have forgotten. Says Peter, "He had a tremendous amount of energy and thrashed away at the kit. But after two numbers he'd completely fall apart and his whole reserve of energy had gone."

Mabel Greer's Toyshop were very psychedelic and did some work for the BBC. John Peel liked them but they never actually made a record. They did land a Marquee residency which went reasonably well. Jon Anderson came along and sang a couple of times before the birth of Yes proper. Says Peter, "He used to sing 'In The Midnight Hour' and it went on for an hour! Actually it went on for 20 minutes. I left Mabel Greer because I didn't like playing with another guitarist. Clive Bailey was the singer and most of the songs were his, but he wasn't really hot stuff on the guitar. So there was a little bit of conflict going on there. When I left Jon did some gigs with them as the lead singer which I never saw."

By now The Marquee was in competition with several new hippie clubs. Mabel Greer's Toyshop played at London's hippie forum, the Middle Earth at 43 King Street, Covent Garden, on February 2, 1968, when they supported headliners The Action. The admission price was 20 shillings and 6d. The gig began at 10.30 p.m. and went on until dawn. The following night Tomorrow appeared at Middle Earth, with singer Keith West and a guitarist called Steve Howe.

"We loved The Action," recalls Peter Banks. "That's the style of band Syn tried to be originally, doing all the Motown stuff. The Action had Reg King, one of the great unknown white soul singers of the Sixties. He was as good as Rod Stewart in his day."

Peter professes not to know the origin of the mysterious Mabel Greer. He believes it was one of Clive Bailey's psychedelic visions. "It was a silly name – and a bit of a silly band. But we did do a Byrds' tune 'I See You' and The Doors' 'Light My Fire' with a very, very long guitar solo that probably lasted 15 minutes. But for whatever reason I left Mabel Greer and went into the Neat Change."

Peter joined Neat Change early in 1968, and they became another resident Marquee band. They were all skinheads with an aggressive Slade style pose. "When I joined I refused to get my hair cut. I was wearing very colourful clothes. Not the kind of stuff a skinhead would be seen dead in. I was still Mr. Psychedelia. Then the band changed and started doing covers of songs by American bands like Buffalo Springfield. We also did a single called 'I Lied To Aunty May' . . . a dreadful piece. Peter Frampton played guitar on the A-side and I was on the B-side."

He was with them for six months, then Peter was unceremoniously thrown out on the day before his 21st birthday. "To my delight, the band broke up a month later. So it was like, 'See – you guys were nothing without me!' For once it was true. Normally when you say that, the band replaces you very easily. 'You can't carry on without me – I *am* the band!' "

Just as Neat Change changed for the worse, Peter had a phone call from Chris Squire inviting him down to rehearse with a new version of Mabel Greer's Toyshop. Peter asked what they were going to call themselves. Replied Chris, "We're gonna call ourselves Yes." Said Peter with alacrity, "But that was *my* idea!" At any rate, Banks was invited to witness the revised group in action with a new lead singer – Jon Anderson. "The name Yes kind of stuck," says Peter. "We used it as a temporary name until something better came along. Nobody has thought of anything better yet."

The nascent Yes were still seeking the elusive perfect drummer who could enhance their new musical style. They found one in Bill Bruford. Peter had not played with Bill before, but the lively young drummer from Tonbridge had already gigged with Mabel Greer's Toyshop. Or so he says. Curiously enough Chris Squire has no recollection of Bill playing with Mabel Greer's Toyshop, but Bill insists he did. It may have been that in Chris' mind the band was already Yes, while it was officially still known as Mabel Greer. At any rate Bill soon learned how to fit in his clean cut jazz style with Chris Squire's increasingly powerful bass guitar work. Compromises had to be made but the result would be one of the most flexible and creative rock rhythm sections known to science.

★   ★   ★

Bill Bruford was recruited via an advert he placed in *Melody Maker*, the weekly musicians' paper. Says Jack Barrie, "I don't remember where Bill came from, but I know that Jon just loved Bill and thought he was the greatest."

Jon rang Bill and asked what kind of drum kit he had. He claimed it was a Ludwig but it turned out to be mainly a set of low budget Olympic drums painted black. Jon was sufficiently impressed to ask Bill to play at the Rachel McMillan College in Deptford, South London on June 7, 1968. It was Mabel Greer's Toyshop's last gig.

William 'Tubs' Bruford would bring a rare intelligence to the Yes rhythm department. He not only ensured Yes swung, he made them sound like a big band. No wonder Jon Anderson was in such awe of the assured young percussionist with the ready laugh and barbed retort. He was probably the only drummer in town who could have brought the putative Yes style to life with such confidence. He wasn't just a drum accompanist, he brought form and shape to the music.

Bill was undoubtedly Mr. Cool. But his occasional outbursts covered an inner sensitivity. He could just as easily be hurt by the machinations of an industry that he now admits, as a naïve young musician, he did not really understand. But he would learn – very quickly. He was born in Sevenoaks, Kent on May 17, 1949, the son of a local veterinary surgeon. A bright and ambitious boy, he went to Tonbridge public school. Says Bill, "I was born and raised in the same house. I started playing drums in the attic – when I was 13!"

Although it amused Bill to be dubbed 'Tubs' in honour of the tools of his craft, he is as far removed from the popular image of the drummer as could be imagined. Highly articulate, armed with a caustic wit, he is very much an enthusiast and a constant source of energy. Sometimes impatient, he tends not to suffer fools gladly. Yet he will freely give his time and encouragement to any project or person he thinks is worthwhile. Of all the bands he has played with, Yes still holds a special place in his heart, even though he has become somewhat disenchanted with them in recent years, mainly as a result of his agreeing to take part in Anderson, Bruford, Wakeman & Howe, only to see it converted back into a less efficient Yes.

A quiet English country town might seem an unlikely place for a bright eyed public schoolboy to be turned onto the modern jazz and hard-core Bebop devised by Charlie Parker and Dizzy Gillespie in the steamy night clubs of New York City. Bill explains it was all because of a long running BBC TV series called *Jazz 625*. Its remarkable roster of guest American stars inspired his burgeoning interest in jazz in general and drumming in particular. The series was so named because the new BBC-2 service launched in Britain in the Sixties was transmitted on 625 lines. Usually hosted by ex-*Melody Maker* music critic Steve Race, the programme featured many of the giants of American jazz, who invariably played wonderfully well in front of an invited audience at the London TV studios.

"I used to sit and watch endless streams of terrific jazz in black and white on Saturday evenings," recalls Bill. "I think I saw everyone I needed. 'Philly' Jo Jones, Max Roach, Cannonball Adderley, Art Blakey – all the good guys. Around that time my sister gave me a pair of brushes as a birthday present. A boyfriend had told her if you swished them around on the back of a thick card album sleeve it would sound like a snare drum. So I learned to play with brushes first on the back of an album sleeve – while watching *Jazz 625*. It was a perfect education."

Bill was given a single snare drum. A full drum kit would have to wait. But gradually he built up his armoury, with the addition of various tom toms, cymbals and a bass drum.

Although the tendency is to assume all teenagers were rock'n'roll fans in the Sixties, in fact many were drawn to jazz music of all kinds, from the big bands to the Dave Brubeck Quartet. Says Bill, "When I went to boarding school at Tonbridge, Kent, there was a very strong jazz thing happening." In Bruford's 'house' at school he found a quartet of 17 year olds who played the kind of music he had been listening to on *Jazz 625*. "They played very well too, although I was very young and no connoisseur. So I grew up learning to play 'ting ting, ta ting', rather than 'boom, boom chick'. In other words I played triple rather than duple pulse music – jazz not rock."

It turned out the regular drummer with the group was leaving and on his way out he kindly offered to teach new recruit Bill how to improvise. He also showed Bruford the Jim Chapin tutor book, the Bible of all advanced drum students. He was simply told 'get to work'. A house master who had a grand piano let them use his room to rehearse and they formed a group with tenor sax, piano, bass and drums.

"That's how we started. And then The Beatles came along and The Rolling Stones and we listened to them. We thought they were quite good but not *nearly* as good as Art Blakey and The Jazz Messengers! Jazz was pretty hip then and we didn't know it was supposed to be an old persons' music. I thought The Rolling Stones looked pretty old. I thought Bobby Timmons looked young. Jazz was American and exotic and we had a stack of jazz albums and only a couple of pop records."

After leaving school Bill went to Leeds University as an economics student and he might have ended up working for British Airways or the sugar giants Tate & Lyle in some senior capacity. That was the career mapped out for him – in theory. However it wasn't long before he succumbed to the lure of the drums.

"I ran both things pretty close up until leaving university. I had a gap year between leaving school and going to university and it was during that year that I did a few gigs. I was full of illusions about the music business and went to Rome to join a ghastly group called The Noise. The guys couldn't play and I had a miserable time. I nearly wept. I had to hitch back home with my drum kit. It was a nightmare journey. I came back in December 1968 feeling bitter. I picked up the *Melody Maker* and placed an ad. And a guy called Jon Anderson rang up and asked me to meet him. We set about forming Yes and we had no idea of the potential."

Bill describes this milestone achievement in an amusingly offhand way. "I believe I can say I helped form Yes – at the Lucky Horseshoe coffee shop in Shaftesbury Avenue as I recall."

Although Bill had started out playing jazz, and likes to say he thought Yes were a 'jazz band' he realised that if he were to make a living and gain experience in the real world, he would have to adapt his style to rock and pop music. It was a practical move that bore instant results. He had already played some gigs with The Savoy Brown Blues Band (and been dropped for messing with the beat). Now events moved at lightning speed. For Bill it all seemed like a blur. Certainly the band that became Yes were desperately anxious to get moving.

Only hours after their meeting, Bill, Chris and Jon did a gig that very night, at Rachel Macmillan's College. Bill remembers they played the 1965 Wilson Pickett tune which Peter Banks also confirms was Jon's big number of the day.

"We played 'In The Midnight Hour' – forever. We only had about one tune we could play. Chris and Jon sang it in harmony. I thought, 'Wow, that's pretty good – they're a vocal group like the Beach Boys.' I'd never really heard vocal pop or harmony singing up until then, and thought it was pretty slick. Clive Bailey was the guitar player then, and he had a bright orange Mini car with blacked out windows – so how could I refuse the gig? And we started work. Clive moved on fairly quickly and then Peter Banks appeared. He and Chris had been in The Syn together. They were exciting times."

★　★　★

With Jon, Chris, Peter and Bill in place, the new band was finally completed with the addition of keyboard player Tony Kaye, quickly known as 'Kaye of the Keyboards' after a particularly naff *MM* headline. Tony would become a much loved member of Yes whose fate was to be cast off like an old shoe, until he was recalled for duty after Yes had gone through at least three more 'keyboard wizards'. Having worked with David Bowie in the meantime, he would take great pleasure in the irony of being back in the band years later when it had its biggest ever hit.

Good looking, affable Mr. Kaye was born Anthony John Selridge on January 11, 1946 in Leicester. He had piano lessons from the age of four. His grandmother was a concert pianist and his grandfather was a jazz saxophone player who went to work in America. Recalls Tony, "My parents never told me much about him. Apparently he was involved in stage musicals and the jazz scene. I got to know my grandmother quite well. She was a splendid old lady. When she died she left me her piano, a beautiful grand which I tinkered around on when I was quite small. My parents sent me to a piano teacher called Miss Flanagan, also a splendid old lady, who taught me a great deal about the philosophy of life as well as piano lessons. By the time I was seven or eight I had mastered quite a few classical pieces and I started to enjoy playing. When I was 12 I used to play at concerts and did piano duets. I was still having lessons right up until the age of 18."

Until he was 17 Tony wanted to be a classical concert pianist, but started getting interested in other forms of music at school. A buddy was a trad jazz fan and another had a collection of modern jazz records. They formed a sort of Temperance Seven style band at Grammar School. Tony had continued listening to classical music until he discovered Count Basie and Duke Ellington. He joined the Danny Rogers Orchestra in Leicester when he was just 15.

"The leader lent me a postal course in arranging and I stayed with them for years. We played four gigs a week. It was a mind blower. I was still with them when I got my first organ, an early Vox Continental. I was really proud of it. Then I started getting into R&B and saw groups like Family."

When he left school Kaye had to decide whether to go into music college or do something else. "There was quite heavy competition in classical piano playing and I didn't think I was good enough. The alternative was a teaching career and I didn't want that." Tony went to Leicester Art College on a three year advertising and design course. He was also playing every night with a group or the big band and in the end was asked to leave the college. "I knocked around Sweden and France with a group and came home not knowing what to do. I was mixed up and dissatisfied."

His musical tastes had by now fully switched from classical to rock'n'roll. He played in several groups including Johnny Taylor's Star Combo and The Federals, who released a series of singles for Parlophone during 1964-65 and backed US star Roy Orbison on tour. Just before meeting Chris Squire in Las Chasse Club Kaye had been with the group Bittersweet and had also played with Winston's Fumbs.

Chris was impressed with his credentials and Mr. Kaye was on the team. The first edition of Yes was complete.

The band always wanted a big keyboard sound right from the beginning and it was often mooted that Tony was unwilling to experiment with a wider range of instruments. It was this that supposedly led to his abrupt departure from Yes. In the meantime Kaye's keyboards added greatly to the rhapsodic sound of the early Yes arrangements which shaped the first three albums.

Says Tony, "I used to go to the Marquee and watch Graham Bond and I liked the sound Bond got from the organ. Until then I had been playing my Vox like a piano." But it wasn't until six months after joining Yes that Tony (or rather their manager) could afford to get him a Hammond organ which provided a range of dynamic sounds.

Once ensconced in their rehearsal room, down in their fetid basement off Shaftesbury Avenue, Yes got to work. The pavement trembled beneath the feet of passers-by, as the band began to thunder and roar through their newly spawned complex arrangements.

Yes were on their way. All they had to do now was find an audience, a manager and a record company. Most bands in their position would beg, scream and pray for help. All they had to do was play.

3

NO EXPERIENCE NEEDED

Jack Barrie had set the wheels in motion but it was down to Chris Squire and Jon Anderson to pull their band together. However they did have help from another source. Recalls Jack, "There was a Northern character called John Roberts who was a great extrovert. Quite how he ended up in La Chasse club I don't know but he had a huge capacity for alcohol, which of course made him a very welcome customer."

Says Jon, "I was in a club and suddenly the person next to me said, 'You must be from Accrington with an accent like that.' I asked him how he knew and he said he was from Skipton in Yorkshire and that at one stage he had been thinking of putting some money into an Accrington band called The Warriors. I couldn't believe it and neither could he when I told him I used to sing with them. His name was John Roberts and when I told him I was in town trying to raise cash for a new band he loaned me £500."

Roberts, who died in the Eighties, was a wealthy paper manufacturer who actually lived in Settle, in north west Yorkshire. He was well known on the local music scene, notably in the nearby market town of Skipton. Assumed by locals to be gay because he preferred the company of young men to men or women of his own age, he was regarded as more sociable than predatory. A jovial, portly extrovert and big spender, for reasons long forgotten he was nicknamed 'Nockets' among his friends and acquaintances.

Among the many places where he used to drink was the Manor House in Thornton near Barnoldswick on the Yorkshire/Lancashire border, a pub where blues and R&B bands from London would perform on Sunday evenings. He befriended many aspiring local rock musicians and those fans to whom rock was becoming more than just something to dance to at a party. A keen jazz fan, he made frequent forays to London to visit Ronnie Scott's Club. There he got to know visiting American musicians including famed singer Jon Hendricks. After meeting Jon Anderson at La Chasse, 'Nockets' introduced him to Hendricks, knowing he was a fan.

Says Jack Barrie, "John Roberts used to tell us stories about the jazz musicians he knew and how he used to go to Ronnie's where he invariably got the best seat in the house. There he'd fall asleep in the front row and Ronnie often used to make a sarcastic comment: 'I see John's enjoying himself tonight.' John also enjoyed the music that Jon and Chris were trying to do and he began part financing them with me."

The £500 was used to buy some equipment and rent a rehearsal room. "The Lucky Horseshoe basement became the rehearsal room for the original Yes," recalls Jack Barrie. "It cost about £4 a day to hire. John Roberts put in some cash at a time when money was short and that helped them get up and running. Although he was from the North I don't think he was known to Jon Anderson prior to the Chasse Club days. He was a wonderful fellow and did a lot to encourage the band when they were penniless."

The group spent hours in the basement perfecting their sound and arrangements. Their biggest ambition was to land a gig at The Marquee. In the summer of 1968 The Marquee, despite the fact it had no bar, no air conditioning and its floors were covered in chewing gum, was the music centre of the universe. If that seems like an exaggeration it has to be remembered that among the bands and artists who played there seven nights a week throughout the year could be found such star attractions as David Bowie, Led Zeppelin, The Who, Traffic, Jimi Hendrix, Jeff Beck, Ten Years After, Joe Cocker, Jethro Tull and the Crazy World Of Arthur Brown – all for six shillings admission and the price of a packet of crisps.

The new band struggling in a basement a couple of streets away on the other side of Soho had a lot to live up to. Although these impoverished musicians came from widely differing backgrounds Jon was determined to mould the group into a team, with his vision of its aims clearly defined. "When we started Yes one of the things I really wanted to instil in the band was my position," says Jon. He'd already suffered rejection from The Gun. Now Jon would make his position quite plain: "First of all – I'm not just the singer. I'm part of the ensemble. I'm interested in writing music. I'm interested in the visual look of the band on stage, I'm interested in the sound." The various members of Yes would always have to take that on board or store up trouble for the future.

Says Jon looking back on those early days, "The whole history of Yes was subsequently built around sacrificing a lot of our finances in order to make a better show and to make a better record. The group always agreed it was better to spend more money on putting on a good show than taking it all home at the end of a tour and putting it in the bank. Whether that's a good thing or not is hard to say, but here we are, still going thirty years later! At that time I had seen enough groups on stage in London to realise there was a big gap and there was a need for a more musical approach. I realised you could extend songs and play longer pieces of music. So when we started we didn't have any boundaries or barriers.

"The main thing was I didn't want us to become one hit wonders. I didn't want to have one hit record and disappear. I didn't want us to be The Applejacks! I remember when Elton John gave us three songs and we never recorded them. They were very happy pop songs and I was frightened of becoming like another Andy Fairweather Lowe with Amen Corner, who were flavour of the month in 1968."

Jon's whole future might have taken a different turn, and Yes might never have existed, if he hadn't been quite so stubborn in his views. "Just before I met Chris I went to see Amen Corner's management to do an audition for a group. They were forming another band and I went to this house in Deptford in South London. There was a big fat guy sitting there with a cigar who was the band's manager and he had the band in the living room all set up. He said, 'Right, I want you to sing.' "

Jon checked out that the band could play a couple of his favourite numbers, 'Hold On I'm Coming' and 'In The Midnight Hour'. He did his audition and the manager took him to one side said, "Well, I think you are very good Jon. You are in the top three. Can you come back next Tuesday for an image test?" Anderson was flabbergasted. "What do you mean – an image test?" Said the manager, "Well, we're going to bring in a hairdresser and a photographer and if they think your image is right for the band, you'll be in." Jon's response was swift. "I said 'screw you' and I didn't go back. I thought if it depends on how I looked – no way. Maybe I didn't look right – I dunno. I probably needed a makeover, but at the time I thought I was a good singer and had a lot of dreams. Within a week I had met Chris."

★   ★   ★

It was pure chance that even before they had ventured out of their basement rehearsal room Yes would be seen in action by a journalist who would one day become the News Editor and an influential music critic on *Melody Maker*. Chris Charlesworth and his best friend, known to all as Twinque, chanced upon Yes rehearsing while on holiday carousing around the West End. Booze and birds were the main items on the agenda for these carefree likely lads from Skipton who knew John Roberts from their home town. When Roberts learned the pair were going to spend a week in London he tipped them off to look up his old friend Jack Barrie at La Chasse. They found the Soho bar a friendly retreat amid the unfamiliar streets of the seething capital.

During conversations over comforting pints of bitter Jack introduced them to his head bottle washer and part time singer Jon Anderson, who promptly invited them to come and see his band rehearsing. The next day Chris and Twinque located the basement beneath the Lucky Horse Shoe and descended into a hot and Spartan room where the band were playing at full volume. Recalls Chris, "Apart from Jon they had no idea who we were. We just thought they sounded better than any band we'd ever heard in Yorkshire . . . such long numbers and very complex. I played guitar myself in a local band up in Skipton, but this was way out of my league. It was incredibly loud and smoky down there but they seemed very professional and they were all very polite and friendly towards us. Of course I didn't write about them as I was working for a Bradford paper as a news reporter at the time. They wouldn't have been interested in some unknown band rehearsing in London. In any case I was on holiday!"

Two years later Chris Charlesworth joined *Melody Maker* and became its News Editor, and later its New York correspondent. He would observe the rise of Yes during the Seventies and write many stories about their exploits. He never forgot his early encounter with the band. He'd even taken a series of photographs of them rehearsing. They would now be of great historical value – if Chris hadn't lost the lot!

Says Jack, "What I remember particularly about those first rehearsals underneath the café was trying to think of a name for the group. We came up with two names. One was Life and the other was Yes. Both Jon and I decided what was needed was a single name. It shouldn't be too long and complicated. We wanted something simple and very much to the point. If we had chosen Life we might have had an advertising campaign for their records showing an embryo in a pregnant woman. I remember everyone laughing about that idea. In the late Sixties we couldn't have got away with it. We were just imagining a heavy press campaign for a group called Life and how it could be done, with a picture of a woman about to give birth." Eventually Life was dropped and the band became Yes. Jack probably didn't know that the guitarist had bequeathed the name.

"Jon had such great musical foresight," insists Jack. "The whole concept of the band was very much Jon's from the very beginning. He only needed to surround himself with great musicians to bring it off. Everyone was then entitled to *his* opinion. That's the best way of putting it!"

The next step was to get the boys some work and Jack Barrie called up all his contacts among London's agents and promoters. They did a few badly paid gigs and eventually got a coveted support spot at The Marquee where they stood more chance of being spotted by journalists, promoters and record company talent scouts. Club manager John Gee wasn't into just giving jobs away, even if he was keen on a particular band. Says Jack Barrie, "He wasn't stupid. He wouldn't give a band a gig just because they were friends. They had to be good and Yes *were* good. Certainly they had the opportunity to be heard. Somebody like John Gee would be invited to a rehearsal and he respected my opinion sufficiently to come and see them. He was sold on their ability and so they played at The Marquee."

While many thought of Jon Anderson as even more shy and retiring than Peter Banks, Jack Barrie disagrees. "Oh no, not at all. Chris was the quiet one. Jon was very much an extrovert. He had to be to get the band gigs. They weren't signed to anybody and everything was done by word of mouth. If Jon and Chris hadn't hit it off from their first meeting, it would never have worked out. They made a good team. However their equipment wasn't very good, and consequently they had to work harder to get their sound and ideas across. The worst thing that happened to groups was when millions of pounds got thrown at them by record companies. They'd then lay back, get lazy and let all the gear do the work. Their performances were dismal as a result. Performances were definitely better from the poorer bands because they had that much more of a struggle. Yes were a poor, struggling band for a long time."

★   ★   ★

Bill Bruford soon revealed his practical nature by keeping a record of all the payments for the early Yes gigs in a notebook which he still treasures and which provides a rich source of information. When I met him at his Surrey home in the Spring of 1998 he produced the book and confirmed that the first gig he played with Chris and Jon was on June 7 at the Deptford college, under the name of Mabel Greer's Toyshop, for which they were paid the princely sum of £11. In retrospect it's a pity that Bill wasn't elected treasurer, secretary or even manager of the fledgling outfit. It would have saved them years of grief and lots of money.

The band rehearsed in the Shaftesbury Avenue basement from June 10–29 and from July 1–9. Says Peter Banks, "That place is now an Italian restaurant. I went down there and met Jon and Chris. Tony Kaye was also there. That was the first time I'd ever met Tony. We got on like a house on fire. I thought he was a very cool guy. He said he had a Hammond organ and we thought that was great. In fact what he had was a Vox Continental!"

During those crucial weeks Chris and Jon were still in the throes of deciding who should be the lead guitarist and drummer. Says Peter, "Having been in two bands with Chris before, I fitted in pretty neatly. We auditioned quite a lot of drummers, but when Bill came along, we thought, 'This is the guy for us.' He was a jazz drummer and had on these plimsolls with 'Moon go home!' written on them in Biro, obviously referring to Keith Moon. That's the first thing I remember about him, seeing these shoes with 'Moon go home'."

This seemed to spark off something of an altercation between the front line and the rhythm section. Says Pete, "I remember saying, 'What's wrong with Keith Moon? He's one of my favourite drummers!' and Bill didn't like that at all. 'He's not a drummer – he just hits things!' But Bill was great. He was the youngest and he had a frighteningly good technique. We just had to get him to hit the drums harder because he was doing all these jazz fills. We'd say, 'No, no you can't do that. This is a rock band!' He still maintains to this day that he thought Yes were going to be a jazz band with good vocals. We all had different influences. Tony was more of a soulful player and was great at filling spaces with his mighty swirling organ."

The first gig under the Yes banner was played at East Mersea Youth Camp in Essex on August 4, 1968. They had a week to get a set ready to play. Few can remember much about the reaction to the band at this less than momentous début. But the second gig at The Marquee a few days later saw the chaps on home ground, playing to people who understood rock music and its aspirations.

Peter Banks: "It is seldom mentioned that Yes basically began as a covers band doing interpretations of other artists' material. But what covers they were, given the full Yes treatment! We had a ton of music to play, lots of changes to relay and to squeeze it all into an hour set. We didn't just rearrange a song – we celebrated it with much enthusiasm. We were doing this at a time when most British rock groups were blues based and very much in a post-psychedelic 'just wanting to rock out man'-mode."

Yes quickly established a band book of material drawn from their favourite artists including The Beatles, ('I'm Only Sleeping', 'Eleanor Rigby' and 'Every Little Thing'), Fifth Dimension ('Paper Cup') and Traffic ('Heaven Is In Your Mind'). They also played songs by Buffalo Springfield and extracts from Leonard Bernstein's *West Side Story*. Says Peter, "We wanted the tightness and controlled power of a jazz band, lots of light and shade, all with great three part harmony vocals. The musicians in Yes had a united ambition to be as good and as versatile on their chosen instrument as possible. It was because of the musical disparity of the five Yes members that this strange musical stew cooked so well. Jon Anderson was always the ring master of the Yes circus. I once unkindly compared him to Napoleon. If anybody did have a grand vision of Yes it would be him."

Although it was quickly discernible that here was a very skilled band bursting with ideas, audiences took a while to cotton on. Says Peter, "People were very bemused because we didn't do the 'covers' like the original tunes. We went down pretty good in London, but outside of town we had a lot of very puzzled faces when Jon would say, 'We're now gonna do a Beatles' tune.' And we'd kind of do 'Eleanor Rigby' at 150 beats per minute. It wasn't quite what they expected. We didn't want to sound like The Beatles. The whole point was 'let's do it our way'.

"When we used to rehearse in this basement, we'd carry all the equipment including Marshall stacks and the Vox Continental up these stairs, put them in the van and then drive off to Northampton or Birmingham to do a gig. Jon was always cracking the whip. He was always planning things and he was two months ahead of everybody else. He likes to give the impression of being a mild and gentle hippie but he was the motivating force behind the band. He also wanted to be the musical arranger, so he would try and tell us what to play and sometimes he succeeded and sometimes he didn't. His technical knowledge of playing an instrument then was negligible.

"He would play open strings on a guitar and say to me, 'Play that chord.' And I'd say, 'Well, what chord *is* it?' If I said, 'Well Jon I don't think that note fits in there,' he'd just say, 'Yes it does fit. It's my song and it fits.' Later I'd change it around and he'd say, 'See, I told you it fits!' Jon was a good communicator, but on most of those early compositions, either I or Tony Kaye would change the chords around so they would fit. Jon was always very stubborn and say, 'No, that is the right chord, because it is *my* chord.' Secretly we'd made it sound more musical. But he was the only one with a concept. The number one priority was to have good vocals because he and Chris liked Simon & Garfunkel a lot. When Crosby, Stills & Nash came out it was like, 'See, *that's* what we should be trying to do'. So having good lead and backing vocals was the priority. Then priority Number Two was not to sound like anybody else. No blues licks. I didn't want to be a blues player anyway, as ninety per cent of the bands in London at that time were playing 'Woke up this morning . . .' I'd been through my stage of trying to sound like Eric Clapton and everybody had been influenced by Jimi Hendrix. I had got through that period and was pretty secure in my own style. I knew I didn't want to play straight blues as it was too limiting."

Jon admits he could be very tough in the way he dealt with the band in their early days. "I *was* very aggressive. That's caused by uncertainty − about who you are and what you are doing. They used to call me Napoleon because I was very aggressive about being committed. When people turned up late and rehearsals then became a joke, I was the one who said, 'I will not stand for this. You are all damn lucky to be musicians and you are all damn lucky to be in a band that's successful. So let's get on with it!' I just used to impress on everybody how fortunate we were to be able to be making music in a band. If anybody didn't want to toe the line then it was his fault and he could move on and do something else.

"That was a hard line but it was the truth. You could not come into the band and expect to make beautiful music without being well rehearsed. If you are not well rehearsed on stage it's a dangerous place to be. If you haven't been practising your football skills, when you get on the pitch then you are going to let your team down. That's all that I ever wanted – that we would be a team. I was not the boss. I was the team captain. Before they were respected, singers were expected to cart the equipment around, drive the van and that was it. I wanted to be more assertive, but I was never personal. It was never a personal thing between me and who-ever. It was simple. You either worked for the group, or you were not in the group. And that's nothing new. It's not like I made that up – ha, ha! It did lead a lot of people to think that the band was always changing personnel. But if one person in the group was not taking care of business, then he really should move on. There had to be a commitment to rehearsing, to creating the music and working as a team."

Jon has been criticised over the years for his disciplinarian approach but it clearly worked for the betterment of the group. "It was never a personal vendetta by me to get somebody to move on or out of the band," he insists. "It could never be said that was the case. The group would sit down and say, 'What are we gonna do about so-and-so?' "

In Jon's view it was not the case that individual musicians were sup-pressed or discouraged from taking a prominent role. "That was the whole idea of the group, that you had five soloists who were also able to work as a team. So you could leave the audience with Steve Howe for ten minutes or with Rick Wakeman for ten minutes. You would create a show around five talented musicians and then show collectively that we could create some special music together. It was never just song after song. Yes concerts then and now were always to do with the individuals within the band and Yes as a whole. There was always space for solos. The music of Yes is so wonderful to perform. You might be playing the same notes every night but you are not playing it the same way every night. There would be subtle differences. Some nights it would be so magnificent, other nights it would just be good. Some nights it would be unbelievable. It's the unbelievable moments that you are looking for – those unreal and spiritual moments. We could play 'And You And I' and every fourth show it will transcend into something else. When we started doing 'Revealing Science Of God' from *Topographic Oceans* during our 1998 tour it was a difficult first two weeks. We felt this music was still *us*. Eventually it became a dream to perform. Some nights it was on such a beautiful level it would take us all by storm. We'd come off stage and go 'Wow! The feeling tonight – what the heck happened?' It was still a tough piece of music to perform."

47

But back in 1968 they could only dream about achieving a major epic like *Topographic Oceans*. Bill Bruford remembers the early Yes rehearsals as a time for getting their stage set together as quickly as possible. "The band started out by playing non-original material, doing various cover versions, for a very simple reason. We thought we'd get more work that way!"

Vanilla Fudge and The Fifth Dimension were their role models. "We'd make various long-winded arrangements of tunes like 'You Keep Me Hanging On', The Beatles' 'Everything Little Thing' and The Byrds' 'I See You'. Eventually we said, 'Let's do some of our own material'," says Bill. "I can't recall what the first tune was that we ever wrote together. It was primarily down to Jon and Chris who wrote some sort of song and the arrangements weren't that complicated. I would just supply the top beat of the day! But then we got a bit more adventurous and I sort of came to the fore around 'Heart Of The Sunrise' where I started bringing in odd metres and supplying rhythmic counterpoint. Then the whole group started to sound more sophisticated. Instead of the drummer just playing the rhythm, Chris and I would set up something and the melody would have a counter rhythm on top. As a result there would be a couple of rhythms happening at once and that would be more fun and exciting and we got better at doing that."

Despite all the tensions, the conflicts of interest and the egos of the various members brought together into this unlikely band, a kind of chemical reaction took place which made the band seem much bigger, more important and more powerful than any of its constituents. It was this chain reaction set off in a West End basement that would eventually lead the band to conquer the rock world in a way none of them could have predicted as they struggled up the stairs, dragging Tony Kaye's organ behind them and grumbling about the latest Napoleonic edict.

For the moment they had the more tangible ambition of simply getting bookings. Jon Anderson set to work. He used every contact he had to secure gigs. On July 20 Yes played at the Market Hall, Kingston, Surrey and on the 26th they played at the Sports Centre, Bracknell, followed by the Municipal Hall, Newmarket (27). Their drummer dutifully noted that his total wage during July consisted of £22 13s 9d. Says Bill, "That wasn't bad – remember, pounds, shillings and pence?"

During the rest of their first formative year together the band persevered with a regular gig schedule while fitting in much needed rehearsals to develop their stage act so it would consist of more than a handful of cover tunes. On August 5 they played their first show at The Marquee. Fame at last! Then a few days later, on August 10, they were dispatched back to the provinces to play at the Red Lion, Walsall. "Ee, what's this tripe. Mine's a pint."

Peter remembers them playing at the now long gone Revolution Club, a trendy West End night spot off Berkeley Square that was often used to showcase new talent. Here they got a very encouraging reaction, at least from fellow musos. "We did two sets and they kept asking us to turn down because it was basically a discotheque. There's us playing very loudly and doing all these unusual arrangements. Then in the interval somebody hit me round the back of the head. It was Pete Townshend of The Who. 'You're a fucking great guitar player!' I was in heaven! He said I had the same attitude as Eric Clapton. I looked kinda shy but was outgoing on the guitar.

"He gave me this five minute lecture on my playing which was really good advice. He loved the band and we later did some gigs supporting The Who. Pete used to come on and announce us and say, 'This is the best fucking band you're gonna see. They've got a great singer and a great guitarist.' He did that for us which was wonderful. We did a few university tours with The Who and by then Bill had got a liking for Keith Moon, so all that changed. It also opened us up to a new kind of audience."

Bruford duly noted in his band book that he earned £32 in August, so clearly Yes were gaining in popularity, at least among bookers. In September they found themselves back at The Marquee.

As Yes began to pick up regular gig money, they could begin to support themselves, although various girlfriends were still willing to chip in with paying the rent. Jon and Chris could at last afford to move into their own place. They took over a flat in Drayton Gardens, Fulham, not too far from a small club in Queensgate called Blaises. It was here that the next and most important step up the ladder took place.

Recalls Jack Barrie, "There was a famous club called the Speakeasy in Margaret Street that everybody went to, which was managed by a chap called Roy Flynn. When the Speakeasy caught fire Roy moved the club to Blaises – which I always thought was rather an apt name."

Of all the hip in-crowd clubs of Swinging London, Blaises was perhaps the most discreet and off beat. Unlike the more raucous Speakeasy or overtly camp Cromwellian (which featured the famed Harry's Bar on the top floor), Blaises seemed to attract a cooler clientele. Rock stars and musicians tended to be on their best behaviour here, perhaps because they were somewhat overawed by the professional gamblers who sat staring intently at the roulette wheels, studiously ignoring the visitors.

A deceptively spacious basement was reached by a set of twisting iron stairs. Once past the eagle eye of the doorman you entered a series of connecting rooms, a bar and lounge with a space for a band at the far end. There was no stage as such, at least not that one can recall. The chrome furniture and luxurious sofas had an Italian style 'Vogue Interiors' look, and it was more a place for liaisons in dark corners than loud, boozy misbehaviour. However it was here that The Jimi Hendrix Experience made their first appearance in London back in 1966, watched by members of The Who, Beatles and Stones. Thereafter and throughout the late Sixties there was a steady flow of clubbers and ravers, welcomed by the regular host Jim Carter Fea, until Roy Flynn took up residency.

Jack Barrie: "There was an act booked to appear at Blaises one Sunday evening that failed to turn up. It was supposed to be Sly & The Family Stone. Roy had a full house and needed some form of entertainment. It was Tony Stratton Smith, a friend of mine, who knew that Yes lived just around the corner. Roy Flynn was desperate and Tony said, "I know a band that lives nearby. I'm sure they'd love a gig if you paid them some money.""

Roy Flynn: "Sly & The Family Stone were due to appear at 11.30 p.m. Then the record company rang me at 11 p.m. to say, 'Sorry, Sly's not coming – he's out to lunch.' I thought, 'Now what?' I walked towards the double doors seeking inspiration – and the first person I saw was Tony Stratton Smith."

The avuncular Strat was a familiar figure in the music business as both a manager and record company boss. He ran the Charisma label and managed Genesis, The Nice and The Bonzo Dog Doo Dah Band. "I said, 'Tony, where the bloody hell can I get a band from at this time of night?' He said there was a band he'd seen at The Marquee who lived nearby. I went down to this scruffy flat and met Jon and Chris. They rounded up the boys and they went on stage at 1 a.m. I was totally knocked out and it was like one of those Hollywood movies as I heard myself saying I wanted to manage them. Normally I never went on stage to announce the bands but after they had played, I found myself willed to go on the stage. I said, 'Ladies and gentlemen, thank you for coming. Tonight could have been a disaster. On the contrary, it has been magnificent'."

Peter Banks remembers that momentous night vividly. "Everyone was living in Drayton Gardens in Fulham but I was still living at my parents' place in Barnet. Jon phoned me up and said, 'Come on, we've got a gig tonight.' This was about 11 p.m. So we all rushed down to play at Blaises. There were lots of famous people there all waiting for Sly & The Family Stone. Instead they got Yes. And we went down very well. Keith Emerson was there and so was Pete Townshend and Eric Clapton . . . a lot of faces!"

Yes made their Blaises début on September 16, 1968. They went down well with the audience, and seriously impressed the host Roy Flynn, so much so that he offered to be their manager on the spot. Says Peter, "Roy immediately said, 'I'd like to manage you' and we said, 'Yeah!' It was as simple as that."

As Flynn would later discover, it would not prove quite so simple but for the moment it seemed the band had reached a turning point. At last the wheels of the music business were beginning to grind into action on their behalf. Bill Bruford: "We really started to take off after that gig. These were the days when you *could* make a big impression on people and cause a stir!"

Roy doesn't even remember if the crowds were cheering. "I certainly was! In a blinding flash their music got through to me. It's very odd. By nature I am very cautious and I had never, ever thought of managing a band in my life before. And yet there I was the very next day − buying them a Hammond organ, a red van (nicknamed Big Red and registered UMD 229F) and a new drum kit. I even found them a place to live. I sunk every penny I had into that band − and they richly rewarded me − ha, ha! Without me they would have broken up. Bruford gave it up as a bad job and went to university. But their music was so exciting. I'd never heard anything like it and I wanted to help them. Because of my running the Speakeasy I had got to know every agent, every manager, absolutely everybody in the music business. So I was in a key position to help this young band."

Banks was impressed by their new manager. "Roy took us in hand, and although he didn't really know much about managing, he learned pretty quick. We used to hang out at the Speakeasy when he re-opened the club in Margaret Street after the fire. Things started to look up and in hindsight I think Roy was a pretty good manager, despite what the other guys said. He took a lot of advice from Tony Stratton Smith, who was desperately trying to get Genesis going at this time. Roy used to say to him, 'What can I do with Yes? How can I get them more publicity.' "

Interestingly Roy Flynn recalls Peter Gabriel of Genesis asking *him* to manage Strat's band. "I said no because I'd never managed a band before. One band at a time!"

The sudden arrival of Mr. Flynn meant that Jack Barrie was now out of the picture. But he knew it was for the band's benefit. "Roy could give them what nobody else could at that time, which was financial backing," says Jack. "Jon came to me and asked what he should do. I said, 'You must go. Roy knows a lot of people and he must be able to help you. Go!' I never regret the day I kind of let him go on to better things. When I look back I suppose I could say, 'God, if only I'd managed them. I could have been a millionaire!' But on the other hand if I *had* managed them − it might have been a passport to oblivion. Everybody was in the right place at the right time. At that particular time Roy Flynn came in and had some money to offer and he built them up from there. I never had a contract with Jon. It was just that as I say, I respected him and wanted to help."

Roy Flynn's impromptu decision to manage Yes led to the band getting a proper foothold in the music industry. He got them prestige showcase spots at London's Royal Albert Hall, courted the media on their behalf and negotiated their all important record contract with Atlantic, one of America's most respected – and hippest – labels.

After their success at Blaises, Yes began to create a stir amongst London's other promoters. The band continued to develop an underground following which in turn drew the attention of the music press. Their gigs at The Marquee Club eventually turned into a residency. Then came a shock personnel crisis, the first of many that would lead all subsequent managers of Yes to tear at their hair and consult specialists in nervous disorders. Bill Bruford decided to quit.

Bill: "We played two or three times a month at The Marquee and then in September I thought, 'Enough of this,' and went off to University. The guys thought they were going to be stars, but I was determined to study and they had to get themselves another drummer."

This was all very sensible from Bruford's standpoint, especially considering the band's financial situation: when they played at The Marquee on Wednesday, November 27, 1968 their takings were £31 and 15 shillings. Out of this they had to pay the support band Van der Graaf Generator £15. After other deductions, including seven and a half pence to the booking agency, Yes were left with seventeen shillings and six pence. The Marquee added £4 2s 6d making a grand total of £5 – less than the average cover band of the day could command at a pub or a wedding gig.

Bill couldn't see this situation getting any better, so he decided to go on to higher education. His departure caused nightmares for Roy Flynn and was a big shock to the band. Says Jack Barrie, "Jon was really gobsmacked. He thought Bill's drumming was absolutely fantastic."

Bruford was already a technically proficient, tasteful and highly motivated player – a rare breed at a time when most rock drummers were still aspiring to the demolition theory of percussion – but he was also a confident young man who didn't feel that playing in a band was his entire life's work, not when his parents were still quietly expecting him to become a captain of industry.

Yes and their new manager were determined to battle on. Their emergency replacement was Tony O'Riley, drafted in from The Koobas, a group who had the distinction of having once toured with The Beatles. Tony did his best but was no match for Bruford.

Bill kept a friendly eye on the progress of his old group. When Yes came to Leeds University to play (for a fee of £50), Bill hastily rounded up all his friends. "I said, 'You've gotta hear this band, they're fantastic.' In fact it was a bit of a mess. They were in trouble and I could tell the drummer was struggling! The problem was he played a quarter note behind everybody else!"

The band were scheduled to play at the Royal Albert Hall, London on November 26, 1968, and after even more serious problems developed with their replacement drummer, Jon and Chris pleaded with Bruford to come back. The occasion was Cream's farewell concert and even though the band would only get a £25 'special fee' there could be few more important gigs that year. It had been Roy Flynn's great coup to get them on an event which would be heavily scrutinised by 'the biz'. Says Bill, "I guessed they didn't want to do it with this guy and they knew it would be okay with me."

Although he tried to appear offhand, Bill didn't really need much persuading to come down to London to do this one-off show. Then, in Bill's words, "one thing led to another." The wavering student asked his university authorities if he could take a year off as a sabbatical. They refused. The response was: "If you want to be a musician – go and do that." So Bill said "fine" and armed with a pair of sticks, rather than a degree, abandoned his studies for music. It was a rather nervous percussionist who came back to London. He found himself in the hot seat at the Royal Albert Hall in front of the nation's most avid and knowledgeable rock fans supporting Cream who had the mighty Ginger Baker on drums. "I dropped a drum stick in the opening measures of one of our first numbers. I still remember the loud clattering sound which a drum stick makes when it falls over a bass drum onto a hard wooden floor. Deafening!"

Sitting in the audience was their old friend Jack Barrie. "Rory Gallagher was on the bill with Cream as well as Yes. The critic Derek Jewell wrote a review of the concert in the *Sunday Times*. He said he overheard someone in the dressing room saying, 'These rock musicians are supposed to be so rich. I can't understand it. They roll one cigarette and pass it round.' It was me. I said it as a joke to Jon."

Despite the effects of smoke and dropped drum sticks the band played well and Bill Bruford was now firmly back in the driving seat. They carried on playing night clubs while their new manager Roy Flynn busied himself drumming up more interest. He got them yet another gig at the Royal Albert Hall, this time supporting Janis Joplin. "It was unusual for rock bands to play the Albert Hall in those days and together with some charity gigs, I think we played there four times in the space of a year," says Peter Banks. "It was almost a residency. Certainly the Cream support show was very good for us. In fact that came through Robert Stigwood who managed Cream. He also wanted Yes on his record label but Roy managed to fend him off."

Of necessity Roy's business negotiations went on behind the scenes, and members of the band remained in the dark. Both Bruford and Banks admit that in those days the workings of the music industry were a sealed book to young musicians. Bill says he left 'the business side' to the management and trusted everyone to carry out their duties on his behalf. There was no conception of musicians studying the business as a profession or gaining an understanding of contract and copyright law. Looking back at his teenage self, Bill sees what he describes as a very green young person. Bill: "I don't recall anything at all about the band trying to get a record deal. It was just automatic. One never sought one. It just came. You just signed something. And I had no idea what I was signing and no idea about publishing agreements. I didn't know that musicians could earn royalties. How would I have understood that? Nobody ever told me."

The people who really knew the ropes were the professionals in publishing and the record business. There was a wide gulf between them and the aspiring band and their manager, even though the latter was determined to do his best for them. He certainly steamed into action once he'd made the decision to manage them after their Blaises début.

"When I first took them over they had nowhere to live," says Roy, who today owns the historic Bull Inn, in Charlbury, Oxfordshire. He sits in the lounge of the inn that he runs with his wife Suzanne and pulls out old pictures, posters, contracts and memorabilia from his days with Yes. Although it proved a traumatic time for him, he is still proud of his early association with a struggling young band whose music had so impressed him. "My first 24 hours with them as manager cost me a van, a drum kit and a Hammond organ!" He also arranged a flat for them in Munster Road, provided two roadies and put everyone on a wage of £25 a week.

A jazz fan with a background in the printing business, Roy's first venue was The Pontiac Club in Putney. He took over the Speakeasy in January, 1967 and celebrated his arrival with a St. Valentine's Day party on February 14. The Speakeasy soon began to attract a stream of star visitors. Over the years everyone from The Beatles and Rolling Stones, to The Who, Cream, The Monkees and the Jimi Hendrix Experience were regulars, jamming, eating, drinking and generally carousing. Going to 'the Speak' was ultimately more pleasurable for most bands and their crews than actually playing their scheduled gigs. Vans would hurtle down the motorways of Britain heading for Margaret Street in the desperate hope of a drink and veal escalope, served by Luigi, the famously rude Italian waiter. A legendary part of the Speakeasy ambience, he clearly felt that most 'rock stars' were just well paid louts and treated them with the respect they deserved. None.

"Oh Luigi!" remembers Roy with a chuckle. "He had a very sardonic face. He had big bags under his eyes and looked as miserable as sin. He'd go round the tables in the restaurant with his order pad and say, 'Whadya fucking want?' That was his way of showing he liked people."

The club became a showcase for new British groups like Procol Harum and visiting American acts. On one famous occasion the entire Stax troupe of artists played there. The only time the author saw Sam & Dave in action was at an afternoon preview at the Speak. It became an exclusive meeting place for all kinds of music biz folk, and Yes became regular patrons, probably because their new manager could usually be relied on to pick up the tab. It's also where they met Michael Tait, a barman at the club, newly arrived from Australia, who would play a key role in the story of Yes. He graduated from driver to tour manager and eventually became their sound and lighting engineer.

Born in Melbourne on March 25, 1946, Michael escaped call-up to Vietnam and got a passport to visit England on a six week vacation, and never returned. When Roy Flynn asked him to drive the band to gigs it was the start of an ever expanding career in the rock business and a long association with Yes.

He began working with the band in September, 1968. "Yes did its first few gigs in June and July that year and then the first one I did was Leeds University. I got hired because I worked at the Speakeasy club and Roy Flynn needed somebody to drive the Transit van he had just got the band. None of the guys could drive, so that's why I was hired."

Tait soon realised that even the best behaved bands had their problems. "I remember we were in the van on the way to the gig and we couldn't get the drummer [Tony O'Riley] out of the pub. He was in there drinking. He had a bit of a drinking problem but eventually we coaxed him into the van and headed up to Leeds. We went to the University and they kind of set up the few speakers they had. In the audience of about fifty kids Bill Bruford came over because he knew the band and had played with them a couple of times. He had decided not to be a musician but was going to be an economist. When he saw the band play, I could see what was going through his mind. He would obviously prefer to be in the band! It took a while but he eventually changed his mind and came back home to the group. Straight after those early shows we went on to play with The Who, Arthur Brown and the Small Faces at the City Hall Newcastle. We only got to play a couple of songs, and the girls were screaming at the other bands – not for us of course! It was the end of the teenybopper era and rock music became more serious and Yes fitted right in that. The timing was great. Their audience was mainly young musicians, rather than young girls – unfortunately for us!"

Michael soon became adept at driving the Big Red Transit. "It was a very impressive vehicle with two rows of seats. There were the five guys and me and the equipment in the back behind a bulkhead. We careered around in that thing for a couple of years. We toured all over Europe. The agent would say, 'You've got a gig at a school.' And that's all they'd tell you. You'd have to go and kind of find the place. You'd have to ask a guy in the street, 'Is there a concert anywhere near here tonight?' It was always a battle to find out where you were playing and then you'd have to drive back to London because no one had the money to pay to stay over. If we did it was in a dreadful bed and breakfast joint where an extra slice of toast cost you sixpence.

"It was amazing fun but we did have our share of accidents of course. Chris smashed up the van once and that's how Tony Kaye broke his foot and appeared on an album cover in plaster. That was a Chris Squire accident. Driving after a gig, if you were tired, you could easily fall asleep. The band had a car for a while and a separate equipment truck. One night after I had dropped everyone off I managed to write off the car by hitting a taxi on my way home from the last drink of the night. The band lived all around London and it was a full circle of town to drop everyone off which was very boring. But they were incredible days. When I look back and compare them to today's tours with 18 trucks and nine buses, I don't know why anyone would want to do it now, because its just a job. Then it was an adventure. I did that consistently with Yes on the road for 15 years and they were incredible days, something I would never trade. They all lived together in Munster Road for a while but often they'd be moving in the middle of the night – Jon especially. He was married very early on to Jenny and when they got their own place eventually, it was always on the fourth floor. Jon would always be moving, and it was always at night. He'd never explain why but we had to get his stuff out in a hurry. He was also famous for plugging so much electrical equipment into one socket, it was like a rat nest of cables. He would wonder why the wires got fused together and there would be smoke coming out of his apartment! But that's because he always wanted his various tape machines plugged in."

Michael grew very fond of his young charges. "They were very well behaved lads compared to other groups. We didn't go around wrecking hotels. The music was everything to them and the dedication was absolutely incredible. You could see it at their rehearsals. For the first five years I'd say the music was everything. When affluence started to rear its ugly head things obviously changed, and that's only human nature. But the music was always very important with Yes and even today they have conversations in the dressing rooms after a gig that are the same as they would have had twenty years ago. When I saw the band play again on their American tour in 1998 they were absolutely stunning."

Michael Tait had a background in engineering and once he had seen the group setting up their own equipment he started doing it for them. "I could then see the possibilities. For instance with Pete Banks he had a volume pedal and then added fuzz boxes and wah-wah pedals which were new inventions. He had one of each – three pedals – so I thought instead of plugging each in separately every night I'd join them to a board and have them permanently wired together. That was possibly one of the very first pedal boards. Eventually I started getting involved with the sound. Mixing was done from the side of the stage with high impedance microphones and the instruments were not miked at all. We were playing some dreadful club in Germany one day and Jon Anderson said to me, 'You know, I can't quite hear the bass drum. Maybe we could put a mike next to the bass drum.' I thought . . . not a bad idea. No one had ever thought of it. To hear the band we only had two PA speakers, but with Jon and Peter there was always a volume battle, and Peter, although he may not remember these days, kept turning up. So there was this battle all the time, which was a difficult one to solve. It made it hard for Jon to be heard and that really did cause problems and may have been one of the reasons for Peter's subsequent departure."

★   ★   ★

Roy Flynn quickly discerned that Jon Anderson was the spokesman and ideas man in Yes, even though he didn't play an instrument. "All the music was in his head! I think the idea of the band really came to him on a trip to Germany when he'd been playing in some seedy club."

After buying new equipment Flynn then put the band with The Marquee-Martin Agency to provide them with a roster of gigs. At least that was the plan. "I used to go in there all the time asking the booker John Martin, 'Where are the gigs?' It was a problem all the time. Years later John Martin and his wife came to see me at my first pub and John confessed that he'd had a problem at the time and apologised for not getting the band enough work. There I was, knocking my brains out trying to get them off the ground, and it wasn't happening. It must have been just as frustrating for the band. However I had this thing in mind about Atlantic Records and for some strange reason I signed them world wide to Atlantic. I say 'strange' because I didn't sort out all the final details. I'm a very trusting sort of person. Having done the deal I thought they would promote the band. However the first two albums we did with Atlantic weren't well distributed and didn't really reflect the excitement of the music. I just think they did a cheap job. I didn't take any advance from them in the first year, and even the second year it was only a very modest advance, which went some way to offset the money I had personally spent on the band."

Says Chris Squire, "Roy Flynn, our first manager, was more of a club owner, but he definitely helped us on the road to being seen around and he helped us to get our first record deal, because Ahmet Ertegun of Atlantic came down to the Speakeasy where Roy was the host and heard us play, and pretty much signed us. Then when we realised we had an album to do, we started working on new material of our own so we could represent our own writing. Obviously it was an achievement to have made an album.

"With the album it was kind of funny actually because it was an example of Roy Flynn not really knowing what he was doing. He had some preliminary negotiations with Ahmet and of course he would have known that the wise thing would have been to have signed us for a three album deal. But I can remember Roy coming into the men's room at the Speakeasy to find me and saying, 'I've just spoken to Ahmet and he wants to sign us for 12 or maybe 14 albums!' I said, 'That's fantastic. He really believes in us that much?' Of course we didn't realise that was the worst thing he could possibly have done. Obviously the rates were very low for a new band just signing its first deal. So we ended up signing this very long contract for very low points. By the time our next manager Brian Lane came along and the band had become successful we managed to negotiate it up by dribs and drabs. The initial contract should have been better but Roy had been very good to us at the beginning. He had all his Speakeasy connections and we ended up playing at the Royal Albert Hall quite a lot, like when we supported Cream and Janis Joplin. It was all because Roy was owed favours by various people. But after this disastrous deal and we realised we hadn't signed the best contract, that's when we had doubts and wondered whether he really knew what he was doing. So his phase drew to a close. Until we did *The Yes Album* in 1970 which was really successful, the people at Atlantic Records at the head office in New York thought we were a folk act. I remember being told that by an employee there, after we had become successful. That was the perception."

Although he had secured the all important record contract, Roy felt frustrated at the lack of commitment from Atlantic. "I was very dis-appointed at the way they treated me. I gave them the hottest band in town. I could have done a deal with Robert Stigwood. He was just starting his own label RSO and he was very keen on Yes. It's easy to be wise after the event, but in retrospect they would have been better served by Robert because he was ambitious for his label, and would have put a lot more behind Yes than Atlantic did at that time. At the Revolution one night Ahmet Ertegun of Atlantic and Stigwood were shouting across to each other that *they* were going to sign Yes. Ultimately I felt we weren't well served by Atlantic Records. It's self evident. The first two albums are just not good records."

The reason for this was not due to the label so much as inexperience in the studio. Says Bill Bruford, "When we made our first recordings with Yes I didn't realise that you could listen to different amounts of different instruments through headphones. I thought you had to listen to what you were given, and what I was given was deafening guitar and almost nothing else."

These were the conditions that prevailed when the band recorded their first album, titled simply *Yes*, and released in August, 1969. Although the sleeve wasn't graced with the kind of elaborate cover art that Roger Dean would introduce on the 1971 *Fragile* album, the bold red and blue 'Yes' in a speech bubble on a plain black cover was most effective. (The digitally remastered version released on CD has a vintage colour photograph of the band taken in a Fulham architectural centre.)

The tracks included 'Beyond And Before', a song by Chris Squire and Clive Bailey, and The Byrds' tune 'I See You'. Jon Anderson contributed 'Yesterday And Today', 'Looking Around' and 'Survival'. They added a dramatic version of The Beatles' 'Every Little Thing'. Two more tunes, 'Harold Land' and 'Sweetness', were composed by Anderson, Squire and Bailey. There were no compositions credited to the lead guitarist but the sleeve had personal thanks to the band's friends and supporters: engineer John Anthony, Jack Barrie, John Gee and John Roberts. No mention was made of Roy Flynn, who had asked that his name be left off the credits.

Although the band were buzzing with ideas, and their career seemed to be forging ahead, making the first *Yes* album with producer Paul Clay hadn't been easy.

Bill: "We had an engineer who Pete Banks nicknamed 'The Weasel'. It was only at the end of the album that he said, 'You know you could listen to the bass as well.' I just didn't think to ask about different levels in the headphones. So if the playing on that album is a little skewed towards the guitar, that's why. On tracks like 'I See You' it turns into just guitar and drums! But if there was any jazz being played in progressive rock I was the guy who brought it in I suppose, in a very naïve way. I didn't know Yes wasn't going to be a jazz group. Nobody told me! I called one track 'Harold Land' which was named after the famous tenor saxophone player. I remember somebody saying, 'What shall we call this? I want to write a song about a man called . . .' and I said, 'Harold Land' as I walked through the room. I also tried to play vibraphone on 'Yesterday And Today'. And I didn't know you weren't supposed to swing on ride cymbals. Eventually I realised it was going to be a rock group. My style was so malleable, I didn't really have a style to adapt. It was just a mishmash of everything I'd heard."

The producer had to cope with a group who seemed to be breaking all the rules. "I don't know where Paul Clay came from," says Peter. "He had previously done movie soundtracks. We *wanted* to get Paul McCartney. This was the idea. We did some demos at Apple for Peter Asher who sat reading a newspaper all the way through. We were very pissed off. I've never heard those recordings but they are around. So instead of Paul McCartney we got Paul Clay. He was a very nice guy who knew a lot about cottages but knew sod all about producing. It was like the blind leading the blind. It was our first album and I think it was his too! Hence the drums sound like biscuit tins – and there is a kind of clangy guitar sound. The first track 'Beyond And Before' was an old Mabel Greer's Toyshop number which we used to start the set. We sang the whole song in three part harmony which was quite effective. The lyrics *are* very strange. I think they are drug induced. Too many Woodbines . . . '*Sparkling trees of silver foam cast shadows soft in winter's home, swaying branches breaking sound, in lonely forest trembling ground. In winter loam, masquerading leaves of blue, run circles round the morning dew in pattern understood by you . . .*' See I can remember the whole thing, but I haven't a clue what it means."

It would be the first of many wonderfully meaningless Yes lyrics; meaningless in the earthly sense, of course, meaningful on a more astral plane. The picaresque words sung in such close harmony with Jon's angelic vocal lines set against such powerful playing were all part of the charm and appeal of the band. "They are charmingly naïve," says Peter, whose guitar has a strangely ethereal violin tone on this magical performance, obtained by judicious use of the volume pedal. It's one of the first examples of this effect, which Steve Howe also obtained in his band Tomorrow and which Banks utilised with Syn. Banks says that influential session guitarist Big Jim Sullivan obtained a similar effect on a 1964 Dave Berry hit single called 'The Crying Game' on which he used a tone control rather than the volume pedal.

A highlight of side one of the first Yes album was a jazzy, improvised interlude played by Banks and Bruford during the superb 'I See You'. It swings with a humour, taste and subtlety rarely heard in a rock context. The guitar solo goes through a range of moods and feelings, with nifty 'quotes' from Wes Montgomery. Banks also utilises the violin tone before leaping into a violent outburst of rock histrionics. Today Peter feels rather uncomfortable about this solo, knowing with the benefit of hindsight he could have done better. At the time it was a welcome blast of improvisational ingenuity.

"It was certainly spontaneous and I tried to make it different every night. We had good nights and bad nights and sometimes if it wasn't happening on a gig, I'd go on longer and longer out of frustration and take all my aggression out on the guitar. And on the audience poor sods! I did some kind of fugue line but none of it was really worked out for the recorded version. On stage I'd end the piece by throwing my guitar in the air and catching it. There were a couple of times when I didn't! This was my post-Townshend angst period and to be honest, it did go on too long. The band used to complain about it and that just used to make me go on even longer. Chris also developed a very long bass guitar solo, but that came after I left. I was an experimental player and not all that would fit in with the concept of Yes. Bill was the same. He would change things around. I can remember him saying, 'I'm going to play everything different tonight' just before we went on stage. It was the sign of a very inventive drummer but of course I'd think, 'Well, so will I!' Poor old Jon would be going, 'What the hell is going on?' We were like misbehaving kids really."

Bill's surging roll at the climax of 'I See You' brought the whole band back with a flourish, as if Art Blakey had flown in for the session direct from a steamy night in Birdland. In fact Bill says that one of his biggest influences at the time was Jimi Hendrix's drummer Mitch Mitchell, who was more of an Elvin Jones man.

Undoubtedly what set Yes apart from other rock groups most at this time was their use of dynamics. Playing soft then loud, they'd leave pregnant pauses and empty spaces. Even today hearing the remixed version of 'I See You' is enough to make you want to leap from your inflatable plastic sofa and yell, "Yeah!" It took courage for Yes to persevere with this sophisticated style. Audiences were still programmed to expect nothing less than stolid blues rock. Yes would tease their audiences and take them on a musical adventure.

"It had shock value," agrees Bill, recalling their increased use of dynamic tension. "It was this idea that we could be like a symphony orchestra. After The Beatles anything was possible. Jon used to listen to his symphonic records and say, 'C'mon lads – why can't we do *this*!' and he'd make all these implausible demands. He had a fist of steel inside a velvet glove. If Jon liked what you were doing all was well. If he didn't you had better find something else – fast. He could be very aggressive. Probably quite rightly so. Jon was very ambitious. Carolyn my wife and I both remember him sitting on the stairs at the flat we shared at 50A Munster Road, Fulham, hustling for work on the phone like a dog. Pushing and hustling, trying to rustle up vans, trying to get another five pounds out of someone for petrol, just trying to keep the thing alive. A very hard worker."

The hard worker was featured heavily on 'Yesterday And Today', a Jon

Anderson original on which Jon sang a gentle ballad accompanied by Bill's vibes. It was never played 'live'. 'Looking Around' began with a funky Tony Kaye organ riff which recurs throughout the piece and has a cheerful Beatles' style tune. This was a popular 'live' piece and was also recorded for the BBC. "We always felt uncomfortable playing this because it was a pop song," recalls Peter. "It had lots of vocals and a lot of strange chord changes. If someone made a mistake it was very obvious. Funny old song! I used to hate playing it 'live' but now I think it's a pretty cool track."

'Harold Land' was the tune Bill Bruford named in honour of the sax player. Jon's lyrics bore no relation to jazz ancient or modern. Peter: "It was a bit of a strange one, with a Western kind of feel in the intro. We were big on Westerns. There was *The Big Country* theme on 'No Experience Necessary', a Richie Havens thing which appeared on the second album. When we couldn't find anything else to fit, we'd say, 'Let's put a bit of Western cowboy music in here.' It's absolutely true because Jon was very much into movie soundtracks. Audiences would wonder what was going on. We used to do that, just to see the expressions on their faces. It's something they just wouldn't expect. Our version of 'Every Little Thing' still sounds good and it was a killer 'live'."

After the thunderous tom-tom and deep-toned snare drum intro from Bill the band jams loosely for a while before the unison theme. Jon sings *"When I'm walking beside her . . . I remember the first time"* and the song explodes into life. 'Sweetness' too is a revelation. It was released as the band's first single with 'Something's Coming' on the B-side. It has one of Jon Anderson's most delicate and wistful vocals. A review of 'Sweetness' stated somewhat regretfully, "An outstanding group who should have made greater impact by now. This is pretty, almost sugary and unlikely to happen."

The last track was 'Survival.' "It didn't quite fit in with the rest of the album," thinks Peter Banks, "although it's very popular with Yes fans today. We played it a lot 'live' but it hasn't made it on to any bootlegs."

The growing army of Yes fans were fairly satisfied with the album and reviews in the British press were encouraging but as far as America was concerned Yes did not exist, even though they were signed to a major US label. "It hardly sold at all," recalls Peter. "All of a sudden Atlantic started putting all their money into the next great white hope which was Led Zeppelin. We were the first English rock group to be signed to Atlantic but all the money went to Zeppelin. There was no promotion and of course Roy Flynn became the scapegoat and got blamed for that. We thought we'd be off to America and we were on our way. It didn't happen. To be honest it was rather a scrappy album. I remember we spent three whole days trying to work the Hammond organ. We hired a B3 for Tony who had still been using the Vox Continental and he couldn't get it to work. Nobody knew how to record the overdrive sound. I think Keith Emerson came down and gave us some tips. The whole thing was done in about eight days with two days mixing. Ahmet Ertegun of Atlantic came down on day three to hear what we'd done. And we hadn't done anything. We tried to put off the inevitable 'Well let's hear something guys'. Here was the President of Atlantic down to see us and all we had done was some bass and drums. The producer had no idea how to record this bloody Hammond organ and we had to find out ourselves. We just couldn't get that gutsy sound and often Tony seems like he's playing a church organ. I found the sessions unpleasant because I was constantly being asked to turn down. I would say, 'Well, I'll turn down if Chris turns down.'

"Here we were doing our first album and the engineer is running around saying, 'Turn down, turn down!' The producer didn't take charge and the Weasel had never recorded a rock band before. He was like something out of the Fifties. He should have been wearing a white coat and rubber gloves. And we were Wild Men Of Rock! We weren't going to turn down. I would pretend to turn down to eight and then sneak back in and turn it up again when nobody was looking. That's how childish it got."

"We were all the same," says Bill. "We all wanted a lot. I remember a lot of arguments and a lot of mis-communication. The atmosphere was always very wired – from drinking too much coffee. We were very edgy people. But the plan was to conquer the world – which indeed we did!"

The album's gatefold sleeve had an attractive Nicky Wright photograph of the band gathered in a leafy floral setting. Flower power was still alive and well in 1969. The fresh faced youths, hair dappled by the sunlight, looked slightly preoccupied, as if worried about making it to the gig that night, or whether they could pay the month's rent and gas bills. Other pictures of them playing under an awning at an outdoor festival were more animated and you can almost hear Bill steaming into the fast choruses of 'I See You', Tony swiping the keys of the Hammond, Peter hitting a series of jazzy Wes Montgomery quotes, Chris kicking his Rickenbacker into overdrive and Jon emitting an exultant "Ahhhh!" from sheer delight.

Peter Banks says the pictures were taken at Parliament Hill Fields on Hampstead Heath. "It was on a Sunday and there was a very big crowd there. They didn't usually have concerts on Hampstead Heath. I remember getting home at 6 a.m. after a night at the Speakeasy. I was staying at Roy Flynn's at the time in a spare room and was woken up at 11 a.m. with cries of, 'Come on – we've got a gig!' We were due on stage in an hour and I was dragged out of bed. It was raining when we got there and I was half asleep and hung over and so was Tony Kaye."

Several photographers attended what proved to be one of the band's worst ever gigs. "I didn't even know we were playing that day. I wanted to be back in bed!" Instead Peter found himself clutching his Rickenbacker. This valuable guitar was coated in white house paint. It looked enormous on the youthful owner. "That's because I was a skinny little wimp. It doesn't look enormous now. I've grown into it!"

The band continued their onslaught on the London clubs. On July 9 they played at The Marquee once more, supported by a band called Hard Meat. On July 11 they supported The Nice at the Lyceum in the Strand. They were back at the Marquee on July 23 supported by Leviathan. This event gained an encouraging *MM* review. Wrote Royston Eldridge, "Yes are a young group who aren't content to stand still. They are constantly improving and re-arranging their material, adding something new each time you see them. Peter Banks on lead guitar is an exciting player who used wah-wah cleverly to add a distinctive sound to the group's tight harmony. Jon Anderson has an unusual voice and the whole adds up to one of the most exciting and promising groups around. Hear them especially on numbers like Crosby and McGuinn's 'I See You' and their own superb arrangement of Bernstein's 'Something's Coming'. Tremendous."

Yes were back at The Marquee only a few days later on July 30, again supported by Hard Meat, followed by more dates there on August 7 and 14. At the end of August they played at the Plumpton Festival when it was reported they were 'The hit of the show with their fresh new sound'. The same month *Yes* was released. On September 27 it was announced in the press: 'Yes, the only British group signed to America's Atlantic Records,[2] are negotiating a massive American tour.' Negotiations would take a little longer than anticipated.

On October 9 they played at the first German Blues Festival with Fleetwood Mac in Essen, and October 30 they were back at The Marquee for their first London show since their Plumpton success. They went to Belgium to make their own TV special and filmed an appearance on BBC2 *Line Up*. Also during October they played gigs in Plymouth, Bristol, Newcastle and Redcar. At the end of the month they were scheduled to join Pink Floyd and Captain Beefheart at the Paris Pop and Jazz Festival held over five days from October 24 to 28. Although Roy Flynn was berated for not getting enough gigs for Yes, it seems that during Autumn 1969 they were run off their feet with work.

During a break in their schedule in October I met Jon Anderson for the

---

[2] The writer evidently forgot about Led Zeppelin.

first of many an interview. He was in philosophical mood as we chatted about the band and he unveiled far reaching ideas that amounted to prophecies. "Life gets faster and harder all the time. People need pop music as a stimulant. People also listen to pop as a serious form of music. I write meaningful lyrics, not just pop songs. We hope to make audiences think. I like to talk to the audience about the numbers first. I suppose I sound as if I'm in a pulpit but each group is doing its own thing. One day I'd like to see all bands and groups get together and create something – do a complete show together. Why not have four organists and four guitars – yeah and four drummers too."[3]

Said Jon back in '69, "We could write music together and spend a couple of months planning and rehearsing. Then we could take it round the world with a big light show and maybe play for six hours." Within a few years Jon and the Yes team would be doing exactly that amidst the huge arenas of the American rock circuit. For the moment they were still playing at the Kings Hall, Romford (October 17) and were lucky if there was a light bulb in the toilet.

[3] It was a dream Jon would finally see come to fruition many years later with the Yes 'Union' tour. When Yes came home to England they played 'in the round' at Wembley Arena on June 28, 1991, with two drummers, two organists and two guitarists.

4

GIVE BOOZE A CHANCE

It was a time of frantic activity for Yes as the Sixties gave way to a new decade. Every day was another gig, another recording session or a long trip to nowhere and back. They often found themselves racing off on a wild goose chase into the midst of some daft situation that invariably reduced them to giggles or apoplexy. But it was all fun and excitement for the ambitious twenty year olds, still struggling to find themselves and their music. As Chris Squire says, "Yes was just five guys learning about music."

It is easy to pass judgement on how in these early days Yes could have done things differently or better. The important thing was always the music which fired up their adrenaline, energised their ambition and sparked tremendous loyalty from their fans and supporters.

Says Bill Bruford sagely, "Looking back on those days, one of the unique things about Yes was that we all came from such different backgrounds. Most bands of that era came from the same street or city block. The Who were a West London band. The Rolling Stones were a South London affair. Black Sabbath were from Birmingham. Yes wasn't *from* anywhere. You couldn't have picked people from a more abstruse social background to gather together.

"Jon was the milk man from Accrington. Chris was a public schoolboy and a chorister. I was also a public schoolboy. Peter was a London boy, a Mod who wanted to be Pete Townshend. Tony Kaye had quite a lot of experience and had been in several bands. In other words we were all from completely different backgrounds musically and socially and therefore the opportunities for mis-communication were rife and rampant, and indeed mis-communication occurred all the time! Plus we were fairly heated and strong-minded individuals, which made things difficult in every conceivable way."

Apart from traumas in the rehearsal room or studio there was the day-to-day running of the band's finances to worry about. Bill Bruford smiles as he remembers how he tried to introduce the concept of Yes

66

running its own cheque book and bank account. "You would have thought I was the devil incarnate! The band limped from one financial crisis to the next. It was a series of disasters really."

After a gig the Yes van usually stopped some thirty miles along the road from the venue in order to split up the sixty pounds in cash they'd been paid by the promoter. It never seemed like each individual's share was enough. Bill's attempts to persuade the others to put 'some aside' for petrol and future bills fell on deaf ears. "It was considered a wholly useless idea. I remember suggesting, 'How about having a band bank account? All the money could go into that and expenses could be paid out from the account.' I nearly got thrown out of the van. It was strictly cash only. So we didn't understand each other socially, musically or financially. And that was the situation right from the start."

Later, of course, the band did have a bank account, opened by Roy Flynn at Coutts in Sloane Street. "Where did they think the money was coming from?" fumes Flynn. "I paid for the wages, the equipment, the roadies, and the repairs. There was nowhere near enough income from the gigs to pay for all that."

One way to save money and cut costs was to share living quarters. Communal living was one of the great dreams of rock musicians during the Sixties. Traffic had tried to get it all together in the country when they moved into a cottage in the Berkshire countryside in 1967. There they could write songs, practise loudly without disturbing the neighbours and smoke without interference. Many other groups followed suit and tried Traffic-style living, if only to share the cost of accommodation.

Roy Flynn paid the deposit on a flat in a terraced house at 50A Munster Road, Fulham. It became a notorious abode. The band occupied half of the basement and half of the first and second floors. The third floor was where the owner, Edwina Carol[4] resided. The band and its entourage of wives and girlfriends lived in a series of bedsitting rooms. "We all lived there except Tony Kaye," recalls Peter Banks. "He was always more up-market and lived in Chelsea. At one time it was Jon and his girlfriend Jenny, me, Chris, Bill and his wife Carolyn. You can imagine the state of the kitchen."

Fortunately not a lot of cooking was necessary as certain members of the band survived on a diet of brandy and Mandrax. "A lethal brew!" recalls the guitarist. Several other bands lived there over the years, including half of Banks' later band Flash. Robert Fripp of King Crimson was another celebrated resident.

---

[4] Edwina Carol is now a shopkeeper in London's Covent Garden.

Never the most tidy set of rooms, the Munster Road 'crash pad' was at its most insalubrious when Jon Anderson was in residence. "Jon would never clean the bathroom," sighs Banks. "And he used to eat lots of fried food. This was way before his vegetarian days. He was a sausage, egg and chips man. He would never clean the kitchen after a big fry up. When he eventually moved out I discovered a terrible smell coming from his old room. I thought, 'What's that *smell?*' Under the bed I found a full plate of sausage, egg and chips which he must have left there for three or four weeks. So whenever I see Jon now I always think of that! He was desperately untidy and I was always running around after him, flicking a feather duster and nagging. 'Don't leave that there – can't you clear up after you!' "

Bruford describes another member of this close-knit community as not so much untidy as 'consumptive', and this didn't mean that he suffered from a wasting disease. "Chris Squire consumed time – a lot. Always late. This was why I eventually left the band. Chris was *always* late. He also consumed money on expensive bass cabinets and so forth. Like many of the bands at the time we were running at a loss. It cost us more to play a gig than we received in payment.

"But because we thought the price was going up and in general the industry was improving and record sales were tripling on an annual basis, it was a kind of inflationary situation. There was a huge boom going on. But further down the line, when we hooked up with a new manager, Brian Lane, we were down to our last twenty five quid. Roy Flynn, our first manager, was upset when we left him I guess, but it was chaos. Jon would have to borrow money from various friends in London like Tony Stratton Smith at Charisma and Jack Barrie at La Chasse Club who helped us out. We were all clustered together in this flat at Munster Road with our wives and girlfriends and it was like a fire station. Jon would hustle up a gig at 24 hours notice. You couldn't leave the building in case they couldn't find you. It was like being confined to barracks! Then the fire bell rang and you set off in this red Ford Transit van to somewhere too far away, like Ireland or Switzerland. It was a dangerous and reckless way to carry on, but nobody knew any different and really – we were all having fun. I was ready to play and I practised all day. I was so eager to put ideas into the songs."

Bill's patience was sorely tested by this experiment at communal living. He got particularly angry at having to wait for Chris Squire to get out of the bath. Chris spent so much time soaking he earned the nickname Fish – which eventually became the title of his famed bass guitar feature. "He was consumptive you see – he would consume all the water and consume all the time and money! He was very heavy in terms of consumption. All the resources went into maintaining Chris. So Chris would be in the bath, Jon would be screaming down the telephone and I'd be practising and Peter Banks would be combing his hair. I put up with all this until 1972."

★ ★ ★

One of the more bizarre Yes gigs occurred in July, 1969, when they were booked to play in Ireland on a package tour that included The Bonzo Dog Doo Dah Band and The Nice. On paper it was a wonderful combination. Indeed, the shows they played in Belfast and Dublin were superb and, with the Bonzos on hand, the tour was rich in comic moments. But the end of the tour was a farcical disaster, the ultimate Yes wild goose chase – or pig chase, as it turned out.

The groups, accompanied by their managers Roy Flynn and Tony Stratton Smith and myself, spent the final day in a hot and stuffy coach, driving endlessly through twisting narrow country lanes between Dublin and Cork where the venue turned out to be a football ground on the outskirts of town. When the three bands arrived on that sunny Sunday afternoon long ago, they were fully expecting to see a massive crowd building up. Instead the ground was deserted; indeed there wasn't a soul for miles around. The roadies discovered a makeshift stage comprising a tangled mass of scaffolding, which had been set in front of the spectator's stand and apparently given up as a bad job. Then they found the power supply: a cable that snaked across the pitch to a small wooden ticket hut where it was connected – incredibly – to an electric kettle flex stuffed into a three pin socket with the aid of match sticks. When the roadies tried to plug in the band's instruments, amplifiers and PA system the whole lot simply fused and went dead.

They tried this three times to no avail. The crew advised the management that there was no chance of any of the bands putting on a show. The troupe of some 14 travelling musicians sat down on the pitch in their satin stage gear and cried with laughter. At that moment an awful stench swept across the empty field. It seemed to be emanating from a nearby building, which on closer inspection turned out to be the 'Cork Pork Abattoir'. The squealing of unhappy porkers rent the air.

All eyes turned on The Nice's portly manager. Tony Stratton Smith sensed he could not escape retribution. He had led us into the valley of doom. The cry went up from 'Legs' Larry Smith and Viv Stanshall of the Bonzos – "Debag the rotters!" The portly manager and his accountant were chased across the pitch by a yelling mob of musos intent on removing their trousers. Nobody had ever seen Strat run before – and he put on a surprising burst of speed. The pair were saved by a sudden diversion. There was a loud explosion and a shower of rust fell from the grandstand roof. Roger Spear, the Bonzos' sax player and special effects man, had let off a cherry bomb. Loud were the cheers as the sun began to set over Cork. Perhaps lured by all this noise and disturbance, a few disconsolate and somewhat tetchy locals turned up demanding to know why the bands weren't giving the advertised concert. When shown the electrical supply they shook their heads as if this was some feeble excuse.

The party repaired to the nearest pub where the pints flowed and Keith Emerson of The Nice began an impromptu performance on an upright piano, playing boogie-woogie and 'Nut Rocker' with such vigour it drove the locals into a frenzy. A version of 'Give Peace A Chance' somehow turned into a chorus of 'Give Booze A Chance!' It was the craziest concert I ever saw – The Nice, Yes and Bonzos in full vocal cry. But when a wild eyed youth started beating time on the piano with glass beer mugs and smashing them to pieces, it was clearly time to escape. As glass showered in Keith's face the roadies managed to get the musicians outside and into the coach to take them to the airport and on a direct flight home to London. I was too late. The bus had sped off and I found myself surrounded by crazed revellers whose mood was starting to turn ugly, despite the unique free concert that Keith had been cheerfully orchestrating.

As the angry crowd chased after the disappearing coach, I was offered a lift and foolishly jumped into a car full of strangers who seemed intent on kidnapping me and dumping me in the countryside. I convinced them to let me out and ran towards the lights of an airport. Quite how I found the elderly Aer Lingus Viscount turbo prop revving up on the darkened runway I don't remember. On board there were Yes, The Nice and the Bonzos filling the twin columns of seats. Viv Stanshall greeted me with a cry of, "We are all nudists and we want our freedom!" which had Peter Banks in stitches. Actually, he remained fully clothed throughout. As we bumped down the runway and up into the night sky, my face evidently betrayed stress and the usual fear of flying. "Don't worry," said Viv seriously, "if we crash, we'll all be fucking legends."

Half way across the Irish Sea the captain made an announcement. "The Americans are about to land on the Moon."

It was a wondrous story and Jon Anderson was greatly amused by the whole episode which seemed like an extraordinary dream. Did we really watch Neil Armstrong make his lunar landing from the safety of London, the same night we had got into a punch-up in an Irish pub?

Says Jon, "I remember that night vividly, especially Keith playing the piano and everybody singing 'Give booze a chance'. Then us getting in the bus and listening to the news of the Moon landings. All of a sudden the bus moved off and we were on our way to Shannon airport. By then we were all so drunk I was just in fits of laughter for about three hours! It was a wonderful, crazy time."

★　★　★

Unlike the Apollo 11 moon rocket, the band seemed to be stalling on the launch pad. The trip to Ireland was great fun but it made little business sense. Says Roy Flynn in his defence, "In fact Yes were the only band to get paid on that weekend. I think we got £75. There was absolutely no publicity for the gig in Cork. All these hairy musicians must have looked like Martians in an Irish landscape. The promoter hadn't told anyone that these three English bands were coming. Even if anyone had turned up, the stand they built was so small only two hundred people would have seen them."

Although I had seen Yes in close-up action on the two gigs they managed to play in Ireland, it wasn't really in the best of circumstances. There was a better chance to absorb their music and get to know the band when I joined them for another exciting foray into the unknown. This time Yes were travelling alone to Switzerland and I could see for myself the kind of frantic pace they endured during that first tumultuous year together.

We met on a cold afternoon in late November 1969 at the Fulham flat, which was indeed very small and packed with people racing around trying to get ready and tripping over guitar cases, bottles and hair brushes. Accompanied by photographer Barrie Wentzell, we set off with Jon, Chris, Peter, Tony and Bill for Heathrow and a hair-raising flight to Basle. The fun started at London Airport when we heard the news that the first snow of the year was falling heavily onto our destination at Basle airport. "A glass of Boozo The Wonder drink I think," said Tony Kaye when it was announced that our flight might be diverted to Zurich. In the event we piled on board the noisy but sturdy BEA Trident for the one hour flight. As we approached Basle the pilot said, "We're just going to go down and have a look." In fact there was nothing to see – except the white hell of a blinding blizzard.

Miraculously and with great skill, the captain got us down onto the runway, to a round of applause from the relieved British passengers. We were met at the airport by a cheerful local promoter called Chris Schwegler who was instantly nicknamed Swiss Chris. He arrived wearing an army uniform and sporting incongruous long hair. He explained that even hippie rock promoters were liable for military service in Switzerland.

It was his job to guide us from gig to gig and guard us from the swarms of police, customs and any other officials who might frown upon visiting English rock musicians. They had nothing much to fear from Yes. I described them later in my *MM* report as, "A happy group of gently extrovert egoless super musicians. The feeling and work they put into every number is matched by a cheerful and essentially adult attitude towards the business of making music. They accept the rigours of pop with good spirit and are determined to enjoy themselves whatever the weather and businessmen are doing."

How true. They were very well behaved, apart from the occasional right hook exchanged in the rhythm section, as I would discover some thirty years later. The trip was described as a promotional visit, although it was difficult to see in retrospect exactly what the band could get out of their visit. Switzerland was never the biggest rock market place in Europe. The band played small venues for very little money and their one TV appearance consisted of miming outdoors in the snow. It was so cold Chris Squire had to play his bass guitar wearing a pair of huge mittens. Nevertheless the scenery was lovely, they made a lot of friends and my report hopefully helped raise their profile. It was impossible not to form a great attachment to such a friendly bunch of people who played such stimulating music with such panache. It was impossible not to be swept up with the enthusiasm emanating from Jon, Chris, Tony and Peter and particularly from their young drummer, who was clearly so proud of the band and thrilled to be playing with them. When he wasn't playing drums he was doing press-ups on the dressing room floor, just to keep fit for the nightly gig.

When you heard Yes play night after night, blasting through the songs from that groundbreaking first album like a supercharged five piece orchestra, you wanted to shout their praises from the rooftops and tell the world – *this* is a great band. *You* dear readers – should be listening to them! It was the same feeling many others would experience, from their manager Roy Flynn to people like tour manager Michael Tait and Roy Clair, the American sound engineer, who was so enamoured with the group when he first heard them in the States, he would work with them for the next thirty years.

One day the entire world would discover Yes. But for the moment the audience at their first gigs seemed to consist mainly of the high society of small town Switzerland, gentlemen and ladies clad in evening dress, furs and jewels, attending what they thought were cabaret performances by a loud but entertaining musical act. The first show was scheduled for the Comedy Theatre in Basle. This was a small, overheated venue with cramped seating that made me think nervously about the apparently non-existent fire precautions.

Yes went down a storm with the upper crust fans but in my review I wrote: "It was not their best performance as Yes had to play for over two hours without a break and some of the solos became over-worked." At this distance in time it is difficult to remember exactly why I said that, but as I recall it was down to Peter getting a little too carried away with his guitar solo.

Of course rock music would depend entirely on long, extrovert guitar solos for the next twenty years, but in 1969 anything more than a chorus was considered rather daring. Peter's playing was terrifically exciting, but if allowed to go into overtime it could unbalance an otherwise tightly drawn arrangement. It would cause problems between him and Jon that often resulted in arguments, even fisticuffs. On one occasion Chris asked me to mediate and I did try to hint to Pete the best course of action was to cool it a bit.

But he could be forgiven for wanting to get his rocks off. After all, why else had the band come all this way – if only to *play*! I wrote later: "At each gig the band played better and better. They have several strong points – a magnificent sense of timing, power, taste and excitement. Peter, Jon and Chris make a beautiful harmony team and Jon Anderson has one of the most expressive musical voices on the scene. Peter Banks' guitar work is always inventive and unique and on the few occasions when the band get into lengthy individual solos, his playing compares favourably with the best of the heavy mob. Chris Squire, the tall quietly smiling bass player with a penchant for straw boaters and an Eskimo coat, obtains a fiendishly fat sound, that rocks somewhere between John Entwistle and Jack Bruce. Bill the ever cheerful drummer – 'If it's good enough for Charlie Parker, it's good enough for me' – is a jazz fan who loves Yes and will talk about drums and the band at the drop of a practice pad. Tony Kaye on Hammond helps to make Yes sound like a big band. While irritated by some equipment problems, the languid off-stage lotus-eater becomes a madman at the keyboard, arms flailing, hair flying, great thundering chords contrasting with delicate passages played with cunning skill. They make a marvellous band and it was a shame some of their appearances were restricted to chic expensive night clubs, village halls and a late afternoon concert at Montreaux Casino. But at each gig they earned an ovation and at Solothol they played brilliantly and tore into an audience seated at wooden tables, drinking Coke."

During an afternoon rehearsal I was able to witness Yes getting down to some creative work at the appropriately named Comedy Theatre. They began work on a new number intended to feature Jon and Peter on acoustic guitars, provisionally titled 'Number 14 Bus'. The rest of the group shouted abuse from the back row of the stalls while Jon and Peter strummed and sang the long since forgotten ditty. "It's bloody Nina and Frederick!" yelled Tony. "Bring back the stripper!" bellowed Bill.

"There's a pig loose in the theatre!" called Peter, invoking the spirit of Viv Stanshall of the Bonzos. There was no sign of the alleged iron fist in the velvet glove as Jon Anderson smiled, even though his latest song was barracked and treated with disgraceful discourtesy by the boys in the band. "Now then!" was all he'd ever say during these rebellious outbursts. As for the gentle song he was putting together – well who knows – it may have been a dry run for 'Yours Is No Disgrace'. And why did they call it 'Number 14 Bus'? I seem to remember someone saying "It's because there'll be another one along in a minute."

When I talked to Bill in a quiet moment between press-ups and paradiddles he told me, "Jon is pouring out new numbers for us to play, but we don't have time to rehearse. Usually he writes a tune and we listen to the tape and take it from there. We use complicated arrangements that can be great or they can baffle an audience."

Bill referred me to a number that would appear on their next album *Time And A Word*. " 'The Prophet' has about five changes of tempo and key changes before the singing comes in. I suppose it is very easy to be too clever. Never mind – it's tough at the top. Day Four of Yes Expedition – going gets tougher. Our roadies have stumbled out into the snow. It's been a great year for the band. Yes are getting more adult and less likely to break up.[5] We have got to know each other and our abilities."

Bill explained that the Swiss tour had been purely for promotion. "You can't really earn much money on these gigs because the country and the audiences are so small. We are primarily here to sell the LP. The last album is so old it is out of date. We are a band that plays songs. I don't play a drum solo and the only instrumental is on Peter's 'I See You' which is completely free and makes a good contrast. We are content to cut good albums and play good gigs. We are happy enough. We could dye our hair green and drop our trousers on stage but we want to try and project excitement, personality and quality." Although we didn't know it, at a stroke Bill Bruford had anticipated Glam and Punk Rock, five years ahead of their time.

Among the crew assisting them on their way was Michael Tait. Strangely enough he doesn't remember an episode that threatened to end the tour rather abruptly. I watched, eyes popping, from the front seat of the band's limo as we raced through an 'S' bend on a snow covered highway, heading down a steep slope towards Montreaux. Another Cadillac shot past in a dodgy overtaking manoeuvre. The driver waved sardonically in his haste to get past. But the heavy limo slid over to the wrong side of the road, then spun round in a complete circle. Instead of

---

[5] This was the first intimation I had that Yes had ever even considered breaking up!

going through the crash barriers and over the mountain, it miraculously came out of the spin and continued its headlong flight to the Casino. No wonder Bill Bruford would later insist on driving himself to gigs.

Yes were not a band of habitually heavy drinkers. They had too much music to worry about to allow their brains to become befuddled. However on the last night they allowed themselves a celebration and we stayed up all night after the last gig, raving in a medieval cellar known locally as the Museum Club, but dubbed by visiting musicians The Monastery Of Labour. How many local girls went into labour as a result of these visits is unknown but I do recall Tony Kaye besieged by a horde of flaxen-haired Rhine maidens. "Well you've got to laugh," said Tony. "Or you get frostbite."

Back in London I discovered that my editor was not best pleased that I had spent three days away from the office, carousing on the road with a band only on the fringes of fame. Thirty years later manager Roy Flynn told me he had written a letter to the editor, advising him that my visit had been of great benefit to the band and assistance to the music industry in general. In other words – please don't fire him. Thanks to Roy, my job was safe. Within a couple of years the 'unknown' band who had taken up so much valuable editorial time, would be regularly winning all of the music press polls.

★ ★ ★

Although Yes were gaining appreciation as one of the great new bands of the age, to the musicians involved it all seemed to be taking an age. Back in London they were still playing such venues as the Croydon Blues Club (December 7, 1969) and a Boxing Day Special at The Marquee. Says Bill looking back, "I thought it all happened very slowly. Yes, King Crimson, Led Zeppelin and Genesis all started at roughly the same time. Led Zeppelin and Yes both signed to Atlantic Records – as did King Crimson.[6] Zeppelin and Crimson both had early success. We were still struggling."

Despite these setbacks the band set about recording their second album *Time And A Word* with high hopes and aspirations. They moved down to a farm in Devon with the idea of getting their act together. But behind the scenes problems loomed. "It was all going pear shaped," recalls Roy Flynn. "I'd had no advance for the first LP and no royalties. We never received a statement from Atlantic and there was no money in fact from the first two LPs. By now I was flat broke and there was a lot of belly aching from the band. They thought nothing was happening. But I was

---

[6] King Crimson were signed to Atlantic in the US; in the UK they recorded for Island.

having problems with the agency. In the end I got a lot of the gigs myself, but by then it was no longer fun. A lot of people started whispering in their ears . . . driving a wedge between me and the band."

As work began on the new album the controversial suggestion was made that the band's sound would be enhanced with an orchestra. One was hastily put together consisting of student string players from the Royal College of Music, together with session brass players. Tony Colton was charged with production, and their future sound engineer Eddie Offord, made his first appearance at the mixing desk, thanks to a suggestion from Phil Carson, who was MD of Atlantic Records in London and a big fan of Yes. Phil would make many far reaching suggestions on behalf of Yes over the coming years.

Says Phil, "I got Eddie in because I used to produce cover records of the pop hits of the day for Saga Records. I always used Eddie when we worked at Advision Studios. I'd book the studio for a late session, bring a reel of eight track tape and finish an album in a night! As long as we got out of the building by 6 a.m. before the cleaners came in we were okay. Eddie and I made a number of albums like that. I remember a budget version of *Hair* we did overnight with student string players. So I knew Eddie was a brilliant engineer."

Eddie would subsequently work on many of the biggest and best-selling Yes albums and actually became a member of the group. He influenced them in many ways, including introducing them to vegetarianism and eating healthy food instead of the usual musician's fry-ups. Unfortunately his personal diet included various substances that worked at odds with the otherwise beneficial effects of organic food.

Time And A Word was the next big step for the band. As usual it was dogged with Yes-style controversy. The surreal album cover was quite striking and Dali-esque, but the black and white chequered design featured a reclining nude that proved unpopular with American distributors. It was artistic, even if it didn't say much about their music or personalities. The back cover photographs weren't much better. A good-looking band was rendered ugly by the use of a powerful wind machine, which distorted their faces into grotesque shapes. There was a handsome selection of songs however. 'No Opportunity Necessary, No Experience Needed', a fine Ritchie Havens tune, was given the full Yes treatment. A dramatic new Jon Anderson special called 'Then' was followed by Stephen Stills' classic 'Everydays'. 'Sweet Dreams', a piece by Jon and writing partner David Foster, concluded side one. 'The Prophet', a powerful Anderson and Squire epic, paved the way for 'Clear Days' and 'Astral Traveller'. The title track 'Time And A Word', by Anderson and Foster, concluded an album full of promise and fine performances but somehow failed to capture that elusive Yes spirit which so thrilled audiences out in the field.

Time And A Word was made in the Advision Studios off Great Portland Street. The arrival of Eddie Offord was regarded as a boon, but Peter Banks was not so sure about the producer. "We had Tony Colton producing who took an instant dislike to me and I took an instant dislike to him. So that was a problem. He was a buddy of Jon's and he suddenly told us he was going to produce our album."

Colton was the singer in Head, Hands and Feet, a touring band with blues and country virtuoso Albert Lee on guitar. "He kind of expected me to play like Albert Lee or Jimmy Page. At the time Jimmy Page was my least favourite guitar player. So there was a lot of tension between me and Tony Colton. He did say later on that the only thing he didn't like about Yes was my guitar playing."

During one fraught session Peter threw a Rickenbacker at Colton and threatened to leave. "That shows how bad it got. I didn't like the orchestra either and I don't think Tony Kaye was too crazy about it. All they were doing was copying the guitar and organ parts and playing them instead of us. A lot of guitar was gone. 'Oh that bit is being played by the string section.' My point was that we were trying to make a five piece rock band sound like an orchestra. So why have these strings? We could do this ourselves. But it was Jon's idea. It was kind of jumping on the bandwagon because The Nice and Deep Purple had both recorded with an orchestra."

Yes did a gig with the orchestra, at the Queen Elizabeth Hall on March 21, which Banks felt was a disaster. "We drowned out the orchestra! I thought it was a daft idea and I was not shy in putting my views forward. So Tony Colton and I didn't get on. We had totally different tastes in music. He even liked country music!"

The concert came after a February tour of Scandinavia with The Small Faces. Yes were joined at the South Bank concert hall in the second half of the concert by a 20 piece youth orchestra, performing extracts from *Time And A Word*. That month the single 'Time And A Word' was released together with 'The Prophet'.

On March 28, 1970 the Queen Elizabeth Hall concert was reviewed in the *MM*: "Yes have scored a considerable success with their first major solo concert. They tried a brave experiment with added strings and brass conducted by Tony Cox. Although it suffered from amplification problems the group scored all the way playing at a peak which earned a kind of 'musical break-through' audience reaction which marks the point when a group have 'arrived'."

I raved over Jon Anderson's vocals and reported that demands for an encore were satisfied with 'Something's Coming'. "At the climax a roar went up for what must now be one of Britain's top three groups."

Heard again today, the much disputed orchestra doesn't sound so bad on the re-packaged, digitally remastered CD version of the album (which has a picture of Steve Howe on the cover instead of Pete Banks). The powerful introduction to 'No Opportunity Necessary, No Experience Needed' is still a thrill. Jon's echoing voice on this piece also sounds unusually deep and the strings work overtime as they embark on the theme from *The Big Country*. The CD sounds much better than the vinyl version and the drums and bass really kick. Richie Havens, who wrote the tune, was one of Jon's favourite artists of the period and Yes later played several gigs with him. The thunderously dramatic Anderson composition 'Then' began with Tony Kaye's Hammond cooking over a rolling Brufordian snare drum. Jon's vocals are interspersed with stabbing swoops from the strings: "*And in a time that's closer Life will be even older – Then!*"

It's a clever arrangement mixing emotion, sentiment and moments of high drama. Banks plays a penetrating descending guitar break before Bill signals an abrupt increase in tempo and Kaye and Banks start an extended instrumental section. Trumpets squeal in a surprise addition to the line-up, before silence falls and Peter plays a few sensitive chords. Jon's voice, ethereal and floating returns to sing another of his most memorable lines: "*Love is the only answer, hate is the root of cancer – Then!*"

'Everydays' gets the kind of jazzy treatment that used to endear the band to unsuspecting toffs when they were accidentally booked into casinos. The strings attempt to create a spooky atmosphere but Bill's smouldering hi-hat and brilliant ensemble drumming launches the piece into the realms of pure big band swing. Tony Kaye's languid keyboards gently usher Jon back in his best Frank Sinatra style. As he sings 'Well, well, well another day', you can almost see him astride a bar stool with coat draped over his shoulders and cigarette dangling between his fingers. The mighty Bruford hi-hat snaps back, to bring the piece to a rousing conclusion.

The Beatle style 'Sweet Dreams' was hardly ever played live although it was released as the band's third single, coupled with 'Dear Father', in June 1970. Says Banks, "In retrospect I really like that song and wish I had got more involved with it at the time. I think it could be much better. David Foster who co-wrote the song with Jon had played with him in The Warriors. It was strange. Here was a guy we didn't know too well and all of a sudden he was an extra member of the band. This was another problem, because David Foster played guitar and there was only going to be one guitar player in the band as far as I was concerned. I had to put my foot down and say, 'No, he is *not* going to play guitar.' But he does sing backing vocals which I wasn't crazy about because I thought Yes was Yes and shouldn't include anybody else. Maybe I was being short-sighted. But this was my stance then.''

'The Prophet' has a lengthy church organ style introduction which shows how much Tony Kaye contributed to the atmosphere and feeling of early Yes masterworks. The strings sound quite superficial here and the drums and organ work well before Peter takes a tasteful solo that leads into Jon's storytelling narrative. 'The Prophet' is perhaps one of the least remembered Yes works. Despite the strings getting in the way, it remains a most attractive and imaginative time piece. Bruford's cymbal work here is particularly nifty and lifts 'The Prophet' into a big stage musical production. Peter scrapes and scratches his strings for a typically witty coda.

The strings come back for 'Clear Days'. Says Peter, "Ah that was a Jon Anderson solo track – because none of us are on it except Jon and a string quartet. Everyone was a bit uneasy, because we thought we were making a Yes album, but it's a pleasant song. My favourite was 'Astral Traveller' which still sounds great." Bruford's Afro-jazz drumming lifts the groove and the mood as Jon sings of the Astral Traveller enjoying a heavenly flight into the wondrous night without the aid of a balloon. A contrapuntal roundelay between the organ, guitar and snare drum creates a most intriguing and delightful moment before Peter launches into an intense series of arpeggios. Bill brings Jon back to centre stage to wrap up the piece and a harsh, echoing blast from the full band brings the 'Astral Traveller' crashing back to earth.

Curiously the title track is perhaps the least effective song of all. 'Time And A Word' has a clumsy structure which made the first few bars difficult to sing. Bill sounds uncomfortable with the rather orthodox Ringo style rock beat. The main theme is stronger, however, and sounded better live. The strings and vocal chorus are overblown and sound more Bee Gees than Yes.

Says Peter, "It was meant to be an anthem. I know exactly where it came from. We were playing in a club in London and heard The Beatles' 'Hey Jude' for the first time on the car radio outside. It was being played on the BBC and really Jon wanted to do 'Hey Jude'. We couldn't really so Jon came up with 'Time And A Word'. He also liked 'Give Peace A Chance' and if you listen to the groove of 'Time And A Word' it's really 'Give Peace A Chance'. To my great annoyance Dave Foster played acoustic guitar on it – very badly. That clunky acoustic rattling away at the beginning was put on while I wasn't in the studio, so I was very annoyed about that. In fact it might even be Jon on guitar! Listening to it today, you can hear it's a nice song, even though I didn't appreciate it much at the time."

Jon's repetition of the phrase 'the time is now' sounds like a warning shot across the bows, a portent of the changes that would soon affect the fabric of Yes. The recalcitrant guitarist was in danger of being fired.

Says Banks looking back on his last project with Yes, "Despite the problems I had with the producer and not liking the string section, the album itself isn't bad and there is some good work there and nothing I'm ashamed of. The re-mastered CD sounds a helluva lot better. The whole album was re-mixed after I'd left the band. Originally I was playing the parts and the orchestra was playing along with me. That sounded okay – loud electric guitar with strings. Then after my departure the guitar parts were taken out. I wasn't happy about that – but who cares now? I'd left by the time it came out, which is why Steve Howe's picture is on the cover in most versions. The band went to America to promote *Time And A Word* and Steve had to come in and cover the parts I'd played. I think he hated every minute of that!"

Despite all the high hopes, *Time And A Word* didn't sell any more copies than the first and got lost completely in America. Says Phil Carson, "Both the first Yes albums were put out in America and neither of them did a thing. We tried hard to promote them in England. I remember that for *Time And A Word* we did the show at the Queen Elizabeth Hall in London which sold out. But there was absolutely zero interest in them in America and Atlantic actually wanted to drop Yes."

All this placed great strain on the band and their relationship with manager Roy Flynn. Says Bill Bruford, "Certainly after two albums and into the making of the third we were nearly lost. The first album was very well received and didn't sell many copies and didn't do much for our booking fee. Then we did an orchestral one with *Time And A Word*, as everybody had to do an orchestra album, and a not very good concert at Queen Elizabeth Hall, with an orchestra. Again not much success. In those days at least you could be given two albums before a record company pulled the plug. Now you are given about three minutes."

★ ★ ★

In the aftermath of the Queen Elizabeth concert and while waiting for the second album to be released, the band played a few more dates, including an appearance supporting Slade at The Marquee on April 10, Poperama, Devizes, on April 17, and then a fateful appearance at Luton College on April 18. A few weeks later on May 2 came the official announcement 'Peter Banks Quits Yes'. It seemed that Luton College was to be his last appearance with the band. Manager Roy Flynn made a press announcement: 'The group and Peter felt their music had begun to stagnate and Yes have cancelled all their engagements and are not taking any more bookings until they find a suitable guitarist replacement.'

Says Chris Squire, "Peter had been sort of against the principle of using the orchestra on *Time And A Word* and that was the main cause of the rift. The rest of us thought it was a jolly good idea, so he was outvoted, which is kind of what happened. Around that time Jon and I started talking about the need to find a guitar player who would be more in sync with the way we were thinking. I had remembered seeing Steve Howe play with Tomorrow who had broken up by that time. I knew Steve was floating, even though he had his own band called Bodast. So that's how Steve Howe came into the band. Then we went down to Devon and started working on the new album."

The threat from Atlantic, the departure of Peter Banks and the band's subsequent split with manager Roy Flynn culminated in the first great crisis to hit them since getting together in the West End basement. Yet these difficult changes led to the refocusing Yes needed to survive and prosper. To the victims it seemed harsh and draconian. To Jon Anderson and Chris Squire it was another step forward in the ongoing struggle to perfect the scheme they'd hatched back in La Chasse Club.

Says Peter, "The problem was we were playing in beer tents in Belgium to twenty disgruntled Belgians who wanted to hear the blues. It wasn't good for band morale. We were playing some very bizarre gigs."

Yes were growing restive. Chris and Jon wanted to find a new manager and a lead guitarist who could change the whole thrust of their musical development. But it was painful for Peter to leave the band he loved as much as the others. Says Peter, "When I was fired we were playing in Luton Technical college. I was in the dressing room and they told me after the gig. It was so sudden that Tony and Bill didn't even know about it. Jon and Chris said, 'We think it would be better for you and us if you left the band.'"

Jon started to explain the reasons but Peter didn't want to discuss it any further. He was even denied the pleasure of storming out in high dudgeon as of course they all had to return together to their shared home in Munster Road. "I was still living there with Bill at this time and that led to a very cold atmosphere for the next few weeks, because I wasn't speaking to him. Tony Kaye was told in similar terms the same thing a year later. He was in bed when Chris went round to see him. When I was asked to go, the gigs were getting bad and we just weren't making any money. We were on a weekly salary and any other money that came in was used to keep the band running, to pay for petrol, roadies, rehearsals and equipment. We were living from gig to gig. Roy Flynn was getting slagged off and we were arguing a lot. I think the second album was the main problem. I later heard that Tony Colton told Jon he should get rid of me.

This sort of thing happens in bands, but it was very sudden and I wondered what I was going to do next. They didn't have anybody lined up. They tried to get Robert Fripp but he turned them down, so they took three months off to re-invent the group. This actually worked very well for them because they brought in Steve Howe and they became a terrific band."

In May I reported on 'Both Sides Of The Yes Split': "When guitarist Peter Banks quit Yes last week and they cancelled all immediate appearances it seemed like another episode in the sad saga of splits that have hit top British groups. The group retired for a couple of months to a house by the sea near Ilfracombe in the west country. The album release was delayed again, this time until June 15. The plan was to rehearse and re-emerge with a new sound and the band now seem more cheerful and determined than they had in some months. Jon Anderson told me, 'We just felt cut off from Peter musically. He wasn't playing our style and there was a feeling we had lost contact with our music. We wanted Peter to get his own scene going. Our material won't change completely.'

"Said Chris Squire, 'We'll keep some of the favourite numbers and use any good new stuff. We'll just sort out the good from the bad.'

"Bill Bruford seemed very upbeat about the changes: 'It's not the end of the group – it's the beginning! I feel ten years younger. When we started out we were told we had a lot of drive and attack. Well we are going to get that back. We'd like to do a big concert when we come back.' "

Peter Banks was hurt by the decision, but tried to appear philosophical. He told me shortly after the Luton bust up, "I hadn't enjoyed playing with the band as much in the last couple of months. I felt my guitar playing was stagnating. I was going on stage each night and repeating myself and the band knew this as well and thought it was time for a change. I had reached my limit with the band. Sure I had freedom but I was lacking inspiration. I was just playing like a machine. It went on and on and got really boring, although it went down well. I was a bit worried about leaving. I really don't know how I rate on the scene as a guitarist, but I have had a lot of offers. I'm looking forward to the new Yes album and I hope it does well. It should go straight to the top of the Kwango Charts – it's got that Kwango beat!"

This latter remark was in reference to an in-joke about a dance craze we intended to invent and then unleash on the public. The Kwango was designed to rival Idiot Dancing as the latest hippie rave. Alas, apart from a few demonstration nights at the Speakeasy, it never took off.

The arrival of Steve Howe into Yes in 1970 was indeed a blast of fresh air. Steve was an underground hero and Bill Bruford had formed the impression that Steve was something of a hippie. Certainly Steve had long hair and played guitar with a wah-wah pedal, but he was also a sensitive, masterful player. He was regarded in some awe in psychedelic circles because he could play the guitar very well indeed. It was Steve who had created the atmospheric wah-wah sounds heard on Tomorrow's classic 'My White Bicycle' which was played non-stop at underground clubs and festivals. But Steve was no Joe Jammer. He treated his beloved guitar as a musical instrument to be cherished. It was this attitude that endeared him to Chris and Jon in their search for a player who could help interpret their musical ideas. It was a shame Peter had to go, but his successor came to embody the spirit of the new Yes.

Jon Anderson was in skittish mood as he welcomed the new recruit. He told me, "We decided to get Steve in when we discovered he was mad. You've got to be mad to join us!"

★   ★   ★

Steve Howe, intense in manner and striking in looks, is perhaps the ultimate British guitar hero. Gentlemanly, elegant and modest, he clings to his unusually large Gibson guitar with a tenacity that exemplifies his determination to hold onto his pre-eminent position. An avid collector, even the delicate and careful way he holds a guitar seems to show his respect for the instrument. Like many self-taught players he has sometimes been wracked by self-doubt and lack of confidence but his self-imposed drive for success and perfection usually win through in the end. Although he takes life seriously and is especially keen on self-discipline in the form of vegetarianism and meditation, Steve is at heart a down-to-earth Londoner with a good sense of humour. He has the well adjusted attitude of someone raised in a large and happy working-class family.

Steve was born on April 8, 1947, and brought up in a three-bedroom flat in Holloway, North London. The youngest of four children he has two brothers, Phillip and John, and sister Stella. "We were always very happy there and it never seemed crowded at home," recalls Steve. While his parents weren't particularly musical they had a big stereogram record player which Steve played as a child. "It had big speakers with loads of bass. It sounded amazing. One of my earliest memories was hearing 78 rpm records of brass bands and I used to march around the flat to the music."

Early rock'n'roll records were also a source of excitement. "I couldn't just sit and listen, I had to jump around. The music seemed so incredibly daring. This led me to want a guitar when I was about ten years old. I got one for Christmas when I was 12. I couldn't play a note but I was blindly confident and for the first couple of months I'd pose with the guitar in the window, while people were walking past, coming home from work.

There was this young kid with a guitar, miming behind the curtains!"

Miming was a rather frustrating business and Steve realised he would have to learn to actually play the instrument. He set about teaching himself, inspired by the guitar work on records by Bill Haley & The Comets. Soon he thought himself ready to play with a group of friends at a youth hostel near his school. "My first concert was so disastrous and it left such a scar that I thought I could never play on stage again. We didn't rehearse, we didn't tune up. We got on the stage and tried to play 'Frightened City' by The Shadows. It was just dreadful!"

For a couple of years Steve steered clear of all public performances. Then, aged 14, he and a friend from Tottenham started a group which played at youth clubs. As they got older they progressed to local pubs and even ballrooms. "One of the first gigs we ever did was at Pentonville Prison. We played there twice a week and the prisoners used to come and sweep up afterwards."

Steve and his group played for young offenders rather than the old lags, and performed current pop hits like 'Bobby's Girl' by Susan Maughan. He was busy on the local gig circuit and he tried to convince his parents that he didn't need a regular day job. He was sure he could make a living as a semi-professional musician. "I only ever had two or three jobs. I worked for two days in a piano making factory which drove me mad listening to pianos being tuned all day. Ding, ding, ding, ding, ding! I kept thinking 'Go on – up, up, down a bit.' I couldn't stop my mind working on these notes, that I could have no affect on whatsoever. Then I had a very convenient job in a record shop which was ideal. There was a very nice manager. I used to beg him, 'Can I have next Saturday off? I've got a gig.' And he'd say, 'Saturday! That's our busiest day!' "

In the end Steve had to leave the store as the gigs began to mount up. His first record, made at the age of 17 with a group called The Syndicats, was produced by the legendary Joe Meek who scored a huge hit in 1962 with the groundbreaking instrumental 'Telstar' by The Tornados. Joe operated from his home studio RGM Sound situated in a flat above a luggage shop at 304 Holloway Road. Here he recorded The Tornados and such successful artists as John Leyton, The Honeycombs, Mike Berry and Heinz Burt. He also tried recording local beat groups like The Outlaws, with Ritchie Blackmore, and The Syndicats. The Syndicats were a North London R&B group who specialised in playing Chuck Berry covers. They formed in 1963 and lasted until June 1965 with a line-up that included Steve on guitar, Kevin Driscoll on bass, Tom Ladd on vocals and Johnny Melton on drums.

Meek subsequently suffered bouts of severe depression, largely due to his homosexuality, and his production style and sound was rendered obsolete overnight when The Beatles and Rolling Stones arrived on the scene. He would die in tragic circumstances. After a tremendous row at the studio he murdered his landlady and killed himself with a shotgun on February 3, 1967.

Mercifully Steve Howe was nowhere near the studio at the time of the incident. Says Steve, "We made three records with Joe. The first was 'Maybellene', the Chuck Berry song, the second was 'Howling For My Baby' which was a great blues song and the third was 'On The Horizon' which came out just when I left the group. It actually got on the Radio Caroline chart at number 17. I thought, 'Have I made a big mistake here?' Joe didn't manage us, he just produced our records. We had a woman manager who was in fact the bass player's mum, Mrs. Driscoll. She spurred us on but somebody left the group and we didn't have a singer for a while and it was all a bit chaotic."

Steve then joined The In Crowd who often played in Tottenham at the Club Noreik, a favourite venue with The Who. This band included Keith West (vocals), Junior Wood (bass) and Twink Alder (drums). The group recorded a cover version of Otis Redding's 'That's How Strong My Love Is' which got to Number 48 in the UK charts in May, 1965.

"Suddenly everything seemed to be happening," says Steve. "When I was asked to join The In Crowd I didn't even think about it. I was straight in because it was the next step on. I then found out what groups were really all about. There were more personality dramas in that group compared to The Syndicats. I realised what it was like for somebody to be fired. When I joined, their guitarist was fired and I heard all these conversations like, 'Well, you're not in the group anymore, we've got somebody else.' "

After recovering from the initial embarrassment of taking somebody else's gig, Steve thoroughly enjoyed his time with The In Crowd. "We went right over the top and did lots of crazy things. But then it was the Sixties! We decided that covering soul music was totally passé and we had to write all our own songs. We changed the way we dressed and changed our name to Tomorrow. Keith West had lots of songs and we did his material. I started to get interested in songwriting too. Keith and I started writing together and came up with our second single called 'Revolution' which was before The Beatles' 'Revolution'. But what most people remember about Tomorrow is 'My White Bicycle' which was my first flop. So many people said it was going to be a hit. We thought, 'We've got *the* single!' "

The record hovered around the bottom of the charts but never got any further. Keith West had written the song with a friend called Kenny Burgess. Although 'My White Bicycle' didn't happen, Steve was intrigued by the idea of writing rather than just playing music and bought his first cassette machine to tape ideas. "We went into the studio to do another single with Mark Wirtz. He was the first producer to ask me to do a guitar session. I arrived and said, 'Where's everybody else?' and he said, 'It's just you! You've gotta overdub a track.' I was thrilled to bits – it was like heaven."

Steve began to record his own singles for EMI, including one unfinished piece 'Mothballs'. Meanwhile a new Keith West solo single called 'Excerpt From A Teenage Opera' got to Number 2 in the charts in August, 1967. Says Howe, "I did play guitar on that record but as a session man. It came out and was such a success people wanted to book Keith West. But what they got was Tomorrow. Or they booked Tomorrow and got Keith West! This wasn't a happy situation because when we went to Ireland as Keith West and Tomorrow we had a terrible time. We were treated so badly we said we'd never go back to Ireland. I don't blame them personally, because they thought they were going to see a pop show. What they got was heads down semi-psychedelic rock! So they were a bit confused to say the least. They started hurling coins at us and it got a bit dangerous. But when we came back we did some nice open air shows and did lots of gigs with Pink Floyd. We also did the big one – Christmas on Earth at Olympia."

It was then that word began to buzz around the underground about the brilliant young guitarist who could blow the socks off most of the spaced out hippies on the scene. "Steve Howe man – phew – far out!" would be the cry as joints were rolled on the backs of Frank Zappa album sleeves in pads from Notting Hill Gate to Manchester Square. Steve was quite proud of his growing status and enjoyed the mystique but insists, "It wasn't premeditated. I was quite shy really and I was trying to discover who I was. I found that very difficult. When I was in Tomorrow and when we were playing clubs, guys would come up and say, 'Do you know what you were just playing then? That was incredible.' I'd just think, 'Who are these weird people!' They could see something in me that I couldn't. All I could see was that I was performing a function in the band and when was the next gig? I was living in a sort of a shadow and this continued for many years. In my own mind I was still trying to get a style and be as good as the great guitarists I admired."

Steve couldn't get a perspective on his ability or talent. "I was just like a lost sheep. I was confused in that sense, but I was very content at being in a group. I even found travelling on the road very easy. I'd get in the van and put me feet up! I loved the psychedelic scene too and I'd go to Granny Takes A Trip which was *the* shop in the Kings Road, Chelsea and they made the most incredible clothes. You could pay fifty quid for an outrageous one-off jacket. I used to like their velvet jackets but in Tomorrow I used to wear a sort of Indian Ghandi style jacket with a beautiful blue design which appeared on the Tomorrow album sleeve."

Steve did the circuit of London's hippest venues from UFO, to Middle Earth and The Round House in Chalk Farm where he met ace hippie promoters like the legendary Joe Boyd. "It was a great time for new discoveries and there were so many aware people around. Hippie promoters would actually come in and say things like, 'We really liked the show guys . . . here's some extra money. Come back next week.' As a young group, what more could you ask for? It was such a change from the old music biz agents who would just rip you off. I enjoyed that rapport. I also remembered when Jimi Hendrix came on stage and played with us one night. He played bass! That was at the UFO Club in Tottenham Court Road. He staggered up on stage and took the bass away from the bass player and started making these weird noises in the corner. That's why I loved the hippie, psychedelic scene. But all too quickly it began to fall apart. By 1969 there was absolutely nothing to do. Keith and I were doing a few sessions with Ronnie Wood on bass and Aynsley Dunbar on drums. That was an amazing combination with great potential but nothing got finished. It was all trial and error stuff. I got a dead end feeling and out of that came my group called Bodast which in itself was a dead end."

Bodast signed with MGM, a label which closed just before the band's album was due to be released. It eventually came out ten years later in 1979 when Steve remixed the eight track tapes himself. "When it wasn't out, people thought it had some chance, but when I did put it out, of course it had no chance at all!"

Bodast included singers Clive Skinner (aka Clive Muldoon) and Dave Curtis, Bruce Thomas on bass, who would go on to play with Quiver and Elvis Costello's Attractions, and Bobby Woodman (aka Clarke) on drums whose pedigree included stints with 'Screaming' Lord Sutch and French singer Johnny Halliday. The group was originally a trio and took its name Bodast from Bo (Bobby), Da (Dave) and St (Steve). MGM had promised them film roles and trips to America that never happened so Steve decided to quit. He briefly joined the Nice with Keith Emerson, who had recently dropped their guitarist Davy O'List. "I joined the Nice . . . and left the very next day. It was all a great idea but when I got home I decided it wasn't what I wanted to do. Even so, I always thought a mixture of me and Keith might have been fantastic. It was brilliant – for a day."

Steve dropped out. But people kept calling him. There were hints of a job with Jethro Tull. Then he got a phone call from Chris Squire who said, "Do you want to join Yes?" Admits Steve, "I had never really heard of them. But they had some money to buy equipment and everything sounded great so I joined Yes – and everything went wrong! We got ditched by our manager Roy Flynn and the wages stopped. Yes reverted back to every other experience I'd had in my life. It was like Bodast, Tomorrow, The In Crowd and The Syndicats all over again. They promised you everything and you got nothing! But I thought . . . no . . . this is something special. This is good. We went to stay in a farmhouse in Devon and rehearsed *The Yes Album*. It didn't feel like a songwriters' band, it was more of a musicians' band. I remember the first time I played with them was in a basement under their manager's house in Putney. Bill Bruford thought I was a bit of a hippie. But I thought they were hippies! I always loved Bill's contribution to the early Yes albums. Alan later took over from him and did great things but there was something about Bill's concept of the thinking musician that we've never had since Bill left."

After the initial rehearsal Steve felt he was definitely in the right musical environment, even if their financial prospects looked bleak. He went to stay with the band in Devon where he got to know more about Jon, Chris, Bill and Tony.

"We borrowed money from people who owned the house for food and we didn't pay the rent for two weeks just so we could scrape through. They encouraged me so much and they wanted input from me as a musician. They didn't just get me in to strum along so I was able to contribute to things like 'Close To The Edge' and 'Siberian Khatru'. The band was always on the edge of new technology and they wanted me to come up with the latest sounds. I must say though that *Time And A Word* was a tremendous album. Before I joined, the group had designed a clever way of breaking rules and changing dimensions, stopping and starting on tunes like 'No Experience Necessary' and 'Astral Traveller'. If I listen to it now, I do hear almost what I do in Yes. Peter Banks did help to design the way the group fitted together and I kind of took over from that. I didn't actually listen to him a great deal at the time but I realise now that he was capable and inventive and imaginative. Obviously when I came in I wasn't going to be thinking about him a lot, as I had my own ideas. But Peter did start the ball rolling. When I joined the band I had to learn a lot of the tunes on the second album and that grated a bit with me, but I think I did a good job."

Steve found himself playing 'Then', 'Astral Traveller' and 'No Experience Necessary'. Later on he also revisited 'Sweet Dreams'. "I always thought we'd do 'Dear Father' because that's one of Jon's favourite songs. It's funny talking about it now, but *Time And A Word* was very dynamic and musically very successful. Of course they asked Peter to leave just when that album came out and when we went on tour we were promoting that record. So that's why I mysteriously appeared on the American

The Syn in 1967, featuring, left to right, Peter Banks on guitar, Andrew Jackman on keyboards, Steve Nardelli on vocals, Chris Allen on drums and Chris Squire on bass. *(Peter Banks Collection)*

Jack Barrie, the manager of La Chasse Club, who in 1968 introduced Jon Anderson to Chris Squire, with Anderson. *(Chris Welch)*

Yes' first manager Roy Flynn, left, with Jimi Hendrix at London's Speakeasy Club in 1968. *(Roy Flynn Collection)*

The first line-up of Yes, which lasted from June 1968 to early 1970; left to right: Peter Banks, Bill Bruford, Jon Anderson, Chris Squire and Tony Kaye. *(Barrie Wentzel)*

Yes Mark I on tour in Ireland with The Nice and The Bonzo Dog Band, July 1969. Also in the picture, just to the right of centre, is author Chris Welch. *(Chris Walter)*

The second line up Yes, with Steve Howe having taken over the all important guitar spot from Peter Banks.
Left to right: Chris Squire, Howe, Tony Kaye, Bill Bruford and Jon Anderson. *(Harry Goodwin)*

Rick Wakeman, the star keyboard player who joined Yes from The Strawbs in the summer of 1971. *(LFI)*

Steve Howe with his favourite instrument, the Gibson ES 175. *(LFI)*

Chris Squire, bass and vocals, the only member of Yes to appear on every album the band has released. *(LFI)*

Jon Anderson on stage at London's Rainbow Theatre, November 1973,
just before the release of *Tales From Topographic Oceans*. *(LFI)*

Drummer Alan White, who with Chris Squire is the only other member of Yes
to have enjoyed an uninterrupted career with the band. *(LFI)*

Yes during the post-*Relayer* period in 1975, with Patrick Moraz (far right)
having temporarily replaced Rick Wakeman. *(LFI)*

Back in the fold: Rick Wakeman in 1978. Rick returned to Yes, initially as a session player, for the recording of *Going For The One* – and was persuaded to stay. *(Lisa Tanner)*

sleeve. They thought the original sleeve was too sexist or something, so they just took a picture out of the file of new Yes shots which featured me. It's a very hippie picture with all of us looking very flower power-ish. I'm even wearing a kaftan! But on the inside of course, you see Peter Banks. Anyway we started a tour for the album and did a gig at a college somewhere in South London. Somehow we got through that year because *The Yes Album* worked and we suddenly became in vogue."

★   ★   ★

On June 20 'Sweet Dreams', the third Yes single, appeared and was given glowing reviews. "Yes seem to have vanished," I wrote in *MM*. "They have gone into hiding down in the west country following the departure of Peter Banks but the record company have allowed a marvellous piece of music to escape. It's a great song by Jon Anderson with fine instrumental support . . . but don't get too excited. We don't want one of Britain's finest groups getting the huge hit they deserve – do we!"

The revamped Yes with Steve Howe played at London's Lyceum Ballroom on July 17, as part of an unlikely bill that included Black Sabbath and Uriah Heep, the monsters of heavy metal. The next day they played a gig in Birmingham and the following month they were scheduled to play at the Plumpton Festival.

I went to interview the band at the Lyceum. This time the headline announced, 'Yes – The Band That's Biologically Improved'. They were described as 'A great original and much respected group who have carved their own niche in the scheme of rock'. Bill Bruford filled me in on events since Peter Banks' departure, the arrival of Steve Howe and their sojourn down in Devon: "We worked so hard while we were away on the farm we were exhausted. It was like four years on the road! Steve is a fine guitarist and very co-operative. Steve talks about the music so we know where we stand. People have said we're a little orchestra but we're still a group. We formed with an idea and we're sticking to it. We will still be playing old material because people like that. 'I See You' has gone but there are new tunes like Chris Squire's 'Adventures' which is a two bass feature. With Steve singing we can get three part vocal harmonies. We are also doing Simon & Garfunkel's 'America' which has been given a great Yes arrangement. Time slips by but Yes battles on! I feel humble that we are going to be paid to do something we like doing and exist entirely for music."

Apart from the occasional festival the band were still playing bread and butter gigs in small pubs. On August 2, 1970 they could be found at the Greyhound, Croydon, supported by Supertramp and on the 14th at the Red Lion, Leytonstone, for the opening of the Chez Club. On Sunday

August 16 Yes played sixth on the bill at the Yorkshire Blues and Jazz Festival, and were back once more at The Marquee on August 18.

Chris Charlesworth, who had first seen Yes rehearsing in their Shaftesbury Avenue basement back in 1968, was now a fully fledged *Melody Maker* rock reporter and he was most impressed by their Sunday evening appearance at Plumpton Festival that August. He wrote: "Yes deserve all the credit that colleague Welch has been showering on them over the past two years. For me they were a highlight of the night. Their rehearsals down in Devon have proved their worth and they emerged as one of the best bands in Britain. Jon Anderson, eagerly tapping a cowbell, encourages the most from his musicians. New guitarist Steve Howe did a lovely acoustic solo with his self penned 'Clap' and the group reached a tremendous climax on 'America'."

The hard gigging continued into September, playing at colleges from Eltham to Bishops Stortford, to Loughborough and beyond with two concerts scheduled for the Queen Elizabeth Hall, London on Saturday, October 31 at 6.15 p.m. and 9 p.m.

★　★　★

More important than all this gigging, was the making of the next album, the first with Steve Howe. In the meantime Yes had finally decided to part company with Roy Flynn and seek new representation. It was a traumatic business. Roy has not wished to talk about his Yes days – until now.

Says Bill Bruford, "When we started writing and rehearsing *The Yes Album* down in Devon, we were down to our last few quid and out of desperation we moved to a new manager Brian Lane whose real name was Harvey Freed."

Recalls Chris Squire, "I found Brian Lane through my hairdresser. It's such a corny rock'n'roll story. There I was in Sweeny Todd's in the Kings Road, Chelsea, which was the trendy hairdressers at the time and this guy Colin used to cut my hair. I told him we were thinking of getting rid of our manager and he said, 'Oh, I know this guy who asked me the other day if I knew any bands looking for a manager.' I said I'd like to meet him and he turned out to be Brian Lane. So that's how I met Brian, through my hairdresser. Prior to that Brian had been involved in song plugging. Brian was a very energetic manager and was a big boost to the whole thing. He was one of those people who always had a phone glued to his ear. He was very impressive because in those days that was the beginning of the age when people were constantly on the phone. It was a new trendy thing."

The split with Roy Flynn left the band's former manager feeling embittered after all his hard work. He found the end of his association with Yes most painful. He was later asked to manage many other people, including the celebrity chef Keith Floyd. But he told Keith, "I've done it once, but it is now my ambition never to manage anyone ever again. It's a pain in the arse. Whatever you do, it's never enough."

The end came during the stay at the Devon farmhouse in March 1970. Recalls Flynn, "I had hired the farm from an accountant. I went down to see the band by train and was picked up at the station by Chris Squire. When I got to the farm I told them, 'This can't go on.' I couldn't go on forever subsidising their stay. They insisted on staying another week. I paid for that but I couldn't go on paying any longer. That's when it finished. That's when Harvey Freed (Brian Lane) came in."

Roy did his best to understand the band's motives in parting company with him. "I admire artists. You need a lot of ego to perform on stage. But what is very difficult for artists to understand is that a third party is needed to promote their careers. They feel that really it's only a question of time before the world recognises their all too obvious talent. This is the problem with management. The situation only really works when the band is *frightened* of the manager. I didn't work like that. Any fool can manage a successful band. The trick is to take a band from £15 a night gigs to the Royal Albert Hall. That's creative management."

Roy carried on supporting Peter Banks financially until the guitarist could form his own band Flash. Says Peter, "One of the reasons I was asked to go was because they started talking about getting rid of Roy. I said, 'Well if he goes, I go.' It was a kind of headstrong thing to say but I thought it was a rotten thing to do to Roy. He had given up his job at the Speakeasy to manage us full time and he'd invested all of his own money into the band. Nobody was more committed to Yes than Roy Flynn. He even gave us the basement at his house in Putney to rehearse in."

Flynn then left the music business completely in 1973 stating that he wanted nothing more to do with it. "I was quite a good manager but I'd never do it again. I wouldn't wish it on my worst enemy. There were a lot of people whispering in the band's ears, undermining my relationship with them. It was no fun for me any more, especially when they were just moaning all the time."

Roy only relinquished his management role after negotiating a deal with the management company Hemdale. "First I went to see Syd Bernstein in New York who had put on The Beatles at the Shea Stadium in the Sixties. I offered him a deal on Yes and he wasn't interested. I went to see Peter Grant of Led Zeppelin and he wasn't interested either."

In the end Hemdale took them over. This was an expanding company run by John Daly in conjunction with actor David Hemmings and Brian Lane. David Hemmings had shot to fame with his starring role in the classic Sixties' movie *Blow Up*. Several years later Hemdale would be responsible for producing many smash hit Hollywood movies. Flynn signed a deal with Hemdale where he retained five per cent of the earnings of the band in recognition of his efforts on their behalf. He also remained a director of their publishing company Yessongs and retained thirty per cent of the shares. It seemed fair to him, although Yes were not so sure and pointedly titled one of the tracks on their 1971 album *Fragile* 'Five Per Cent For Nothing'. Roy almost grinds his teeth when he recalls this episode.

"The problem was – I never got paid. Even when the band went to America and enjoyed big record sales, nothing ever came back to yours truly! There were no company meetings called and there were no accounts provided, so I brought an action against them. I had spent all my money on the band. I'd given up running the clubs. I'd given up everything to manage Yes and because I didn't have any more money to spend on them, I was pilloried. I had thrown my life away but obviously it wasn't enough for the gentlemen of that august orchestra!"

The legal action lasted for some two years but in 1973 Hemdale finally made an offer. "It was peanuts and I didn't want to take it, but I owed over £6,000 to my lawyer so I was advised to accept."

Flynn settled out of court for $150,000 dollars. After that he walked out of the music business. "It left a very unpleasant taste in my mouth and it's now a part of my life I'd rather forget. Even so I always liked their music and I thought Yes were a great band. I loved the dynamics of their performances. They had so much colour and texture. The sad thing is there aren't really any records that show how exciting and wonderful they were at the beginning. I saw Jon Anderson years later at the Reading Festival with his wife Jenny and we spent the whole afternoon talking about what happened. I just know I had done more than anybody else could have done for them at the time."

Roy still keeps as a memento a piece of shiny blue wrapping paper that once held a gold Dunhill cigarette lighter – a Christmas gift to him from the band which he received in 1968. A simple inscription says: "To Roy Flynn, who has done more for us than any other man put together in the pop music business. Looking forward to a long and happy association. Hope this small gift will enlighten you as much as you have enlightened us. A very happy Christmas from Yes. Chris, Jon, William, Tony and Peter."

"That's why I feel so sad about it," says Flynn. "I saw them on BBC 2 on their *Family Trees* TV documentary. I didn't recognise them, but they were still moaning!"

Although Michael Tait came to the band through Roy Flynn, he would remain closely involved with Yes for many years to come. Roy was not best pleased at what he saw as Tait's attempt to undermine his position but Michael says he had no personal ambitions to become the band's manager. Says Tait, "Roy was a very nice guy and he had faith in the band in the beginning but he didn't have any real knowledge about what to do with them and he wasn't going to put everything on the line for them. He wasn't going to mortgage his house to promote this band. I don't think he was dedicated enough to do that and risk everything. Therefore the band had a very slow start, especially with the record company. He had done a deal with Atlantic but they didn't really care. They had got the band for basically nothing so whether they were a hit or a miss didn't really matter to them. If they hit, great they made a profit. If they missed they didn't lose anything. What the band needed was a real go-getter and that led to meeting Brian Lane. He was a go-getter and a deal maker. Some people would say he had a lot of faults as well but he had a vision and the gift of the gab with people. He did very good deals for the band – and himself. He definitely got the band noticed."

During this fraught period Tait went back to Australia to sort out his immigration problems. "The band were down in Devon and I came back via New York and dropped into Atlantic Records. To be honest they didn't know who Yes were! I said, 'Well they've been signed to you for two years.' They thought it was a folk act. They really didn't know anything about Yes. It was astonishing. I was flabbergasted. This was after Roy Flynn and just before Brian Lane. I could have been their manager if I'd been that kind of person. They looked to me to help them, but to be honest it was not my job. I was more on the technical side and dealing with that business thing was not what I wanted. It's an art and not what I wanted to do at all. There was a void to be filled but Brian came along."

Yes quickly formed a new, long-term partnership with Brian Lane at Hemdale. Says Bill Bruford, "It was a case of us asking him, 'What can you do for us in the next six months? If you can do a lot we'll sign with you.' So he said, 'I can get you into the chart.' "

Bill and the rest of the band were nonplussed at this confident assertion. "How do you do that then?" they asked in wide-eyed bewilderment.

Brian Lane would become a major factor in turning Yes from a London based gig band into an international supergroup. He had previously worked as a song plugger and had managed successful pop singer Anita Harris.

Says Bill, "I didn't understand what was going on, but suddenly we were on a stronger financial footing and Brian became our manager. Brian was a plugger and got artists' records played on radio. He had worked on Jimi Hendrix's 'Hey Joe'. He also had one record away called 'Arnold Layne' by Pink Floyd, so instead of being A. Lane he became B. Lane . . .

you see? I loved all this. I thought it was very colourful. You see in his mind the public was an ignorant beast missing all this good music. All they needed was to be led into the thing by getting a record away. Then everybody would love Jimi Hendrix or Pink Floyd and we were next in line. Once we'd appeared in the album charts we were up and running. We just needed a helping hand. Everyone knew Yes was going to be a great band eventually. So why not get a record started?"

But there weren't that many singles from Yes to hype into the chart. Since 'Sweetness' in June 1969 there hadn't been another single until the title track from their second album *Time And A Word* came out with 'The Prophet' on the B side in March, 1970.

"It was a bit unhip to release singles," explains Bill. "I like *Time And A Word* the album. In fact I loved it because there was a lot of drumming going on. I loved 'Then' which I played more or less on the snare drum throughout. Tracks like 'Sweet Dreams' I thought was very groovy and 'Astral Traveller' I loved. Everybody bitched a bit but I thought this was a great album. We had strings and whether the violins were good, bad or indifferent, I could only see the strong ideas which were recorded really nicely. From my point of view I liked the sound of the drums which were way better than the first record. I was learning fast."

As part of the 'helping hand', Yes were provided with £5,000 worth of new equipment ready for a series of much bigger and better dates, like Van Dyke Hall Plymouth (November 22), Newcastle City Hall (December 8) and Hull University (9). The news was also trumpeted in the music press: "New Yes manager Brian Lane is presently negotiating their first American tour to start next March 31. A British and European tour with a top American band is now being set up by Lane in conjunction with Atlantic Records for January."

It was revealed that the American band would be Atlantic stable mates Iron Butterfly, famed for their smash hit album *In-A-Gadda-Da-Vida* (loosely translated from the Brooklyn as *In The Garden Of Eden*). It was the first rock LP ever to go platinum. American critic Lillian Roxon rather unkindly referred to them as ". . . the original heavy-metal Cro-Magnons. Their low-browed, jut-jawed sound conjured up visions of steamer trunks being dropped down several flights of stairs."

Amidst all the talk of massive 12-date British tours and an appearance at the Royal Albert Hall (scheduled for January 13, 1971) there was a curious footnote to their proposed third album. It was announced: "Yes have started work on their third album provisionally titled *Stunt Of The Month* which will be the first featuring new guitarist Steve Howe." The title was clearly a very silly stunt indeed and hastily abandoned before show time.

In November, 1970 the band played two gigs at London's Queen Elizabeth Hall, London, and received a glowing review. "After the changes that have taken place some fans felt that the band might be in danger of losing some of their established identity. Not so. With Steve Howe Yes have reached a new peak. The guitarist proved something of a show stealer with his unaccompanied acoustic tour de force 'Clap'. He ranged over a whole gamut of country rag licks and it was done with such speed and aplomb he gained an ovation. The second show was better. 'Astral Traveller' opened, followed by Jon Anderson's beautiful new work 'Yours Is No Disgrace'. 'All Good People' featured Steve's mandolin and the vocal choir of Anderson, Howe and Squire. Chris Squire and Steve took part in a phenomenal battle of the bass guitars in what Chris called 'A Bass Odyssey' showing how the rock bass can become an exciting lead instrument. The climax of their show was a dramatic arrangement of Simon & Garfunkel's 'America' which opened with a strange 1930's Berlin style intro played by Tony Kaye on organ and Steve leading into Jon's simple emotive vocals. Bill Bruford was a tower of strength throughout."

Supporting Yes on these two entertaining shows was a new band called Dada featuring Elkie Brooks and Robert Palmer, both destined for stardom. The week after this review appeared I kept up the Yes media bombardment by interviewing 23-year-old Steve Howe for the first time. We met over a glass of wine and a Chinese meal in the bar of the Red Lion, a fine pub in an alley off Fleet Street sadly long demolished. At that same bar I had previously interviewed David Bowie, when he was still a nervous young hippie involved in Arts Labs and Bhuddism. Steve reminded me a lot of David. They had the same intensity about their music, the same London charm and sense of humour.

At this time Steve was already married to wife Janet and they had a bouncing baby son called Dylan. Some twenty-three years later I would interview Dylan when he had become a brilliant jazz and rock drummer, wowing London club crowds with his drive and technique. He had been tutored by a good family friend, William 'Tubs' Bruford.

Introducing Yes fans to Steve back in 1970, I reminded them that Howe had been something of an underground legend since 'My White Bicycle' created such a stir. His old band Tomorrow had only just split up when we met. Since his arrival in Yes audiences had been delighted by Steve's displays of solo virtuosity. "Lots of people think I've had classical training, but I picked it up myself. I just worked on my technique," he explained.

As Steve Howe settled into Yes he was understandably keen to get on with new material. He told me back in 1970, "Some people who come to see us are disappointed that we don't do more of the old material. We do 'Astral Traveller' but we dropped 'Then'. It was more important for me to rehearse new numbers with the group when I joined them than to spend time doing numbers they already knew and they played differently from the records I had heard anyway. 'Clap' is slightly influenced by Chet Atkins. It's a simple little tune I used to play and expanded by putting in stop time breaks and bits from Mason Williams' 'Classical Gas' which I have always loved. Down in Devon the boys said they wanted to find a solo for me and this came up. I started playing it on a couple of gigs and it always goes down well. People don't know what to associate my guitar style with, blues or the underground. I want to do a solo album one day, but there is no hurry."

Now began the serious work of heavy touring. On November 13 they played at the City of London Students Union. On November 27 they were at Southend College and the following day at the Starlight Rooms, Boston, Lincs. All this travelling was of course very risky. Bands were forever involved in 'shunts' on the motorways as fog and tiredness took their toll on their driver's concentration. On December 5, 1970, the *MM* headlines bellowed 'Yes Man In Crash'. The story below read: "Yes organist Tony Kaye received a broken foot when the group were involved in a head-on collision with another vehicle at Basingstoke last week. The four other members of the group were treated for shock and the group were forced to cancel a show at Bradford University the following evening. Tony Kaye now plays with his foot in plaster and has to be carried on stage for subsequent live commitments."

Apart from jokes about Tony being plastered again, it was a painful business. At least he didn't have to play with his elbows in plaster.

On December 20, Yes played a special Christmas show at London's Lyceum which started at midnight. Around this time it was reported that the band planned to record their fourth album, *Fragile*, with Tom Dowd of Atlantic Records at his new studio in Miami. It all seemed very exciting, and yet as 1971 dawned the band were back at the Greyhound, Croydon, being supported by Curved Air. They still had contracted gigs to fulfil. Hollywood would have to wait – and in the event, no Tom Dowd-produced Yes album ever materialised.

Nor did it need to, for Yes' third album, *The Yes Album,* would see the band achieve the kind of success they had only dreamed about in La Chasse, Blaises and the Speakeasy. But first they had to hang on to the dream, and their Atlantic contract. Phil Carson worked behind the scenes to ensure the label didn't drop them.

"Ahmet Ertegun dropped Yes right after *Time And A Word,*" reveals Carson. "I called up Ahmet and was able to convince him to withdraw the drop notice, which he did. Then we made *The Yes Album* which most Americans think is still the *first* Yes album."

The record unveiled some wonderful new songs as the band went into creative overdrive. 'Yours Is No Disgrace', the three part 'Starship Trooper', 'I've Seen All Good People' and 'Perpetual Change' were among the more astonishing pieces that have since become part of Yes lore. Most of the material was done in cahoots with producer Eddie Offord at Advision Studios, London, during the Autumn of 1970. Steve Howe's acoustic guitar feature 'Clap' was recorded live at the Lyceum Theatre.

Heard today, *The Yes Album* still has the power to amaze and delight. The staccato introduction to 'Yours Is No Disgrace' builds the tension to the point where the piece suddenly shoots into swirling layers of sound. Steve Howe's spine tingling guitar swoops joyously, like some graceful bird floating over a landscape of canyons and mountain peaks. Chris and Jon's unison vocals exude a sense of optimism as if all past battles are finally over and nothing can now stop the band's musical odyssey. "On a sailing ship to nowhere," sings Jon before the band free falls into a series of violent guitar chords. This nine-minute masterpiece packs in more music than most bands could manage in a lifetime. All the while Bruford's precision snare drum patterns chase the most intricate guitar licks Steve can summon. Jon brings it all back home with his cry of 'Yours is no disgrace' before a snapping, snarling Howe signals one more aerial flight around the cosmos and the whole piece spins into another galaxy.

The famous stop time passages on 'Yours Is No Disgrace' were worked out while the band were at the cottage in Devon. Recalls Steve, "All the guys had gone back to London for a day and I was entirely on my own for the first time. For a while I was quite frightened with the place being so silent. I had so much to let out, I played alone tremendously loud with two amplifiers and that repetitive figure cropped up."

After this liberating display, Steve was unleashed on 'Clap'. This Chet Atkins influenced *tour de force* has graced many Yes shows since this début appearance. On the album Howe was bursting with ideas and at his cotton pickin' best. The final chord was always a signal for tumultuous applause. After this 'live' interlude the rumbling bass of Chris Squire led into the opening flourishes of the astonishing 'Starship Trooper'. Fans who had already been captivated by the band's first two albums were knocked sideways by the sheer confidence and flow of ideas that characterises this ultimate Yes vignette. Every few bars there is a change of sound, style, mood, atmosphere, tempo and rhythm. Yet it all hangs together in a brilliant atomic flash of creativity, a phenomenon now almost totally lost to rock music.

The grinding intensity of 'Würm' during the third part of this remarkable construction has no equal. If some found this almost too much to take on first hearing, Yes provided gentle light relief with 'Your Move' the first part of 'I've Seen All Good People'. "*Move me onto any black square, use me any time you want . . .*" sings Jon enigmatically, as recorders played by Colin Goldring pre-date the instrument's use on Led Zeppelin's 'Stairway To Heaven'. The abrupt stop and launch into the chanting 'All Good People' is one of their great moments and still sounds irresistible.

Steve's country rock guitar solo here is a gas. Chris bounces a descending bass line while effervescent Bill kicks into stop time on his choked crash cymbals and bass drum. Tony Kaye's magisterial organ provides a floor shaking finale as the vocals fade down the scale into a tonal abyss.

In contrast 'A Venture' is somewhat awkward and is one of the band's least memorable pieces. However, Kaye of the keyboards hammers out some pub piano and provides a jolly three minute interlude before 'Perpetual Change'. This section sees Jon descending from the heavens to dispense peace and harmony. Undoubtedly the first four tracks on *The Yes Album* are among the finest the band ever devised and represent a peak that British rock music has yet to equal.

Reviews were mostly ecstatic and I hastily advised readers: "Now they have managed to combine all the delights which make Yes such a popular and satisfying stage act, one can enjoy their album without the feeling that it isn't doing them justice, or that some of the spontaneity is missing. There is a lot to discover in a Yes performance."

The Yes Album, released in January 1971, caused a sensation and even if it didn't sell in millions it certainly repaid all the faith put in the band by its supporters within the industry. It got to Number 6 in the UK charts and made its US chart début at Number 40.

Recalls Phil Carson, "I went to Advision Studios everyday to hear the music being made because I was so into the band. I remember making Steve Howe double the length of his fantastic guitar solo on 'I've Seen All Good People'. When the album was finally mixed Eddie Offord came into my office and put it on. Just one track after another was incredible."

Despite Phil's enthusiasm tour manager Michael Tait did not trust Atlantic's promotion department and decided to take matters into his own hands, even though Atlantic had taken full page advertisements for the album in *Melody Maker* and *New Musical Express*.

Says Michael, "When *The Yes Album* came out I went round with another guy and personally went into all the record shops in London with these posters and got them stuck in the window, because the record company hadn't done anything. We pounded the pavements and put up hundreds of these posters and that record got on the Virgin chart from that effort. It was one of the few times a Yes record was on the chart. *The Yes Album* was the one that had Tony Kaye with his broken foot in plaster on the cover! The album was quite successful in England and the band were hot. When we went to play somewhere like Redcar or Nottingham, the audiences were spellbound. You'd see jaws drop when they went into these songs because there was no other music around like that."

Chris Squire: "We were kind of lucky with *The Yes Album*. When it was released there was a two month postal strike in England. None of the record stores could mail in their chart returns. So the music papers took their charts from Richard Branson's Virgin store. Whatever he sold there *was* the chart. Fortunately because we had most fans in London obviously our album sold really well in the Virgin record store and for that reason it got to number one in the chart. By the time the strike was over all the other record stores accepted it was the number one record and they all stocked and sold it too. Everyone thought it was a great record to go out and buy because it was number one. There was a lot of luck involved there and that got us noticed over in New York by the American staff at Atlantic. 'Oh my God, this little folk group seem to have a number one album! We'd better do something about promoting them in America.' I have a lot of fond memories of that album. We felt we were making a statement and it was our third album for Atlantic and if it hadn't been a success I'm not sure they would have kept on financing us. Even though they had signed us for 14 albums, if it wasn't going anywhere, they have ways of getting out of that."

Even if Atlantic weren't prepared to slog the streets putting up posters, they had bigger promotional plans up their sleeve. Says Phil Carson, "After the album came out I put the band on a tour with Iron Butterfly, an American band who were also on Atlantic. I knew Butterfly could fill the venues. At the same time I was really trying to break Yes. After the tour Iron Butterfly more or less broke up! We then bought the band a PA system. In those days bands carried their own PAs. Even Led Zeppelin carried their own tiny PA consisting of Watkins speakers. Iron Butterfly insisted they wouldn't tour without their own equipment. It was the first real PA system that Europe had seen. It had huge speaker cabinets and monitors and mixers and Yes had a great time playing with it."

The days of Chris Squire driving the band to a gig and trying to get there on time for the opening number were over. The gear was now transported in trucks while the band travelled on comfortable coaches or jet planes. They aimed to get to a gig five hours before the doors opened to give them two hours to set up, feel the vibes and get a balance. It's the sort of routine that all bands now take for granted, but in the early Seventies it was a novel procedure. Even so Yes were still at risk from the perils of intensive travel. In February 1971 the band had to issue an apology in the press for missing a gig at Llandaff Technical College in

Cardiff due to a serious road accident involving their truck on the way back from France.

This latest crash worried Bill Bruford. He tended to blame the need for fast driving on Chris Squire's unfortunate habit of being late. "It's the grossest insult one musician can give another," he says firmly. "It's probably the grossest insult anybody can give to anybody else, to keep them waiting. 'Cos all you are doing is implying your superiority. This went on for so long it was just a joke. It even started to endanger the car rides. We had to drive too fast – or we'd be late for a job. Life started to get dangerous."

Bill was haunted by memories of the tragic death of Fairport Convention's drummer Martin Lamble in a motorway crash. "He was in a Transit van, exactly like us in our early days. There was something about Martin's death that made me feel very jumpy about this road stuff. People were falling asleep at the wheel. When we started out there was no money for hotels so you had to drive back from Newcastle to London often through fog. There were no central crash barriers on the motorways then. You could cross the central reservation very easily. It was dangerous as hell and made *more* dangerous by the fact that we had one person who was consistently making the band late. So we had to run red lights and this was very dodgy. Eventually I decided to make my own travel arrangements."

These were in place even before Peter Banks had left the group. One day the drummer announced: "I'm going to the next gig on my own." The band was due to drive to Germany. He got on the ferry and turned up half a day early to ensure he would be on time. The band had not arrived. Eight hours later he was informed they had driven off the road and crashed. "Mercifully they were alright but they'd ended up in a muddy ditch," recalls Bill.

Peter Banks was travelling in the car with Chris on that eventful journey, not long before he left the band. "It was a near fatal crash that could have been the end of the band. Chris was driving in a Volvo car which originally belonged to Roy Flynn. It was a long day. We had come from London and crossed the North Sea on the ferry and were heading for Hamburg. It was night time and I was asleep in the front seat. All I remember was waking up and finding that we were going sideways and branches of trees were hitting the car. It was like a ghost train ride. I thought, 'This is interesting, I wonder what's happening?' "

Chris had fallen asleep while driving at 80 mph and the car was hurtling sideways along a ditch, crashing through the undergrowth. The car finally came to a halt and the band got out. Incredibly nobody was hurt and the car survived, but they had left a 200 yard swathe of destruction behind them. They discovered they had missed a concrete post by a foot after skidding off the road. They called the emergency services, the car was dug out of the ditch and they drove on to play the gig. It wasn't until after the performance that delayed shock set in and Banks found himself shaking uncontrollably.

Says Bill, "So that's why I preferred to travel on my own. It was getting really unpleasant. It was part of the general hysteria. Added to which Chris was consuming the band's resources, which I don't resent him for. That's the way he is. But I couldn't put up with it anymore. It wasn't so bad later on in the States, as we were flying everywhere, which was much more comfortable. But even then Chris was late for the plane. He'd keep it waiting on the tarmac while all the businessmen were saying, 'Come on, let's go!' "

Despite all the risks, the heavy touring was worthwhile. Says Phil Carson, "Their touring certainly broke them in Europe. Then, after the album came out, the group caught fire in America. From then on it was a really tremendous time for Yes."

5

CLOSE TO THE EDGE

It was an unusually mild January when Yes and Iron Butterfly set out on the 'Allies Of Rock' 28-day rampage across the Continent that would 'break' Yes outside of the UK for the first time. Mercifully the British and American bands got on well together. On their first show in Holland Iron Butterfly were so impressed by Yes they immediately asked the English band to jam with them in a grand finale. On their return to London at the end of the tour the two groups even planned to record together.

Newly installed Yes manager Brian Lane flew to Amsterdam in pursuit of his charges, only to find both groups had gone on ahead to the next city. He had to catch up with them in Eindhoven by taxi. At the venue he found the band keyed up and ready to play the crucial opening salvos of their most important tour to date. Yes opened up with 'Astral Traveller' and 'Yours Is No Disgrace' and the hordes of stoned Dutch fans were suitably impressed. Even more impressed were the guys from Butterfly whose jaws dropped at the swirling rhythms, complex arrangements and Jon's astral vocals. During 'Yours Is No Disgrace' Jon began playing what was quickly dubbed his 'Meccano Moog'.[7] It was a kind of home made synthesiser which he used, rather pointedly, alongside Tony Kaye's more traditional Hammond organ. Steve Howe caused a sensation with his acoustic showcase 'Clap' and wowed Butterfly's Mike Pinera with his blazing lead guitar solo during 'America'.

Iron Butterfly, from San Diego, featured Doug Ingle on vocals, Larry 'Rhino' Reinhardt and Mike Pinera on guitars, Lee Dorman on bass and Ron Bushy on drums. Mike Pinera liked to use a voice bag on their eerie stand out number 'Butterfly Blue' which incidentally was played a lot in Soho strip clubs.[8] A fascinating device, the voice bag was later used to good effect by Peter Frampton on his hit 'Show Me The Way'.

Butterfly were a confident, hard rocking outfit. They concentrated on

---

[7] For the benefit of American readers, Meccano is a British-made children's construction kit.
[8] Don't ask how I know, but DJ John Peel can be my witness.

material from their *Metamorphosis* album, which went down extremely well with the youth of Eindhoven. Then at 3 a.m. Mike Pinera called Yes back on stage and Bill Bruford took over the drums to swing the massed bands into a steaming jam session. This incited the fans to leap on stage and start a wild version of Dutch idiot dancing.[9] The day after the Eindhoven jam we drove to Amsterdam for another midnight concert at the prestigious Concertgebouw. On the coach after a slightly less successful gig – due to the hall's echoing acoustics – I talked to Jon, Chris and Bill on the way to the airport. Jon mused over the band's state of progress: he was disappointed that their records hadn't sold well in the States and he could sense Butterfly were doing better with audiences than Yes at some of the gigs.

"They know a bit about us. But we're not a group that caters for hysteria. We could try and play a rock-blues and see what happens. It gets better communication because people can understand it more. I suppose if we really wanted to play rock-blues we would have done it by now. But we are making it. I just hope we can carry on making music. We're not after status or position."

Chris and Bill both thought that Yes might be two steps ahead of its target audience. Although Yes were well received, the more direct style of Iron Butterfly tended to get a bigger response. Said Bill, "The music's complicated man. If I was a little Dutch kid brought up on Shocking Blue – maybe I would find it difficult."

Said Chris more reflectively, "We often think we're too complicated for audiences that may not have seen us before."

The last night of their visit to Holland took them to Rotterdam. Once again the two bands jammed together after Iron Butterfly had delivered a powerful set to the most responsive audience thus far. Curiously enough, as I studied both groups' performance, it seemed to me that Yes were getting heavier, while Butterfly were getting lighter.

"The whole thing is one great big paradiddle really," said Bill Bruford, neatly summing up the paradox.

One reason why the American band made a greater impact was their far more sophisticated and powerful sound system. Yes were greatly impressed and tour manager Michael Tait's eyes and ears were popping. "Iron Butterfly actually had a monitor system," recalls Bill Bruford. "They brought a terrific PA system with them from the States and part of it included monitor speakers so the band could hear themselves. This was all new to us! We just played with bigger and bigger amplifiers, which was how we thought the audience heard the music – from the amplifiers on stage.

[9] Clifford Loeslin, Seattle-based expert on all matters pertaining to Yes, advises me there is a bootleg recording of this historic event.

"We didn't know what was coming . . . a system where you had little amplifiers and microphones that put the sound through the PA. So *that's* how it got broadcast to the public! At that point we started to have microphones on the drums. The tour with Iron Butterfly was an eye opener, it was so high tech.

"The Americans all had great sound and when we used it, suddenly you could hear Tony Kaye for the first time! So monitors and microphones came in. Until then I had been playing rim shots on the snare drum to try and get through Chris' high frequency bass sound. That's why I developed that rim shot style – a bit like Stewart Copeland twenty years later."

In their desperate attempts to improve their stage sound Yes had tried a stop-gap ruse devised by Michael Tait which involved rigging up a series of domestic hi-fi amplifiers. Clearly this wasn't sufficient and they decided to buy Butterfly's PA complete with big speakers and monitors. Now they were equipped to face America – except it wasn't worth taking the gear to the States when they were only going to be a support act.

Recalls Michael, "Iron Butterfly's PA system was like nothing we'd ever seen before. It had horns, 'W' boxes, electronic crossovers, all new stuff. We were using just three 4x12 cabinets as guitar speakers. But we saw this PA system that they were actually mixing from inside the audience. Recognising the quantum leap in equipment here, we bought that PA from Iron Butterfly. It allowed us to mix the sound from the front of the house and allowed us to have more than three microphones. It led to DI-ing (direct injection) instruments direct to the PA and using monitor speakers for the vocalist. It also had a limiter compressor which was unheard of in England. It meant the 'louds' weren't so loud and 'softs' weren't so soft. The volume was compressed into a narrower band which made it sound much better."

Tait knew that Jon Anderson had been getting depressed with the band's sound on the road. "Having a new PA made such a difference to the band. They enjoyed playing much more because they could hear each other. Unfortunately in order to get the money to buy the equipment, the management company negotiated with the band for a bunch of the publishing rights in return for this PA. Today a deal like that would never happen. One wonders if the management company had the group's best interests at heart or their own. If you look back at all the mega groups of the late Sixties and Seventies and ask them, 'Well lads, where is the money you earned in those days?' they can't show you any, because they didn't get any. Management companies used to give 'em houses and Rolls Royces, but no real money, because they kept it all! It took a while for bands to realise that they should be keeping the lion's share. Of course when you toured, the promoters used to keep the lion's share. Now it's the absolute reverse. The bands make all the money now."

On their return from Holland Yes were scheduled to play more dates in Britain with Iron Butterfly. When the two bands played at the Royal Albert Hall, London, Led Zeppelin came along to cheer their fellow Atlantic artists. Everyone shacked up in a VIP box stocked with champagne, overlooking the stage. Robert Plant got so carried away by the performance he decided to venture on the stage at the end of Iron Butterfly's set to start an impromptu jam session. I joined him and began bashing inexpertly on Iron Butterfly's see-thru plastic drum kit, while Robert grabbed the microphone and began singing Elvis Presley's greatest hits. It was all a great laugh, but before Plant & Welch could really begin to rock, a surly American roadie stepped in to stop the fun.

"Nobody touches Bushy's drums," he glowered. Well if you say so squire. I hastily relinquished the kit and even Robert looked bashful as he stepped smartly away from the mike. And so one of the world's greatest supergroups was nipped in the bud. Neither Bill Bruford nor John Bonham were on hand to see me in my moment of glory – just as well really. I often wondered whether any of the audience was left to see this disgraceful exploit.[10]

On March 4, 1971 Yes began a series of UK dates at Liverpool Stadium. This was followed by shows in Brighton, Redcar, Birmingham, Bournemouth, Doncaster, Blackburn, Guildford and Nottingham. Yes then ventured into Scotland, finishing the tour with a show at Glasgow City Hall on March 22.

During March a row flared up between Atlantic Records and the BBC over the band's mooted appearance on the prestigious *Top Of The Pops*. The producer refused to give the band the coveted 'album spot' on the show. This item was intended to allow hard rock bands and more esoteric artists to play two or three tracks from their latest album. It was meant to reflect the more serious aspects of the music biz – a policy long since forgotten. *The Yes Album* was at Number 6 in the charts, so the group felt entitled to appear. Atlantic's Phil Carson fumed. He had been trying for five weeks to get Yes on the show. The producer came up with various excuses but it was plain the Beeb had no stomach for Yes music on a popular chart show. The BBC primly told the press: "There is no ban on Yes. The album spot on the programme is not governed by the charts. We've often had albums featured that aren't in the charts. It's entirely up to

---

[10] For years afterwards I was plagued by a horrible dream in which I was playing drums on stage with Led Zeppelin. Just as I was about to take a Bonham-esque solo, my sticks turned to rubber and I couldn't play a thing. In fact I *did* actually once play conga drums with Led Zeppelin in Germany on 'Whole Lotta Love'. And I was so nervous, I couldn't play a thing!

the producer. We have to consider what is suitable both visually and musically."

*   *   *

More important to the band's future than an appearance on *Top Of The Pops* was the chance of making their mark in the States. They were dying to get across the Atlantic. Says Bill Bruford, "We *had* to get to America. We had done too many English gigs. It felt like we had done Birmingham Town Hall six times already! The band had done a lot of work at home." Bill's diary reveals that Yes played 187 gigs in 1969, followed by 131 shows in 1970, 166 gigs in 1971 and 104 in 1972.

Bill's personal earnings had gone up to around £260 a month. Handy but not a fortune. During a bumper month, though, he'd earn £600 from gigs and one October he worked 22 nights with the band and made £889. "That was a lot of money but it was still playing at the Central Hall, Chatham. We were going around the same places a lot and knew we had to get to America. But we couldn't find the right agent or the right tour. All British acts had to have success in the States, so they could come back as conquering heroes, but we couldn't quite get started."

Eventually Yes made their US début in April, 1971. They played their first date in Tennessee and thereafter went out supporting Jethro Tull, Ten Years After, The J. Geils Band and even Black Sabbath. "We were an immediate success and we wiped the floor with the other bands and everybody loved Yes," says Bruford gleefully. He recalls one hot night when Yes played the Whiskey A Go Go in Los Angeles in November, 1971. "That was our West Coast début . . . we'd finally made it in America. We did a six week US tour in December and it was very hard work. We went all over the place from New York to Chicago and Florida."

Chris Squire, too, remembers how quickly they gained support. "By then a lot of the East Coast cities like New York, Philadelphia, Cleveland and Pittsburgh had taken to the band. We had a lot of DJ support and we were quite surprised when a lot of people showed up who knew what we were doing. A couple of times Ian Anderson of Jethro Tull wasn't totally happy with the way we went down. We did a few gigs where – after we'd done our set – half the audience left. Well, it wasn't *quite* like that but we were definitely going down as well as he was. We were just supposed to be the opening act!"

One of their earliest American converts was sound engineer Roy Clair, now president of Clair Brothers Audio Enterprises Inc. who would be associated with the band for the next three decades. "We heard the buzz and all over the States people were saying, 'There's an incredible new group coming from England,' " recalls Roy. "The first time I heard them I was most impressed, because the music was so different. They were so talented and they worked really well together. We developed a new system that gave them a big sound. They'd already had a sound system they'd just purchased from Iron Butterfly. But when they came to America they didn't bring it along because they were only second on the bill to Jethro Tull."

Clair Brothers built them a new system similar to the one they had in England. "It was more compact and had more devices. That's why they chose us, because we could provide a system similar to the one they'd used on their successful tour with Iron Butterfly. At this time our company also worked with Elton John, Cat Stevens and The Moody Blues. Yes were so professional and it was such a joy to work with them. They believed in the people they were touring with and gave them a wide latitude. They also brought their producer along. Most groups would hire a sound engineer to go on the road. They brought Eddie Offord who used to produce them. The sound was so good, they got a lot of good reviews in the States."

Roy Clair became the band's sound doctor. He studied their arrangements and came up with what they needed to get the music across to loud and demonstrative US audiences. "Their music is very dynamic and they needed a lot of power. So we used big amplifiers. This enabled the speakers to cope with the dynamics of the band, quiet sometimes and then remarkably loud. Yes was famous for that."

As Roy regularly travelled with the group he grew very fond of his new English mates. Roy was house engineer, working alongside Eddie Offord. He remembers the daily routine of keeping the complex Yes sound requirements ticking over. "We had to set up every day and make sure everything was ready for Eddie to mix. Eddie was great. His only problem was drugs. Every now and then he'd fall onto the faders! And then we'd have to mix for him. But he was a great character, that's for sure."

Roy witnessed the growth of the band in America to superstar status. They started out playing at colleges and supporting often unsuitable groups. "We were doing small venues but they were selling out instantly. You just knew they were heading for coliseums because they were becoming so popular. When we started we could fit all the equipment into a 24 footer truck. Then it just kept growing. After the second tour they were doing the big indoor venues and then outdoor shows. With the coliseums came the multiple trucks. They just kept getting better and better and the kids were fanatical in their support. To me a Yes audience is almost the same as a Grateful Dead audience. Really loyal. They bring all their friends and move from city to city. They wouldn't just go to Madison Square. They'd go to Philadelphia, Pittsburgh, as many cities as they could on a tour. In fact Philadelphia became Yes town. There was a DJ there called Ed Sciaky who was an incredible Yes fan and played their records all the time. He made them really big in Philadelphia."

Now that Roy Clair and Eddie were operating an effective sound system together, Michael Tait could concentrate on providing a suitable light show to complement the music. These were pioneering days for rock band lighting, the start of a process that expanded into a huge business. Michael now heads Tait Towers, a production company based at Lititz, west of Philadelphia, close to Clair Brothers Audio. His operation is housed in several large buildings with over 100,000 square feet of manufacturing facility. Michael and his staff design and build rock'n'roll stage shows for clients that now include Madonna and Michael Jackson.

Says Michael, "The first couple of years in America, when we were supporting acts like Jethro Tull, there was no lighting for the band. If we played a big arena the only lights were the follow spots left over from the ice show! I remember being asked at one show, 'Who is going to cue the spotlights?' We didn't know about such things. I was the only one standing there who wasn't in the band, so I got the job and started cueing spotlights. Because I knew the songs intimately I had a gift for operating spotlights and not getting confused. All of a sudden I realised I could do a lot with lighting and that took my interest. I got into building lighting systems because you couldn't actually buy anything off the shelf then."

Michael Tait, and Graham Fleming from Pink Floyd, took matters into their own hands and started building lighting equipment expressly for bands. "The only lights you could get were for the theatre and they weren't really suitable. We wanted more power and it grew from there. We used laser lights very early on and Jon Anderson was usually the initiator of all these ideas. Jon would come up to me and say, 'Micky, what about using lasers?' And I'd figure out how to do it. He must have stayed up nights thinking of things. It could drive you nuts! But I loved it because the cutting edge was coming from Jon. He was the one who thought of having multi-keyboards as a concept. Rick had a couple, but he joined Yes because Jon wanted all these keyboard sounds. 'How can I get multi-keyboards sounds? I gotta get Rick Wakeman!' We also dreamed up a whole bunch of effects. I remember he wanted to get smoke effects when you just couldn't buy dry ice machines."

Tait spent ages experimenting with water and dry ice in his bath tub in London and worked out how to build his own smoke machine. He also built a special 'mirror wheel' which old Yes fans fondly remember from many a spectacular show. "Instead of a mirror ball, it was a flat thing which we used on 'Close To The Edge'. It was a great effect. In fact on some of the band's 'live' recordings you can hear the applause . . . for the mirror! The mirror wheel would reflect the light beams right back into the audience instead of scattering them."

The band made two US trips that year and the pace was exhausting. They often played two shows a night and one particular tour lasted a full seven weeks. Steve Howe became quite ill with the strain. He told me on a return trip home: "One thing the American trip did for me was to see the various rock styles in perspective. We did some shows with The J. Geils Band and the audience liked them as much as us." Steve also dropped a hint about an important future project that would materialise a year later . . . "In America Jon and I were working on some new songs which possibly will have a religious feel . . ."

On the band's return to England in August, 1971 Tony Kaye played with the group at Crystal Palace Bowl in South London where they were supporting Elton Hercules John and his band. In the VIP area behind the stage old friends like Jack Barrie and Peter Banks came to reminisce. Elton appeared in the hospitality tent and announced that he was looking for "a naked man" and as none were available, he stomped off and played the piano instead.

★   ★   ★

It was shortly after the Crystal Palace show, scarcely a year after Peter Banks' departure, that the second personnel upheaval shook the group. This time it would affect Tony Kaye whose rhapsodic, grandiose Hammond organ and funky piano solos had contributed so much to the unique Yes sound. But the 'Meccano synthesiser' Jon had been using on tours was a hint that he and Chris wanted to experiment with the new electronic sounds then coming on stream. Tony wasn't keen on giving up his beloved Hammond.

There were other problems to contend with of a more personal nature, as Chris Squire reveals. "Tony did the first US tour and then there was a general area of disagreement between Tony and Steve Howe and I never quite fathomed what the problem was. It was more of a social than a musical thing. They just didn't get on very well. By then Steve had very much established himself as a guitar star and when it came to deciding on who was gonna stay and who was gonna go, I suppose that's when Steve stayed and Tony went. It wasn't really my decision but I remember having to go to this dreadful meeting and having to tell Tony that we'd decided to make a change. But it was mainly because there was the lack of a good relationship between Tony and Steve. We tried to repair the relationship but it seemed to get worse. Tony had a lifestyle that was a little different from Steve's. Tony liked to drink and he enjoyed the company of women. The problems arose when Tony and Steve were sharing a bedroom which they did in those early days of touring and staying at Holiday Inns. They'd have these queen sized beds in the rooms I remember."

The rooms were small and if anyone wanted to bring a 'guest' back to the room to spend the night it would be a great disturbance for the other person sharing. Chris: "I used to share with Bill, and Tony shared with Steve. Jon and Brian Lane shared a room. That's how it used to work. Then I realised if we wanted to carry on working with Steve we'd have to change the keyboard player. I started looking around when we got back from that American tour. At that time Rick Wakeman was getting a lot of attention and was on the front page of *Melody Maker* because he had a fantastic act with The Strawbs. Of course Rick was always very good at milking the press. He went down Fleet Street and hung around the pubs. I wondered why he used to do that, until I realised it got him a lot of press. I didn't do a lot of interviews myself because I didn't have the taste for being that exposed. I guess I was more of a private person than I later became. Rick was a wild character but the strange thing was Steve managed to cope with that, probably because by then the albums were successful and the next time we went on tour, we had separate rooms!"

Tony Kaye left Yes just as the band was cracking America. It was announced his new band would be called Angel Dust, until the drug implications became plain and Tony quickly vetoed the idea. His second choice, Badger, seemed much more down to earth. This latest departure was unsettling for Bill Bruford who perhaps didn't fully appreciate the underlying personal problems: "So Peter Banks had gone and the next thing you knew the keyboard player is going. Why? Because somebody has found this guy called Rick Wakeman. So . . . out with Tony Kaye! Tony hadn't done anything wrong. It was just that this guy Rick was a whole different ball game. I could see this was going to happen around the entire band. The only one left would be Jon! It was definitely a case of ambition and there was no loyalty at all. If Mitch Mitchell had become available, I would probably have been history. It was like . . . get the best people in town – and Rick Wakeman was a real scoop. The scent of success was in the air, and now it was like a pack of hounds in full cry. We had been grinding away for two years and it was beginning to get exciting. Success was within our grasp and yet time was running out. We had to pull something off with the next album."

Despite their achievements with *The Yes Album* and putting aside all questions of personal difference, Jon and Chris were still driven to make Yes even better – literally the best band in the world. Bill did not have quite the same ambitious instincts. "No, I don't think so. I was very ambitious on the drum set. My entire focus was on playing. I couldn't give a monkey's about the violins! Or the lyrics! I was obsessed with the drum set to be honest. *Now* I seem to know a lot about what was going on. At the time I was just caught up in the general push and shove. It was aggressive, and fast moving and exciting. There was still no money.

Nevertheless, it was a great time to be around. *The Yes Album* was going pretty well and after that *Fragile*, our first with Rick Wakeman, was a huge success and went to Number 4 in the US chart. I had a third share of one of the songs 'Heart Of The Sunrise' which produced a great deal of revenue for me!" Bill says that in the early days he didn't fully appreciate the importance of publishing rights. "A lot of the music we did was credited to Anderson and Squire – and rightly so. But in all fairness nowadays you would have credited the drummer and keyboard player as well, because the arrangements were so peculiar to the band. I could probably have had a claim on some of those early publishing royalties, but I was happy enough with 'Heart Of The Sunrise'. And Jon was always on at me to write. He'd say, 'Come on, you've gotta write. It's not enough just being the drummer.' I'd say, 'What's the matter with you? If it's good enough for Philly Jo Jones, it's good enough for me!' But he was right, because writing was the thing and that's of course where the money lay, eventually. I think Squire and Anderson did very well on the original albums. No hard feelings there . . . I just didn't understand the system. We were learning so much about everything, from microphones to recording, from business and finance to publishing. We had to learn all that stuff very fast."

★   ★   ★

Rick Wakeman's arrival in Yes made headlines in the music press but behind the scenes there were protracted negotiations between various record companies. Once he'd settled in, however, Rick became one of the most popular figures in Yes mythology and one of the most controversial. An instant hit with fans at home and abroad, he was outgoing, personable and charismatic. But he could be just as stubborn as Jon and Chris. He was forever falling out with the band that he admired so much; indeed, he stormed out on at least three separate occasions.

His assets were obvious. Rick was not only a gifted piano player, he utilised the whole spectrum of electronic and acoustic keyboards. With his dazzling classical technique, he was just as much at home on a synthesiser, Hammond organ or Mellotron as he was on a church organ, harpsichord or grand piano. There had been great keyboard players in rock before him, like Graham Bond, Keith Emerson and Jon Lord, but none had made the same personal impact. When Rick was featured on the front page of *Melody Maker* in an article by young reporter Mark Plummer, he became a star overnight.

Wakeman's visual impact was striking. Fans loved the imposingly tall figure with long flowing blond hair, shiny capes and conical caps. Surrounded by keyboards on stage, weaving a torrent of blistering notes, he seemed a magical figure and became hugely popular with audiences. Rick was popular with the music press too. He was a man after their own hearts. He was always free with the latest gossip, happy to buy a drink and swap outrageous jokes and stories. Unlike so many musicians, he never seemed mortally wounded by criticism. If he got a bad review he'd turn it into another joke. "Hitler got worse reviews for the Second World War!" he'd quip.

Rick wasn't all about showmanship and gags. A serious musician and composer in his own right, Wakeman regarded it as a great honour to be invited to join the ultimate 'group's group'. But he had a great sense of humour and lived life to the max. Tony Kaye had been known to imbibe the odd glass of beer and laugh readily at any joke, witty retort or comical remark. If Jon and Chris hoped their new keyboard man would prove to be a more serious academician they would be disappointed. Rick Wakeman was even more convivial than Tony Kaye, and could drink them all under the table, including the road crew, and the entire London Symphony Orchestra – if they happened to be in the bar. Rick brought not only a much needed lightening up of attitudes, his dazzling finger work almost threatened to blow the band away.

Although Rick had a well established career as a session musician before he joined Yes, he was clearly made for the band which could best utilise his talents. He was born in Perivale, Middlesex, on May 18, 1949, and from an early age it seemed he would establish himself in the world of classical music. Educated at Drayton Manor County Grammar School, he took piano lessons from the age of seven and in 1963 he joined his first rock group, Atlantic Blues, who played at youth clubs in North London. In 1966 he joined The Concord Quartet dance band where he was featured on a Hohner Pianet.

After leaving school Rick went to the Royal College Of Music and was expected to become a concert pianist. But he carried on playing with rock bands in clubs and pubs and was dismissed from the college for neglecting his studies. It wasn't long before he became one of the most prolific session musicians in London. On the busy studio scene he became known as 'One Take Wakeman'. He played with a huge range of artists including Kenny Lynch, White Plains, Brotherhood Of Man and Edison Lighthouse. He played Mellotron on David Bowie's first hit 'Space Oddity' in 1969 and played the sensitive piano solo on Cat Steven's 1972 hit 'Morning Has Broken'. In 1970 he joined folk and bluegrass act The Strawbs whose leader Dave Cousins wanted to turn into a folk-rock group. The band had started life as the Strawberry Hill Boys in 1964. Rick's keyboard skill and striking appearance made him the focal point of the band's performances. The Strawbs attempted to blend rock guitar with classical piano and the results were fresh and unusual. Wakeman's exuberant piano and organ

112

playing were demonstrated on albums like *From The Witchwood* (1971). But Dave Cousins' vocals still took precedence and Rick clearly felt the need for greater musical freedom. He also felt the need for more cash from session work. He quit The Strawbs intending to return to the security of the studios. Then he was invited to join Yes in August of 1971 and found himself back on the road.

"It was a weird one," recalls Rick. "I had already decided to leave The Strawbs. I had joined them in April, 1970, and left in July the following year as I couldn't survive financially. We were only on £20 a week and out of that we had to contribute to the cost of the van and the road crew. I had much higher expenditure on equipment like a Hammond organ and I just couldn't do it any longer. I had been making a good living doing sessions prior to that and I had actually decided . . . okay I've tried being on the road, but I'll have to go back to sessions."

Rick went to see a top 'fixer' David Katz who filled Rick's date book with work for the next eight months. The Strawbs were upset and couldn't understand why their star keyboard player was going back to the anonymity of the studios, but he had to pay off mounting debts. "I was quite sad because I liked being on the road with them," says Rick. One day he had three sessions which took all day. He got back home to Harrow in North West London at about two in the morning. The next day he was due to get up at six for a jingle session which would pay £6. "It was for a toilet roll in Germany – really exciting!" He crawled into bed and had been asleep for half an hour when the phone rang. It was Chris Squire of Yes. Rick had met Chris before when The Strawbs had supported Yes at a gig in Hull. What Rick describes as a bizarre conversation ensued.

"He said, 'We've just come back from America and we are looking to change the personnel of the band. We've noted that you are really keen on the wider side of keyboard instruments and that's what we're into. We wonder if you'd consider being part of the band'. I said, 'Do you know what time it is?' He said, 'Hold on a minute . . .. er it's a quarter to three.' I said, 'I know what the bloody time is, I've got to be up at six o'clock for a jingle session!' " Rick thanked Chris for his call but said he'd had enough of being on the road. He promptly forgot all about his late-night caller and went off to the studios as dawn broke. He came back to find both Chris Squire and Yes manager Brian Lane had been leaving messages on the phone. He knew Brian well, having done many sessions for singer Jack Wilde who Brian also managed. He'd even seen Yes performing when he had supported them on tour.

"When I first saw them in action I was still in The Strawbs. I was a bit stunned really. Everything they did was different from what rock bands normally did. In the days when every guitarist sounded like Clapton or Jeff Beck, Steve Howe was totally different. He used a little Fender amp miked up and got his own sound. Chris too had his own bass sound which was basically the bass full on, the treble full on and all the middle cut out so it cut through everything. It was the most astonishing bass sound I'd ever heard. Yes were also one of the first bands to mike up a drum kit. Bill Bruford's snare drum sounded like a cake tin – so it would cut through everything. Then on came this diminutive five foot four singer who had a voice like a choir boy! The straightest element then was Tony Kaye who played straight blues style. I met Tony later and we got on very well. When he left the band he went to the management and they helped him form Badger which supported Yes on quite a few shows. So it was all very gentlemanly. Meanwhile I phoned back and spoke to Brian. He said, 'Look, it's fifty pounds a week.' Well I liked *The Yes Album.* They were a good band and I could see where I could fit in musically. But no, no – I was going to stick to the sessions!"

Brian Lane changed the subject and asked Rick to come in and see him about a new Jack Wilde album. Wakeman agreed and went to Hemdale's office in South Street which Brian shared with John Daly and David Hemmings. "I arrived there and sat in Brian's room. He started rambling on about Jack Wilde."

Suddenly Brian mentioned Yes and said that by chance they were rehearsing just around the corner. "Are they?" said Rick innocently. At that moment the door opened and in came Chris Squire and Jon Anderson.

"It was beautifully stage-managed by Brian," says Rick. "We all said hello and they asked me round to have a listen and a play. Over the remainder of that day 'Roundabout' was written. It was astonishing."

Rick has many other memories of that strange and momentous day. "I remember we were rehearsing in Shepherds Market and downstairs there were lots of ladies in fur coats even though it was high summer. They smiled sweetly and seemed very busy, and then I realised we were rehearsing above a brothel. It was quite interesting. I'm not sure who made the most noise – us or them! It's funny . . . Brian came and paid us the wages and when Steve Howe arrived he said, 'Well I won't be needing this then.' He had a handful of change in his pockets and he threw it over the other side of the room. And I'm thinking, 'That's my milk bill.' I was wondering, if they all go away I can grab that and I can pay my milk bill . . . but Bill Bruford beat me to it!"

Rick thoroughly enjoyed the impromptu rehearsal and when they finished playing he offered to give Steve a lift home to Hampstead. When he dropped him off, the guitarist asked Rick: "The next rehearsal is at 11 o'clock tomorrow. Do you think you could pick me up? I remember driving home and thinking, 'I've joined the band.' And that was it. Over the next few days we put together pieces like 'Heart Of The Sunrise'. All that incredible music for *Fragile* was done in a very short period of time."

Rick and his new Yes confreres went into Advision studios to record *Fragile* almost immediately after his arrival. They stayed there for a month, which was unheard of at that time. "I remember when we set the gear up, Chris' stuff was really noisy, but it was a wonderful sound. Steve also used to play at a deafening volume and so did Bill. We'd set up in the studio and play 'live' as a band. Even if we only managed to play twenty seconds, if it fell apart we'd stop and try again. We'd record a bit, then move on so we'd always have the best bits on tape. If you could get hold of some of the early Yes 16-track tape I'd say 'Roundabout' has about 16 edits on the multi-track where it was put together. It was the Yes way of getting perfection and making sure it all worked. This was way before digital editing and it was the only method to be sure of getting a really good performance out of the piece.

"The tragedy was after that and *Close To The Edge* nothing was ever written with all of us in the same room at the same time. Those two albums were done like a giant jigsaw with everybody linking up ideas and it was very exciting. But after *Close To The Edge*, probably because the band had real success and everybody was doing their own things and to put it bluntly making the most of their stardom, everyone's lives changed. So we never again sat in a room together to write, which to some extent I think was quite sad. Hindsight is a wonderful word but it's useless. You can always think how you could have done things better."

'Roundabout', the opening track on *Fragile*, is one of the most popular of all Yes tunes. The surging chords and delicate acoustic guitar notes that presage the opening theme are almost unbearably tantalising. The old firm of Bruford and Squire set up a crisp riff for Jon to cling onto while singing at the top of his register. Wakeman's slippery keyboard interjections give way to a tumultuous burst of Brufordian drum power. A brief return to the acoustic guitar, then Rick's Hammond howls like the ghost of Tony Kaye seeking vengeance. Steve and Rick blast back in a wonderfully exciting duel. A wordless choral coda signals the end, until Howe pops back for an acoustic guitar tag. It's a rare and perfect piece of work.

Given the reserves of talent pent-up within Yes, it was decided that there should be five individual 'solo' tracks on *Fragile*. Steve Howe had been introduced with 'Clap' on *The Yes Album*. Now Rick was piped aboard with 'Cans And Brahms', a witty foray that revealed his classical roots. Multi-layers of keyboard tracks blended into an entertaining two minute piece extracted from Brahms 4th Symphony in E Minor, Third Movement. It seemed out of place in the context of a Yes album but it was a fun interlude. Jon Anderson was then unleashed on 'We Have Heaven', a plaintive piece lasting barely two minutes during which Jon chants "*Tell the Moon dog, tell the March hare*" over the cry of "*Yes, he is here*". Described on the sleeve as 'A personal idea by Jon Anderson on which he sings all the vocal parts', its message is decidedly mystical and possibly the work of an initiate into magic. Footsteps run away and winds howl and thunder roars, leading into the angular and aggressive 'South Side Of The Sky'. Steve offers some dazzling runs played with an almost barbaric intensity. Rick's grand piano looms large and the whole arrangement sounds like it might be suitable for some dark Hollywood psychotic thriller. The theme Wakeman plays here is one of countless pieces of Yes music that stick into the consciousness for years. 'South Side Of The Sky' seems almost neurotic on first hearing, but like so many Yes arrangements of the period is full of satisfying surprises, like the sudden use of backward tape during Steve's final outburst. 'Five Per Cent For Nothing' is 33 seconds of Brufordian angst which seems to say, 'I don't much like the music business, and I'd rather be with King Crimson.' 'Long Distance Runaround' is a more digestible work closer in spirit to 'Roundabout' and this quickly became a popular live item. A nifty unison theme set to a rumbling, busy bass line gives way to a staccato rhythm broken up with unexpected accents as Jon sings at the far end of the studio. More simple but memorable licks from Steve cut through this perky tune.

The digitally remastered version on CD is particularly successful in enhancing all the subtleties of a piece that moves seamlessly into Chris Squire's solo piece 'The Fish (Schindleria Praematurus)' which has the vibes of a Bhuddist Temple imbued into its hypnotic theme. Each riff, rhythm and melody is produced by using different sounds from the bass guitar. Steve's 'Mood For A Day' is a more considered classically inspired piece than 'Clap' but equally popular. On the CD re-mastered version you can actually hear Steve breathing as he concentrates on the more demanding parts.

Rick Wakeman's presence is strangely missing from much of side two of the album but his Mellotron dominates the forbidding and slightly ominous opening choruses of 'Heart Of The Sunrise'. Once again Bruford's inventive drumming takes the band into new dimensions as Rick, Steve and Chris lock into a startling burst of speed during a long and complex instrumental. In typical Yes style this frenzy gives way to Jon at his most vulnerable and innocent as he sings, "*Love comes to you and you follow . . . lose one on to the heart of the sunrise*".

Apart from getting to grips with the technicalities of Yes music, Rick also had to get used to the personalities. He told BBC TV in their *Rock*

Family Trees special on Yes[11] about a confrontation he witnessed between Bill Bruford and Chris Squire shortly after joining the band.

"Bill came up to Chris and said, 'You missed out such'n'such.' Chris: 'No I didn't. You didn't listen to what I played.' They had a blazing row which culminated in Bill hitting him. He gave Chris a right chinner. I thought this is great. The drummer has just hit the bass player – it's all going to fold up. But apparently that was the norm."

Rick didn't have any composing credits on any of the tracks on the album, even though as he says, he contributed to the music and in particular the creation of 'Roundabout'. "That was a strange one. Basically Yes had a publishing deal with Warner Brothers. The deal stated very clearly that any new pieces of music had to be published by them. It's water under the bridge but there are two areas here that have long been a bone of contention. Everyone was going to have a little segment on the album. Some critics thought this was just being flash. The thinking behind this was that we realised there would be a lot of new listeners coming to the band. They could find out where each individual player's contribution lay. I had all sorts of problems. I was signed to Rondor Music and I couldn't write anything for Yes, so we took a classical piece for me to play.

"In fact I wrote half of the piano section for 'Heart Of The Sunrise' and a few other bits and pieces. The record company and management said, 'Don't worry, we can't give you a credit but we'll sort you something out on the publishing side.' Well of course I was never, ever sorted out! I enjoyed the music too much to want to create a tremendous hoo-hah about it, although it was worth a fair amount of money. I was just pleased to be part of the music and the fans could recognise which were my bits. When we did *Fragile* there were loads of kids lined up on the pavement outside the studio. We used to invite twenty in at a time and they sat round listening while we were recording. It was a fantastic time because the record company had no idea what we were doing. To some extent *we* didn't have any idea what we were doing. It was that wonderful time when musicians were ahead of technology."

Despite the apparent sophistication and complexity of the music Yes played on *Fragile* (and *Close To The Edge* which followed) it was largely an instinctive process of creativity. "If the truth be known I don't think we really knew where we were going," says Rick. "It was just all wonderfully new and exciting and the record company left us alone because we were selling bucket loads of records. They didn't understand a word of it!"

★   ★   ★

---

[11] Screened in Britain on BBC 2 in October, 1998.

Apart from Mr. Wakeman, among the other innovations that came with *Fragile* was the arrival of artist Roger Dean whose distinctive artwork and designs would contribute hugely to the image of the band. His calligraphed Yes colophon logo remains one of the most easily identifiable symbols in rock. Roger and his brother Martyn would later help design and create many of the band's stage sets.

Fantastic landscapes, elaborate drawings and meticulous artwork were all attributes of the craft of Roger Dean, long recognised as one of rock's foremost creative designers. His imaginative paintings done in an instantly recognisable style were eagerly sought by many bands to give their work stature and a classy quality they hoped would complement their music. He would design a grand succession of Yes albums: *Fragile, Close To The Edge, Yessongs, Yesterdays, Tales From Topographic Oceans, Relayer, Drama* and, most recently, *Open Your Eyes.*

Roger Dean was born in Ashford, Kent, England on June 31, 1944. His mother had studied dress design at Canterbury School of Art before her marriage and his father was an engineer in the British Army. Much of Roger's childhood was spent in Greece, Cyprus and Hong Kong where his father was on duty. Apart from his brother Martyn, Roger has two sisters, Penny and Philippa. In 1959 the family returned to Britain and Roger went to Ashford Grammar School and in 1961 he entered Canterbury School of Art to study silversmithing and furniture design before arriving at The Royal College of Art in 1965. He was still a 24-year-old art student in 1968 when he was given the project to design the interior of a disco room, where bands like Genesis played. This led to his first album sleeve, by coincidence for Gun, the very band that Jon Anderson joined for a day. Recalls Dean, "Gun were managed by Ronnie Scott Directions and at the time I was busy designing the discotheque upstairs at Ronnie Scott's Jazz Club in Soho."

The furniture in the disco was designed like a landscape in foam, not unlike his later landscapes for Yes. Says Roger, "There were murals on the wall, and seats filled with foam. The fire brigade who inspected the club were very concerned about the amount of foam we had used. Then inevitably there was a fire at the club. The foam furniture wasn't touched, but the murals were burnt off the walls!"

One job led to another and after Gun, Roger produced album sleeves for Atomic Rooster, Babe Ruth and Osibisa. He did his first cover for Yes in 1971 which led to everything else. Says Roger, "My brother Martyn does more work on my projects than most people think. For example I often get credited for doing the space sets for the Yes shows, whereas in fact I had nothing to do with them. He did them all. I just jump in and take all the credit! I was still learning at this stage. At college I studied three dimensional design. Coming out of college and doing paintings and graphics intrigued me, but it wasn't something I was skilled at. I'm not a bad calligrapher but I couldn't spell to save my life so I was for ever redoing things."

The connection between Yes and Roger Dean was forged by the ever ready Phil Carson at Atlantic Records. He had wanted to use Roger after the first Yes album but artist and band did not meet until two years later, just after *The Yes Album* was released. When the band returned from America manager Brian Lane asked Dean to do the cover for *Fragile*.

"I showed them what I did and they asked me to come up with some ideas, which they liked," says Roger. "*Fragile* was quite a complicated cover because there was a book inside. It was elaborate although it wasn't one of the most striking of all the Yes covers. I was kind of learning my trade at the time. The main feature on the cover was a little Bonsai world with a wooden space ship flying overhead! It was literally meant to be a fragile world."

The band had wanted an image of a fractured piece of porcelain. In a compromise move Roger drew his miniature world and then broke it in two pieces. The idea of the fragile, broken world would be continued on the subsequent *Yessongs* album. By this time the planet had disintegrated but the inhabitants had built a spaceship which guided fragments of the planet, drifting as spores through space and aeons of time. Such imagery would play an important part in giving Yes a mystical image that suited Jon Anderson's increasingly metaphysical lyrics.

Many fans assumed Dean listened intently to the band's music before he put brush or pen to paper. "No – but I listen to the music before I finish not before I start. People always ask me that. But throughout my whole career it has been impossible to listen to the music before I do something, because it is never ready! The thing about *Fragile* is Yes had a title which the whole band was very keen on. Quite a few Yes titles relate to band activities. *Fragile*, *Close To The Edge*, *Union* and *Talk* are all descriptions of the band's current state. I've got a whole list of logos based on other working titles like *Communication*, *Hanging In*, *Hanging Out*, *Falling In* and *Falling Out*. Actually I was making those up, but in principal that's the idea. It's a psychiatrist's couch in logo land. When I did *Close To The Edge* the main image was an overflowing lake close to a mountain top."

Although a hand drawn Yes logo appeared on *Fragile*, the version that is most familiar to aficionados first appeared on the cover of *Close To The Edge*. "I didn't do the logo until after I finished *Fragile*," says Dean. "I was looking at it one day and thought, 'God, I should be able to do better than that. I'll have another shot at it.' So when Yes went into the studios again I was able to go in and sell them the idea of a new design which became the famous Yes logo. The original Yes covers and logos are now in the permanent collection of the Victoria & Albert Museum in London which is a nice buzz!"

The logo has been described by experts as a 'calligraphed colophon' but Roger is rather baffled by this term. "I'll let you call it that. I guess I'd better look it up! I have heard the word 'colophon' but logo is the word I use and even if it's not accurate, it's certainly widespread." Roger Dean has worked with all the band's members but found himself becoming closest to Steve Howe. "I was involved with them a lot but not always. Apart from Chris Squire, every single person involved with Yes has left the band at some stage. There have been different managements, different guitarists, drummers and singers. Certainly different keyboard players. Yes is a different beast every day. But the line-up which includes Steve is I think the traditional Yes."

Roger Dean also organised merchandising for the group which he says was an innovation for a touring rock band. "Brian Lane was a little bit nervy about it. He was pretty keen that it didn't happen because they used to make money by selling the rights to different promoters. Each promoter did his own tee shirt or whatever. We did a trial run in England which wasn't so good because the bits of merchandising weren't great. But I made up my mind if we were going to America we should do it right. We did every-thing . . . tour programmes, posters, tee shirts and badges. We made ten times more money than Brian was expecting, so it went incredibly well. We were flying in two tons of paper a night at one point!"

★　★　★

Back in 1972, with Rick Wakeman now part of the band, Yes were dying to get back to America. In January they did more European dates includ-ing two nights at the Rainbow Theatre London (14 and 15). On February 15 they started their third American tour in Providence, Rhode Island. They had already started putting down tracks for *Close To The Edge* in Advision studios on February 1 and 2. In between all these tours, re-hearsals and recording sessions Jon Anderson and his new wife Jenny were trying to lead a normal married life, with some difficulty. Over a period of several months they had to move home at least half a dozen times. It wasn't so much a case of a moonlight flit as being 'gazumped' during a period of rising property prices.

By April 1972 they had ended up in a basement flat near London's Earls Court Road. When I went to visit them for coffee and scrambled eggs one sunny afternoon, Jon was reflecting on the changing fortunes of Yes while Jenny was busy booking a two week holiday break. Liverpool born Jenny had first met Jon on the London club scene during the formative years of Yes. Jolly and extrovert, she and Jon made a contrasting but happy pair. She was hoping they could fit in a much needed break after the band's third and most successful tour of the States and before Jon disappeared once more, this time into the studios to record their next album.

Jon was still recovering from the culture shock of a visit to Las Vegas, which he pronounced in his amused Lancashire tones as "Daft!" As he lit up a Benson & Hedges he seemed to drift away in a reverie and I asked, "Where are you Jon?"

"I'm sitting in the pictures in Accrington," he sighed. "I wish myself away and think I'm going to play a gig in America tomorrow, but everybody else in the pictures will be staying at home." It was the sort of scenario that Jon used to imagine when he was a lad and working on a farm. It was still only just beginning to hit him that he wasn't sitting in the pictures watching a movie. His life of travel and adventure with Yes was really happening.

"Sometime it's going to hit me that I really don't have any financial worries anymore. But there are always other worries which are equally frustrating. Sometime the crunch will come. But I've never been concerned about money anyway. All the energy I have put into my life for the past five years has come back to me and now all the good things are coming into my life."

The rewards came as the result of *The Yes Album* and *Fragile* that had enabled Jon to move to a more comfortable flat but despite the fact that both were represented by framed gold albums on his apartment wall, he still had doubts about the band's status. "Those gold albums are probably sprayed copies of *Bing Crosby's Greatest Hits*," he smiled. " 'The Who' smashed theirs up. They've had so many I suppose. But they are nice to keep. I was very surprised that *The Yes Album* didn't take off in the States. But *Fragile* is there. We were lucky to tour with Jethro Tull the first time because we were virtually unknown there a year ago. In a way something was bound to happen when we got there. It isn't a question of how many records we sold but whether the group is fulfilled and honest in making the LPs as compatible entertainment on plastic. Basically we are an entertainment. We can be self-indulgent or we can work for the people. That's what we want to do. Yes are a people's band. We haven't had any hype. We've just moved on the music and tried to improve it. That's what we set out to do from the first. We never became a blues or jazz band. Basically we have no direction. We can go anywhere. If we have a direction, its towards good singing and good music. I wouldn't say we are doing anything new. We just hope it's the kind of music where all the barriers have fallen down."

Jon liked to see artists from different strands working together. "I

121

remember seeing Jimi Hendrix and Roland Kirk. I was utterly amazed at how well they blended together at Ronnie Scott's Club. Jimi just got up and started to play and it was tremendous. If we can learn from all this music so we teach our audiences to respect music other than rock. The finest singer I know is Gilbert Becaud. I wish I could do what he does. I'd be too afraid to go on a stage with just a guitar and sing. I've never done it and the nearest I came to it was with Peter Banks, when we did an acoustic number together. I was always scared then and my knees used to tremble. I've got a lot to learn about being an entertainer. That's why I stand pretty rigid on stage. I haven't got much stage presence, especially when you see somebody like Rod Stewart. But I have been going crazy with my tambourine lately!"

Jon was increasingly proud of Yes at this crucial stage of their development. "The musicians in the band are getting so good but as more people buy our albums then we have a greater responsibility to the public. The only thing we can do now is make good music. It's not an egotistical thing, it's a sensible attitude. I just feel a little humble that ten years ago I was working on a farm in Accrington. Rock musicians today are very lucky. Most young people in the past would have been fighting wars."

The following month – May, 1972 – Yes began rehearsing more material for *Close To The Edge* at the Una Billings School of Dance in Shepherds Bush. The whole of June was spent in Advision recording. The new album's title was certainly appropriate, as Roger Dean thought when he went to the sessions. Despite Jon's avowed delight at the progress of the band, Bill Bruford remembers it was a torturous process in the studio.

"We started recording a piece of music, got half way through it and nobody knew what the heck the conclusion was. We'd break the drums down, do a couple of gigs. Get back to the studio, set the drums up again, put the microphones back, go to the middle of the same track and then continue. Nobody knew what the end was and we'd never complete a tune all the way through. We couldn't play any of the tunes all the way through because nobody knew what they were. They were being invented in the studio. You only learnt to play it later. It would have been better if we could have played it through first. But we could only figure out how to play the music by doing it in the studio. There were no computers, so tape editing was the thing."

Rick Wakeman: "When we did the loop tape for *Close To The Edge* it must have been forty foot long. It went all round the room, just to get all the birds and things you hear at the beginning. Now you could do it all with one sample and it would take about two seconds. Then it took us two days to get the loops going. It was ever so difficult. We'd think of ideas at a brainstorming session then wonder, 'How on earth can we do this?' The thing about technology going ahead of musicians is it has taken away the human element. What can we do that technology can't do? The answer is nothing. That was a wonderful period of time. In the order of things there was the record company, the media and the band. The band would present the record to the label and they'd say, 'How can we best market this?' and they'd present it to the press and radio and it would stand or fall on the reaction of the DJs and journalists. All that has changed."

★ ★ ★

In June I went to Advision Studios see the band at work on *Close To The Edge*. It was immediately apparent a great deal of stress was being generated and outbursts of anarchy came not only from the drummer, but from Rick Wakeman and even Steve Howe. At the time I put this down to high spirits and suggested the band were suffering from an ailment known as 'Studio Stupor'.

Certainly Yes weren't about to put on a show of unanimity and conformity. This was no polite interviewing session. This was the nitty gritty. It was also the best possible insight into the way band members interacted with each other. Here at first hand I could see them battle to put ideas into coherent shape and get them on tape. They were aided in their task by engineer Eddie Offord, now an official band member. Anybody who has ever watched an engineer having to spend anything up to eight or more hours at a stretch, trying to match tape edits, drop in solos, mix vocals, guitars, drums, basses and keyboards and keep a grip on reality could only sympathise with Offord's Herculean task. There can be few more maddening experiences than hearing the same piece, indeed the same few seconds of music over and over again, only to find that the completed 'take' or mix doesn't satisfy any one member of the group at any given moment. Having various members of the group seizing control of the faders couldn't have helped either.

Judging from the conversations at the time and the final verdicts given later, it seemed that only Jon Anderson and Steve Howe really knew what *Close To The Edge* was all about and only Chris Squire and Eddie Offord could pull it into shape. As for Rick and Bill – they seemed more like innocent bystanders.

When I arrived at the studio the band were in the throes of cracking up. Bill was playing with a mountain of paper cups, hammering a precious hand-carved harpsichord and loudly announcing his ultimate aim of blowing up the studio. Not to be outdone Rick Wakeman wandered around mouthing silently, pretending to be dumb, while mixing soup and chocolate in the same cup, which he proceeded to feed to unsuspecting visitors.

The dark and rather spooky studio had a large mixing console in the centre of the room, which would nowadays probably appear quite basic. The instruments were set up in separate rooms and it was clear the band weren't playing together as a unit, just contributing pieces to a vast jigsaw puzzle of sound that perhaps only Jon and Steve could visualise as a completed picture. Yes had been locked away in their dungeon for days. Shortly after I arrived to hear a preview of the completed sections, there was a dull thud as Eddie Offord fell to the floor. He had slumped asleep over the mixing desk, leaving music from the spinning tape deck blaring at an intolerable level.

From the depths of the studio Bill Bruford wandered around playing tunelessly on a wooden North African flute. It was so irritating that normally mild mannered Steve Howe suggested that if he were to keep up this din, it would be better for everyone if he committed suicide. Bill then loudly proclaimed his boredom with proceedings and was still stomping around when Eddie roused himself sufficiently to play back one of the album tracks called 'Total Mass Retain'.

"What does 'Total Mass Retain' *mean!*" protested Bill.

"What's wrong with 'Total Mass Retain'?" demanded Jon. "I had to think of something quickly." The name of the piece was only chosen after some argument and at the time I misheard the title which I thought was 'Total Mass *Return*'.

"Why not call it 'Puke'?" asked Bill.

Jon and Chris began singing their parts to the microphones, sounding strangled and out of tune when the backing track was faded out. "Turn around – Glider!" they roared. Out of context it didn't make much sense but Jon persevered. "Try again!" he said. His voice cracked and he failed to make the right notes.

"This is the silly stage," said Bill pacing about in his clean white tee shirt, clearly wishing he was behind a kit with a pair of clean sticks.

"Look, this is really hard work," said Jon getting red in the face. "I'm getting pains in my head."

Who wrote these lyrics, I wondered?

Chris Squire waved in the direction of the singer. "Jan Onderson on lyrics. Good old Jan!"

"Our fifth album," mused Jon, remaining remarkably even-tempered despite the grumbles from the ranks. "I thought we'd only ever do two!"

The sound of *Close To The Edge* booming from the speakers brought the band rushing to the control console. Steve, Rick, Jon and Bill began playing with the sliders on the control desk, suffocating the engineer in a tangled mass of arms and fingers.

As the strains of the last few notes died away Bill Bruford ceased idly flicking paper cups at Eddie Offord and said, "Well, it's a long way from

West Side Story." Before I left the studio Eddie played me 'And You And I' for the first time − ten minutes of stunning music which reached a shattering climax.

"Play that ending again," said Steve "because you'll never hear it again. We've got to make some decisions about that one."

Said Jon quietly as I prepared to return to the relative sanity of Soho's rain swept streets, "We've got a long way to go yet with our music. Nobody is getting lazy and we're not resting on our laurels. In a couple of years, well it should be tremendous. We're only just beginning."

★   ★   ★

What stuck most in my mind about that evening at Advision some 26 years ago was Bill Bruford's mischievous and sometimes grumpy attitude. But nobody knew at the time he was planning to quit the band.

"I did get irritated, but then I was an irritable guy," admits Bill. "I was very pompous and arrogant and like all 20 year olds, I thought I knew everything. But it was all so *slow*! We had to work all night and knew it would take at least three months to make this record because Simon & Garfunkel had taken two and a half months to make theirs. We were being egged on by the press, because there was this sense that bigger was better. We had a bigger PA, bigger crews, and bigger wages. There was more equipment and longer albums. It was all going that way and you kinda sensed that it was wrong. I wasn't fussed by the money. I seemed to have plenty by then. Everybody says, 'So you're the guy who left Yes and turned your back on a fortune.' That's not it at all. People forget that I got very well paid. But I was screwed rotten for leaving the band."

Although Bill states this tersely, his decision to quit was a bombshell for everyone. A few weeks after sitting in on the Yes Advision sessions, I was in a Tokyo hotel, covering a tour of Japan by Emerson, Lake & Palmer. A girl from a top Japanese music magazine asked me to name my favourite drummer. "Bill Bruford," I replied firmly, hoping Carl Palmer wouldn't hear.

She smiled and said, "Oh, he just left Yes." I was shocked, and the news left me feeling quite depressed. If you cared about British rock music at all it was a cataclysm that ranked with the departure of Steve Winwood from the Spencer Davis Group, the break-up of Cream and Peter Gabriel's split from Genesis. It wasn't just the case of one dispensable musician moving on to another gig, in this case King Crimson. Bruford's drumming was an essential part of Yes' unique creativity. He was the spirit of the band made rimshot. I returned from the East a sadder but wiser man.

Bill was sadder and wiser too when he realised the ramifications of quitting a top band in the throes of a major assault on the American market. The management were not pleased. "I had no idea that I had to pay to get out of the band. Brian Lane made me pay to leave." Even now, some 26 years later, Bill still winces at the memory. "It was a little unfair."

Yes had a tour booked when Bill decided to quit, but he been very careful to make sure a suitable drummer was in place to take over. Finding a replacement was no problem. But there was a severe penalty in store. Bill says he had to pay ten thousand dollars in compensation. "This was to leave the group I helped form. I also had to give [replacement] Alan White the set of flight cases I'd just ordered *and* give Alan 50 per cent of my royalty share from *Close To The Edge* which I thought was very steep. You couldn't possibly do that to a young band now. But Brian Lane said, 'This guy is going to leave. I'll make him pay.' So over the years Alan and I have split the royalties from *Close To The Edge*. It's probably fair. I originated it and he's had to slog round the world playing it for all these years! He was a harder hitter than me on the drums, but then of course he had been working stadiums and I never did. I had a light jazz touch and never hit anything very hard. I was not interested in that at all. I was more into the effortless approach."

Bill would not have been happy playing at full volume night after night, and if he didn't much like 'Total Mass Retain' then he certainly wouldn't have liked *Topographic Oceans*. That was the 'religious music' that Jon and Steve had been secretly cooking up on tour.

Bruford muses on the role of drums in rock: "Stadium work tends to encourage people to plod a bit and you have to strip down the beats so much. If there is any confusion or ambiguity in the beat it gets lost in the roar. So really you are left with '1,2,3,4' beats to the bar and a big crash on the 'one'. That's all you can do. A lot of that American stadium rock success spoilt musicians. On one hand you get paid a lot, but on the other hand you turn into this hotel room wrecking idiot on tour, almost incapable of thinking. I don't mean Alan! I mean . . . anybody. If you are the keyboard player in Dire Straits and you are going to do 126 shows, you are gonna be *dead* physically from the neck down. I mean, it's not hard keyboard playing in the first place!"

Although Bill welcomed Alan White as his replacement and thought he was the best man for the job, it seems Alan was already waiting in the wings and had already been under consideration by Jon and Chris.

Bill: "I didn't actually recommend Alan to the group. He was pals with Jon Anderson and Eddie Offord. He came with the kudos of having played with a Beatle – John Lennon. He'd been hanging around Advision, and I knew if I took the opportunity to leave he'd come in. I was dying to join King Crimson anyway. I just needed the right time to go. Everything was booked months in advance and there seemed no possibility of getting off this thing without causing a minor rearrangement. In March '72 we went on a tour of America with King Crimson. Robert Fripp and I were friendly and I had approached Robert a year earlier saying, 'I wanna be in King Crimson.' That was the band for me – the one with a dark, jazz element. It was the less singing, more playing element. Yes was like this A major, sunny, diatonic kind of yellow group. It was very attractive. But everything you saw was what you got. King Crimson was darker . . . much bleaker. You couldn't quite understand them. There was more mystery and I preferred that a lot. It was much more obscure. I knew that the change would do me good. I had only ever played with four guys in my whole life.

Bill also felt he'd done his bit musically for the band. "To do another album with them would simply be repetition. All I could foresee was more trouble. It was like drawing teeth to get *Close To The Edge* made. Yet it turned out really well! It was an excellent album. How it got to be so was simply a miracle. There must have been some grand co-ordinator up in the sky because we barely knew what was going on. But it was very exciting and I wanted to leave on a high note. By the time we did *Close To The Edge* Yes had beaten the world into submission. There was a strange feeling once we'd made it. This was like a successful bank raid. There was an air of terrific self-congratulation. 'We've done it – we've pulled it off! Well done fellas. After all those nights in the van on the M1 we are Number 4 in the American chart. Great.' At which point I felt like saying, 'Okay, let's have a pint. Goodbye.' I didn't see it as the start, but rather the end of something. Chris Squire thought it was the start of something. For me, once we'd arrived, the interest was gone."

Crimson supremo Robert Fripp had often gone to see Yes perform in their early days and it was even once suggested that he might join Yes to replace Peter Banks. Says Bill, "They asked Robert and he said 'no'. Anyway, I told him that one day I'd really like to play with King Crimson. Come our tour of America in March, 1972 we were co-headlining with King Crimson and I said to Robert at the last gig in Boston, 'Well, what do you say?' And he said, 'I think you are about ready now Bill.' He'd seen me growing up in Yes and now I'd made all my mistakes I was ripe for King Crimson – like a tomato. I was still only 22."

Despite any past differences over time keeping and crashed vans, Chris Squire was very sorry to hear that Bill intended to quit the band after *Close To The Edge*. "Sadly Bill departed at the end of that album and that came as a surprise to me," says Squire. "We had just finished making the record and he showed up at Advision Studios and said, 'I've decided to join up with Robert Fripp and King Crimson.' I said, 'Seriously Bill, what are you talking about? We are doing very well here and we are going to be making a lot of money.' I could never see the logic of what he did. I think it was just because he was a jazzer at heart and wanted to go more in that musical direction. He had become frustrated with some of the songwriting I think. During the writing of *Fragile* Jon and I had been close as a writing team and then when it came to *Close To The Edge* it was mainly a Jon and Steve collaboration. I was more involved with tracks like 'And You And I'."

As the news broke of Bill's departure Chris told me back in October 1972: "Bill leaving was very odd. Funnily enough Yes seem to thrive on setbacks. The more that gets thrown in our face the harder we work and try to come up with something better. I really hope this will be a lasting situation now. I can't see any reason for anybody else leaving the group, until whenever it breaks up. There is so much potential in the band and I still can't see why Bill left. There was no bad personal relationship. I can only think he wanted to take a look at music from a different angle. He could have advanced himself with us just as much as with Bob Fripp. Yes is a well balanced group and is the reason we're successful. It's not a good thing to abuse it. We should think of the public who put us there. We should try our hardest."

During the making of the album the lyrical content in particular seemed to bug the drummer. Certainly the lyrics had became more philosophical on *Close To The Edge* which included the eight minute epic 'Siberian Khatru'.

Chris Squire laughs. "Philosophical? Vague is the word I think. Ha, ha! I don't think anybody has ever worked out what a 'Siberian Khatru' is exactly. I have seen interviews with Jon over the years when he's been asked that question and he once came up with quite a clever answer. He said that Khatru is Siberian for 'As You Wish'. But I don't know if he was just saying that. It could mean whatever you want it to mean. I think that's what he was trying to say. Really he just liked the sound of the word. I don't think he cared too much if 'Siberian Khatru' really meant anything. Jon went through a phase where he looked upon his voice as another instrument in the band, as opposed to being there to deliver love songs. He wanted to use his voice as an instrument and therefore he went for pure sounds. His favourite words had those sounds. Quite a lot of the songs have similar words. He read a lot of books which gave him ideas for lyrics. It's quite funny when he talks about it now. He used to be a lot more touchy, serious and protective about his lyrics but he's more open about the funny side of it now."

★ ★ ★

Close To The Edge was released in September, 1972 and swiftly rose to Number 4 in the UK charts and Number 3 in the US. When Yes had finished the album they set about welcoming their new drummer.

Chris Squire: "Alan White was a very good friend of Eddie Offord who was our engineer and producer and they shared an apartment. Alan had popped into the studio on a couple of occasions and hung out and when Bill left we asked him if he'd like to join. We just said, 'Are you interested?' He had been playing with Joe Cocker at the time as a sideman, so the idea of being a full member of a band appealed to him. I remember he had to learn the whole Yes set in three days before we had a show in Dallas, Texas, in July, 1972. It was the beginning of the tour and I'll always remember this. The first night he was *fantastic*. He hardly gave any hint of a mistake and I said to him afterwards, 'That was unbelievable. How did you manage that?' He said it was just nervous energy. Of course for two weeks after that it was dreadful! After the first night it all fell apart. Actually it wasn't that bad but he went downhill before he started to go up. He had just psyched himself up to get it right the first night. Then he breathed a sigh of relief and relaxed. Everything was fine from then on. He's been with us so long now it's hardly fair to think he hasn't *always* been with us. Out of the thirty years Yes has been together, Alan has been there for about 27 of them. People always say Yes had two drummers, but actually – Bill was only there for four years."

It was on July 19, 1972, that Bill Bruford packed his stick bag and left Yes to join King Crimson. Flags flew at half mast. Many felt Bill had been hijacked, but he was a willing party to the move. Bill had played 594 concerts with Yes. It was time to move on. While he may not have fully understood the depth of feeling his decision aroused among fans, he knew it was a shock for the group.

"This was somebody actually leaving the band. They were used to the idea of people being kicked out. It was okay to kick people out but it wasn't okay to leave. Jon was very sweet. He was genuinely astonished. We had come so far together. Why could I possibly want to leave? He couldn't understand it at all. He came round and we sat and talked. It was just a feeling that I had to move on. How could I develop on the instrument unless I changed? I firmly believed it is a musician's obligation to do so. I'm not an entertainer. I'm not a juke box. There is a difference. Your obligation is to move on, otherwise audiences can rightly demand their money back! I respected Jon Anderson, but I really had to leave Yes."

The fact that King Crimson ceased operations two years later didn't bother him in the slightest. "I was on a roll by then and learning to play with other people. In big bands you can become institutionalised y'know? I learnt a huge amount from '72 when I was the drummer in a good rock group through to '76 when I was able to write my own album. Now I'm 14 albums into my own solo career. And you don't get to here . . . by staying there. I think you are obliged to have an output. I've now developed as a composer and a band leader. But it's important to get across that I was thrilled with Yes. It was my favourite band. When I left it was one of the best bands in the world. I'm certainly not blaming anyone for what happened. Sure, Chris was late, yes Jon was like Hitler on some occasions but that's not the point. Generally the band was bigger than the sum of the component parts and it really was a terrific organisation. I was very sad to leave it, although I sensed I absolutely had to at that point. I wished it no ill and wanted it to go on and do great things."

While Bill loved Yes and enjoyed his time with them, he did not like the business side of affairs. "There was a lot of nonsense going on in the band. The decision making process was mostly a reign of terror. It was a bit like Stalin. It was okay if you agreed. If you disagreed you did so at your peril. You'd be excommunicated and sent to Siberia. Aside from all those moans, the fact is it was a great start and I was thrilled to be joining the music industry in 1968 with Yes. It was all so exciting and for five years it was heaven. But after five years all progressive rock should have stopped. In 1974 King Crimson was recording *Red* which might not have been thought much of at the time, but 20 years later Kurt Cobain of Nirvana cited it as one of his favourite records. Things had changed and it is a musician's job to spot these changes and ride with them. From 1974 onwards you were left with Yes and Genesis not doing very good versions of progressive rock. All the creative stuff had already been done. It's always like that if you look at any art movement. With jazz-rock there were two or three great years when the thing was invented. After that all the late comers arrive and copy the original and you may as well move on because there is nothing new left. So I was quite happy to leave Yes and had no regrets at all. I was screwed financially which I have never forgotten. To be taken advantage of in that way was very sad."

At the time, Chris and Jon both hoped this would be the last of the band's upsets. Although in some odd way Yes actually thrived on setbacks, there was no doubt Bill's departure was unsettling. Rick Wakeman, who was by now hailed in the music press as 'The Wizard Of Yes', certainly felt the pressures.

"Until we did the *Close To The Edge* album I felt very secure with Yes," he said back in February, 1973. "When Bill suddenly left I couldn't believe it. I thought the band would crumble. For the first time I had started to feel part of the band and then it seemed it was about to end. When Alan White came in I was really worried because it had taken a year for me to settle in. But Alan was great and worked really hard. The real test of the band comes when we are touring, living, eating and sleeping together. We all get our little miserable moods, you're bound to. But if you concentrate on the music you're bound to overcome them.

"I went through a terrible period when I was almost too frightened to go on stage, especially in the first half of 1972. I was having a lot of equipment problems at the time. I felt as if people were waiting for me to play a wrong note. Yes teaches you self discipline, and I've changed substantially. I'm a lot more involved, disciplined and careful."

Rick's policy of turning over a new leaf at this time also included trying to get personally closer to Jon Anderson. "For the first few months we had a shaky beginning which was more my fault than Jon's considering he can't play an instrument – well he can strum a guitar – he has so many ideas about music in his head, that he comes close to being a genius. So I'm a lot happier but I worry a lot more. I worry about my music. I have to keep on top of it all the time. I try to be doing something all the time. Music has become so much more important to me and everything has to be right. Sometimes I get into a trance from playing and the more perfect things become the more I can get involved."

Bruford's departure also shook Steve Howe. "The biggest shock I ever took in Yes was when Bill left. We were all pretty close at that time and what Bill was doing for Yes, no other drummer could do. He was saying 'no' to things – 'I'm not gonna play that! Don't ask me to play 4/4.' That was the trait in him that I liked. Let's steer away from every cliché. That was my philosophy on the guitar too. I knew all the clichés. I wanted to play the alternative."

Alan White might have felt he was in an unenviable position being summoned to step into the shoes of a founder member of the band. And yet he did the job with a calm professionalism and musical strength that has seen him remain as the band's linchpin for the rest of its existence. He was able to give the band the necessary power to cope with gruelling tours in huge venues. He could interpret a vast array of music from the demands of complex albums like *Topographic Oceans* and *Relayer* to the later more pop rock orientated works like *Drama, 90125, Big Generator, Talk* and *Open Your Eyes*. Above all he was a down-to-earth guy, able to cope with the tantrums of others. He had no particular desire to whiz off and start forging a meaningful solo career away from the band. He'd already done that well before he joined Yes. He was after all, the man who'd played drums for John Lennon during his hottest post-Beatle years.

Says Trevor Rabin, "There's no such thing as a bad thing about Alan White. That's the only bad thing about him!"

★　★　★

Alan White was born in Pelton, Co. Durham on June 14, 1949. He was educated at a technical school and took piano lessons from the age of six. His father was a pianist who played in local pubs. Says Alan, "You could hum a song to him and he could play the thing and knew all the chords!" Alan's uncle was a drummer and he was given an Ajax drum kit of his own when he was 12 years old. "I had that for about three months and my parents thought I was playing well enough to be given a metallic silver sparkle Ludwig kit. I still have that kit today. I sent it back to Ludwig and they did it up for me, so it's now in mint condition."

Alan took a lot of drum lessons but he felt that his teacher was trying to make him play his way. "I wanted to be more individual, being a bit of a brat. So I developed my own style which paid off eventually." Only three months after he had begun playing drums he joined a group called The Downbeats, who became well known in the Newcastle area. At one point he was playing seven nights a week. His schoolteachers only found out about it when they read articles about him in their local newspapers. They were most concerned when they saw a picture of Alan billed as 'The Youngest Drummer In England'. They were even more worried when they discovered the 13-year-old schoolboy's busy schedule. He got up at 6 a.m. to do a paper round, went to school all day, did his homework in the evening and then went to play gigs until 11 p.m.

Alan: "When it came to sitting my school exams I laid low on the drums for a while and got through all my grades. But gigging at that age was a great experience for me." The bands were mostly playing Beatles tunes in working men's clubs. After school Alan went to college for a while and studied technical drawing. He was planning to be an architect. Then his band The Downbeats, who later changed their name to The Blue Chips, went to London to enter a *Melody Maker* band competition. "We won the contest and got a contract with Polydor. We were the underdogs but we had a whole bunch of screaming fans who came to support us. It was at the London Palladium. We were competing against bands from all over the country and we won the whole thing. I think it was around 1965. We later recorded a song as part of the prize."

After The Blue Chips Alan played with Billy Fury's backing band The Gamblers. "When I was 17 I was playing with Billy Fury on the cabaret circuit around England. We also went to Germany for three months. It was great experience and we grew up very quickly." He remembers playing at a club in Cologne where The Warriors with Jon Anderson had just played. "The Warriors included Jon and Ian Wallace on drums. But I didn't meet Jon at that time. We were moving into the German club circuit at the same time The Warriors were moving out."

Alan was much in demand. During the late Sixties he played in a remarkable variety of bands including Happy Magazine, Plastic Ono Band, Balls and Ginger Baker's Airforce. He also worked with George Harrison and Joe Cocker and played with Terry Reid's band for almost two years.

In an age of frequently erratic and unreliable drummers, Alan combined powerhouse playing with a solid sense of time. "Terry Reid was very big in those days. He had a jamming band and every night it was something different. It was a fun band to play with and I got a lot of experience from that. Then I went to work with Alan Price for 18 months. We made records like 'Don't Stop The Carnival' and 'Tickle Me' and played all the clubs. I go back a long way!"

When he was with Ginger Baker's Airforce in 1970 he was teamed up with four drummers. They weren't all easy to get on with. "I played keyboards, tubular bells and log drums. On every number I changed into a new position and was wandering all over the stage. I also did three or four songs on the kit with Ginger during a double drummer thing. But Phil Seaman, one of the other drummers, used to steal my drum seat! He was quite a character and an amazing player."

In the summer of 1970 Alan joined an Airforce spin off group rather inelegantly called Balls with Denny Laine on vocals and Trevor Burton on bass. "There were a lot of people coming and going in that band but I remember Graham Bond was on keyboards most of the time. It changed around a lot but I spent about three months touring with them. Then the Joe Cocker gig came up and I played on the European dates of the Mad Dogs & Englishmen tour."

Then came Alan's biggest break. He was invited to play with John Lennon and Ono in the legendary Plastic Ono Band. Formed in 1969 this was an outlet for John and his wife Yoko Ono during the last days of The Beatles. Their début single 'Give Peace A Chance' was recorded live in a Montreal hotel room during a 'Bed-In' session. Then a more structured group was put together to play a Canadian concert featured on the 1969 album *Live Peace In Toronto*.

"I played with John for over two years. If anything came up with the Plastic Ono Band he called me to play drums. The first thing I did was *Live Peace In Toronto*. He'd seen me play somewhere and it was a call out of the blue. This voice on the phone said, 'Do you want to do a gig with me – it's John Lennon' and I thought it was a friend of mine playing a trick on me. Actually it was him and he called me back five minutes later and said, 'No . . . it's me man, John Lennon. We're gonna do a gig tomorrow. Do you wanna do the gig?' Then I realised it was the real thing. All the guys in my band got really annoyed because we had a gig that night and we had to cancel it because I was going to play with John Lennon. The Plastic Ono Band was John & Yoko, Klaus Voorman, Eric Clapton and myself. It was a unique band. Very unique! Eric had never played with John before either. So nobody had played with each other in this band that was on a plane flying out to Canada. We rehearsed everything on the plane and when we got to Toronto we just did this gig. It was recorded for the album but the first studio thing I did with John was 'Instant Karma'. After that it was Jim Keltner or myself who played on his stuff. I played on 'Imagine' and 'How Do You Sleep'. It was all done down at his house at Tittenhurst Park. I spent ten days down there. We'd get up each morning and work in the studio all day. John would come up and give me the lyrics to the song we were doing that day and say, 'This is what we are saying to the whole world. You can play on it or not.'

"He'd explain that 'How Do You Sleep At Night' was all about Paul — just to make sure everybody knew what was going on. He was very open about things. He'd either have some kind of rough demo, or he'd play through the song on the piano and we'd gradually get into it. Everything seemed to work really well. He'd never say to me, 'No, no, don't play that.' He'd say, 'Just play what you feel.' Everything you hear on the records is what we just got into playing. There was no controlling factor and playing with John was a very friendly, enjoyable experience. He was very serious about the band and the album. He was totally into it and he knew exactly what he wanted to do. It was as if he had already been through the album in his head and knew what he wanted it to sound like. He was very happy then because he was doing his own thing and had probably wanted to do that for a long time. Now he had freedom and was very happy about everything that went down. He was having all this building work done."

Alan remembers clouds of dust and lots of rubble everywhere. One night John wanted to watch something on TV and there was only one set working. So he lay watching TV with the band on a huge king-sized bed.

"There was me with Eric Clapton, John and Yoko and I'm thinking, 'I'm sitting on John Lennon's bed watching TV!' It's one of those moments you can never re-create. During that whole period in my life I was so young and naïve I didn't realise what I was experiencing until years later. Wow . . . I was part of history! It was mind blowing at the time and I was living in a kind of dream world."

One of Alan's fondest memories of the Sixties dream concerns a remarkable day at BBC TV's *Top Of The Pops*. "I was doing the show with John Lennon. But I had done a lot of albums at that time including some tracks with Gary Wright of Spooky Tooth, George Harrison and Doris Troy. They *all* happened to be on *Top Of The Pops* the same week and so when they used their videos it turned out I was appearing on the same show with four different people!"

After his John Lennon experience Alan worked with Joe Cocker and then joined Yes in 1972. "From then on the band took up most of my time. I went down to a rehearsal with Eddie about two weeks prior to joining the band. Bill was having his problems with the band and he left early. They were playing 'Siberian Khatru' and there was nobody to play the drums. So they asked me to sit in. I played the piece and obviously did it well enough to make an impression. A couple of weeks later Bill finally left and joined King Crimson and they came and asked me to join. They were still rehearsing *Close To The Edge* in a basement in Shepherds Bush. I just went down with Eddie to hear a couple of songs. Bill played on the album but I sat in at the rehearsals. The music was quite different from what I had been doing with John Lennon and Joe Cocker, which was very basic. But at the same time I'd had my own band out in Suffolk and I was playing more Yes type music with them. So that was a good preparation for me to step in and play in different time signatures and arrangements."

Alan's band was called Griffin and featured Peter Kirtley on guitar. It had been called Happy Magazine, and it was produced by Alan Price. White had played with Price on the road which is how he got involved. "There was another band called Gryphon who actually toured with Yes at one stage. Guys with bare feet who played the flute as I recall!"

Alan quickly settled into Yes: "I had a different style from Bill and even though I can play that kind of stuff, I knew the band wanted a drummer with a little bit more weight than Bill anyway. I was more of a rock 'n' roll player. When I joined there was a kind of mutual agreement. I gave them three months and they gave me three months and then we said we'd kind of match our files together. And here I am, still in the band 27 years later! The first gig that I did was in Dallas. When Jon and Chris asked me, they said I'd have to join or they'd throw me out of the third floor window of Eddie Offord's apartment. Then I said, 'Okay, we'll try it out.' Then just as they were leaving and walking out the door they said, 'Oh and by the way the first gig is in three days' time. You've got to learn the whole repertoire in three days.' I only ever had one rehearsal. The rest of the time was spent listening to the albums. It was very funny as Chris says, I managed to make it through the first show but the second and third deteriorated somewhat! It took me a few days to settle in."

6

STORMY SEAS
AND TOPOGRAPHIC OCEANS

1973 was the busiest and most successful year in the career of Yes but it was also the year in which serious cracks appeared in the glittering musical edifice that Jon Anderson and Chris Squire had built with such painstaking care.

For the moment everything the Yes men touched turned to gold. In February Rick Wakeman released his début solo album *The Six Wives Of Henry VIII*. Although it was a set of instrumental performances, it proved a resounding success, much to Rick's delight and the astonishment of pundits. Rick proudly delivered the tape of keyboard vignettes to his record company, only to be asked by nervous executives, "Where's the vocals?" It was a Top Ten hit in the UK and even got to Number 30 in the US album chart. It would set a pattern for Rick's future 'themed' albums and encouraged him to contemplate an independent solo career that he would pursue come hell or high water for the next 25 years.

Yes, meanwhile, embarked on a frenzy of group activity. During the year they toured Japan, Australia, America and Britain. In May they released the triple live album *Yessongs*, originally intended to placate the band's hardcore following. It became their biggest selling album thus far, soaring to Number 7 in the UK album charts and Number 12 in the States.

During the summer they began work on their sixth studio album, an ambitious concept devised largely by Jon and Steve Howe called *Tales From Topographic Oceans*. In the midst of these intense recording sessions, the band was showered with accolades. They won a string of music press awards and Yes were photographed together, smiling and content. Audiences loved them, tickets and records were selling in droves and critics were united in their praise.

Yes were front page news as they swept the board of the prestigious *Melody Maker* 1973 Pop Poll Awards. They were voted top band in two categories. Rick Wakeman was the top keyboard player and headlines proclaimed 'Yes Men On Top!'

The awards ceremony took place in September at the Global Village, a cavernous venue located underneath London's Charing Cross Station, now better known as gay night spot Heaven, where the awards were presented by jazz singer George Melly. As Rick balanced a pint of beer on top of his award he cheerfully announced, "I'd like to thank Watney Mann and everyone who has helped my career." The big guns of the music business were on hand to toast both Yes and Rick. Ahmet and Nesuhi Ertegun came hotfoot from New York to represent Atlantic Records. Yes manager Brian Lane and Led Zeppelin supremo Peter Grant were seen sharing a wink and a nudge. Zep's Robert Plant was pictured alongside Jon Anderson and his wife Jenny. If ever there was a moment when Yes had something to laugh and smile about it was now.

Yes were feeling a tad humble; dazed and confused that they had usurped such giants as Led Zeppelin. The most they could do was mumble polite thanks. Said Jon, "Next year it is most important for us to give back to the people what they have given us."

Steve Howe thought the poll results "incredible". "I think my mum sent in quite a few votes!" he quipped.

Said Rick, "We're all acting very cool. Really the whole group is over the moon about the poll results. It means a lot to all of us."

Nothing, it seemed could possibly go wrong yet within a few weeks all the celebrations and bonhomie turned sour. And it was all down to the double album which was designed to put the seal on their success, the hoped-for crowning glory of their artistic achievements. All at once praise transmogrified into condemnation as critics and fans turned on the record with furious dissent.

The mighty work was released in November. *Tales From Topographic Oceans* was presented in a lavish gatefold sleeve designed and illustrated by Roger Dean. His main design consisted of a rocky landscape under a dark blue starry sky. A waterfall descended from the central rocks while huge fish swam in a kind of curved space. In the distance a setting sun illuminated a stepped pyramid in front of mysterious lines in the desert. These were details stemmed from suggestions by Jon Anderson and Alan White. Inside the lyrics were printed in white on a black background. There was a kind of gloomy, forbidding tone about this design which might have complemented the music but failed to draw the wavering listener into the concept.[12]

Dean's artwork was an important selling point, but when the band

---

[12] In fact, the artwork looked much better when reproduced in Roger Dean's 1975 book *Views*, published by Dragon's Dream, where the white bubble seen like a wake behind a shoal of flying fish on the LP sleeve had magically disappeared.

performed vast chunks of *Topographic Oceans* during their next British tour many found the intense, long drawn out performances all rather oppressive, although a switch to more traditional Yes material ensured they ultimately went down well. However, it transpired there was more tension backstage at two showcase dates at London's Rainbow Theatre on November 20 and 24 than there was in the audience.

The UK tour was a complete sell-out as press advertisements for the shows proudly boasted. A further announcement informed patrons: "It is essential that all ticket holders be seated prior to the time of performance. Nobody will be admitted after the start of the performance." This was the sort of stricture expected at a performance of Wagner's *Ring Cycle*. Rock fans felt rather intimidated by the vibes even before they heard the music.

The tour began at the Winter Gardens, Bournemouth, on November 16 and progressed around the country via Bristol, Portsmouth, Sheffield, Liverpool and all points north, ending up at the Empire Edinburgh on December 10.

For the first time since the group had hit the road back in 1968 they received reviews that were less than enthusiastic. The Rainbow shows in particular proved hard work rather than fun for audiences. At the same time my review of the album was surprisingly harsh: "Chanting voices lead us into 'The Revealing Science Of God' and the marathon Yes epic that has occupied so much of their time this summer. Was it all worth it? Even after hearing the concert and playing the four sides of the album several times it still somehow fails to make an impact as an entity. It is a fragmented masterwork assembled with loving care and long hours in the studio. Brilliant in patches but often taking far too long to make various points and curiously lacking in warmth or personal expression . . . the music is more of a test of endurance than a transport of delight. I just wish they'd make it easy on themselves. The strain is becoming unbearable."

Shortly after this review appeared I met Chris and Jon for an interview. I half expected to find a bucket of water balancing over the door as I entered the room at their London office. Yet they took the criticism surprisingly well. It seemed I was not the only one who had fired a broadside. My December 1973 report stated, "The critics slammed *Topographic Oceans* but thanks to the fans Yes go sailing on. For the second time in a few months an important, respected rock band has unveiled an extended work and failed to win the critical acclaim one would expect. Jethro Tull released *A Passion Play* and nobody liked it. After spending six months and 18 hours a day in the studio on the LP *Topographic* – the double LP and the gruelling tour – has gained a lukewarm response from critics who until now have been hard put to find anything but praise to shower upon them. Said Jon Anderson, 'We haven't had one good review.' The Rainbow concert had been particularly difficult. It was cold backstage and Jon was clearly irritable before the show, facing the hard task of playing to a mainly music business audience. Said Jon, 'One of the first things I wanted to do after the Rainbow was read the reviews. I just wanted to see if they were capturing what we put into it. It was a pretty heavy night for us in a few respects. We had a party afterwards and a few things became upsetting. Physically we were all very tired and worried that what we had been working on might not have got over. It wasn't musically a bad night for us. It was just the atmosphere.'

"Chris Squire said their manager Brian Lane and others beside had advised them to drop 'Side 3' of the album. 'It really is a bit of a drag,' admitted Chris. But would Yes write another piece as involved and complicated as *Topographic Oceans* again? 'Oh yes I hope so,' said Jon. 'You see, to us it wasn't that complicated. Steve and I had a basic cobweb of ideas and we filled them up. We actually had a lot more music than we finished up putting on the record. We are aware there are a few mistakes in it but as a piece of music we stand by it.'"

During the performances there was mounting tension among the performers. One eyewitness backstage during the *Topographic* tour says: "The band had to climb all over Jon and say, 'Please don't talk about the meaning of God – tomorrow night!' The public loved Jon so they were very tolerant but he pushed their patience every night for the first part of that tour. When he started talking about God it didn't get a very enthusiastic response. Somehow the band managed to stop him. There were many attempts to curb Jon on that tour, apart from his going on about the meaning of God and the universe and everything. They also wanted to limit the number of instruments he played. There was a discussion with Brian Lane about it. The problem was – what was Jon going to do on stage while the band was playing? Steve Howe said: 'What is he supposed to do – read a newspaper?'"

Despite all the criticism Jon, Chris, Steve and Alan resolutely stood by *Topographic*. But their keyboard player had other ideas. The first the public knew about the latest spot of internal unrest came in October with music press headlines that read: 'Wakeman to Go Solo'. Rick was to star in his own show at London's Festival Hall in January 1974. He would perform his latest solo work *Journey To The Centre Of The Earth* which was to be recorded for a live album.

What the public didn't know was that matters had already come to a head during the *Topographic* recording sessions earlier in the year. Says Rick, "Despite all our different lifestyles, we had survived because when we got together musically, it all worked. We had five totally different people in the band. Usually the music brought us together. Then we did *Tales From Topographic Oceans* which to put it bluntly was not my favourite album. I'll own up. Jon and I have had some conversations about this since. We both agree that if CDs had been available then there was enough good material on that album to make a 50-minute CD. We had a bit too much to go on an album of 36 minutes but not enough for a double album. So it was padded mercilessly. And that really upset me."

Such was the difference of opinion between Rick and Jon about *Topographic* that it would lead to a seismic shake-up within the band. Not only was the main theme difficult to comprehend, Rick says the entire album was made in the most bizarre circumstances. "Jon and I wanted to record it in the country. But Chris and Steve wanted to record in the town. Alan didn't care where we were recording. So there was a compromise . . ."

Yes finally agreed to record the album at Morgan Studios in Willesden, North London, but studio boss Monty Babson was bewildered by the spectacle that met his eyes when he dropped in on the start of the *Topographic* sessions. Rick arrived early in the morning, knowing he could get a quick drink in at Morgan's private bar. The band were not due to arrive until midday. "I got down about 9 a.m. and went to the bar for a drink. Monty Babson comes in and says, ' 'Ere, can I have a word? Those guys in your band. Are they er . . . all right? The crew have been loading in all morning. Have you seen what they've done to the studio? Come and have a look.' "

Rick and Monty went into Studio 3 with the road crew and their jaws dropped. "It looked like a farmyard. There were white picket fences. Hay bales. All the keyboards and amplifiers were set up on stacks of hay. I was the only keyboard player who ever had to send his keyboard back for repair because it had lice. It was unbelievable. There was also a full sized, cardboard cut out cow with electrically powered movable udders. It was hilarious! It was absolutely ridiculous."

So who conceived this rural transformation scene?

"Jon. 'Oh, it is nice, it's just like being in the country. Don't you like it?' I mean we were in Willesden of all places."

According to Chris Squire, their manager organised the farmyard effects. "The cows and stuff were a Brian Lane joke because Jon wanted to record in the country. Brian had got a great deal at Morgan and I wanted to record there even though I hated Willesden because I lived near there as a kid. I always thought it was a very dull place. But Morgan Studios had the very first 24-track tape machine in England made by Ampex. So I was keen on the technical side and wanted to go there, although Jon still wanted to record in the country. Brian Lane compromised by getting a bunch of cows and putting them in the studio to make Jon happy. I think they ended up being shoved in a corner after a couple of days!"

Jon says that he actually wanted to record *Topographic* in a forest at the dead of night. The themes were all about mother earth and the ritual of life and he wanted to get in the right frame of mind and closer to nature. "When I suggested that, they all said, 'Jon, get a life!' "

Despite the worthy intention of bringing some rustic vibes to the sessions, *Topographic Oceans* proved to be such a difficult album that in some eyes it marked the beginning of the downturn in the band's fortunes. Its critics were confused by the size and scale of the work, the complexity of the music and the thinking behind the lyrics. Says Rick, "I was upset because I thought we weren't properly prepared for that album. There wasn't enough music. What happened was I spent most of my time over the road, playing on a Black Sabbath album.[13] I was playing darts with the guys and playing on their album as they were in the studio at the same time as us. What happened then was real stubbornness set in. And I take a lot of the blame. Instead of me saying, 'I think there are a lot of nice things on this album and it has its good points,' I just said, 'It's crap.' And Jon in defence said, 'It's a work of art.' "

Jon Anderson felt besieged. Elements of his own band and even a previously supportive music press seemed to be turning against him. Yet the album was by no means a disaster. By December it had become the first album to qualify for gold disc status on the 'ship-out' sales alone. By January 1974 it had topped the UK album charts for two weeks and got to Number 6 in the US *Billboard* chart. In February the band played *Topographic* for two nights at New York's Madison Square Garden to hugely enthusiastic crowds.

The problem, according to Rick, was that the whole concept was based on Jon's somewhat cursory reading of the Shastric Scriptures. When the band toured the UK in December 1973 they presented *Close To The Edge* in the first half of the show and *Tales From Topographic Oceans* in the second. In a telling aside in the programme notes Jon Anderson explained the origins of his band's major new work. "We were in Tokyo on tour and I had a few minutes to myself in the hotel room before the evening's concert. Leafing through Paramhansa Yoganada's *Autobiography Of A Yogi* I got caught up in the lengthy footnote on page 83. It described the four part Shastric Scriptures which cover all aspects of religion and social life as well as fields like medicine and music, art and architecture. For some time I had been searching for a theme for a large-scale composition. So positive in character were the Shastras that I could visualise there and then, four interlocking pieces of music being structured around them. That was in February. Eight months later, the concept was realised . . ."

---

[13] Rick played on *Sabbath Bloody Sabbath.*

While touring Australia and the US Jon spelled out his idea to Steve Howe. The pair began holding candlelit writing sessions in their hotel rooms. By the time they reached Savannah, Georgia, the main idea had come together. During one six hour session which carried on until 7 a.m. they worked out the vocal, lyrics and instrumental foundation for the four movements. Said Jon, "It was a magical experience which left both of us exhilarated for days. Chris, Rick and Alan made very important contributions of their own as the work evolved during the five months it took to arrange, rehearse and record."

As he was about to unveil the completed album, Jon asked me what I thought the word 'topographic' actually meant. I thought it was to do with the features of a landscape. The topography of an ocean, apart from the waves, is generally rather featureless. The title therefore should have been *Tales Of Oceanic Topography*. An ocean cannot of itself be topographic. If this was to be a story about life on the sea bed then it might make some sense. But that wasn't the intention. And in any case Jon's title sounded better than mine.

Rick was doubtful about Jon's ability to fully comprehend the Shastric Scriptures after leafing through a few footnotes. "It's reckoned that if somebody sat down to study the Shastric Scriptures it would take eighty years, reading non-stop to get through them all. I said to Jon, 'You've sat down and read a *Sunday Times* colour supplement article about them and suddenly you are an expert.' It was really sad because I went one way and Jon went another and never the twain would meet.

"And I resigned. After we played at the Rainbow Theatre in London, I quit. Brian Lane, Steve Howe, Chris and Phil Carson of Atlantic sat me down and said, 'Look, we've got a big European tour and some American dates. Why don't you do the dates and see how you feel at the end of the tour?' So I said I'd do those two tours. But to be honest I'd made up my mind about the music before I went. Jon wasn't budging an inch and I wasn't budging an inch."

Rick remained at his keyboards but under protest. Eventually the protest spilled over into one of the most talked about episodes in Yes lore. Rick: "Ah ha! The curry on stage! Funnily enough this has been refuted by a few people but it is all true. It happened at Manchester Free Trade Hall. Incidentally this story has also been exaggerated and blown out of all proportion. I've heard that truck loads of stuff arrived . . . and that's not true. It is true I used to be a real heavy drinker and one of the lads. I was down the pub every Sunday lunch time playing darts, eating curry and being a bad boy. This was totally the opposite to all the other guys, who were getting into vegetarianism. They were going towards the cosmic stratosphere and I was going down the *Dog & Duck*!"

142

Rick's face was a picture of misery during these *Topographic* performances. He now says, "That's because I *was* miserable. And that's where the curry came in! There was one particular piece – I can't remember what it was called – where I had little or nothing to do. And what I had to do, I didn't particularly like. It was at Manchester Free Trade Hall and I was sitting there bored rigid. I'd sunk quite a few pints while we were playing away and lager does have a remarkable mental effect on people. Normally after eight or nine pints the word 'curry' flashes into your brain. Suddenly it flashed . . . *curry*."

Rick's keyboard tech John Cleary came to the rescue. It was his job to lie under the equipment on stage during a performance, in case of a breakdown. Rick looked down at his loyal servant and said, "John, we'll go for a curry when this is all over." However, with all the noise of the *Topographic Oceans* breaking over their heads John could only catch the word 'curry'.

Rick: "The next thing I know he's handing me up a chicken curry, a few poppadoms and an onion Bhaji. In fairness I'd never actually planned for him to go and *get* a curry. I said we'd go for one after the show. But he vanished and came back twenty minutes later and there was this *lovely* smell. John's under the keyboards handing it all up to me. So I laid it out on the organ . . . and ate it. Jon came over . . . and he did have a poppadom. But I don't think Steve Howe was very amused. It was harmless fun really."

Steve certainly took the album seriously, as he had devised most of the instrumental work: "Even though the album was knocked a lot by Rick, side two had these marvellous sections in it which were full of colour. We were colouring a big landscape in *Tales* but we went for some stark realities too, like on side three where there was some very weird instrumental progressive stuff. But when Jon sings 'Nous Sommes du Soleil' that's really romantic. Yes music has those contrasts. There is the beauty but there is also anger. When we did the next album *Relayer*, we did some of the most outrageous stuff ever. There was a piece called 'Soundchaser' and the guitar solo still shocks even now. How we got to that I'm not sure. The group let me go wild!"

Whatever the critics thought and despite Rick's criticisms the band was ready to surf the *Oceans* on a massive tour. When, on February 18, 1974 Yes played the first of two nights at Madison Square Garden, New York, it was the first time the band had taken a full sized stage show to America. In the Big Apple they stayed at the Warwick hotel and that week *Melody Maker* celebrated their American success with a front-page story indicating that the gross takings from the two Garden shows would exceed $200,000. Chris Squire was less than happy that *MM* had chosen to 'reveal' Yes' earnings and at a pre-show party in their hotel 'hospitality' suite he berated Chris Charlesworth, now *MM*'s American editor based in New York.

"I kept telling him that anyone with a calculator could work out what they were grossing, simply by multiplying the average ticket price by the number of seats," says Charlesworth. "Chris seemed to think that we had exposed some dark secret. He didn't like the idea of the fans knowing how much money they made but there really wasn't a secret about it. I thought it was a bit rich coming from him as he always seemed to me to be the most money-conscious member of the band. He was a bit flash and drove a yellow Lotus Elan! The others didn't care about the story at all, and neither did Brian Lane. Rick certainly didn't care and he joined in the argument on my side."

The party ended in disarray when Harvey Goldsmith, the London-based promoter who promoted Yes' UK concerts and who was visiting them in New York, was thrown fully clothed into a bath tub. "I'm sure it was Rick who instigated that," says Charlesworth. "Harvey was all dressed up, ready to go to the Garden when suddenly Rick and some of the others in the room picked him up and threw him into a bath full of cold water. He was furious . . . really angry. He was soaked and had to change his clothes. Lots of people used to take the mickey out of Harvey in those days but this time they'd gone too far and he didn't see the joke. Personally – after the row I'd just had with him – I'd have liked to see Chris Squire dumped in the bath too!"

Down at the Garden the stage set was quite unlike anything most fans had ever seen before. Roger Dean and brother Martyn had created stage scenery with a visual impact worthy of their fantastical new music. They came up with a glowing landscape that looked like the album cover come to life. The band even emerged from a tunnel with a cave-like entrance, rather like five of the seven dwarves emerging from the gold mines in *Snow White*. It was wonderful viewing but the stage set led to practical problems on the road.

Work on the concept for both the *Topographic* stage set and album cover design had begun the previous year. Roger Dean had gone to Japan with Yes in March 1973, to discuss various proposals. Roger's idea was for a design that worked as a drawing in its own right and would be a code for patterns 'located elsewhere'. He ended up with a complex collection of landmarks. The idea was to make a Yes concert a total experience with the music enhanced by the visual effects. The first Yes stage sets designed by Roger and Martyn Dean were intended to be a three-dimensional fantasy landscape. The stage for the *Topographic Ocean* tour was composed of ambiguous shapes meant to be transformed by lighting, so they sometimes appeared as flowers or animals or even machines. When the band toured Britain with the set, audiences saw only a fraction of the shapes the Deans had designed and built as there wasn't room for them on stage in the relatively small venues.

Castings for the final version used on the 1974 American tour were made of translucent walled fibreglass and lit inside and out. Martyn Dean produced a finned shell that formed a pavilion for Alan White to sit inside with his drum kit. Alan said the fibreglass canopy actually sharpened his drum sound, making it more resonant. At the climax of 'Ritual' the shell opened out to release a cloud of fire and smoke. Roger contributed a series of illuminated islands that covered the stage and there was a series of organ pipes in undulating, shifting colours that were intended to be an extension of Rick Wakeman's keyboard set-up. Behind it all was a screen for lighting effects and slide projections. This was pure showmanship but it had practical value. When the band began heavy touring of America it was quickly appreciated that in the vast auditoriums that could seat up to 30,000 people, many of the fans might be sitting a long way from the stage and there wasn't much to see apart from the dots on the horizon that represented Chris, Jon, Steve, Rick and Alan. At the larger open–air concerts it was even worse. Sections of the audience might actually be a quarter of a mile away and could see nothing. A large stage set at least provided a long distance spectacle accompanied by music. Those close up could see the full details of the shapes and changing colours and lights. It was not an entirely new idea. Martyn Dean was fascinated by tales of Wagner who carried two train loads of monumental scenery around Bavaria to stage his epic operas in the 19th century.

When the Dean brothers began work on *Topographic Oceans* the pressure was intense to get the work ready in time and within the budget. In their wonderfully illustrated book *Magnetic Storm* (Pomegranate Artbooks) they tell how they had to work through the night with cups of coffee to keep them awake. They would often doze off with their hands covered in fibreglass, only to wake up and find a coffee cup stuck to one hand and the other hand stuck to the side of a chair.

The first version of the set was strengthened with a steel framework which they had to build themselves. They often took risks with hot welding equipment used next to buckets of inflammable chemicals. Says Roger Dean, "Building the stage was certainly interesting but it became a nightmare carrying it around England in different trucks and vans because it was so heavy. By the time we got it to America we had ironed out all the problems. It was now super lightweight and very elegant. No one had seen anything like it and no one has seen anything like it since, because there are few dramatic stage props used in rock anymore. There's great lighting but there isn't much in the way of landscaping on stage. We had a kind of fantasy landscape where you could never be sure what things were. One of the set pieces was the huge 'thing' behind Rick's keyboards which could have been a plant, or it could have been organ pipes. Over the drums a weird shape opened like a beetle and there were other various bits of glowing landscape dotted around the stage. The band emerged through a specially constructed tunnel. The tunnel snaked around and glowed in the dark. It looked really good! We used it at the Rainbow Theatre in London for the English tour but it looked much better when we went to America and rebuilt the staging. It was made from fibreglass, very thin skinned with carbon fibre reinforcement."

Michael Tait was involved with the lighting on this tour as usual but there seemed to be a lack of co-operation between him and the Dean brothers. "Did he work with us? Never enough!" says Roger. "I don't know if he felt his territory was being invaded but I felt we could have used the illuminated stage to more dramatic effect. I always thought he did good lighting and I just wished we had worked closer together, but that's partly the story of Yes I think. Looking amazing . . . but knowing it could look that bit more amazing. That was always the way."

Martyn was placed in charge of actually building the sets. "Occasionally I interfered – and got thrown out! During *Tales* I worked on the UK tour dates but in America Martyn took over completely. In fact on the next tour for *Relayer* Martyn did the staging which was even better and I wasn't involved in it at all. I did the backdrops which were made off site." Roger regrets the lack of proper filming during those days, which means many of the great rock shows of the Seventies must remain dim memories.

In 1975, a *Yessongs* movie was released, containing 80 minutes of concert footage which became a surprise box office hit. Says Steve Howe, "In 1972 we filmed *Yessongs* which was the first and almost the last thing of its kind we did. It is very much a document of the times. People filmed and filmed us after that and it was all going into the archives. Years later there was a big to-do about a concert that Yes did at Queens Park Rangers football ground in London. It turned up in Japan on video and none of us knew how. It was a bit of a rip-off. The guy collected the money and we didn't see any of it! I went to look at the Yes film archives kept in storage, but unfortunately there wasn't much left. We did release a concert from 1979 called *Yes In Philadelphia '79* and that is like an in-house video. The texture is pretty thin and the sound is raw. That's the kind of thing that got released and hasn't done us any favours. It is semi-historical but one day we should put something better together."

"The tragedy is that the guy who organised the filming of *Yessongs* also organised the filming of the *Relayer* tour but there was a falling out at some point and they never completed the film," says Roger Dean. "They shot quite a few concerts but the film has never surfaced and I would love to see that because the staging was amazing. There are rumours of an 8 mm pirate copy. Even though they never completed filming the tour, they shot a lot of footage."

Roger believes the kind of stage sets used on the *Topographic* and *Relayer* tours were a kind of art form in themselves. But he still feels they could have done so much more. "When you think we worked on minuscule budgets, compared to what other people were getting, we achieved quite dramatic effects. Some designers were working with budgets literally a hundred times greater than we were spending. That was frustrating. You see the record company didn't pay a cent. It was all paid for by the tour promoters and the band. That's why money was so tight."

After the American *Topographic* dates Yes set off for Europe. By the time they got to Frankfurt, Germany, they had only four shows to go before the end of the tour but Rick Wakeman was at the end of his tether and called a meeting. "I said, 'No, I can't do it'," he says. "So I left. I felt we were cheating the audiences. There *was* some good stuff on the record. Years later Jon said he would personally like to re-mix *Topographic* as a single CD, but said he couldn't get permission to do it."

As far as Jon Anderson was concerned the issue of Rick's departure from the band had less to do with curries and boredom than the fact that Rick couldn't get a crucial keyboard solo right. "I said to him, 'Please get the keyboard solo right. Why don't you just learn it?' I must have asked him a dozen times. I kept pushing him all the way through the tour to the point where he said, 'You're driving me crazy. I've had enough. I'm leaving.'"

Jon was then full of apologies. "But it was too late. I'd pushed him over the edge."

★   ★   ★

Tales From Topographic Oceans was re-issued on a double CD in 1997 having been digitally remastered by Joe Gastwirt. It was long overdue for reappraisal. Some of it now sounds less daunting and intimidating than it did in 1973, although there is no doubt the individual pieces are far too long and lack focus. 'The Revealing Science Of God (Dance Of Dawn)' fares better than most of the tracks. It is the sort of melodic arrangement The Beatles might have developed in their *Sgt. Pepper* period and as such harks back to the very early Yes. Jon's voice has distinct overtones of Paul McCartney as he sings the complex lyrics aided by the choral style harmonies from Chris and Steve.

What is noticeable is the almost complete absence of keyboards during the opening salvos. This failure to use Rick Wakeman's talents properly on the piece was either an oversight on the part of Steve and Jon, or the result of Rick's own failure to involve himself more seriously in the project. There are touches of Mellotron of course and spots of piano and synthesiser but the emphasis is on a relentless rolling tide of lyrics. It's not so much a song as a saga, a tale told by Jon amidst endless waves of drums and guitar.

The second piece, 'The Remembering (High The Memory)', clocks in at twenty minutes and is vague and uneven. The band fails to develop even a tentative grip on a melody for longer than a few seconds at a time. Seven or more minutes into the work there is only a wash of tonal colours to support lines like "*Softer message bringing light to a truth long forgotten.*" It has its moments, of course. Steve Howe kicks in with some animated guitar work at the 13th minute. Alan White battles manfully with his kit trying to bring some life to proceedings but it is an uphill struggle. Without a strong theme and without an independent producer calling for heads to be knocked together 'The Remembering' simply weakens and distorts the Yes concept. The will o' the wisp of their magical flame recedes into darkness.

Time has not healed the wounds of 'The Ancient (Giants Under The Sun)' either. This commences with frenzied, neurotic percussion pounding behind some of Steve Howe's least attractive slide guitar playing. When I mentioned this album to Michael Tait, the band's long serving sound and lighting engineer he succinctly described it as "rubbish". I thought this quite hurtful and abrasive – until I replayed 'The Ancient'.

Says Michael, "We used to go into the studio without any ideas. On *Topographic Oceans* there were no ideas and the studio was costing five hundred dollars an hour. It was ludicrous. In those days no one would even speak to each other. Rick wouldn't even come in and if they were in the studio – he wouldn't be there. Everyone worked separately. It was nuts. Absolutely nuts. We were there for months making that album and it was a load of rubbish! But you see by then they were out of ideas. What made you mad about it was that you knew the potential. You knew what could be done. Because of the personalities involved you knew it was not being done and you think, 'These guys are nuts! What an opportunity is being squandered here.' "

There is little respite on the final piece 'Ritual (Nous Sommes Du Soleil)', which drags on for a further 21 minutes. It was ironic that just when the band had reached its largest imaginable audience they were, musically speaking, at their lowest level. Even so, this piece eventually begins to pick up with a locomotive drive lacking during the previous 18 minutes. And when Jon Anderson begins to sing 'Nous Sommes Du Soleil' you are at once ready to forgive and forget. But as the mighty work reaches a long drawn out crescendo of strange percussion effects you can imagine ticket holders in the back row of the Apollo Glasgow debating the merits of staying the course or repairing to the nearest bar. If proto-punk rockers heard this record – perhaps at a party or music biz reception – it would not be difficult to imagine their scorn and pent-up frustrations.[14]

Indeed, a new breed of street-cred performers were soon champing at the bit for recognition. Artists like The Sex Pistols, The Damned and Elvis Costello saw the music industry dominated by these untouchable cosmic beings and clearly resented them. Operating in their own sweet world, Yes were blissfully unaware of the subterranean underground movement plotting to unseat them. It would take a few years to materialise but the revolt had begun, without and within. And the backlash could be unpleasant.

A lone Jon Anderson once encountered some of the avowed enemies of progressive rock. "It's funny the impression people have of you," says Jon. "I always remember meeting Elvis Costello and Ian Dury while doing a charity concert in London. I said I'd get up and sing and it was something I'd never done before in this situation. Meeting Elvis Costello was like meeting this incredible brick wall. He was very cold and distant. He came from that aggressive, punk thing. But within five minutes I think he understood I was just like him and he actually became a very sweet friend. Within the space of an hour we were chatting. Ian Dury was there too and he was quick to have a go at me. He didn't even know me. Within an hour we were all mates. We're all in the same business together. I think initially their aggression was towards what had gone down in the past. Yet when Yes started, we felt *we* were the new wave. All you think about is who you are trying to beat. But when I met Elvis and Ian it was a wonderful day for me because I was able to get rid of all the crap. I'd been really hit by this anti-progressive vibe that was going round at the time. We were these pompous techno flash people, but all we were trying to do was become better people and better musicians and just trying to utilise our talents and realise our potential. They've all learnt since. I've always admired Elvis Costello's songwriting but you go through those hard, sharp aggressive periods. It's caused by uncertainty . . . about who you are and what you are doing. I was very aggressive myself in the early days!"

★ ★ ★

[14] I was at a party attended by young record executives, one of whom was vitriolic in his condemnation of Yes. I was eventually silenced by his barrage of criticism larded with expletives, but I remember my friend and *MM* photographer Barrie Wentzell being quite upset and saying: "Hey man, Yes are great!" But to no avail. The loudest critic of the band present would later become head of one of Britain's biggest and most successful labels.

Long before Elvis Costello and Ian Dury found themselves on the front pages of the music press, the Yes men were hitting the headlines regularly and there was plenty to report in spring 1974 when the band were hit by the most damaging split in the ranks since the departure of Bill Bruford.

Rick Wakeman: "When I left Yes I was very sad. It was May 18, 1974. I was sitting all on my own at my place in Devon. It was actually my birthday. I'd phoned the Yes office the day before and said I'd made up my mind . . . I wanted to leave."

Manager Brian Lane called and begged Rick to come to the rehearsals for the new album *Relayer*. "I told him I couldn't. I'd heard some of the material being put together and it wasn't the kind of music I envisioned Yes doing. 'I can't be part of something I can't contribute to, so I'm out', I told him."

Brian was very blunt: "You're crazy. You've done all the hard work and this is going to be the year when everybody earns money, and you're going to give it to somebody else?"

Rick: "Well, I just can't do it."

Brian Lane then asked Wakeman to do him a favour and not announce his departure until they had found a replacement. Rick put the phone down in the kitchen at his country farmhouse and felt utterly dejected. Then it rang again a few minutes later. This time it was Terry O'Neil from A&M Records.

"Rick, I've found you," he said. "I've got some unbelievable news. *Journey To The Centre Of The Earth* is number one in the charts. It's the first number one album for A&M. We're having wonderful celebrations . . . fantastic!"

Wakeman was sunk in gloom and couldn't share the festive mood. "I just left Yes half an hour ago," he told O'Neil. It was one of the strangest days of his life. "I had a hit record and yet I felt I had failed in what I wanted to do within the band. Shortly afterwards I had a heart attack."

The official announcement of Rick's departure came on June 8, 1974. The following month he was admitted to hospital with suspected coronary pain. The moment the attack came on he was actually in the throes of an interview with *Melody Maker*'s veteran journalist Chris Hayes. A reporter with the *MM* since the Thirties, Hayes was still working for the paper as a semi-retired freelance in the Seventies. Each week he assiduously compiled a column known as 'Expert Advice' for which he interviewed musicians about their equipment. In this role he talked daily to more stars than the average rock critic does in a year, regularly bombarding the likes of Eric Clapton, Jeff Beck and Pete Townshend with probing questions about their wah-wah pedals and preferred brand of strings, pick-ups and plectrums. Over the years Chris had compiled a phone book of home numbers that would be the envy of anyone on Fleet Street. He would treat his subjects with little respect and persevere with his questions, often at a time of day when most rock musicians were sleeping off the previous night's excesses. Perversely, it was an attitude that appeared to gain their respect, albeit not so on the famous occasion when he tried to interview jazz trumpeter Dizzy Gillespie. The tetchy bebopper came to his hotel bedroom door and threatened to whack Chris over the head with his trumpet. "As I ducked to avoid the blow I noted that he played a Conn trumpet," he reported later in triumph.

Rick Wakeman is far too polite to whack a journalist or ask him to desist from his questioning. "I remember saying to Chris in the middle of the interview, 'Excuse me. I don't feel very well.' As they carried me off in the ambulance I suddenly remembered him and told the crew 'Oh no . . . I've left Chris Hayes of the *Melody Maker* hanging on the phone!' "

Rick's heart attack at such a young age was no laughing matter. It came as a devastating blow to his family, friends and colleagues. It seemed that the tensions, pressures and his frantically busy, and singularly unhealthy, lifestyle had finally caught up with him. Rick was laid up in Wexham Park Hospital near Slough. However the band had to carry on. By the time they announced his departure Yes had already found a new keyboard player, the jovial Swiss émigré Patrick Moraz.[15]

Even this wasn't a clear-cut decision. While the band were planning to bring in Patrick they had another keyboard player in the frame and for a while it was even hoped they might not have to make any changes at all.

Says Rick, "I remember being in bed in hospital and not feeling very well. I was only allowed a few visitors but Jon came to see me. I can remember him coming into the ward and sitting down. Our parting had been rather acrimonious over *Topographic Oceans*. He just said, 'How are you? Do you want to come back into the band?' He was really concerned that my heart attack had been caused by worry and concern over leaving the band and maybe I'd had second thoughts about the whole thing. I said it was very kind of Jon but I had made my decision and I could not be part of the musical direction that Yes was going in. He said that's all he wanted to know – and there was a look of relief on his face. I realised then that Jon did have a heart and he really was concerned about me. Nobody knew he had come to see me."

Phil Carson recalls another curious episode. "When we realised we had to replace Rick our first thought was Vangelis." Vangelis Papathanassiou was a gifted Greek composer and musician whom Jon greatly admired.

---

[15] I recommended Patrick to the group's manager, Brian Lane, when he asked my advice on a suitable replacement.

Vangelis had been in the group Aphrodite's Child. He and Jon would later work together as Jon and Vangelis and they had a hit with 'I Hear You Now' in 1980 and cut an album together. In 1982 they had a top ten hit with 'I'll Find My Way Home'.

Says Carson, "Jon and I went to Paris to try and get him to join the group. He was an amazing character. As I recall, he had a Daimler limousine with a female chauffeur. We had a great meeting with him in this bizarre apartment where he was surrounded by young women. He also had an archery target set up in the living room of this huge room. During the conversation he kept loosing off arrows which flew across the crowded room and always hit the centre of the target! Anyway we talked him into giving it a try. He came over to London and tried out with Yes but it didn't really gel. One of the problems was Vangelis wouldn't get on a plane and wouldn't fly anywhere and Yes were about to go on tour. That's when they brought Patrick Moraz into the equation."

Patrick Moraz, born on June 24, 1948 in Morges, Switzerland, was a virtuoso pianist who had already worked with British musicians in his group Refugee. Keenly ambitious, he would top his career by becoming the ninth member of Yes. Naturally, he was delighted at being asked to join a prestigious band at the peak of their international success.

Patrick came from a sophisticated and highly musical background. He studied violin, piano and percussion as a child and at the age of five was already composing pieces of music for the piano. He learned the rudiments of jazz and studied classical music but his rapid development came to an abrupt halt at the age of 13 when he broke four fingers of his right hand in a roller skating accident. "I was told I could never play classical music again," he says.

Fortunately, with therapy and hours of practise, Patrick's hand healed. "I practised my left hand like crazy and I eventually became ambidextrous. Did I go roller skating again? Oh yes, of course I did! I even broke my arm skiing. That slowed down the learning process but I got into jazz and was rehearsing with local bands. I also learned to play classical organ with a priest."

At the age of 17 Patrick won a prize as a young jazz soloist at a festival. The prize was a couple of lessons with Stephane Grappelli. "He was not only the greatest jazz violinist ever, he was also a fantastic pianist and he showed me a lot of stuff. I learned from him all I needed to know about jazz and rock."

Patrick later won an even more exciting prize. In 1965 his quartet was invited to be the opening act on a European tour by American jazz tenor sax player John Coltrane. He was absorbed in jazz but like most musicians he was turned on by the elegant simplicity of The Beatles. He yearned to visit England, home of all those wonderful rock bands. Never afraid to take a plunge into the unknown, at 17 he bought a ticket, packed his tooth brush and set off for England. He travelled all night by train and boat and somehow ended up in the south coast resort town of Bournemouth. "I didn't know a word of English and the only job I could get was as a cook!" he says. He stayed in Bournemouth for six months, learning the language and about the country. He also fell foul of the Musicians' Union.

"I was kicked out by the MU because I accepted a job playing in a bar. I didn't have the right visa to be a pianist in a pub. I then started to play in a restaurant and the secretary of the Musicians' Union actually came along and kicked me out! I had to leave the country for a while. Then I came back and applied for membership of the Union, which was denied. I wanted to stay in England because all the great groups were there. I was invited to jam with a group in Bournemouth called The Night People but there was no possibility of me joining them because of the Union. It was extremely strict about musicians coming from abroad."

Moraz wasn't able to return to England until 1969 when he auditioned players for his progressive rock group Mainhorse. He settled on a line-up that included Bryson Graham on drums, Jean Riston on bass and Peter Cockett on guitar. They signed to Polydor records and in 1970 recorded an album at Deep Purple's studio in Kingsway. It was not a great success but they worked on film scores and played club gigs in Germany. In the back of Patrick's mind he may have already been thinking about a liaison with Yes. He had already bumped into the band when they played at the Golden Rose in Montreaux, Switzerland in May, 1969. When they met again in Basle, Patrick was greatly impressed. He was also blown away by another dynamic British progressive band The Nice, led by organist Keith Emerson. He even jammed with Keith's rhythm section of drummer Brian 'Blinky' Davison and bassist Lee Jackson. Mr. Emerson was not best pleased at these incursions into his territory.

In 1973 Patrick returned to Switzerland from a tour of Japan and Hong Kong where he had been working as musical director of a Brazilian ballet. In the summer, four years after his first meeting with The Nice, their bass player and singer Lee Jackson called him and said, "Hello, remember me?" He asked Patrick if he'd be interested in forming a group with him. Moraz immediately got on a plane to England and teamed up with Lee and Blinky in a promising new trio called Refugee. They signed to Charisma Records, released an excellent album and went on tour, performing as a more structured and updated version of The Nice. The group proved very popular and all three put much hard work into rehearsing the material. Alas it all came to an abrupt halt when Moraz was asked to join Yes. Davison and Jackson were so disillusioned they withdrew from the music scene. It had all happened to them before when Keith Emerson broke up the Nice to form Emerson, Lake & Palmer in 1970.

Patrick always regretted his decision to leave Brian and Lee but he had to make a move that would ultimately benefit his career. The opportunity was simply too good to turn down. But it left him feeling somewhat remorseful. "Refugee did a lot of disciplined work, rehearsing six days a week for at least three months before we recorded our album," recalls Patrick. "So it was a very strong album and I really enjoyed working with Lee and Brian. I had much more scope in Refugee and everybody said I was crazy to join Yes. They might have been right. I worked better with Refugee because I had more freedom."

He arrived back in Britain in June 1974 and quickly settled in for a three year tenure with Yes during which time he was cheerfully dubbed by the crew 'the Swiss Poodle' due to his distinctive hairstyle. Patrick was a loveable character who had mastered several languages, but his English was always a little eccentric. His old drummer in Refugee, Brian Davison, used to chuckle heartily at Patrick's pronunciation of words like 'rhythmically' which came out as 'Ritt Mickley'. This became the title of the fourth track on the 1974 album *Refugee* which, incidentally, included Patrick's impressive 'Grand Canyon Suite'.

Publicist and ex-*NME* journalist Keith Altham remembers Patrick's penchant for malapropisms. "I remember driving through Holland with him and he suddenly said, 'Where are all the turnips?' I said, 'What do you mean *turnips*?' Eventually I realised he meant tulips!"

There was no mistaking Patrick's musical intentions. He steamed in with great gusto to record the tracks for the next Yes album *Relayer*, which was released in November, 1974. Such was the popularity of Yes that even after the abrupt departure of the much loved Wakeman, the album shot straight to Number 4 in the UK charts and to Number 5 in the US.

It was a single album but that didn't stop the band once again indulging in massively long and, in some cases, indigestible pieces. It was almost as if Yes were defying the critics. At least this time it was recorded without cows or bales of hay. Alan White remembers how the sessions developed: "All of the *Relayer* stuff was recorded at Chris Squires' house. We'd drive down there every day and we'd spend eight or nine hours in his studio with Patrick on the keyboards."

Polite and friendly, Patrick Moraz got on well with the band. However it wasn't easy to blend into Yes, especially when he began to realise there were other players vaguely waiting in the wings. Says Chris Squire, "Patrick was a different kind of keyboard player but, prior to him joining, Vangelis was going to come into the band. Jon and he had become very good friends and they went on to work together later. I liked playing with

Vangelis and thought a lot of the stuff he was doing was really great when we rehearsed together. But once again there wasn't a bond between him and Steve, who wasn't very keen on Vangelis' style. That didn't work for Steve, so Vangelis didn't happen and we started looking around for another replacement. Patrick came along and at that point Steve liked what Patrick was doing. I thought he was a nice chap so we got on with it!"

Moraz was overjoyed at the prospect of playing with the ultimate musician's band. Says Patrick, "I really enjoyed my three years with Yes . . . it was a fantastic experience. People still talk about it to me and recognise me from those days. I'm better known as an ex-member of Yes than an ex-member of The Moody Blues, who I joined later and played with for 13 years! I saw Yes as a school. I recorded an album with them and did many tours, and really got into the way they arranged and composed their music. It gave me a deep insight into that kind of music. Yes music is vastly superior to any other group's music I have heard. They are a kind of exponential development onwards from The Beatles. Funnily enough I didn't want to join Yes right away. Apart from the band I was also into film music and by then I had done 25 music scores for movies. Joining Yes came as a very hard debate with my conscience."

Patrick was invited by Brian Lane to attend a rehearsal with Yes to see how he'd fit in. Moraz vividly remembers it was on a Wednesday in the first week of August 1974. At the time Patrick still had some gigs outstanding with Refugee and material ready for another album for Charisma. "We decided to call it a day because we didn't have the necessary management and we were being offered a pittance for the record. I thought if we did a second album with Refugee it would be a downer from the first one. Bearing that in mind I went to the rehearsal and later Brian Lane called me and said that I had got the gig. I said, 'I don't want the gig! What would happen to the guys in Refugee?' I was still debating what to do. But all the legal work was done by the time I had my next meeting. I had told Brian I wanted Lee and Brian Davison to be taken care of financially. At the time I didn't really understand anything about contracts and the English used in documents was very complex for me. Brian Lane said he would take care of them but I think Lee and Brian were both upset."

Patrick finally made his decision and told Brian Lane he would be happy to join Yes. "I was always fascinated by their music and I thought they were brilliant. I went to the rehearsal and Brian Lane almost ran over me in his car! It was late, it was raining and he didn't recognise me. He took me in his car to Rickmansworth and saw the very core of the band at work. They had already been preparing material for the *Relayer* album. When I heard them play 'Sound Chaser' I was blown away. It was unbelievable. They had already been there a couple of months so they had the best sound possible." Eddie Offord was there with a 24-track recording desk and Patrick's contribution to 'Sound Chaser' was recorded that same day and ended up on the album.

There were only three items on the entire album: 'The Gates Of Delirium' which ran for 21 minutes and 55 seconds, 'Sound Chaser' at 9.25 and 'To Be Over' at a mere 9.08 seconds. The latest Roger Dean cover depicted a snake curling around the rugged rocks amid a spooky landscape of caverns and cliffs. Despite Roger's policy of producing the art work without having heard the music, this scene must surely have been inspired by the lyrics: "*Snakes are coiled upon the granite horsemen ride into the west. Moons are rising on the planet where the worst must suffer like the rest . . .*"

Unfortunately for Yes *Relayer* appeared at a time when the curt brevity of pub and punk rock was beginning to make the work of the classic bands seem overblown and in some eyes irrelevant. Yes still held a commanding position and the fans who had been with them since the Sixties retained their loyalty and were still prepared to listen, even if the catchy themes that had graced their earlier work were now sadly missing. One of the biggest fans of the album turned out to be a young itinerant bass player called Trevor Horn who played 'The Gates Of Delirium' at full blast while driving in his van along the motorways to his next gig. He wasn't to know the part he would one day play in the Yes story.

Relayer was beautifully recorded and engineered by Eddie Offord. Steve Howe's guitar work echoed with a bite that is especially impressive when heard on the digitally remastered CD version. 'The Gates Of Delirium', inspired by Tolstoy's *War And Peace*, reaches a fever pitch of instrumental intensity in which Patrick Moraz fights to be heard amidst the dense layers of guitar tracks. With the drums and bass also fighting in the background, there is very little left for space and syncopation. This was neurotic, disturbing music full of nightmarish clattering and howling that sounds like a soundtrack to an *Eraserhead* style movie. During the final chorus Jon Anderson's silvery vocals elevate the piece into something rather more pleasant as he sings and repeats the line "*Our reason to be here.*"

'Sound Chaser' contained some brilliant instrumental work and some of Chris Squire's best bass work on record. Patrick Moraz also made his presence felt here. But the confused structure of the piece, with its changes in tempo and violent excesses, helps explain why Rick Wakeman didn't want to be involved.

Even Steve Howe is not a big fan of the album, even though he was heavily featured. "It was a bit of a mixture and record sales started to drop . . . but we had been through lean times before. Even *The Yes Album*

156

didn't sell when it first came out. *Topographic* was rather smooth to our ears but *Relayer* was total speed, especially on tracks like 'Sound Chaser' and we started to get a bit angular and sharp. We were making ferocious, frightening sounds, like the battle in 'Gates Of Delirium'. It was all a bit horrible and one of the first big arguments Jon and I ever had was about the explosions on 'Gates Of Delirium' and the amount of echo. I was hearing a tight group and Jon wanted to hear explosions of sound. To my ears Yes was going over the top."

Patrick Moraz toured with the band from 1974 to 1976 and during his last year with Yes he played some 75 concerts. During 1976 the band set off on their biggest ever American tours which included a spectacular concert at Philadelphia's vast JFK Stadium. They were seen by an estimated 150,000 cheering fans in the blazing sunshine of a June afternoon. Backstage there were barbecues, a make-shift swimming pool for the sweating crews, dustbins full of iced beer and a massive fireworks display. The whole tour was a sell out and the band played to over 1.2 million people. It was the Indian summer of progressive rock, before the nuclear winter of punk set in.

"We played some very big gigs in Philadelphia and Chicago, playing to 100,000 people at a time," recalls Moraz. "We needed 16 different PA systems from Clair Brothers just to cater for all the various concerts. At Philadelphia it was the Bicentennial year and we had Peter Frampton opening for us and Gary Wright.

"I got on very well with all the guys in Yes and had a great time. But when I joined the band in August 1974 it was hard for me to learn all the previous material. I wrote the arrangements down on maps and charts and listened to all the keyboard solos Rick Wakeman and Tony Kaye had laid down before me. Their music was extremely subtle, like classical music in a way. You have to feel the music from the inside because it is very emotional. It took me several weeks to get into it. I think I did what was required of me at the time and performed really well from the third or fourth concert onwards. The first few gigs were very hard. I was like tap dancing!"

Although Patrick had integrated well with Yes he was destined to record only one studio album with the band and he left after the 1976 summer tour. In an unexpected twist he was replaced in November that year by Rick Wakeman. Says Patrick, "What happened was that in 1975 we all decided to do solo albums. Alan White did *Ramshackled*. Then Steve Howe asked me to do the orchestration on his album called *Beginnings*. Chris asked me to contribute to his album too, so I was always going back and forth between England and Switzerland. At the same time I was working on my own solo album. Then we went on the road in the States and we finished in Miami. I went off to South America to record my album and finished it in Switzerland."

Patrick's eponymously titled album got to number 28 in the UK charts in April, 1976, the same month that Rick Wakeman's *No Earthly Connection* was in the UK Top Ten. A couple of months later Jon Anderson's solo album, *Olias Of Sunhillow*, peaked at number 8 in the charts. It seemed Yes fans were hungry to buy anything by their favourite artists in the absence of a full blown new band album.

Patrick: "In 1976 we started rehearsing for an album that eventually became *Going For The One*. We were tossing some ideas around. We also rehearsed the next big stage show which would have included a lot of *Topographic Oceans* and *Close To The Edge*. We went on the road until October of that year. Then all our equipment was sent to Switzerland to start recording *Going For The One*. I was living in Brazil at that time but when I got to Switzerland for some reason they wanted Rick back into the band. I think he needed to come back. He'd had a big hit with *Journey To The Centre Of The Earth* but I personally think Brian Lane wanted Rick back in Yes because he didn't know what to do with him! He was losing money doing these Cecil B. DeMille style shows on ice. I didn't feel so good about being in the band at that point."

Patrick left and a year later joined The Moody Blues. In 1984 he began working in a duo format with Bill Bruford and they recorded two albums *Music For Piano And Drums* and *Flags* and did three well received US tours. Later in 1985 Bill formed his own band Earthworks fronted by jazzmen Django Bates and Iain Bellamy. Patrick returned to The Moody Blues for some years before relaunching his solo career. He remains a big fan of Yes and when Rick Wakeman left again in 1997, he offered his services, but was pipped at the post by Russian keyboard wizard Igor Khoroshev. Today Patrick lives in Florida, tours as a concert pianist and has released many albums over the years.

Says Michael Tait, "Patrick Moraz was a sweetheart but he wasn't a Yes man. He never had a chance of being fully accepted. He was too foreign! Yes is an English band, that's all there is to it. Patrick was a lot of fun and technically a good player and a lovely guy. But it just wasn't the same."

★ ★ ★

Despite doubts about *Topographic Oceans* and *Relayer*, the mid-Seventies was a fruitful period for Yes. In 1975 Atlantic released the compilation *Yesterdays* featuring tracks culled from their first two albums. Rick Wakeman, recovered from his health scare, was scaling new heights of popularity and unsheathed his latest blockbuster concept *The Myths And Legends Of King Arthur And The Knights Of The Round Table* which was staged on ice at Wembley Arena. In November came a whole series of solo Yes albums including Steve Howe's *Beginnings* and Chris Squire's *A Fish Out Of Water*. They were followed by Alan White's *Ramshackled*, Patrick Moraz's *I* and Jon Anderson's *Olias Of Sunhillow*. It is an indication of the hold Yes had on rock music that so much related material could find a market.

In the few years since Yes had become a supergroup, the touring business had grown into a million dollar industry which drew upon many ancillary services. The success of mega rock bands brought work and custom to airlines and hotels, trucking, car hire, sound, lighting and musical equipment companies, caterers, accountants, tax advisers and lawyers. It also required the right people to book and co-ordinate all these services. They couldn't rely any more on a couple of roadies armed with fuse wire and a bottle opener. Yes had their manager Brian Lane, based at his London office, ready to fly out to oversee their US and European tours. But they also needed people around to take care of day-to-day business. Michael Tait concentrated on the band's lighting effects and the regular roadies had their hands full just looking after the equipment.

They needed a tour co-ordinator and found one in Jim Halley, whose job was to get the band from A to B, at the right time and in good shape. Over the years Jim would become expert at handling difficult situations with skill and diplomacy, whether it was fending off a disgruntled roadie armed with a fire hose or coaxing a recalcitrant superstar to come out of his bedroom and make an album. When it came to dealing with angry hotel managers, booking executive jets or ensuring a supply of dancing girls for the band's entertainment, Jim could fix it.

Yet when he joined the Yes organisation in 1974 it was only as a favour to his new found mates and he took some persuading to give up his 'day job'. But having done one tour he found himself so embroiled in Yes affairs that he couldn't leave. Quietly spoken, with an impish smile, Jim was precise, organised and businesslike, as befitting someone who had previously been running a health food shop. He was hip to the particular fads and fancies of a band that had become increasingly concerned with their wellbeing in an attempt to ward off the perceived ravages of rock'n'roll.

Musicians had spent years living on a diet of truck stop food and knew more than most the effects of large quantities of pig meat, grease and ketchup. They had the acne and rumbling bowels to prove it. So while most of the population were still tucking into a cholesterol filled diet, certain rock musicians – and most famously four fifths of Yes – were trying to make amends. But in the early Seventies they found it almost impossible to find vegetarian meals on planes or in cafés. They had to be ordered especially in advance, and when they found at least one place in London that could cater for their needs they descended en masse at regular intervals to stock up.

Yes found Jim Halley working at Whole Food, a specialist shop located in London's Baker Street. At that time it was the only organic health food shop in town. The main store comprised a book store, a restaurant and – rather less appealing perhaps – a butcher's shop. "This was around 1973, before health food shops became commonplace," says Jim. "Yes in those days were already vegetarians except for Rick Wakeman of course. I was managing the store and they all used to come into the shop to get their week's shopping."

Jim first got to know the band just after they'd finished *Topographic* and were about to start work on *Relayer* at Chris Squire's studio, in Virginia Water. "They used to come to Baker Street to buy food for the whole entourage including the road crew and the technicians. Virginia Water was a small village and as they didn't have anywhere else to eat, everyone dined at the studio. The band would visit Whole Food on a Friday and stock up. It was quite a small shop and they'd arrive in their Rolls Royces and Bentleys and do the shopping for an hour and a half. Everything ground to a halt in the shop until these people left!"

Jim thought it would be more sensible for them to telephone their orders so he could get them ready in advance. When the band arrived they went into the restaurant while staff put the sacks of tofu, bran and organic vegetables into the cars. Then came frantic messages. "Jim, we can't come into town to get the shopping, do you think you could come out?" Jim loaded up his car with fresh supplies of munchies and drove down to Chris' house. He became friendly with his rock star customers and was invited to stay overnight. He would hang out with various members of the band, in particular Chris and his wife Nicki. "I would stay with them for weekends and even went to Crete with them on holiday," he says. "I also went to gigs, just as *Tales From Topographic Oceans* was finishing. I remember going to see them play *Topographic* at the Rainbow Theatre just before Rick left."

Jim would deliver the food, hang out in the studio and watch them recording. "It was very interesting for me. Then it turned out they were looking for an assistant tour manager." They called him at the shop and asked if he fancied going on tour with them. "I said absolutely no way!" Then Alex Scott of the management company called him again and explained they wanted him to come along because they preferred to have someone they knew, rather than a stranger. Jim insisted that he had to stay to manage the shop but eventually agreed to go on the one tour. "So I took leave of absence from Whole Food and went on the 1976 Bicentennial tour of America. I went out on Concorde, on to the Yes private jet which flew us to the best hotels in the United States. Once that tour was finished, I said thanks very much guys – nice tour! Then Brian Lane said, " 'Ere, Jim, we are going out of the country to make the next album.' "

Yes were going to Switzerland and needed someone to co-ordinate finding the accommodation, organising the travel, rehearsals and recording sessions. Halley left Whole Food and went to Switzerland in September and stayed nine months until the following May. During that time he got used to life with a supergroup. It was a high old time – up the snow clad mountains. "I learnt to ski with Alan White and Jon and some of the crew. We'd meet at nine o'clock in the morning and go skiing up the mountain and then back into Montreux, shower up and start the sessions at 1 o'clock in the afternoon."

Patrick Moraz was still part of the Yes team that descended on Switzerland – his home country – to start work on what would become *Going For The One*. The music was recorded at Mountain Studios in Montreux, the picturesque town nestling beneath the snow clad mountains and beside Lac Leman (Lake Geneva) which was host to the annual jazz and pop music festival. Says Jim Halley, "But there was a slight upset at the beginning of *Going For The One* because when Patrick started the album it didn't work out. Then it was decided, 'Oh, what's Rick Wakeman doing?' So Brian Lane called Rick and asked him over. I picked Rick up at the airport, took him to Montreux and *Going For The One* was the result. Rick really liked Switzerland and he stayed on there for a while. As soon as we finished the album we went on the 1977 tour."

It was Alex Scott, the band's personal road manager, who called Rick in October to tell him there had been yet another change in personnel. Patrick had gone. They weren't planning to get another permanent keyboard player, but would he come over and do the sessions for their next album? They'd pay him a handsome fee to come to Switzerland. Once again Rick demurred, reminding Alex he just didn't like Yes music anymore. Scott then said that Jon Anderson would send him tapes of their new songs. Rick received a cassette which had the basics of 'Wondrous Stories' and 'Going For The One'.

Remembers Alan White, "Rick came back to do *Going For The One* in 1976 which was recorded in Switzerland. It was expensive – that's for sure. We were all doing tax years out of England and had to spend so many days out of the country. But the album produced a hit with 'Wondrous Stories'."

Says Rick, "I thought, 'Oh, we're doing songs again – yeah!' So they flew me to Switzerland." Wakeman was pleased to be back. The blond giant could be seen driving a sleek Rolls Royce between his rented house

161

and the studio, cracking a handy bullwhip (that he kept in his boudoir), cracking jokes and cracking open the odd can of refreshing lager. Rick was enjoying himself but he thought he was doing a session, not officially rejoining the band.

"Contrary to popular belief there hadn't been any recording done before I arrived," he recalls. "They had rehearsed but nothing was put down. So we started playing and it was really going well. Then we went up to a party thrown by Claude Nobs who was head of Warner Bros in Europe. Chris was always really the spokesman of Yes and a great manipulator. I like Chris a lot and if the truth be known he was always best at running the band, because he could stand back and see what was going on. I remember him sitting next to me at Claude's party. He said, 'It's a shame you know. Here we are doing these sessions and already we've got a problem. If we go out on the road we've got to find somebody who can play this stuff. Would you be interested in doing a tour with us?' I said I would . . . very much. He then said it would be pointless me being a guest session player. It would be better all round if I joined the band again. I said, 'Well . . . yeah . . . okay fine.' "

The following morning Rick went down to the studio and spotted the latest copy of *Melody Maker*. There was a picture of all five sitting in the studio in Montreaux and the front page headline was simply 'Wakeman Rejoins Yes'. Rick was stunned: "And I'm thinking . . . Chris Squire spoke to me last night – and this paper was out in England four days ago. It would have gone to press the day before that. So somebody had told them *five* days before I had rejoined the band. I called Chris over and showed him the paper and said, 'Oi, you only asked me last night!' And he said, 'Yeah – good job you said yes wasn't it!' "

Says Jim Halley, "We spent the whole winter in Switzerland and the band were getting on really well with each other. There was a lot of rehearsing and writing in the recording studio itself. People would come along with ideas and be in the studio actually composing and writing the songs. Jon and Rick wrote together but one of the best tunes, 'Turn Of The Century', Alan White was instrumental in writing. It was a joint effort though, and they'd all gather in the studio at one o'clock in the afternoon and say, 'Right, what do you think of this?' Someone would play a riff and Alan would start playing along and that's how they created in those days. People would come in with little ideas and the others would augment it to develop the songs. My impression was they would all contribute to each song. It seemed to be a very happy time. They had their families there, the children would come out." Jim would drive back and forth to Geneva airport six times a week ferrying the extended Yes family when they returned to the UK or collecting new visitors. "We even had a film crew there for a long time. We had a whole entourage of technicians including the band's crew."

Jim Halley also remembers how during the Swiss adventure Yes' entourage began to rival The Who or Led Zeppelin for destruction and mayhem. Apart from Rick cracking his whip, there were the wrecked cars. "We used to hire cars and race them around Lake Geneva and wreck as many of them as we could! I remember Claude Johnson Taylor, who was Steve Howe's roadie going out of the studio, across the road to Avis and winning the world record for wrecking a car from a rental company. We came out of Avis, turned right and within 50 metres we crashed into a big bollard beside the lake. Within ten minutes we were taking the car back to Avis, absolutely wrecked!"

★ ★ ★

If fans were disturbed by the frequent changes in the line-up of Yes, so were the regular members, particularly Steve Howe. "It started to get very complicated," says Steve. "When Rick rejoined after Patrick left, I thought, 'This is very strange. We keep going through people and now someone is actually coming back!' " Indeed, Steve soon became tense and unhappy. Asked the cause, he replied, "Touring . . . and Brian Lane!" So he began to take positive steps to combat the physical and mental stress of life in Yes, and found the answer in Transcendental Meditation. "When we flew to Switzerland to record *Going For The One* I got into meditation and began to think more deeply about life. I had done all sorts of interesting meditation without any real guidance. Many things contributed to make me think that life shouldn't just be a rat race. But there are always so many things to achieve."

Steve has always tended to look worried on stage as he concentrates hard on his playing, and in recent years he looks as if touring has become even more of a physical strain. But he denies that he suffers from stage fright or nerves. "I profess not to have stage fright but people do say I look tense." He insists on having his stage equipment well organised and his beloved guitars tuned and in good order for a show. It worries him if things are not set up properly and he combats Yes stress by using a combination of exercise and meditation to relax himself for each performance.

"Preparation is the thing. I see a lot of guitarists clenching their fists before they go on which is the worst thing to do, it's just tiring and not therapeutic. I don't drink alcohol or take heavy drugs before I go on stage. I tend to meditate which is something few rock musicians do. It's the Yehudi Menuhin approach. If you can't think of anything better – don't do anything. Meditating is the epitome of not doing anything. You just stop and shut the whole system down. Then you come out refreshed instead of being tired and overheated. I've done that for years with Yes. In the early days I used to rush around like a blue arsed fly. We were trying to eat, drink, change clothes for the show . . . doing too many things at once. When you can organise the space around you, then you can say, 'This is my dressing room. This is my corner. Thank you very much. Piss off!' Later on when I joined Asia in the Eighties, I didn't always have my own dressing room and would muck in with the guys but I'd always have my own section. Preparation is where classical musicians score. They don't have this hyped up feeling of, 'Hey man, I'm going to blow them away tonight!' They have a collective feeling. 'I'm going to go on, sit there and play my instrument. I hope you all like it because I'm going to.' With that attitude you get on much better. Secretly I have very high expectations of myself but I can only achieve things by being at ease with no distractions."

Whether it was the mid-Seventies upheavals that saw Patrick Moraz and Rick Wakeman coming and going, or just the exhaustion of a daily flight, bus journey and gig, Steve began to suffer physically as well as mentally. "This started when I used to finish Yes tours with back aches, shoulder cramps, spasms and tense and twisted arms. I was in awful physical pain. An Indian lady in Finchley who was a chiropractor told me I was a complete mess. I couldn't stop doing the tours but I *could* change the way I did them. I now know there is no such thing as wasted time. In your free time you can be preparing for the next important thing. When you are on tour the only important thing is the show and an awful lot of energy is put into a show. So during time off I go to visit guitar shops, or natural healing centres – anything to break it up. I always used to think I was just a guitarist and until I was 28, never realised I was a human being too! I can understand why some rock guitarists have lost their lives. You can get to the point where being good at any instrument is actually a big worry. You want to keep on being good and you also realise you are not the same as other people. When you realise that you are good you are at a crossroads. You can either carry on giving your heart and soul to it, as I did, and at worst risk going completely mad, or just lose sight of what your life is about.

"What I tried to do and I have not always been successful, is try to live a full life doing lots of things and staying in touch with people in different fields, not only musicians. Many of my friends aren't musicians. I'm not some kind of perfectionist mentor. I'm still looking for the way ahead. There is a danger in saying, 'I am now this person'. In fact I'm still beginning."

While Steve wrestled with his physical pains the band struggled to complete *Going For The One*. It was their first studio album in two and a half years and the new work proved quite a radical departure in several respects. After the intensity of *Topographic* and *Relayer* many welcomed the new material as a return to the kind of melodic simplicity of the *Time And A Word* era. It was a breath of fresh air and still sounds dynamic and pristine all these years later, especially on the remastered CD version.

The cover was important too. Gone were the elaborate Roger Dean landscapes. In their place came stark, geometric simplicity. Anticipating computer designs of the future, it showed a nude male figure contemplating a towering vista of shiny skyscrapers set against a clear blue sky. A typical product of the Hipgnosis design team, famed for their work with Pink Floyd and Led Zeppelin, it symbolised a new look for Yes and prepared listeners for a revitalised attitude.

There were just five pieces on the album, but there was much greater clarity than on previous Yes works and a much more generous use of Rick Wakeman's talents. His flowing rhapsodic keyboard playing was a crucial part of such attractive and inspiring pieces as 'Turn Of The Century', and he could be heard prominently in the uplifting 'Going For The One'.

There seemed to be less of a fight for solo space, and Rick and Steve complemented each others' playing. Acoustic guitar was featured in the opening and closing moments of 'Turn Of The Century', while Rick's piano playing was both tasteful and inventive. Jon's vocals sounded at their most childlike and mellifluous on a song which saw the balance between romanticism and power neatly maintained. Wakeman's dramatic use of a church organ sets the scene on the gothic sounding 'Parallels' and Alan White's drums set up a kicking back beat that holds the piece tightly in check. Jon sings *"To build a shining tower"* (a phrase reflected in the sleeve design) before Steve launches himself off the top of the tower in a vertiginous guitar solo of dizzying power. Rick then shows that even a church organ can rock. He shook St. Martins' Church, Vevey, to the foundations when he was let loose on their mighty organ. Strange voices pop up in the final moments of this stomping piece, presumably the Richard Williams Singers. Jon Anderson shines on the relaxed and melodic 'Wondrous Stories', one of those fortuitous tunes that enabled the band to fly without really trying.

Gone were the restrictions of *Topographic* days and Wakeman was allowed to shine, notably on 'Awaken'. Here he plays one of his most striking piano introductions since the days of *Fragile*. 'Awaken' is one of those long drawn out soundscapes full of declaiming lyrics that can either enthral or send a listener into a trance depending on their mood and attention span. The final tranquil moments are quite beautiful, the kind of music making now almost a lost art. This track set the seal on what is perhaps one of the band's most overlooked and yet consistently satisfying albums.

It also saw Yes in the British top ten singles charts for the first time ever, facing down the challenge from the punks who would have the readers of the newly hawkish music press believe that the days of Yes and their ilk were numbered. Unlikely as it might seem in that summer of punk, the summer when Johnny Rotten sneered in contempt at musicians who had taken the trouble to learn to play, 'Wondrous Stories' reached number 7 in September, 1977, and *Going For The One* topped the UK album charts in July, and reached number 8 in the US. Even the single 'Going For The One' reached Number 24 in the UK in November.

The punks might have drawn blood, but Yes weren't going down without a fight.

7

DON'T KILL THE GOOSE!

Blockbuster albums like *Topographic Oceans* and *Relayer* sold in great quantities throughout the world in the mid-Seventies, despite the grumbling complaints of critics. Money from album sales, ticket sales and merchandising showered over Yes in a golden cascade. It also flowed remorselessly away from them in a deep oceanic current of expenditure.

They were spending freely, not just on running a rock band with all its attendant costs, but on their own personal needs. In the heady atmosphere of fame and success it seemed the rock business would forever be a great source of wealth. These were the days of wine and roses. No one could conceive the idea of a Great Depression, least of all a debilitating social revolution.

Yet the bleak reality was that in later years many rock stars would find they had lost all they had gained. Yes were not immune from this process. The big houses went and with them the trappings of stardom. Gone were the Rolls Royces and Lotus sports cars. They weren't quite back to queuing for a Number 14 bus in the Fulham Road in the rain, but it was a close run thing.

Old friend Michael Tait muses on the band's latter-day condition. "Did they miss opportunities? Sure they did. They could have capitalised a lot more in the Seventies when they were really hot. But everyone was a bit near-sighted. And it was hard to control those guys. Everyone wanted to do something different. It even affected things like picking a studio to record in. The only reason they went to Switzerland to record was because it was the only place no one wanted to go to! It was the only thing they all agreed on. No one wanted to go there. So that's where they went. It was those kind of silly and expensive decisions that plagued them. Also, it was harder to come up with new ideas. I always say you have twenty years to write your first album and only six months to write your second – and so on!

"Unless you are a damned genius it gets harder and harder. They use up all their ideas and as they have success it goes to their heads in such a way they don't even understand. They want to take too much control of the part of the industry that they're not good at. They want to start managing themselves instead of sticking to what they know best. Even producing themselves. All musicians end up taking themselves a little too seriously. They think their success is because of their pure talent. They don't realise there's a lot of other factors in there. It's human nature and you have to accept the different personalities in bands. But you can almost foresee what's going to happen to them. U2 is a good example. When they started there was a big family feeling between the band and the crew. Before you knew it, that feeling was gone. It's to be expected. Money is a terrible corrupting influence and there's no way round it."

Yet in some respects Yes were quite canny and there was invariably a method to their madness. Tour manager Jim Halley was able to observe the band's affairs at close quarters and reckons they knew what they were doing. "Once they'd had big success it made sense for them to work out of England for tax reasons. Because of all their earnings they decided to go out of the country for a while. In the Seventies you were only allowed a limited period in the UK, so that's why they went to Switzerland to record and then immediately went on a tour of the States."

In the meantime, before the grim tax reaper took his cut, Yes enjoyed the lifestyle of *nouveau riche* rock stars. Remembers Chris Squire, "We all had big houses and stuff. It took some getting used to, having been from one end of the scale to the other. We were all still in our early twenties and that's not an easy age to cope with having money. You tend to think you have more to spend than you really do. You think, 'Oh that's good, I'll spend that!' And you forget about taxes. We all spent our money on houses, although Bill of course had always been very frugal with his money and later on I wish I had taken more of a leaf out of his book. You think everything is going to carry on at a certain level and of course it doesn't. I bought a big house and I'd never even owned a small house before! I'd never even owned a car until I bought a Bentley. I really went from having nothing – living in rented flats – to having a big house and a Bentley. Although they say youth is wasted on the young, I was able to take advantage of it, so that was good. I bought my house in Virginia Water in Christmas 1972. I built a studio there too."

Chris's house, called New Pipers, had what was reputably the biggest thatched roof in England. It was used as an American Embassy during World War II. The dining room was like a baronial hall with heavy gothic furniture. A bell under the table summoned worried looking servants who came scurrying to their master's bidding. Alan White also had a splendid home near Oxford, not far from Virgin's Manor Studios. Alan's abode, an old Mill House, had a cider cellar and a river running under the building.

There was a glass floor in one of the rooms so you could watch the water flowing beneath. Alan even had his own hovercraft so he could avoid traffic jams and skim up and down the river. His hobby was sailing and he was often heard threatening to take a year off to sail the oceans into the sunset. Later he moved to Seattle where there was plenty of opportunity to sail and enjoy the wide open spaces.

At Jon and Jenny's English country mansion, there was little talk of sailing but a ceaseless round of parties were held and guests were entertained with fireworks and champagne. It was all a far cry from Munster Road and fried eggs left under the bed.

In August 1977 this lifestyle was boosted by a particularly lucrative US tour. The band played a whole week of sell-out performances at the 20,000-seater Madison Square Garden in New York, the Coliseum in New Haven, Connecticut, and at the Boston Garden. It was a great time to be alive and in a successful rock group. Yes flitted from city to city in their Gruman Gulf Stream G2 private jet. If this was not available they'd take a couple of smaller Lear jets, one with all the seats taken out for the luggage. The G2 was equipped with a kitchen where the crew could make breakfast. The pilot usually volunteered to do the shopping, not the sort of treatment you'd expect from British Airways. Spending freely on private jets – which would be curtailed dramatically in later years – was the only way to fly!

On one memorable occasion they actually flew a *guitar* first class. By Concorde. It sounds like the ultimate extravagance but there was a logical reason. Steve Howe's favourite guitar is his Gibson 175. It travels with him everywhere and he never lets it out of his sight. Just as a violinist might have a precious Stradivarius, so Steve has his 175. Flying home to London from Washington on Concorde, Steve wouldn't hear of his guitar being put into the luggage compartment, where it could be crushed or subjected to extreme cold. The airline wouldn't allow Steve to take the guitar into the cabin without a ticket. So he bought a ticket under the name of 'Mr. Gibson' and the guitar was carefully strapped into its own Concorde seat. Among the first class passengers amused by this extravagance were Johnny Dankworth and Cleo Laine, fellow British performers who were also enjoying huge success in America at the time.[16]

The private jets sounded like an extravagance too, but in the Seventies it made reasonable economic sense in terms of speed and convenience.

---

[16] Buying an airplane ticket for an inanimate object was not that unusual for rock groups in the days when money was no object. I once sat next to a 'Mr. Carson' which was in fact a piece of antique furniture purchased by Jimmy Page, which flew under my watchful gaze from Frankfurt to London.

Most of these planes were as safe as the major airlines, but with the vast amount of aviation traffic in America there were occasional scares. Just two weeks after assistant tour manager Jim Halley flew in one such plane on Yes business in January 1977, the same Lear jet dived into the mountains of Nevada with Frank Sinatra's mother, Dolly, on board. The crash killed both her and the crew. She was taking a 20-minute flight from Palm Springs to see Old Blues Eyes singing in Las Vegas. Only a few months earlier Yes had run into Sinatra, Jon's old idol, when they arrived at the swanky Carlyle Hotel on Madison Avenue in New York. As the group checked in they spotted Rock Hudson in the elevator, Frank Sinatra at the bar and Warren Beatty in reception. The hotel later became Princess Diana's favourite haunt in New York. Yes only stayed at the best places. But they weren't always on their best behaviour.

If the band were wound up after a gig there would often be horseplay of a kind that would have shocked earnest students of 'The Revealing Science Of God'. There might be an outrageous food fight with entire buffets demolished as Jon, Rick, Chris, Steve and Alan played baseball with the bread rolls and cucumber sticks. A Yes fan arriving at such a scene bent on inquiring of Mr. Howe the nature of the dotted crotchet played in the 16th bar of the first chorus of 'Gates Of Delirium' might find a cheese and onion quiche splatted in his face. Similarly those seeking enlightenment from Jon Anderson on the spiritual values of Indian folk lore could easily suffer the indignity of a plate of muesli being tipped over their heads during these moments of abandon.

"Actually there was no serious destruction," says Jim Halley, whose job it was to clear up the mess – or at least warn the hotel manager in advance there might be trouble. "When you are in the middle of Wyoming on a Friday and you've been away from home for six weeks, the band needs to release some steam. I would warn the hotel managers. 'You know the food room? It could be a bit of a mess tonight.' He would check it out in the morning and we'd pay for the damage.

"We never left a bad name because they were good hotels and they were good to us. We'd always pay for any problems." But one intractable problem occurred when Steve Howe freaked out and attacked a hotel with a pickaxe. Says Jim, "The hotel was being renovated and there was endless hammering and banging and crashing. It was driving us all mad. We were walking down a corridor and there were some building tools left lying around. Steve in frustration put a pickaxe through the ceiling and left it there . . . sticking out."

It often took the band three hours to 'come down' after the adrenaline rush of a performance. If there wasn't a fully equipped roller disco handy or any dancing girls with balloons to provide distraction then it was a Yes 'red alert'. This was a dangerous time to be around. Even the best hotels faced the eve of destruction. On one famous occasion a Yes roadie went berserk, demanding a bonus that hadn't been paid. He burst into the restaurant armed with a fire hose, threatening to soak the band and their parsimonious management. There were yells of alarm. Somebody went to grab the roadie and pushed away the spurting hose. Somehow in the melee the fire alarm sounded. It was late at night and out into the corridor poured guests in their night clothes, many of them women and children screaming in fear, convinced there was a major hotel blaze that would engulf them all. Jim Halley plunged into the corridor begging them to return to their rooms. "It's okay ladies and gentlemen, don't rush. It's a false alarm – there isn't a fire!" In the end he gave up and, realising the authorities would be on their way, grabbed the band's smoking materials, pushed his way down the emergency stairs and out into the car park. Fire trucks and cops were streaming towards the hotel expecting to cope with a major disaster. As Halley stood panting a cop grabbed a glass of beer out of his hand and warned him he could be arrested for drinking in public. At least the band weren't smoking in public. Jim had it all stashed in his pockets.

"We had a laugh on the road," says Halley. "Yes were serious musicians but we let off steam on the road like any other band. We used to hire whole cinemas on a night off and the band, crew and friends would go down to watch a new movie like *ET*. We'd have the whole cinema to ourselves."

Despite these high jinks there was sometimes a sense of isolation about Yes on these endless American tours. As headliners on increasingly long shows, they hardly ever saw any other bands on the road. Says Jim, "We wouldn't have people walking on stage to guest. We just didn't have a lot of time to socialise like that because the travelling was so intense. We never did big festivals but we would do outdoor concerts, maybe supported by The J. Geils Band. But again there wasn't much socialising because Yes would be in their trailers backstage and then go out and play and after the show they'd go back to the hotel. We did get quite close to Peter Frampton and have dinner with him and we had Donovan and his band on tour with us sometimes."

It was like a military operation as the group hopped from city to city playing to larger crowds with bigger and bigger shows. Michael Tait remembers the sheer scale of operations: "In America we'd have a three or four truck tour although that is nothing by today's standards. The biggest development was the rotating round stage, which I thought of back in 1976. We were trying to come up with a new stage design and I picked up a can of film I was taking to a studio and was on the seat of my car. I looked at it and I thought, 'That's it!' I put the idea on paper and showed

171

it to the band. 'Look, we can play in the centre of the arena – in the round.' We'd have Jon in the centre, with Alan behind him. To his left would be Chris and to his right would be Steve which was the normal set-up. The only difference would be the keyboard player would be in front of Jon, but that's how they set up in the studio anyway. They said it couldn't be done, but I said if it worked in the studio, it would work outside. And it did. What that rotating round stage did for Yes was to make them a lot of money. The late Seventies were their golden years in America and Yes were doing big, big business. Sell out business in the round is worth a lot more than sell out business in a proscenium set-up. The front row is 120 feet long instead of sixty! You scale up the tickets and sell more seats. We broke box office records all over the country, including playing to something like 22,000 people at Madison Square Garden in New York. We were doing the business!"

The fun continued as the band alternated between the States and Europe. At the end of one marathon they organised their own '1977 European Tour Awards' ceremony. Special end-of-tour presentations were made to Michael Tait and Brian Lane. Rick Wakeman dreamt up some of the festivities and ordered Jim Halley, "Get me four dancing girls, make sure they are dressed in gold and get me 400 balloons."

"Gimme a break," was Jim's response. After much rushing around both girls and balloons were duly delivered.

As well as awards ceremonies there were other special events organised on days off. In Montreal Yes booked an entire snooker club for a day and organised their own band competition. A rare photograph was taken of Brian Lane dishing out the prize money. "I bet he hated every minute of that!" observed one grizzled Yes man. He wasn't grizzled then but he is grizzled now. In the Seventies there was so much cash to dish out that the media were feted and joined in the fun. On a trip to the States to cover the 1977 tour, rock writer Steve Clarke of the *NME* was cheerfully informed by a welcoming US record company executive, "Money is no object." He could travel wherever he pleased at their expense. Steve and myself (no bitter rivalry between *NME* and *MM* in those days), spent several days commuting between New York, Boston and Los Angeles chasing rock stars and drinking champagne.

After one evening spent with Peter Frampton and his band in a Greenwich Village bar we all ended up rolling around on the floor, helpless with laughter at the sheer decadence of it all, yelling "Money is no object!" Those were the days when Alice Cooper's former publicity guru Ashley Pandel used to run his own star studded New York club called Ashley's at 5th Avenue and 13th Street. John Lennon sometimes popped in for a drink, Lou Reed was among the regulars and it was a regular haunt for all visiting British rock stars. It was here that the visiting Yes party, including legendary Beatles PR Derek Taylor, Peter Frampton and guests, caroused until the early hours, drinking the cocktail of the month Tequila Sunrise. If you drank enough of them you were guaranteed never to see the sun rise.

As the Yes team staggered around Manhattan by yellow cab we were refused entry to trendy disco Studio 54 as we were 'inappropriately dressed', much to Chris Squire's chagrin. We may even have been inappropriately drunk. I wondered whether the manager knew they had turned away The Beatles' right hand man and half a dozen of the richest rock stars in the known universe. Ashley was much more accommodating. Around 4 a.m. I asked him what happened when they finally closed up the joint and the stars went home. "Oh we just hose the place down," he said and we all burst out laughing again.

★ ★ ★

But they weren't laughing back home. In London and Manchester a whole bunch of sullen geeks with chips on their shoulders were having a miserable time, and they were determined that everybody else should be miserable too. By 1978 The Sex Pistols were dominating the headlines in England, and in the aftermath of their success the whole thrust of the music business had changed. Pop music had always been a welcome and cheerful alternative to the more serious aspects of rock. Nobody liked a good pop record more than the Yes men, who had after all been raised on The Beatles. But punk wasn't just about bringing back the earthy three minute record. It was a kind of Cultural Revolution in which the Red Guards wanted to destroy everything of value in a great purge. Already undergoing their own crisis of confidence and not quite sure which direction to go in, Yes were particularly vulnerable. Suddenly, overnight, nobody cared about who was the top international band or who might win the *Melody Maker* award for top bass guitarist. Anybody who dared put such an award on their mantelpiece would risk being greeted with a cry of 'Boring old fart!'

'Anarchy In The UK', the Pistols début single, had appeared in November 1976 and their album *Never Mind The Bollocks* in October 1977. By the time *Tormato*, their ninth studio album, appeared in September 1978 Yes were already losing ground in terms of street cred. Of course their fans didn't disappear overnight and in America and the rest of the world their stock remained high. But instead of representing high fashion, Yes were now yesterday's news. Except in *Melody Maker*, whose readers voted Yes top in the annual poll once again! In terms of appreciation, hard sales and fan base, 'traditional' rock music was much stronger, as magazine publishers and

173

record companies would rediscover a decade later. In the meantime they were all quick to demoralise and demean the bands who had only the day before been a rich source of income. Much to their chagrin, they would rise again, but only after a long and exhausting battle.

Yes were in a strange situation. They still had their solid mass support as was proven by the *MM* poll results for 1978. Jon Anderson was top male singer (ahead of David Bowie and Bob Dylan). Steve Howe was top guitarist, Rick Wakeman top keyboard player and Chris Squire top bassist. *MM* editor Richard Williams wrote, "Yes and Genesis share many characteristics; for the best part of a decade both have struggled up from the ranks to develop music which is fresh, articulate, inventive and unmistakably British – and both have conquered the world."

Yes received their awards from Peter Cook and TV personality Janet Street-Porter at The Venue, Victoria Street, London on Wednesday, November 8, 1978. Interestingly, DJ Alan Freeman's progressive rock show was voted top Radio One show, even though it had been taken off air earlier in the year. Said Richard Williams, "Obviously the *MM* readers are giving the thumbs-down to the BBC's programmers . . ."

It seemed that in the teeth of punk, Yes fans were fighting a rearguard action on behalf of their favourite group. All Yes had to do now was come up with a first class album. It was not to be. Not quite.

Rick Wakeman: "Everything was going well and then we did the *Tormato* album in 1978, which was potentially one of the best Yes albums ever. But it suffered from appalling production. By that time Eddie Offord had gone to Mars and was unavailable. Everybody was using their own engineers, so you never saw so many hands on faders. The whole thing ended up so compressed it was tragic. I would love to get hold of that album and have it remixed. There is some fabulous stuff on there. 'Arriving UFO' is a great track and could have been one of the great Yes stage features of all time, but it suffered on the record."

Says Steve Howe, "*Tormato* had the same line-up as *Going For The One* but it was made under difficult circumstances. People didn't want to be in England. Chris and I said we had got to do it in the UK and we couldn't go to Switzerland for seven months. So we finally agreed to do it at home. But *Tormato* was kind of unsatisfying for everybody, although I thought Chris's track 'Onward' was rather good. But on most of *Tormato* Rick and I were in each other's way every flipping second. He was playing one thing and I was playing something else. To mix the tracks we had to tear each other's hair out. A lot of engineers got the wrong end of many sticks in Yes very unfairly, because the real problem was in our arranging and how we transformed that to production. We would use whatever we thought of and then say afterwards, 'How are we gonna produce this?'

174

Tormato was a complex thing with lots of ideas that never got heard because there was no room for them."

Steve admits there was a disjointed quality about late Seventies Yes. "That was because we did everything too long. We'd either repeat ourselves or start introducing ideas that didn't really sound like part of the song. We sort of calmed down on *Going For The One* and the second track 'Turn Of The Century' was like a high spot for me. The way that was constructed was so complex that even when we'd just played it – nobody knew how to play it! It was born out of many people's ideas. 'You do this, then go back to the beginning and do that!' I loved that piece. But then we did *Tormato* and the final insult was that Hipgnosis, who had done wonderful sleeves for other people but were not suited to Yes, finally threw a tomato at the cover and called it *Tormato*. For me that was an insult."

Steve's original idea was to call the album *Yes – Tor* after a famous pile of centuries old rock called Yes Tor which is located two and a half miles from Okehampton in Devon. "I complained about Hipgnosis," he says. "They knew I was the most awkward one, because I was the most pally with Roger Dean. They knew he was my friend as well as somebody who worked with the group and I was not happy that Roger didn't do those two album sleeves. Roger had fallen out with other people in the group for reasons not connected with Yes. Of course, when we changed direction and did the *Drama* album in 1980, Roger did the cover picture. I felt that once again we had continuity."

Alan White also has unhappy memories of *Tormato*. "It was done at Micky Most's studio in St. John's Wood. That wasn't the best album we ever made. We kinda got into some crazy stuff on that one. There are some good tracks but it was a throwaway album. Funnily enough in certain parts of America that's the album people bring for us to sign and they think it's amazing! We couldn't decide on the cover. I think Po[17] of Hipgnosis did that. He put a picture of a guy with divining sticks on the front. He took it home one night and decided it wasn't working. So he threw a tomato at it – and that was the album cover! *Tormato* actually came from all the Tor points in Devon and around Glastonbury that link up."

For the *Tormato* sleeve Yes were originally pictured wearing black bomber jackets and dark glasses standing in front of the mighty Yes Tor rock. Except they weren't in Devon. They were actually a hundred miles away, standing in a London park not far from Rak Studios where they had been recording. Says Jim Halley, "If you look at *Tormato* you will see them supposedly near the Yes Tor. In fact the pictures were taken in Regents

[17] Designer Aubrey Powell.

Park and superimposed on the cover." There was another little subterfuge. The black jackets had each wearer's name on them. But Chris Squire had forgotten his jacket and had to wear one supplied by Halley which had 'Jim' on it. In case the public were confused as to the identity of the mysterious 'Jim', when it came to preparing the artwork 'Chris' was drawn onto the jacket seen in the picture. Perhaps because of these manoeuvres everybody said the cover was a load of rubbish and as a result the artist blew his top and threw his fruit. "There were bits of tomato all over it!" chuckles Jim.

Tormato is a strange mixture of good, bad and indifferent material. There is a strong pulse to pieces like the opener 'Future Times'/'Rejoice', notable for Alan White's heavy snare drum patterns and Chris' deep toned bass guitar. Jon's lyrics remain high, light and airy and the arrangement is full of stops and starts. "*In the fountains of the Universe sits the boy child Solomon . . . dreams he of glory*," sings Jon while Rick hammers his Polymoog and Steve nips in with a blast of lead guitar. Mr. Howe plays tasteful country rock guitar on 'Don't Kill The Whale', the nearest the band had got to a hook line in years with Jon adding, 'Dig it, dig it!' for good measure.[18]

Rick's synth solo here is rather corny but it is Rick who shines on harpsichord on one of the album's success stories 'Madrigal'. Steve Howe's Spanish guitar work blends well with Rick's keyboard flourishes. Yes accelerate into top gear for 'Release, Release' with almost Zeppelin-esque alacrity. It's an odd mixture of styles and even includes an unexpected Alan White drum solo, complete with cheering crowds. As Steve picks up the rhythm with a stadium rock guitar riff, for a few bars the band starts to sound like The Doobie Brothers. This is an album full of such surprises, none more so than 'Arriving UFO'. The highly unusual thermionic valve sound used in the introduction is produced by Chris on his harmonised Rickenbacker, aided by Wakeman on polymoog. Or it could be Steve on paper and comb.

Jon sings, "*I could not take it oh so seriously really when you called and said you'd see a UFO. But it dawned on me the message in writing spelt out a meeting never dreamed of before.*" It reaches a stunning climax, a core of energy exploding into a fireball before that mysterious harmonised riff returns to take the UFO back into space.

It remains an imaginative and exciting piece, unlike anything Yes had done before. It even impressed those who were largely hostile and uninterested in the band. Next came one of the most controversial of all

---

[18] This was the tune that young Trevor Horn, still driving his van to gigs, would find a complete turn off.

Yes pieces, often cited by ex-fans as one of the reasons why they were ex-fans. 'Circus Of Heaven', rather twee in sentiment, has a lilting reggae rhythm. With Alan White playing bell-like crotales this is light years from punk or The Doobie Brothers. However, taken at face value it has charm and includes Jon's baby son Damion Anderson making his vocal début reciting the line, "*Oh! It was OK. But there were no clowns, no tigers, lions or bears, candy-floss, toffee apples, no clowns.*" Many years later I met Damion, by then a hip and noisy young dude into Beat Box and rapping. He'd never forgotten this magical moment from childhood, captured on record for all time and for all to hear.

A highlight of *Tormato* was one of Chris Squire's finest songs, the slow moving, stately 'Onward', arranged and orchestrated by his old friend Andrew Pryce Jackman. It contains simple but effective sentiments: "*Contained in everything I do there's a love, I feel for you*", a line echoed in a certain Bryan Adams hit of twenty years later. Chris' superb bass playing is to the fore on the brisk and businesslike 'On The Silent Wings Of Freedom' which also has some of Rick's most fluent and stabbing keyboard work.

Tormato is a strange album that contains moments of genius and certainly didn't deserve to be splattered with a ripe tomato. It puzzled everyone who saw it, and that single act of effrontery seemed to signal the crisis that lay ahead. The first great age of Yes was drawing to a close. The future now looked dark and confusing.

★　★　★

At first all seemed perfectly normal. Or as normal as life got in Yes world. Many claim the shows performed during this period were among their finest. The band toured using Michael Tait's revolving stage upon which Jon Anderson, his voice soaring and dressed from head to toe in brilliant white, would gently pluck the strings of a small harp while clouds of dry ice billowed around him. One cynical critic suggested he resembled an angel on the point of rising unto the heavens, but fans flocked to the shows and the charts even remained open to their singles output. Trevor Horn's fave 'Don't Kill The Whale' got to Number 36 in the UK chart in September, 1978.

Then an eerie silence seemed to fall. During 1979 Rick Wakeman cut his latest solo album *Rhapsodies*, released in June, and in November Steve Howe unveiled his second solo effort *The Steve Howe Album*. Then the band decided to go to Paris to record another Yes album. It would prove to be destination doom. Says Jim Halley, "They asked me to go over to find out where the best place was to record. So first I went to the South of France and found accommodation for them." He also found a recording studio owned by Jacques Loussier, the jazz pianist. "The studio was in the middle of a vineyard, which was very nice. I spent four or five days there with an estate agent and an interpreter checking out the area which was on the road to Nice and Monte Carlo. Jon Anderson loved it and stayed at Bill Wyman's old house nearby while Bill was having a new house built. David Niven also lived locally."

But instead of staying on the Riviera the band relocated to Paris which was felt to be more central. They had been assigned a new producer, Roy Thomas Baker, fresh from his successes with Queen, but he didn't seem quite the right sort of chap to handle Yes. His favourite expression during sessions was 'take-ee poos' which might have appealed to Freddie Mercury, but irritated the hell out of Yes. Instead of saying 'Can we do that one again' it was a shrill cry of 'Take-ee poos!' which emanated from the control room. The recording process was also disrupted by having to work in a busy city as opposed to being in a small town like Montreux. Says Halley, "Transportation was more difficult and it was stressful getting all the guys from the hotel to the studio. We tried to co-ordinate things through the local WEA office."

Getting across town in the rush hour was the least of their problems. Certain members of the band absolutely hated what was going down in the studio. Rick Wakeman for one was clearly unhappy: "After *Tormato* everything started to go horribly wrong because punk was hitting big time and Yes were out of fashion. We were trying to record the new album in France and there was dreadful animosity. Jon and I teamed up tightly together and although we had written a lot of stuff, it wasn't liked by the other guys and they didn't even turn up to the studio. It all became a mess."

Then Rick didn't want to turn up either. Says Jim Halley, "I can remember one day trying to get Rick to come out of his room. I knocked on the door and said, 'Please come down to the recording studio Rick and make this album.' Then all sorts of notes came back to me under the door, telling me to 'Fuck off' and questioning whether my mother and father were married – that sort of thing. References to female genitalia also came into it, if I remember correctly. Basically he was trying to tell me to go away. But the music was quite interesting. Some of it came out on a bootleg tape later and some of the tunes they developed formed parts of later solo albums by Jon. There was one track called 'Richard' which was possibly about Richard The Lionheart. Another called 'Tango' was very interesting. The trouble was Roy Thomas Baker wasn't tough enough with them. He had an assistant with him and he needed more taking care of than the band themselves. It wasn't the ideal studio either. They'd never had a big rock band there before."

Eventually the band was put out of its misery. Says Rick, "The situation was saved and destroyed by Alan White, funnily enough. He went off roller skating and broke his ankle. So Jon and I got paralytic on Calvados in the bar and left."

Says Jon, "The producer and the other members of the band weren't turning up on time, so we'd just go to the bar. We had lost respect for each other and then we broke up."

Rick remembers that the Calvados had the effect of making them both very depressed. "We began crying on each other's shoulders. Jon was saying, 'This isn't the band that I loved'. "

Jim Halley watched events with a mixture of bewilderment and despair. "Roller discos were the big thing in those days. Then Alan White came in one morning and discovered that he'd broken his ankle, so that's how the album failed to be completed. It was Christmas 1979 and that was the end of the project."

It seems strange that manager Brian Lane didn't take a firmer grip on proceedings and knock heads together. Says Halley, "He wasn't in Paris. I was his representative there as the personal manager. I was co-ordinating the transportation, rehearsing and recording. I was on the phone quite a few times to London saying, 'Brian, you'd better get your ass over here. They're not happy bunnies.' And he would come over. But it was a difficult situation for anyone to deal with because the band just wasn't happy. There were musical and personality differences and it wasn't the best time to be recording in Paris. They just weren't in the right mood to make an album. We spent Christmas wondering what was going to happen next. Who was going to be there when it was time to gather again after the holidays?"

Says Brian Lane, "When Yes came along they were the first band to play music that was completely original. Yes could have been as big as Pink Floyd but they were their own worst enemies. They never toured for long enough, only enough to recover their costs and then they stopped. They never took advantage of the opportunities that were presented to them. 1979 was the worst year of my life. I had to go into hospital for a growth under my arm and while I was recovering Chris Squire, Alan White and Steve Howe came to my house to tell me they had fired Jon Anderson in a row over money! I had an American tour booked for them which had sold out in advance."

After Christmas the crew went to Redan Studios behind Queensway in Bayswater, London, wondering who was still in the band. Rick and Jon decided they weren't. But instead of the band breaking up as everyone close to them expected, steps were taken to ensure its survival.

Says Jim, "Nobody really knew what was going on at the time. We'd be sitting in the studio waiting and saying, 'Is Jon in the band or not?' We didn't know from one day to the next whether Jon would show up or

Rick would show up. Brian Lane happened to be managing The Buggles at the time which consisted of a vocalist and a keyboard player, and we were short of those! We didn't have to search for replacements. They were on our doorstep. They came down, started rehearsing and suddenly they were in the band."

★   ★   ★

It was unthinkable. How could Jon Anderson, who with Chris Squire was the sole remaining founder member, and Rick Wakeman, their star keyboard man, quit after all their hard work? Things had come to a pretty pass. Nevertheless, those who remained in this group of erstwhile poll winners and gold album makers had somehow to pick up the pieces. It was a grim prospect for Chris, Steve and Alan. Their record company, too, was bemused by events. Phil Carson was still holding a torch for Yes at Atlantic but even he couldn't sort this one out. "There was a lot of acrimony. The band had completely burnt themselves out. They just weren't relating to each other. They went into the doldrums after that."

Says Steve philosophically, "Well Yes had come to be a regular trauma. There would often be a really big upheaval, usually unknown to the public or even the fanzines. It would be totally in-house. *Somebody* would be on the cards to be axed! The musical standards were very high and if people were not cutting it, there wasn't a place for them. We had seen a preview of how Yes could end in 1979 when we went to Paris and started work with Roy Thomas Baker and nobody could seem to do anything. Rick Wakeman had become very distant. For a start he lived in Switzerland at the time and he wouldn't even come to England until we were actually playing because he was a tax exile. That's a very dangerous thing, because you start to make yourself unavailable. Anyway we had some songs but Roy Thomas Baker the producer wanted us to keep it really simple. It was like 'don't play anything . . . add it all later'. There seemed to be an element missing from Yes which we couldn't define. Was it me – was it Chris? Then people started falling out with the producer and the Paris sessions ended and everybody came home and we said, 'Well, let's start again.' "

When the final attempt at Redan failed it seemed as if this was the end of Yes. In fact it was the beginning of a period of transformation both bizarre and strangely productive. Says Steve Howe, "When we started again there was a total transformation of Yes and Trevor Horn and Geoff Downes came in. It was meant to be a change from Jon and Rick. But it was much more difficult to split with Jon than it was with Rick. There were certain things that had to be done to right Yes and really we all fell out with each other."

180

The rows which led to Rick and Jon's departure were not entirely to do with the problems of the Paris rush hour nor their producer's cry of 'Take-ee poos!'. Financial matters also played a part, and Steve Howe confirms the bust-up with Jon resulted in awful friction. Says Steve, "The change of line-up was hard because of Jon's involvement and all the work I'd done with him on songwriting. The final upheaval was all about saving the band because things were not so good for Yes. The lean years were coming. The album sales had dipped and if we wanted to continue we had to invest in the group.

"The falling out was about how much people were prepared, then and there, to say, 'I'll help the group that's helped me.' Much to everybody's surprise, people you would have thought would say 'yes' instead said, 'No, I'm not going to do this.' So if they didn't, then everybody had to leave. It was no good anymore and it all collapsed. People got very suspicious, there were accusations and the whole thing escalated into a major problem. We were analysing, looking back into the past, dragging out skeletons from cupboards and absolutely nothing was achieved by this. It was all totally negative. I believe just before the next album we did [with The Buggles called *Drama*], if everybody had been able to see clearly we might have stayed together and done another four great albums. But as it happened, we couldn't see eye-to-eye at that time and we couldn't make it right, and therefore we couldn't carry on. Then the people that were left started making deals with each other and nobody was happy. By February 1981 that was it. There was no more Yes."

Chris Squire was particularly saddened by Jon's move. It was almost impossible for him to accept the departure of the singer and songwriter he had teamed up with in La Chasse Club on Wardour Street all those years before. It was also difficult for Chris to explain. He tries to simplify the reasons for Jon's departure. "You know what I think? He just wanted to go off and be a solo artist. He had a lot of work to do and Jon just felt if Rick can do it, so can I. That's really all it was. He wanted to get his own backing band and tour. The rest of us were left standing there and thinking, 'Well we'd better find a keyboard player and a singer!' "

But Jon has his own explanation for what triggered the bust-up, potentially the most damaging in Yes history. Over the years he'd said goodbye to Peter Banks, Tony Kaye, Bill Bruford, Rick Wakeman and Patrick Moraz. Now he was going himself but he saw it more as the result of a breakdown in communication than any direct plot to unseat or fire him, as some have suggested.

Says Jon, "It's very simple what happened. In 1979 the band was emotionally very tired. We hadn't stopped since the beginning and we'd been on the road for over ten years. We had been recording and touring without really being able to assess and take stock. Our children were growing up, and we were stuck in this twilight zone of being pushed into making another album. The idea was to bring in a big producer and try and get a hit record. Groups like The Cars and Foreigner were having big records with sales of eight million. The record company said, 'This is what you've got to do.' They put us with Roy Thomas Baker as the producer and that was a complete disaster. The band was just not built for that way of working."

Jon points out that in the thirty years of Yes history they have only ever had two big hits, 'Wondrous Stories' and 'Owner Of A Lonely Heart'. He felt they were being pressurised into going for a hit in 1979, as they would be again in the mid–Eighties. On both occasions Jon would quit the band. Anderson always felt that hits came naturally. They couldn't be forced. The concept went against all his gut feelings.

One version of what really happened in their dark years after 1979 comes from honest, blunt-speaking Michael Tait who had observed all the goings-on from a position that enabled him to step back and analyse the problems more rationally than most. "If you want to be truthful about what happened – did they start running out of musical ideas? Possibly. Had they been regurgitating their original concepts for a few years? Absolutely. Were there problems with affluence and wives being jealous with each other? Positively! Show me a band that doesn't have jealous wives and I'll show you a band that's not married! There were those kind of problems and it got worse and worse. Eventually it all fell apart.

"The band could have split up like so many other groups, with each member going off to do something different. But let's face it . . . individually they are not strong enough. Their strength is as a band. They all tried doing solo albums and that was a big mistake. Their solo albums happened before the band broke up and that too was a mistake. If anyone thinks their success is entirely due to themselves – and some people thought Jon believed that – well is that true? I dunno. He was a big part of it but without Chris Squire in there playing bass and Steve Howe playing guitar, I don't know what you've got. The main bad vibe was between Chris and Jon. They live with it. There's always something going on between them. They are just different personalities. Chris will think what Jon does is silly and vice versa. It's like being married. No one's partner is perfect. You just live with those defects and deal with it because you need to."

Some members of the band would suffer badly when the albums stopped selling. Says Tait, "The guys had the cash flow but not the back-up in the bank. That was the problem. They lived on the cash flow and didn't let the capital build up. When the flow stopped, they were in deep trouble. Another thing was that people would draw more than their share and get ahead of the game, leaving the other guys short and that caused problems.

"Jon was famous for going on huge vacations, taking the nanny and the kids and flying off first class to Barbados at vast expense. Then Steve might think – well he's doing that on my share of the money! That didn't go over too well. It was always the cash flow problem, because in reality all the money came from touring. There was no big money from albums because they never sold a *big* amount of albums and that's all there is to it. A gold album means nothing, because they probably spent most of that money before they got 'em. Towards the end, in the late Seventies. I could see the writing on the wall. I realised what was going on and had to do something about it. If you look on people who write songs, you have to ask do they have a life time of writing songs, or do they just have a few years? Paul Anka and Paul Simon will keep on writing good songs. But even they slow down. And most people only write a couple of albums which have one or two good songs if you're lucky. 'Roundabout' was a fantastic song but there were some lemons there and some copies! Jon wrote 'Harold Land' and another song that was almost identical and he didn't even know it."

As an old hand from the earliest days of the band, Tait has his own insight into what made Yes special. "They forgot the original Yes sound was a treatment. Just like you can play any song with a tango beat, you can play any song with a Yes treatment. A typical example would be 'America'. Everyone recognises their version has the Yes sound, but it's not their song. When they started writing songs they forgot the Yes treatment and they got confused about the two things – writing and treatment. *Topographic Oceans* was really just bits of tape from the bin that Eddie spliced together. I think he cut up the tape into one foot lengths and put it back together! They'd take a melody line from here and another from there and join them together. There was no cohesive force. There was no song that you could take to a publisher and say, 'This the top line of my song. This is the verse. This is the chorus.' You couldn't find that anywhere. It was like confused overture music. There was nothing there. It was background music – but in the foreground and that's because there was no cohesive writing. It was writing by committee. Two people can collaborate on a song, but I'm not sure you can have a committee write a song. Most songs have a germ of an idea that comes in a flash and then you work on it."

Michael Tait was not impressed by the arrival of The Buggles. "That was stupid. That was really, absolutely stupid. But economics had taken over everything. One could argue that things haven't changed. Put yourself in the situation of being a musician in what was once a big, successful band and things are falling apart. What do you do? Well you don't want to be a taxi driver. You want to keep playing music and making a living. So you do whatever needs doing. The days of saying, 'I'm only going to play what I want and I don't care about anything else' . . . those days are gone! You need to make a living. The reality is the band *should* have broken up and that should have been the end. That was the honest thing to do. But who could accept the alternative life?"

The problems had been brewing for some years, probably since *Topographic Oceans*. Put simply, when the band had been earning good money and Yes was still the 'big generator' they were happy to spend freely without compunction. They would be the first to admit they spent on luxury houses, cars and holidays. After all, they had worked hard for their success. The band members and their families grew accustomed to a jet-set lifestyle that became increasingly difficult to sustain. Yes as a business was still spending huge sums. Studio time and touring costs ate up their profits. They had to pay for flights, hotels, sound, lighting, artwork, scenery, instruments, trucking and wages for the crew. They also had a hungry manager, agent and promoters to support. The money they were spending was generated by album sales, publishing royalties, concert receipts and merchandise. When the band's record sales dipped in the late Seventies Yes found they had overspent. There were internal rows about who was being profligate and who should put some of the money back into the pot for more even distribution. Nobody wanted to put money back, especially when it had already been spent.

Even today the band find it hard to discuss these sensitive matters, except in the most oblique way. After all, when friends fall out and then make up, raking over the coals is an undesirable exercise. Rock musicians are notoriously sensitive about discussing their wealth and Yes are no exception, although some Yes men seem more prepared than others to discuss this issue, as is Brian Lane.

Lane has been criticised for his part in the financial confusion that afflicted Yes but he offers a version of events that sheds new light on the circumstances of Jon Anderson's departure. "All Yes' finances were handled by a firm of accountants," he emphasises. "I went round to see Jon after this row happened and Jon didn't really understand accounts and finance very well and to a certain extent neither did the rest of the band. They are musicians. They are not investment bankers. Basically, their accountant who shall remain nameless, would never say 'no' to Jon or his wife Jenny's needs. They obviously thought that there was a bottomless pit. The money would continue to be spent – more than his share. Even if he was aware of this, Jon in his own mind would rationalise it as 'I am the singer and the life of the band so in theory I am entitled to spend a bit

Various members of the group, sound crew and management personnel make up Yes United in 1976.
Top row, left to right: Nigel Luby, Ken Adams, Roy Clair, Barry Clair, Jim Halley, Mick Roth, Brian Lane,
Alan White and Jon Anderson; bottom: Jake Berry, Rick Wakeman, Paul Adams, Toby Ellington,
Nunu Whiting, John Martin. *(Scott Weiner)*

Buggles join Yes. The 1980 band that recorded *Drama*, left to right: Steve Howe, Geoff Downes,
Alan White, Chris Squire and Trevor Horn. *(Atlantic Records)*

Yes manager Brian Lane aboard the group's private jet. *(Jim Halley)*

Yes' first ever roadie Michael Tait, who would go on to become their lighting engineer. *(Jim Halley)*

Jim Halley, whose vegetarian food shop became a magnet for the group and who eventually became their tour manager. *(Jim Halley Collection)*

Patrick Moraz, Yes' Swiss-born keyboard player in the mid-Seventies. *(LFI)*

Geoff Downes (left) and Trevor Horn on stage with Yes in 1980. *(LFI)*

The revitalised mid-Eighties Yes with guitarist Trevor Rabin, and Tony Kaye and Jon Anderson back in the band.
Left to right: Kaye, Rabin, Chris Squire, Alan White and Anderson. *(LFI)*

Jon Anderson, vocals and incidental percussion, evidently pleased to be back where he belongs. *(LFI)*

Rick Wakeman and his wife Nina in 1984. *(LFI)*

100% Yes but not Yes at all: Wakeman, Anderson, Bruford and Howe in 1992.

25% Yes, 25% ELP, 25% King Crimson and 25% Buggles, Asia in 1982,
left to right: Steve Howe, Carl Palmer, John Wetton and Geoff Downes. *(LFI)*

The *Union* tour, 1991, left to right: Steve Howe, Trevor Rabin, Alan White, Jon Anderson, Bill Bruford, Rick Wakeman, Tony Kaye and, seated, Chris Squire. *(Jim Halley Collection)*

Four members of the Yes quintet that recorded *Talk* in 1994, left to right: Jon Anderson, Tony Kaye, Trevor Rabin and Chris Squire. *(LFI)*

Yes in 1998, still touring and releasing albums 30 years after their inception, left to right: Billy Sherwood, Steve Howe, Jon Anderson, Chris Squire, Alan White and Igor Khoroshev. *(Eagle Records)*

The Old Firm: Jon Anderson, Chris Squire, Rick Wakeman, Steve Howe and Alan White. *(Brian Rasic)*

more'. But a democracy doesn't quite work like that. In any case they were all buying big houses. It wasn't just Jon.

"The thing is, if they had worked to capacity they could have covered their needs. Frankly, all they had to do was add a few more dates onto a tour. I said to Jon: 'I'll try and sort this out. We'll put a few more dates on the tour, you give up your share to the band and you'll be sorted.' He said that was fine. But nobody wanted to know and he was a bit pissed off. Jon and I fell out over this. He may have thought I supported the other side. Well I didn't. I was the piggy in the middle."

Studying veiled references, it is possible to gain a broader understanding. The main difference of opinion – as far as financial matters were concerned – seems to have been between Steve Howe and Jon Anderson. Howe was a relatively frugal man whose sole extravagance was his ever increasing collection of guitars (which in the fullness of time would turn out to be a very wise investment). Anderson's carefree attitude evidently rankled. If hard evidence of the ill feeling between them is hard to come by, consider this: after their parting of the ways this particular pair of Yes men who were once so close would not perform together again for 11 years, until 1989 and the formation of the short lived quasi-Yes group Anderson, Bruford, Wakeman & Howe.

But that was a long way into the future. Back in 1979, Chris Squire refused to accept that Yes was over, even if his original partner in the band thought otherwise. The tall bass player would fight on.

185

8

DRAMA

When Jon Anderson and Rick Wakeman quit Yes in March, 1980, Jon was already heavily involved with the Greek composer and keyboard player Vangelis Papathanassiou. Rick, of course, had been running a parallel career almost since the day he joined Yes. Anderson hadn't been on his own since the birth of the band and going out alone might prove a nerve-wracking experience. However it held out the promise of peace and independence. Who needed that ungrateful band and their endless arguments? Now he was free to face the challenges of a new decade without interference!

In February that year Jon & Vangelis were greatly encouraged when they hit the UK singles chart with 'I Hear You Now'. Their album *Short Stories* was also doing brisk business. Jon and Vangelis would also record two further albums, *The Friends Of Mr. Cairo* and *Private Collection*. Vangelis, born Evangelos Papathanassiou on March 29, 1943, in Valos, Greece, had formed the group Aphrodite's Child in France with Demis Roussos in 1968. He would enjoy a huge hit in 1982 with the instrumental theme 'Chariots Of Fire' from the Academy Award winning movie, which topped charts around the world.

Jon also cut two solo albums between 1980 and 1983, respectively titled *Song Of Seven* and *Animation*. He also wrote music for a ballet company and won a San Remo Festival prize for his collaboration with poet Andre Verdet. Jon's new found solo status surely signalled that Yes was now an ex-group. Peter Banks' joke 'See, you are nothing without me!' seemed to be holding true. Yet the old group was only biding its time.

In May 1980 came the astonishing announcement that two rising young musicians known to the pop world as The Buggles would join Yes. The reaction was swift. As one American writer put it, in rhetorical terms: "How dare these two hack purveyors of ear-candy defile a band of Yes' legendary status!"

Trevor Horn would take over Jon Anderson's time honoured role as lead singer. His partner Geoff Downes would replace Rick Wakeman on keyboards. Yes fans were stunned. Some were outraged. But it was not as daft as it sounded. Geoffrey was a brilliant, classically trained musician with a wide range of experience. Trevor was a bass player and singer, who was also a long standing Yes fan and budding record producer. The pair would leave their mark on the music industry in a variety of unexpected ways over the coming years.

These Buggles would find their stint with Yes a mixed blessing, but like all who came in contact with the band at various stages of development, it was a period of unforgettable excitement, nervous activity and intense challenge. As each started out on their individual musical careers, hoping and dreaming of success in the future, they could hardly have imagined quite how it would all turn out, or that the mystical band that had been an inspiration since their teens would play such a direct role in their lives.

Like many of the players drawn to Yes Geoffrey Downes, born in Stockport, Greater Manchester, in August 1952, came from a musical family and had impressive early musical training. His father was a church organist and his mother was a piano teacher. She taught him his five finger exercises and later he studied with Manchester Cathedral's organist. He bought his first Hammond organ at the age of 16 intending to play it solely at home. He would later take this same rumbling piece of 'furniture' – as such instruments are referred to in the trade – around the world on tour with Yes.

He went to Leeds College of Music in 1972 to study classical, jazz and light music for three years. "I did the course because they concentrated more on modern music," says Geoff. While at Leeds he studied the work of jazz-rock keyboard player Herbie Hancock. For more practical experience he also joined a local student group called She's French, which gained a short-lived national reputation for originality. Having completed his college studies in 1975, Downes moved to London at the age of 20, where he quickly worked his way into the music business. He wrote jingles for TV commercials as well as playing with club bands to pay the rent.[19]

"We used to play things like 'Viva España' in the famous Roy Carter Band!" he recalls, "all lashed together as a finale, which Roy the sax player used to refer to as 'a cavalcade of crap'. He was a very funny guy! At that time I was doing sessions and jingles to make a living. I also started getting interest in some of the songs I was writing and got a publishing deal with April Music. That's where I met up with Trevor Horn."

[19] The author played drums with Geoff when he was playing organ at a pub gig with Roy Carter in Penge, South London, in the mid-Seventies.

Trevor's previous experience included playing bass in the resident dance band at the Hammersmith Palais. The pair hit it off and began making disco records together. They also played in the backing band for singer Tina Charles, along with guitarist Bruce Woolley. Geoff: "Trevor was actually going out with Tina at the time and he had the job of putting the band together. We played on some of her later singles like 'Dance Little Lady'. We toured with her for about a year until she stopped gigging and Trevor and myself thought we'd carry on doing our own thing. That's how we started The Buggles."

At first Geoff, Trevor and Bruce wrote material together, hoping to find a way out of the pubs and clubs and into the charts. Bruce subsequently left the team to form his own band while the other two continued to work together. They landed a deal with Island Records where astute label boss Chris Blackwell quickly spotted their potential and paid for them to spend three months in the studios working on just one track 'Video Killed The Radio Star'. Released as a single under the name of The Buggles it became one of the most talked about hits of 1979.

The catchy theme and hook phrase seemed to epitomise the transformation of the music scene, as new technology came in and old stars were replaced by new faces and even machines. "It was originally called The Bugs," says Geoff explaining their odd choice of name. "The Bugs were studio insects – imaginary creatures who lived in recording studios causing havoc. Then somebody said as a joke that The Bugs would never be as big as The Beatles. So we changed it to The Buggles."

'Video Killed The Radio Star' hit number one in the UK and got to number 40 in the US in 1979. The video of the song was premiered on MTV's first show in January, 1981. Their album *The Age Of Plastic* was also a Top Thirty hit in 1980 and included another hit single 'The Plastic Age'.

"It was quite an exciting period," says Geoff. "We were also in-house producers at Island so we were doing quite a lot of other bands. We did a few bits and pieces on our own under different guises but The Buggles was the first one we were serious about. Trevor sang the lead on 'Video Star' through a Vox AC 30 amplifier. When it was a hit everything went crazy and we were on *Top Of The Pops* and loads of other TV shows. The record did well initially in the States and then for some reason it petered out. Although the record came out in 1979 it had an Eighties theme, that's for sure."

Many predicted a bright future for the inventive pair, but later singles never quite matched the impact of 'Video'. Then coincidence and chance meetings led the upcoming Buggles to their unexpected liaison with the elder statesmen of rock. Says Geoff, "Because we were managed by Brian Lane, Chris Squire heard bits of our album *Age Of Plastic*. He had a mate in

American radio, a guy called Lee Abrahams who was a big Yes aficionado. He advised Chris that The Buggles was the direction Yes should be going. I think they all took that idea a bit too seriously."

Squire was particularly keen that The Buggles should become co-opted into Yes as part of his plan to keep the band alive. Chris: "It just so happened that Geoff Downes and Trevor Horn had come to Brian Lane and asked him to represent them for management, so they were in our office. We said, 'Why not get together with us then?' Trevor Horn kept saying to me, 'I can't possibly fill Jon Anderson's shoes.' I used to keep telling him, 'Yes you can, yes you can!' I'd tell him to go away and sleep on it and then he'd come back to me and say, 'You know, you're wrong. I can't do this!' Later on in life he actually thanked me for getting him to try. It gave him a lot of confidence which allowed him to go on and become a hugely successful producer."

Trevor later said, "I agreed to do it as I'd never get a chance like that again in my life. But what clinched it was when Chris said, 'Haven't you got the bottle to do it?' "

Alan White remembers the atmosphere of confusion that reigned during this period. "Everybody had gone their separate ways to do solo albums to get the excess material out of their systems. Then Jon went off on his own solo career for a while. Steve Howe and myself and Chris were left with a rehearsal room booked and we said, 'Well whoever turns up is in the band!' So that was the beginning of our period with Trevor Horn and The Buggles. They were in the next studio and they were big fans of the band. We were rehearsing for a new album and they came in and said they had a song for us. Within two days they had moved their equipment in and that was the new version of Yes. We ended up writing new material and doing a new album called *Drama*. But Trevor didn't feel he matched up to what Jon did on stage, singing things like 'And You And I'. In fact we went down very well when we did three nights at Madison Square Garden during what was a very successful tour. He just felt he couldn't match what Jon used to do."

Chris Squire looks back on it all with his customary cool demeanour. "The famous Buggles period with Geoff Downes and Trevor Horn coming in . . . was a bit confusing for everybody, especially as we already had a huge tour of the States that had already been booked and sold out before Jon and Rick had left. Brian Lane, in his wise way, said, 'Don't tell anyone we've changed the singer and the keyboard player!' So we just showed up and there were like two different people in the band and the audiences were saying, 'What's going on?' So that was a little bit of a tricky time. Of course we had just made the *Drama* album with Trevor and Geoff prior to that tour and we were very rushed doing that. It actually turned out to be a very good album but we could have done with a little bit more time. We were working 18 hour days to get that finished before we had to do the tour."

When Brian Lane and Chris brokered a deal to bring Geoff and Trevor into Yes the news proved immensely puzzling to the outside world. Buggles fans thought they had sold out by siding with the old guard. Many Yes fans couldn't accept these merchants of techno pop invading their territory. Only a few thought they might inject new ideas and were prepared to listen. The vast bulk of fans, particularly in America weren't even aware of the changes, until confronted with a new line-up when they arrived for their scheduled 1980 tour.

Geoff and Trevor were excited but apprehensive. "The situation was that Anderson had left and Wakeman wasn't going to do it without Anderson," recalls Geoff. "When we met the guys they were just record-ing stuff as a three piece at the Town House studios. They were obviously looking for a singer and a keyboard player. Brian Lane said, 'They haven't got much material – can you guys write a song for them?' So we wrote this song called 'We Can Fly From Here'. We did a demo with Chris Squire and Bill Bruford, funnily enough, because Chris wanted to do something with Bill. We carried on for a while and then they asked us to join the band. Bill wasn't in the band though, he'd only come in for the demo."

It was pretty clear to Geoff and Trevor that the surviving members of Yes – Chris, Steve and Alan – were still in a state of shock. "They were confused . . . that's why a lot of people were suggesting directions for them at that time. It was okay doing stuff as a three piece, but a band like Yes is song-orientated. It was largely Chris' idea to swell the ranks again. Jon had left because he was engrossed in the Jon & Vangelis thing and that was taking up a lot of his time. The mood was also pretty bad because the previous album *Tormato* really got slammed and didn't do very well at all. It was their worst album in terms of the career of the band. They were just looking to revamp the whole picture really. Once we had written a song we went in the studio and started working with them and it kind of went from there."

After the official announcement that Geoff and Trevor were joining Yes, the band and their manager had to convince Atlantic Records that the new line-up would be viable. Ahmet Ertegun flew from the States to London to check out the situation and he gave his seal of approval.

Within a few months of the shake-up Yes recorded and released *Drama*. Geoff: "The band had a few tracks they'd written before we arrived and Trevor and I had two which we brought to the party. Then we vamped up a few more. In the event it was only a six track album but it did very well. It was called *Drama* because the situation was so dramatic. Eddie Offord

came in to do the album to start with and then he left in strange circumstances. It was a fraught, manic time. Yes have more crazy moments
than the average rock band. They can be very tense – very self-centred.
They had been a very big band in America and lived their lives in an
extreme way. They all had their own limos and in 1979 they were still
very much buried in that 1970s rock-star-with-a-big-house image. This
was the way these bands had built their lives and it affected them. If you've
come from humble origins, money kind of unsettles you."

Tour manager and faithful servant Jim Halley was still in attendance as
the band began work on the new album at SARM East studios in Commercial Road, near London's Tower Bridge. "We recorded quite a bit of it
there and I remember we had four or five recording studios on the go in
London. I was going from one studio to the next delivering two inch
tapes, so Steve Howe could do his overdubs in Chalk Farm while Chris
was doing his at the Town House and the others were working at SARM.
It was tough going."

At SARM East Trevor Horn could be seen desperately writing the lyrics
for a song that everyone was waiting for with bated tape recorders. "I can
remember Trevor walking around reception thinking of lyrics and then
going in and singing them hot from the note pad. He was under a great
deal of stress and I had great respect for the work he put into *Drama* and
how he coped with that whole situation, taking over from Jon. He did
extremely well considering there was already an American tour booked. It
was a daunting task for him but he coped admirably."

Geoff: "The album was a lot more song orientated and helped shift the
band towards a new generation of fans. They showed we weren't just
locked in the Seventies' stuff. Yes had a new sound, which was despised
by some and accepted by others."

Astonishingly, given the outrage expressed at the changes of personnel
and the hostility of the music press, the album went straight to number 2
in the UK charts and 18 in the US. It came complete with a striking new
Roger Dean cover. Says Roger, "After that I didn't actually have much to
do with Yes during the Eighties because I was working with Steve Howe's
new band Asia. It's interesting because Asia didn't want to look like Yes so
I did something completely different for them. Yes went off in a completely different direction too with a very cool cover for their next album
which was *90125*."

Drama is perhaps one of the band's most neglected albums and yet it
contains elements of both traditional Yes values expertly blended with
a highly organised, more contemporary approach. This is revealed on
the driving opening number 'Machine Messiah' which has unexpectedly
heavy metal guitar work from Steve Howe. Divided into three parts

'Machine Messiah' has exceptionally tight and hard hitting drum play from Alan while Steve, Geoff Downes and Chris Squire spin around each other in a giddy romp before crashing out into the grinding metal theme. The lyrics are crisper, more direct and less complicated and Trevor sings them with charm and sincerity. Oddly enough, certain eerie moments here sound like elements from *The Ipcress File*, Michael Caine's famous spy movie. But generally this tour de force shows Geoffrey well suited to taking over the Yes keyboard role. The vocals, too, are excellent on 'White Car' and the echoing 'Does It Really Happen?' The most original and unusual track is 'Into The Lens' predicated on the hook line "*I am a camera*". There are echoes of early Genesis in some of the staccato, angular themes contrasted by musical box interludes, but it remains a remarkable piece of work. Apart from the sprightly vocal sections it is interesting to hear how the keyboards, bass, guitar and drums work in common cause. They deliver the tricky theme without trying to battle for space. This is ego-less Yes music, yet even at this distance in time it still sounds surreal, like a surrogate Yes; wonderful to behold, but what were we to make of it all? What price loyalty? It was clearly a problem for certain sections of the band's audience when they went on tour.

The remaining highlights of *Drama* included the Sting influenced 'Run Through The Light', notable for its clipped beat and warbling synthesiser effects. 'Tempus Fugit' has Chris working overtime on the bass and the organ kicks in over a driving Police style beat. It's remarkably attractive theme has some of the band's best unison playing, with Downes in particular playing with all the speed and dexterity of his illustrious predecessors.

Phil Carson was watching developments closely. "The album did well and most of the tour dates sold out before anyone knew that Jon had left the band. The interesting point was who owned the rights to the name. But there was never a fight over it. You can't stop anybody else working. If you try and pass something off that it isn't — well that's against the law. Providing you are up front there's no problem. So a few people in the band have changed. So what!"

In September 1980 the band, fronted by Trevor Horn, would play three sold out nights at New York's Madison Square Garden as part of a lengthy US and Canadian tour. It showed the continuing power of Yes music to win hearts and minds. Even so, many of their oldest American friends were puzzled by the turn of events. Says sound man Roy Clair, "They went through what all bands go through . . . politics. First it was the keyboard people leaving and then Jon and Chris weren't seeing eye to eye. There were so many changes people started getting tired of the whole thing. When you start substituting lead singers for Jon Anderson then the people get confused!"

Before the tour the new boys had to learn the set. Says Geoffrey, "I remember all the stuff was drawn from earlier albums. It wasn't even from the Wakeman era. There was a lot of stuff from *Time And A Word* and *The Yes Album*. We played a few tracks from *Fragile* and *Close To The Edge*. There was a lot from the Tony Kaye era and we had to learn it all from the records. There was nothing written because none of the members could read music. That's very surprising when you think it's a band with incredibly high standards that plays very complex music. Yet there was nothing ever written down. I just listened to the records on headphones and tried to 'vibe' my way through. It wasn't as hard as you might imagine."

Geoff's style was largely built on the kind of progressive rock that Yes pioneered and he could quickly pick up on their arrangements. Trevor Horn, too, had a great pair of 'ears' and was a huge fan of Yes. He had been ever since he had first heard the group playing live at a concert in the early Seventies. So far from being the alien outsiders, the duo were admirably suited to the task. In the studio all worked well. But when they hit the road there were problems.

The biggest hurdle was that Trevor Horn was expected to sing like Jon Anderson. This resulted in immense personal pressure. His voice was similar in some respects, although he is quick to deny this. There was also an image problem. He didn't dress like Jon Anderson and he looked uneasy hiding behind dark glasses. He was understandably nervous and this feeling was communicated to audiences.

Geoff: "It was more difficult for Trevor going out on the road than it was for me, because he had to fill Jon Anderson's shoes. Trevor, in all honesty, wasn't that kind of front man and he got panned quite a lot, although it wasn't so bad in America. It was only on the English leg of the tour that there was a bit more resentment, particularly in the press."

Says Steve Howe, "The two failings in that version of Yes were that when we came on stage people were quite disappointed that the Jon Anderson larynx wasn't there and that old twiddly fingers Wakeman wasn't there either. But we went to America and somehow did a blinding tour! We walked in everywhere and seemed to slay them. We did three days at Madison Square Garden in New York with this hodge-podge version of Yes. It was quite an experiment but it seemed to come off. When we came to England we couldn't make it work. There were certain elements that were way out of sync. I remember talking to Trevor Horn in Newcastle and saying, 'Just imagine this is your dream come true – you are playing and singing in Yes. Just go on and enjoy yourself.' So he looked at me and said, 'Don't you think I've tried everything to make it work for those people?' It wasn't that Trevor had any shortcomings. He was an amazingly talented writer, producer, singer and bass player. But when you put people under undue pressure like that . . . replacing Jon Anderson, writing all the lyrics for an album, virtually producing it because Eddie Offord only did the backing tracks – the guy had lead boots on.

"Meanwhile the audiences in England were shouting out 'Jon Anderson – we want Jon!' And then they shouted 'We want Rick!' usually at the most crucial moment. They really did it to us on that tour. One of the worst places was Lewisham in South London and the other was Brighton when we got a grilling from the audience. It wasn't like it all the time, but there were people who were being unkind to Trevor. And it's a long way when you have to go up those steps and onto a stage. I guess the people shouting out had paid to see a show. But if they were expecting it to be like the old days they were mistaken.

"We did have a whole new album, none of which was written by Jon or Rick. We thought we were going out on those terms, but of course we weren't. We were going out with a history and with expectations."

Says Chris, "A lot of Yes fans who came to see the shows with Trevor singing thought it was really good. They actually enjoyed the change. But I am sure there were an equal number who looked forward to seeing Jon and Rick and were disappointed. It was hard to know what to do really. We had the tour ready which was sold out. We could have told audiences they might want to take their tickets back because the band had changed, or just go ahead and do it, and see what happened. So we opted to do that. It didn't really get too much bad press, as it happens. Punk rock had come in while we were doing our mega tours of America. It was a good thing for the evolution of music as a whole but it wasn't the best thing that could have happened to us at that point. But we managed to weather that storm, like many other bands, including Genesis. There were enough music fans out there to carry on supporting us. I liked a lot of the punk rock stuff myself."

Says Geoff, "Both myself and Trevor Horn were fans of Yes and there were some good moments during the US tour, like playing at Madison Square Garden. But I always felt I was kind of filling in on a high level session gig."

★ ★ ★

Suggest to Trevor Horn that actually playing and singing with the band he once loved must have been a dream come true and he snaps: "It was more like a nightmare come true!" Today Horn is one of Britain's most success- ful and respected record producers with a string of hits behind him. Famed for his work with Frankie Goes To Hollywood and their ground breaking dance hits 'Relax' and 'Two Tribes', Trevor has also worked extensively with ABC, Dollar, Grace Jones and the singer Seal, who is signed to Horn's own ZTT label, as was Frankie. He was born in Durham on July 15, 1949, and like so many others who became involved with Yes came from a musical family. His father was a professional double bass player who taught his son to play the instrument, and though Trevor subsequently joined a local youth orchestra he soon began gigging on bass guitar with semi-pro rock bands. At the same time he began taking an interest in studios and sound-recording techniques. He helped to build a recording studio in Leicester but before it was complete he moved to London where he found work as a session musician. The Buggles were formed after he met Geoff Downes.

Trevor Horn is usually reluctant to talk about his period as the lead singer and producer of Yes as it brings back painful memories. He became seriously disenchanted with both the business and managerial aspects of the band. However he still has great respect for Yes music and remains fond of the musicians who called him up in their hour of need nearly twenty years ago. "I was an utter fan," he confesses. "I read about them in the music press first." Then came an event in unlikely circumstances which fully converted him to Yes music.

"I remember it happened in a pub in Margate. I took some LSD one weekend and went to this pub where groups played. A group called Tristram Shandy came on and played a song with lots of changes. It was called 'Your Move'. I said to the girl I was with, 'That's fantastic. What a brilliant song.' The girl said, 'That's by a group called Yes. You'd like them. They've got a good bass player.' On Monday I went out and bought *The Yes Album* and more or less played it non-stop for months. It just blew me away. The bass player was fantastic and I also really liked the singer. What surprised me was it was poppy in one sense, because it was tuneful. I was playing in bands myself at this time and I'd been a professional musician for four years. I had started out in dance bands, but I'd never heard a group that was as musical as Yes. If you are a musician you can tell if somebody knows what they are doing. It was very different to the normal run of the mill thing. And the bass playing was wonderful. To this day I haven't heard bass playing to turn me on like that."

All through the Seventies Trevor Horn remained "a huge fan" of Yes and went to see them play on the *Yesterdays* tour of 1975 when Patrick Moraz was in the line-up. "It was one of my all time favourite concerts. I thought they were terrific."

Trevor loved the *Relayer* album. When it came out he was having to drive to Birmingham four nights a week for a regular gig and then drive back home in his Robin Reliant van. He would play the latest Yes album all the way. "I used to love 'Gates Of Delirium'. It was great when you were driving a very noisy three wheeler van! In the very early Seventies when I was building a recording studio up in Leicester, every day I used to play *Tales From Topographic Oceans* to warm up the room. When you are working with a drill every day, putting up stuff, it's great to have a long album to play. So I was the most abject, pathetic Yes fan! I really did like them a lot. I loved *Going For The One* as well, particularly 'Turn Of The Century' which I thought was a lovely track."

But Trevor started to lose interest in Yes towards the end of the Seventies. "*Tormato* I hated. I just hated it and in a way I had kind of written them off. What happened was the songs were no good anymore. Whoever was writing the main themes had run out of steam. The songs were pretty crap and a bit stupid. 'Don't Kill The Whale – dig it, dig it?' No I didn't get that. Times were changing and at that point in time I thought, 'Well, that's the end of them.' I wouldn't have bought another Yes album – unless circumstances hadn't made me bump into them."

The Buggles/Yes connection might never have come about had not Trevor's wife Jill Sinclair reasoned that he should have a manager. Trevor: "For some reason she thought Brian Lane would be a good one. We now had the same manager as Yes and I was very curious to meet the band to see what they were like, as I'd been such a huge fan. It's funny, when you get a hit record it's suddenly like getting a diploma. Everybody talks to you and wants to be nice to you. It's like getting membership to the club. People don't have to worry about you hitting on them. So having had a big hit with The Buggles I was able to be friendly with everybody."

Trevor was curious to see what Yes were actually like. "The first guy I met was Chris Squire and he was the one I liked the most in the band. As I got to know him I was invited to his house and he said he liked the production on our record. I told him I had a song for Yes. That's what I'd thought had been so bad about their previous album . . . the songs. I played him this song called 'We Can Fly From Here' which we never really recorded, although there is a 'live' tape around somewhere. He really liked it and said, 'You sound a bit like Jon Anderson.' The thing is I *don't* sound a bit like Jon Anderson. He's got a much higher voice than me, at least three tones higher than mine. I was a record producer. I could just sing a bit . . . that's all."

Trevor was pleased at all the sudden interest in his work. But he didn't actually know when he played his song to Chris Squire that Jon Anderson had left the group. "That was because they had fallen out over money. They had this stupid business arrangement where nobody knew what the other one was doing. That's the way it operated. Suddenly the records stopped selling. It's alright if you've got a great big bin full of gold coins.

Every day people go to the bin, dip in and get a few gold coins – right? Then your records stop selling and there's only a few gold coins left in the bin. So everyone starts arguing. 'Ere, you had more than me! You've got to pay some of it back!' Getting a rock star to pay back the money he's had is as difficult as getting Bill Clinton to keep his trousers done up. Those guys live large and they spend large and boy do they get mean if they have to give some of it back! Immediately you've got the beginning of this huge bitterness. 'How could you say that to me, after I gave you parts of all those songs that made you a fortune?' "

Trevor believes that the underlying reason for Jon Anderson's abrupt departure was his anger over all the rows and accusations. "This was what had happened, and I didn't know any of that when I came along. I was just a starry eyed, naïve little Yes fan from the Seventies. Then suddenly Chris Squire is saying to me, 'Why don't you join the band and do this tour?' The reality was the tour had been sold out and the money was in the bank. The money had probably already been spent and they had *got* to put on a show and make an album. So me and Geoffrey were a kind of lifeline. It meant they could hold on to the money and something could happen."

And so this was how Trevor Horn found himself the lead singer in Yes, the band he had always loved and facing audiences who didn't always love him. The gruelling *Drama* tour began in Canada and reached its dramatic conclusion in Britain. The first date, at Maple Leaf Garden, Toronto, Ontario on August 29, 1980, was followed by the Forum, Montreal, Quebec (30). The US dates started on September 1 at Hartford, Connecticut. They played Madison Square Garden, New York on September 4, 5 and 6. These three dates took on special significance. They completed a run of 16 sold out performances at Madison Square which Yes had begun on February 18, 1974. The band was presented with a commemorative certificate which proclaimed that these sell outs were 'The most in Garden history!' They played the Philadelphia Spectrum on September 12 and 13. The tour continued across the States throughout September and October. The 23-date UK tour began at Bristol Hippodrome on November 16 and finished at London's Rainbow Theatre on December 17 and 18.

Among those working behind the scenes on this uneasy tour were many old faces and friends, including Roy Clair as supervising engineer, Nigel Luby as sound engineer, Michael Tait as lighting designer and Jim Halley as personal manager. The band's manager Brian Lane was assisted by Sandy Campbell and Phil Straight and secretary Fiona Sanders-Reece. Helping with the band's equipment were Nu Nu Whiting, Richard Davis, Stuart Young, J.J. and Claude Johnson-Taylor. For them it was another round of dashing from point A to point B with frequent cries of "Hurry up and wait!" the slogan most heard in the Army or on the road with a rock band. For the crew it was just like old times. For the musicians it was a nervous ordeal as they waited to find out if the fans still wanted them.

Says Brian Lane, "So we did this tour of America with Trevor Horn doing the lead vocals. For Trevor Horn to make his début on stage at the Maple Leaf Garden in Toronto was something even Elvis Presley hadn't done. We got away with it in places where the dates were sold out, such was the strength of the Yes cult, which was even more frustrating. But when we got to the places where they knew about the changes, whereas before we were used to playing to 20,000 people, only 3,000 people showed up."

Says Jim, "Trevor was very nervous before that Toronto gig, but they went down well because in North America they loved Yes. It didn't seem to matter that Trevor was there. It was only when we came to Europe and did the UK that Trevor came under pressure. During the quiet bits people would be shouting 'Get off – we want Jon' which must have been rather daunting."

The band battled on but the strain was immense. Says Trevor Horn, "The idea of sticking somebody who was a second rate singer, who was really a producer, up front in a band like Yes and sending them out on a 44-date tour of America playing every song in the original key was ludicrous. In three or four days I was absolutely knackered. I couldn't talk. I had to whisper. The opening note in the set was a B and the highest note I can sing is a B. The minute you get tired your upper and lower register goes. So if you say it was 'like a dream come true' it was certainly a fascinating experience. Considering what they had to put up with the audiences were pretty nice to me. Occasionally people would shout 'wanker' and 'fuck off'. But I understood. I wasn't bearing them a grudge. I was a big Jon Anderson fan too. I was in a very odd situation but by and large the Yes audiences were very nice to me."

Once the tour was over Trevor soon found he had more to worry about than losing his voice and suffering from loudmouth hecklers. "When I came back I had to do something quick, 'cos I was broke! During the whole of that year I earned ten thousand dollars and that was given to me in cash on a plane." Trevor states that his wages for the 44-date tour of America should have been around £14,000. But he was advised he couldn't have the full amount as there was no money left in the tour. "Why was there no money? Because people had flown out their children and their nannies first class and put it on the tour. People had even paid their mortgages from the tour. Meanwhile I was asked to sign a document to pay $25,000 towards the cost of the production. So I said, 'Let me get this straight. The production costs $125,000. So what am I getting for my $25,000? What part of the stage will I own? Do I own any of it? Who owns the stage? Oh . . . Yes owns the stage?' Well I refused to sign that document."

The Yes wives enjoyed being with the band on the road. Some were there for the shopping. Others took a keen interest in the band's business affairs. Jim Halley, the ever busy tour manager, had to look after the orchestra wives and cope with the distractions they might inadvertently cause. "The wives used to come over to the States and that used to be a nightmare for me because they'd all go off shopping in the afternoon of a gig at Madison Square Garden. I daren't leave my hotel room and had to have extra lines put in so I could keep in touch with the limousine companies to find out where each member of the group was, what they were doing and whether they would get to the gig on time! Some of the wives didn't speak to each other. But you can't love everybody you have to be with. Just because you are forced to work with people it doesn't mean you have to like them. But generally everybody got on, and we'd have parties and receptions where everyone would dance and have some fun together. The whole period I was involved with Yes I saw many rows and arguments but never any violence."

It got close at times. Trevor Horn remembers being in a hotel room in New York, unable to speak because he was trying to rest his voice for the Madison Square Garden show. "I heard my wife Jill saying to Brian Lane, 'I know what you've been doing and you're not going to do it to my husband! Don't think you can pull the wool over my eyes like you have with all these schmucks in this band.' That was the flip side of the dream come true. I'm not saying Brian wasn't instrumental in getting them going and I'm not saying he isn't good to have dinner with, because he can be very funny. He's also very expensive."

Brian Lane says that US tour was not a big money earner. "When we got to the end of the tour the band came out making a very small profit. We didn't lose money. But somehow or other I seemed to end up taking the blame for this situation. The band blamed me for not making the tour happen. Anyway we came back to London and I then got a visit from Trevor Horn, Jill Sinclair and Geoff Downes. They announced that they were firing me as the manager of The Buggles. I said, 'Why?' They said for the past few months I had been neglecting the band and had been on tour with Yes. I said, 'Hold on a second. Didn't I see Trevor and Geoff every single day of the week for the past three months?' And I'd been on the telephone acting for them and I'd had this guy working for me called Phil Straight who had done a fantastic promotional job getting 'Video Killed The Radio Star' played on the radio all over Europe. But I think it was a ploy on Jill's part. She was about to make her move to become a rock'n'roll entrepreneur. Okay . . . so they left. A couple of weeks later I got a call from Chris Squire and the whole band came round to see me. Chris said, 'We've all had a meeting and we've decided that enough is enough and we've decided to fire you as the manager of Yes.'"

Brian was taken aback but decided to offer them some parting advice. "I said okay, fine, if that's the way it is. Yes have peaked so it's a good time to get off the boat. But let me give you some advice. If you are going to continue as Yes, can I suggest that you get down on your hands and knees, kiss Jon Anderson's feet and beg him to return to the band. So Trevor Horn says, 'Well, what am I supposed to do?' I said, 'Why don't you become a fucking record producer?' Chris Squire says to me, 'Making dumb remarks like that is one of the reasons we're firing you.' So they all left but Steve Howe and Geoff Downes must have agreed with my thoughts because a few weeks later they were back in the office with John Wetton and we formed the embryo of Asia. Then Carl Palmer joined the band and suddenly I had the first corporate rock band of the Eighties. Then eventually the other guys did reform Yes and they *did* kiss Jon Anderson's feet, he did rejoin and Trevor Horn produced the record!"

Touché.

* * *

Trevor Horn found his whole involvement with Yes a very odd experience. "It was even odder that I should end up producing *90125* with them after all that, which was their biggest selling album. It happened I suppose really because of Chris Squire. Anything that happened with me and Yes happened because of him. I have a lot of affection for Chris and I've always stayed friends with Steve Howe who I like a lot. In fact he played a bit on the Frankie Goes To Hollywood records. I adore Trevor Rabin too, even though I still prefer the Seventies' Yes."

After the *Drama* tour, by January 1981 when the latest recruits planned to defect, the Yes saga seemed to be finally at rest. Rumours of their demise began to sweep the music business. The Yes office issued a press release saying, 'There is no question of the band splitting.' The statement was memorably derided by Pete Frame in his Family Tree chart of Yes antecedents: 'Arrant bollocks. It was all over.'

Says Geoff Downes, "By the time we'd done the UK tour at the end of 1980 the word was . . . 'Is this going to work? Shall we carry on and do another album?' The general consensus was 'No!' After that it all kind of fell apart."

Steve Howe recalls that after the *Drama* tour the band went into limbo for three months. "We began to wonder 'Is this going to hold together?' 'Is Trevor going to produce. Is he going to leave?' 'Where does Jimmy Page fit into this!' The rumours were flying."

Indeed Geoff Downes and Chris Squire *had* started working with Jimmy Page on a short lived project. When that fell through Trevor Horn and Geoff started work on another Buggles album. By January 1981 Steve Howe decided he had had enough. He was out of the band and began looking for employment elsewhere. With the redoubtable Brian Lane as his manager he set about forming a new band to be called Asia with John Wetton, singer, bass player, composer and veteran of such bands as King Crimson, Roxy Music and UK.[20]

Howe and Wetton were the prime movers in Asia, their clear intention to make the band a logical successor to Yes. They would, however, take a simpler, more commercial approach, with emphasis on songs and as their drummer Carl Palmer would say, playing the beat 'four on the floor'. Geoff Downes joined on keyboards and they were managed by Brian Lane. Later, around 1985, Steve would leave Asia and form the group GTR with fellow progressive axeman Steve Hackett, a veteran of Genesis.

It was Brian Lane who actually came up with the name Asia. Much to their satisfaction, and despite the direst predictions of industry buffs, Asia was a big success. Their March 1982 début album topped the US charts for two months. They also scored a Top Ten hit single with 'Heat Of The Moment' and their next album *Alpha* was a palpable success during 1983. Steve Howe was able to experience the joy of having a second career away from Yes that could match and even beat the achievements of his old Yes colleagues Jon and Rick.

Asia would prove to be a welcome home for these able-bodied rock musicians, all still in the prime of life and anxious to carry on playing. They could work in an organised, productive and less stressful environment. They were tired of being shunted around in self-destruct mode and wanted to get on with their musical lives. Asserts Geoff, "We really felt positive about it and I certainly felt more comfortable as I didn't have to fill the shoes of somebody else. It was actually my own band and I could be myself."

Jim Halley, who had worked for Yes for so many years, now found himself involved in the creation of the new group. "Jon Anderson went off and did the Eighties Yes with Trevor Rabin, whilst I went off with Steve Howe and Geoff Downes to work in Asia with John Wetton and Carl Palmer. I co-ordinated that whole thing. The first drummer was going to be Simon Phillips. We were also looking for singers at one stage. We had people in like Robert Berry from the States and we even had Roy

---

[20] UK had at one stage included ex-Yes man Bill Bruford on drums, together with Allan Holdsworth on guitar and Eddie Jobson on keyboards.

Wood from The Move. He came down to try out for the singing job but John Wetton eventually became the singer. We recorded the album with producer Mike Stone who had worked with Foreigner. The first Asia album was incredibly successful. It became the biggest selling album in the United States on *Billboard* by a début band. They were all 'known artists' but they were a new band. We booked a small theatre tour of America after going to Michael Tait and Roy Clair's place to rehearse and we noticed that the album had gone in at number 28, much to everyone's shock. We went on the road and found we were selling out all the theatres, so we had to go back and tour all the stadiums and arenas. We were at number one in *Billboard* for eight weeks with the Asia album so we were all very excited. But we all travelled on buses this time. Private jets had become too expensive!"

Nobody was happier in the new band Asia than their star guitarist Steve Howe. So it was a hideous shock for him to discover in the summer of 1983 that his past was coming back to haunt him. Yes suddenly announced they were getting back together – with a bright new guitar player called Trevor Rabin. When asked what he thought of these developments Steve responded, "It's one big ugh!"

★　★　★

Strange things had been going on since April 1981 when it was generally believed that Yes had 'officially' broken up. Yet the remaining members, who now numbered only Chris Squire and Alan White, were determined to carry on making music together. Under conditions of great secrecy plans were hatched which involved some of Britain's finest rock musicians, all in imminent danger of being left high and dry. Eventually rumours leaked out. Astonishingly it seemed the surviving members of Yes were teaming up with two of the most influential rock stars of the Seventies, Jimmy Page and Robert Plant of Led Zeppelin.

Explains Alan White, "At one time there was just Chris and myself in the band! We kind of kept Yes happening and that's the period when we began playing with Jimmy Page. Led Zeppelin had folded because of the death of John Bonham and Jimmy, myself and Chris were working on music in Jimmy's house."

Alan says the material taped by this secret mega band was of the highest quality. "Some of the material I wrote around this time appeared later on the *Keys To Ascension* album. At one time we were going to call the band XYZ meaning Ex-Yes and Zeppelin. We did eight or nine good songs in Jimmy's studio. This was the interim period but when Robert Plant came and listened to some of the stuff he thought it was too complicated. It then all got messed up. Brian Lane, our manager, began talking to Peter Grant,

Led Zeppelin's manager, and then it kind of fell apart. Then in around 1982 we were recommended to meet Trevor Rabin and check him out. Chris and myself met him together. We'd heard a tape of his two years prior to that, when he was shopping his tapes around. Somebody from Atlantic Records said we should get together. They flew him to London, we had some food in a Japanese restaurant and then we went down to Chris' house and jammed for the night and that was the beginning of the next Yes."

Alan insists that Yes had never 'officially' folded because he and Chris were keeping it going. "Everybody else was doing something different. So we just carried on. After we met Trevor, Chris had the idea of calling Tony Kaye up. 'Do you want to come and play keyboards?' Tony flew in and there we were doing a completely new thing. We had this idea of calling the band Cinema and we rehearsed for nine months at John Henry's rehearsal rooms in North London. We changed the direction of the music a little bit, mainly because of Trevor's writing influence. We recorded most of the backing tracks for the album. Then Jon Anderson met Chris again in a bar somewhere. They went back to Chris' house and Jon heard a couple of the tracks. He came down and sang on a couple and there was the new Yes! That's when we did 'Owner Of A Lonely Heart' which was a huge success. It was the biggest hit single the band ever had and so was the album *90125*. We kept a lot of stalwart Yes fans and we also made a lot of new fans."

The revamped Yes was a wonder to behold: Jon back home and Tony Kaye back from the tennis courts, where he had become an expert player. Chris and Alan were on form and they had the added miracle ingredient of guitarist, composer and producer Trevor Rabin. Chris Squire explains that the decisions that led to the new Yes were sparked by the desire to do something fresh, a fortuitous coincidence and practical considerations.

"After the *Drama* tour we were just a bit tired. We had been very busy and we were considering whether to do another album with Trevor Horn and Geoff Downes. Steve really didn't have the same kind of confidence in Trevor as I had, so we just put things on hold. What ended up happening was that Steve and Geoff strangely enough, got together and became involved in the Asia project while Alan and I had a bit of a rest after all those years of making records and touring constantly. We then got together with Jimmy Page and we were experimenting with starting a new band with Page and Plant. We did quite a lot of work on that for a while but there came a point where it was obvious that Robert Plant wasn't ready to come back to work. John Bonham's death had affected him quite badly. Jimmy wanted to get back into the saddle and try and do something fresh with me and Alan but Robert wasn't ready to jump into that.

Because of that – after working on it for a year – it sort of fell apart. Alan and I made a Christmas single called 'Run With The Fox' which they dig out every year and play on the radio. The next thing was Alan and I said we'd better think about putting something together. We weren't thinking about reforming Yes but that's when we got involved with Trevor Rabin and we started on a band with the working title of Cinema."

The indefatigable Phil Carson played an important role in helping Chris reinvent the band. Musing on the fate of the great rock bands he had championed throughout the previous decade, he decided to embark on a new crusade. It would start with a gamble and end with the band's greatest success. It was largely through his efforts that Yes were introduced to Trevor Rabin and their hit album was given life. Says Phil, "Around 1980 I woke up one morning and thought, 'We've got these two great bands on Atlantic who haven't made a record for years and yet have sold millions of albums. They were Emerson, Lake & Palmer and Yes. So I went to Ahmet Ertegun and said, 'These bands should be out there working'." Atlantic boss Ertegun agreed that something should be done and sent Phil some help in the shape of A&R man Richard Steinberg who had been in a group called Tycoon.

"Richard came over and set to work. The first thing he did was completely piss off Keith Emerson. So I went and talked to Keith and tried to get ELP back together. We couldn't get Carl Palmer as he was with Asia, so we got Cozy Powell on drums. I put them together for Atlantic but they got a better deal from Polygram. So I didn't stand in their way."

Phil continued working behind the scenes to assist Yes and made contact with top producer Mutt Lange, production genius behind Def Leppard. "Mutt introduced me to this kid Trevor Rabin who was in a group called Rabbit that had been very big in South Africa. Trevor played me these songs including 'Owner Of A Lonely Heart'. Chris Squire then decided he wanted to put a group together with Trevor but he did not want to call it Yes. He insisted on the name Cinema, which consisted of Chris, Alan, Trevor and later on Tony Kaye. Tony was in one minute and out the next!"

Kaye Of The Keyboard left after a month of recording sessions. Said Trevor Rabin later, "Basically Tony is a great Hammond player which is fine as far as it goes but we were getting involved with Fairlight computers, the Synclavia and there was a whole area of technology that Tony didn't know enough about. It was a mutual parting really." Tony was replaced by Eddie Jobson for a while but most of the keyboard work on the new album was by Trevor Rabin.

Carson says that Atlantic wouldn't put up enough money to make an album that the musicians could be proud to call their own. "They were all living at my house at one stage. I actually funded the album myself. But when it got finished – and it was still called Cinema – I was listening to this tape and thought the record was amazing. There were four or five hits on the thing. I called on Chris and Trevor and said, 'Look, this is crazy. You've got this great album and it could be the biggest thing you've ever done. We've gotta get Jon Anderson back.' They both looked blankly at me. But Trevor, who had written the songs and was singing them on the album, said, 'Wait a minute, maybe Phil's right here.' He was not only a brilliant musician, he was a consummate businessman as well. He could see the up side to this idea. So I got hold of Jon through his roadie. I hadn't spoken to Jon for three years."

Tracking down Jon Anderson was not easy. His wanderlust and habit of frequently changing addresses had continued unchecked. Phil: "It was funny. I spoke to his roadie and he said, 'Well Jon is in a phone box in the Kings Road, London right now, waiting for me to call him!' So Jon Anderson picked up the phone and said, 'Ullo, who's that?' I said, 'Jon, it's Phil Carson here'."

The pair started chatting and Phil told him about the new music Cinema had been recording. He urged Jon to listen to the tapes even though the last meeting between Chris and Jon had apparently been very acrimonious. It was explained that the songs were complete, with vocals by Trevor Rabin. However if Jon liked the songs, Trevor was open to changes. Jon later admitted he had no idea who Trevor Rabin was. But he was prepared to meet him.

Says Phil Carson, "Trevor was absolutely fabulous about all this stuff. His version of 'Owner Of A Lonely Heart' was exactly the same as the final version, with the chorus and everything. Jon then insisted that Chris bring the tape round to him. Chris arrived but Jon wouldn't let him in the house! That was because of the acrimony between Chris Squire's wife Nicki and Jenny Anderson. Eventually Jon came out of the house and listened to the tape in Chris' car."

The next day Jon called Carson and said casually that he quite liked the tape but wanted to make a few changes. This was agreed and it transpired Jon was all ready to go in the studio and sing. He went into ZTT the very next day with Trevor Horn to add the vocals to four songs including 'Owner Of A Lonely Heart'.

Says Carson, "Trevor Horn came to see me with the tape and by then I had spent all the money that Atlantic had given me and $150,000 of my own money. It had by now cost $300,000 and we had to record it all again because we now had Jon Anderson in the band. We had actually been mixing the album when I got the idea of putting Jon back in. Unfortunately I had now spent all my cash."

Phil then heard that Ahmet Ertegun was in Paris so he flew over to play him the tape. Ahmet was astounded to learn his company had only authorised a mere $150,000 to record an album featuring Jon Anderson and produced by Trevor Horn, and even more shocked to hear Phil Carson had paid for the rest. Once in Paris Phil called up the French office of WEA in urgent need of assistance. He explained he had to play Ahmet Ertegun a vitally important tape. He asked them to ensure that the president of Atlantic had a suitable sound system installed in his hotel suite.

"I got to the Plaza hotel and we decided to have lunch because the machine hadn't arrived. After lunch he asked to hear the tape. Mercifully there was a message to say the French staff had set up the stereo. So we went back to his room looked round and . . . no stereo. He looked in his bedroom and came back with this thing that looked like a purse. It was a little portable mono machine. It wasn't even a Walkman. No headphones. Nothing."

The senior record executives put the tape in the tatty machine. It wouldn't play. The batteries were flat. They ordered fresh batteries sent up from reception, while Phil Carson was grinding his teeth with fury at this display of Gallic incompetence. "I had practically given blood to put this tape together and we couldn't play it! But at last 'Owner Of A Lonely Heart' came on and Ahmet listened to the whole thing. I was pulling my hair out by now, but he just said, 'You know what? It sounds great on this. So what's it gonna sound like on a proper machine? How much do you need?' "

Understandably Phil said he'd like to get his own money back first. Ahmet told him to ask for whatever he wanted to finish the record. "We put it out and it became the biggest record in the history of the band. It sold about eight million world wide. It was a *big* record and the best production Yes ever had."

The album was named after the catalogue number but the original working title was *The New Yes Album*. Eventually this was abandoned after much discussion and it was decided to be very minimalist and use what was expected to be the album's allocated catalogue number. Even this simple idea led to complications. Says Phil: "Funnily enough the number was NOT 90125. For some reason we got a different number. Then there was another mistake made. They'd given the number we wanted to another band. I had this bizarre conversation with Chris Squire. We were going to call it *90104*. We couldn't use that so it had to be *90125*. He said he didn't like that and he was dead serious. He said it was not as good as *90104*! As if it made a fucking bit of difference! The record sold very quickly and I then gave my friend Tony Dimitriades a call and they brought him in as their manager and he did a great job with the group."

Shortly after achieving his aims with Yes, Phil Carson left Atlantic to manage Jimmy Page and Robert Plant and subsequently joined JVC to set up the Victory record label based in Los Angeles. However his path would cross with Yes once again, a few years later. It had been a commendable idea to call the new group Cinema, but the reality was the name Yes would mean instant commercial acceptance, whereas a new band would have to struggle, as Jimmy Page would discover when he tried to form a new group called The Firm in the mid-Eighties.

And so Cinema eventually gave way to a revived Yes and to complete the transformation they brought back an old friend from the original Sixties line up. Says Chris Squire, "Because of the kind of guitar player Trevor Rabin was I realised that we didn't need an over complicated keyboard player. So I thought let's give Tony Kaye a ring and see if wants to come back. That's how it started coming together. Then Trevor Horn got involved in the production of the Cinema album that we had started. We had pretty much done the whole thing when Phil Carson at Atlantic said to me, 'Why don't you ask Jon if he wants to come back and call it Yes again?' So literally two weeks before we finished the album Jon sang on the tracks and it was finished. *90125* was our biggest album ever! It sold seven or eight million copies. I thought it was *amazing*. We were given a re-birth."

Said Trevor Horn in a 1998 BBC TV interview, "It was obvious to me that Trevor Rabin was not ready to be the lead singer in the band. It wasn't going to work. Either Chris Squire would have to sing and he didn't want to, so after some terrible arguments Jon Anderson was brought back in and I finally got to meet him!"

Says Jon, "Chris gave me a call in London while I was doing some work with Vangelis. Chris asked if I'd listen to his music. I said 'yes' and it was really good stuff. I said, 'What's the band called?' Cinema! I said if I'm going to sing on the thing it's going to sound like Yes. Is that the deal, do you want to do Yes again? He said, 'Yeah.' "

Says Trevor, "So it was Yes again but it was never quite the Yes that it was before because Jon wasn't ever quite in charge again. Trevor Rabin was much too forceful and after all – he'd written the hit song."

The overnight financial revival of Yes created by Rabin's hit song had some curious but highly welcome side effects on their standing within the record industry and in particular in the matter of royalty payments. Chuckles Chris, "Suddenly they found tons of money that was owed to us in the past. They realised we could now *afford* to take them to court – ha, ha! It's funny how that happens. As soon as they think you've got enough money to afford a lawyer they suddenly find all these royalties that they'd 'lost'. It was all from the Seventies era, but that's the way the business works. Trevor Rabin and Tony got on well and the band then did a very successful touring cycle and went everywhere around the world."

'Owner Of A Lonely Heart' was number one in the States and it also achieved the distinction of selling a million singles in France. Yet when Trevor Horn was asked to work on *90125* many friends questioned his sanity. "At the time everybody told me I was mad, because I was having such a successful career as a producer. When the idea came up of me going back and working with those old 'guys' people were just furious with me. But Brian Lane wasn't managing them anymore. They had been taken over by Tony Dimitriades and that was a huge step forward for Yes because he is what a manager should be. But of course it wasn't Yes. It was Cinema and there were just three of them. It only gradually became apparent that really it was a Yes album. To be frank, if it was going to sell it *had* to be a Yes album. Trevor Rabin wasn't used to being a front man for a serious rock band. He couldn't cut it and they needed somebody good. So Jon came back in again. It was one of those once in a lifetime things where Jon came back at just the right time. We could get the thing finished fairly quickly and because I was involved, Chris could have some serious, concerted influence. That's his problem. He can never really have consistent influence when there isn't anybody there to look after his end. I always thought Chris was the real talent in the band, but it's a case of whatever shape he happens to be in. Since I was such a fan of his, while we worked on *90125* I held up his end, if you see what I mean. Even so most of the recording was by me and Trevor Rabin. For months on end it was just me and Trevor. The keyboard player left after we had a row and that was the end of him. Trevor Rabin was such a good keyboard player anyway."

The stunningly powerful dance influenced sound achieved on *90125* was light years ahead of what most bands could achieve in the studio. Most attributed this to Trevor Horn's skill as a producer but he insists, "It's all the band playing live. We just took a bit of time and trouble over the recording. Mind you, the band sounded great on the early albums too. It's just a producer working hard. It was Eddie Offord on the early albums and it was me on *90125*. Any band needs a good producer, I don't care who they are. Once the music is on tape it's in a different medium and you need people who are experienced at working in that medium."

The light, skipping feel achieved on 'Owner Of A Lonely Heart' was interspersed with cosmic bursts of sound that still have the power to shock and surprise. Trevor Rabin's harsh, angular guitar solo is brilliant in its execution. The diamond hard sound achieved by Trevor Horn set off Jon's vocals like a jewel in the Yes crown. It was an example of what could be achieved once the band was given set targets with no room for arguments and distractions. They could even rock hard as they showed on 'Hold On' which laid back on the beat with all the raunchy power of a Bon Jovi or Aerosmith. Strange vocal treatments in the background sustained the air of Yes mystery. This was the spirit of Yes hoisted into the mid–Eighties and injected with rocket fuel. The confidence and sense of purpose permeated such powerful pieces as 'It Can Happen', strong on structure, enlivened with a tinkling sitar and not overladen with solos. 'Changes' has a brash mid–Eighties vibe, the stomping rhythm interspersed with immaculately tasteful guitar work.

'Cinema' the fifth cut is heralded with exuberant drumming and layers of sound, somewhat in 'Relayer' mode. It's a poky two minute instrumental and, interestingly, Trevor plays the same sort of guitar whoops and howls that Peter Banks used to play way back in the late Sixties. The piece serves as a dramatic introduction to the astounding vocal feat 'Leave It'. If Jon and Chris had always wanted Yes to be strong on vocal harmonies, they fully realised their dream with this inspiring, off the wall piece of work. Credited to Squire, Horn and Rabin this a cappella performance is one of the truly outstanding tracks on an outstanding album. "*One down, one to go, another town and one more show . . . leave it!*"

'Our Song' is another bright gem of construction and performance. Jon sums up his philosophy as he sings 'Music has magic!' He may have felt he was brought into the band just to perform and not take decisions, but being unburdened from his old role as musical director, somehow enabled him to soar like a free spirit once more. He also wrote, with Trevor Rabin, the funky 'City Of Love' which sounds like a movie soundtrack with overtones of Talking Heads. Rabin's guitar work is totally controlled and yet exudes power and menace. Once again the sound quality and production is exemplary and has rarely been equalled. Jon takes the lead on 'Hearts' a swirling finale that put the seal of distinction on a magnificent album.

★   ★   ★

All this was music to the ears of Chris and Jon who had been through so many tempestuous situations since the start of the band, but the Yes comeback left one ex-member of Yes quietly seething. Steve Howe was just launching his own career with Asia when news reached him that Cinema would now be called Yes. He had been under the impression his old group had long since ceased to function. Steve had put the past behind him and the way seemed clear for Asia to take the high ground in a brave new Yes free world.

I met Steve in July 1983 when he was busy making a promotional video for Asia's single release 'Don't Cry'. I found him ensconced with Asia chums John Wetton, Carl Palmer and Geoff Downes at Twickenham Film Studios. They were having great fun making the expensive promo which looked to me like a re-run of *Raiders Of The Lost Ark*. It was a chance for me to catch up on Steve's career and to see how movies were made.

The large studio was packed with musicians, film technicians, extras and assorted directors and cameramen. The group were in make-up and costume and Steve was having the most boyish, carefree fun since the days of The Syndicats. The khaki-clad musos were expected to act like silent movie stars on an elaborate set depicting the African jungle. Wearing shorts and sweating under the arc lights they were hemmed in by palm trees overlooked by a huge mock pyramid. The set was alive with jets of water and sheets of flame and the extras giggled as the group tried out their acting skills. Steve looked very natty, like a British expedition leader about to discover the source of the Nile.

As 'Don't Cry' echoed tinnily through monitor speakers the band were expected to wade through a 5000 gallon swamp while miming to the song. The story line behind the $35,000 mini epic (shot on 16 mm film) was inspired by Roger Dean's cover for the band's new album *Alpha*.

Although John Wetton was put off by the giggling onlookers, it seemed clear that the band members were more relaxed than they had been for years. Steve Howe in particular had been wound up like a watch spring in the last days with Yes. Now he was wreathed in smiles. Until the news of a Yes 'reunion' was raised. One of the best songs on *Alpha* was 'The Smile Has Left Your Eyes'. The smile left Steve's eyes as soon as I mentioned the latest plan to kick-start Yes.

Brian Lane, now Asia's manager, was also on hand to dispense his thoughts about the latest developments. Jon Anderson teaming up with Chris Squire, Trevor Rabin, Tony Kaye and Alan White? Brian could hardly conceal his disbelief. "It's like Joe Bugner[21] trying to make a comeback," he said scornfully.

Said Steve: "I knew about this on the grapevine ages ago. I think they are jumping back into the frying pan. This isn't a thoroughbred Yes project. They just looked up in their phone books for a lead singer and thought, 'Oh yes, Jon Anderson.' I think their coming back is one big 'Ugh'. It's taken me all this while to stop talking about Yes when I mean Asia because after ten years it was hard to drop the habit."

Steve pondered on the chain of events that led to the reformation. "It started out as Cinema and then it got into deep water and for six months they went no further. They didn't have a singer, so when they asked Jon he said he'd only do it if they called the band Yes. Now everybody is

[21] A former British Boxing champion.

rubbing their hands thinking they'll make a million dollars. But they've not checked it out. For a start Rick Wakeman isn't in the band or Geoff, and I certainly am not. I'm in Asia – playing the guitar! But why should I worry about Yes anymore? Yes was a big section of my life. How can it come back, when it was called Cinema only a few weeks ago? Yes was from a certain time in history. Those first three LPs I did with them were the real golden days of Yes. That was the creative time for the band when everybody was pulling together. That's what is good about Asia. We all have something worth fighting for. We're all in a hole and we've all originally worked our way out of bedsits. But I'm not doing Asia for the money, it's because I want to play in a good band."

Steve reiterated that his days with Yes had not left him 'made for life'. He roared with laughter at the idea of being a rock millionaire. "We never dug a gold mine with Yes. We never created any Empires. We grossly mismanaged ourselves. We had an endless string of bills and huge running expenses." Steve offered sage words of advice to anybody new coming into the music business.

"Believe me, all you young groups out there, you are doomed. For the first 20 years of your life you have absolutely no concept of what it's all about. If you're in a successful group, you mustn't pull out all the profits and lash out on 20 Rolls Royces. The money either goes to the tax man or you just squander it on yourself. I never wanted to go to the bankruptcy court, so I was intelligent with my money. But there are no hundreds of thousands in Panamanian bank accounts. I never wanted a Rolls Royce or Cartier watch. All I ever bought were guitars. I suppose I could have rushed out and bought gold bars, but I'm not a businessman. I never wanted to be a superstar with Yes and it would worry me if my children thought me superhuman. In fact my children have helped me a lot. They're like a mirror offering a glimpse of reality. They make me realise who I really am and I have had so many years of confusion. The most important things to me are my family and giving my utmost on stage."

It was a touching, revealing statement. Many years later Steve would be reunited with Yes, but in the early Eighties he felt like he had been excluded from a band that was still such an important part of his life. When Jon Anderson heard of Steve's cry of 'Ugh!' to the reformation of Yes he told an American reporter, "If he wants to say that fine. In the heat of the moment you tend to say things that sometimes later on you regret. Your mouth keeps opening and things come out and you can't help it. Steve's a nice guy. We became a bit unhappy with each other though, so you get these little bits of frustration."

★ ★ ★

With *90125* deservedly topping the charts, the latest version of Yes set off on their biggest ever tour. According to Alan White, on the *90125* tour they did almost two hundred gigs within a period of 15 months. They hit the road just as 'Owner Of A Lonely Heart' was blasting the airwaves and bringing the band a whole new audience, most of whom had never even heard of Yes before. As a result of all the renewed interest *90125* went platinum. Amazingly, Yes were still only at the halfway point in their career.

The man who had unexpectedly arrived on the scene to revive the fortunes of Yes had a tough job. Somehow he had to remain true to his own musical beliefs, coax Yes out of its backwater into the mainstream, fend off resentment from past members and stay cool. He did it with a combination of self-motivation, diplomacy and strength of purpose.

Trevor Rabin was not the studio bound technocrat that he has some-times been portrayed. He had already enjoyed success as a teenage pop star in his native South Africa and had learnt how to fend off screaming teenage girls when Yes were still signing autographs for teenage boys. But that was in the Seventies. By the end of the decade Trevor had moved to London to establish himself on the studio and production scene. He also had a shot at working as a solo artist with his own band. As a singer, guitarist, keyboard player and producer he was well equipped to take on the pop scene during a confusing time for everyone. He had no hang ups about past glories and was much more up to date with studio techniques and market changes than any of the members of Yes. They still had their innate talents intact, but given all the upheavals of the previous six years it was no wonder they were overwrought. When Rabin came on the scene he provided clear cut songs instead of rambling overdubs; definitive hooks instead of cut and pasted themes. He was one of that rare breed: a musician who knew how to edit his own work. His approach, together with Trevor Horn's production ideas, might have made it seem as if the old traditional Yes was being lost in the march of progress. Given the climate of the mid-Eighties, that was no bad thing. There were no radio stations on the planet that would play a new *Topographic Oceans* but they would fall over themselves to play 'Owner Of A Lonely Heart'.

For the next few years Yes would become an important part in the life of Trevor Rabin. It was a strange twist that someone who had no part in the early evolution of the band should suddenly become the single most important member who would dominate the band for the next decade of its existence. And yet Trevor was not the 'world domination' type. He'd already outgrown his taste of stardom as a teenager growing up in South Africa where he was highly successful with his first important group

Rabbit. They had their own TV show, number one hit records and money spinning tours.

Despite his forceful reputation, Rabin is just as sensitive about his work as any other musician and he remains very proud of his contribution to Yes. He was born in Johannesburg on January 13, 1954, and like so many others who make up the Yes family he came from a musical family. His father was a conductor and lead violinist with the Johannesburg Symphony Orchestra. "All my family are pretty musical – except me! I'm the black sheep of the family. I'm joking because none of them became professional musicians except me. When we were young my brother was a very fine violinist, and my sister a fine pianist."

As a child growing up in a happy family Trevor wasn't fully aware of South Africa's underlying political problems. But his cousin was famed activist Donald Woods, a friend of Steve Biko who died in police custody. As a young man Trevor became allied to the anti-Apartheid movement. "One of the first calls I got when I moved to London was from Peter Gabriel who was doing a tribute song called 'Biko'. He wanted me to help him contact Donald Woods."

Meanwhile rock 'n' roll was his consuming passion, rather than politics. Trevor studied piano from the age of six then at the age of 12 he began to play electric guitar. One of his earliest idols was Hank Marvin of The Shadows. Within six months he formed his first group Conglomeration. Says Trevor, "I got a Fender Stratocaster guitar and Hank B. Marvin was my absolute inspiration. He had a very clean, clear sound as opposed to mine, which was really filthy! I really got into guitar and practised all the time. I taught myself how to play by taking churning piano exercises and doing them on the guitar. After listening to Hank I moved on to Wes Montgomery and John McLaughlin. I then got into playing in different bands with my brother."

At 16 Trevor was discovered by a record producer and went on to become one of the top session guitarists in South Africa. He began playing jazz-fusion as his session work led him to play with many older musicians. "I was about 18 years old at the time and there were some incredible jazz musicians around. They would play at the jazz club on Sunday nights and do all this amazing music. I was lucky enough to be invited to play and became quite a regular on that scene."

The following year he joined rock band Freedom's Children then reunited with his friends from Conglomeration to form pop group Rabbit. Although unknown outside of South Africa and Rhodesia, Rabbit rivalled The Beatles in popularity at home, and enjoyed multi-platinum album sales and sold out stadium concerts. In 1975 Trevor won an award for the best orchestral arranger of the year for the first Rabbit album.

Trevor had written a song called 'Charlie' which was a big hit and helped the band break through. Rabbit had their own weekly TV show and South Africa's teenage girl population thrilled to their exploits. But they were a very hip rock band as well as being a teenage attraction. Says Trevor, "Funnily enough we had a number one single with a song called 'Locomotive Breath' which was a cover of a Jethro Tull song. Later on we put out a couple of albums and then I left the country to go to London in 1978. The band then split up and it was kind of my fault. But I really wanted to explore and play somewhere else. We had tremendous success in South Africa and they were enjoying that. I said, 'It doesn't have to end. We can just explore other areas.' But they weren't really interested in leaving to come with me. So I moved on. But I am still very friendly with the guys in the band."

Trevor had got used to being a pop star in South Africa and it was a shock to the system when he arrived at London Airport. "I'll never forget arriving at Heathrow. A bunch of pretty 16-year-old girls walked past me. I kind of ducked and dived, trying to hide in case they came up to me. This guy who was with me said, 'What are you doing? You're in London, you can't get arrested!' That immediately put me in perspective. I was being naïve. But my plan was to go to London and do my job. I was going to play shows, make records and sell them, and that wasn't an easy thing to do. I opened my own record company called Blue Chip Music with some partners from South Africa and did a deal with Chrysalis. I released some records with them and I also did three solo albums. I then toured England opening for Steve Hillage."

Ray Davies of The Kinks co-produced Trevor's first album *Trevor Rabin* which was released in 1978. This was followed by *Face To Face* (1979) and *Wolf* (1980). Several years later, in 1989, he released his fourth solo album *Can't Look Away*. "When I arrived in London I produced records with Manfred Mann which was a lot of fun and we have remained close friends. I also produced a band called Wild Horses and a very good singer called Noel McCalla."

After a few productive years in London Trevor decided to move on to base himself permanently in Los Angeles. "What happened was David Geffen was planning to sign Manfred Mann who I was producing at the time for an album called *Chance*, and it didn't work out. Geffen then asked me if I'd like to go out to LA to write some songs for an album. I went to LA and wrote what landed up on *90125*."

It seems the talented Rabin was already being head-hunted by the rock industry, and many thought he might be the ideal man to boost the fortunes of other groups being postulated at the time. This led to some odd situations and quite a few 'what might have beens'. "I was asked to join a band that funnily enough included Carl Palmer, Rick Wakeman and John Wetton. I wasn't really that keen on the idea. I wanted to do a solo album but the company thought that the material I was writing was a little left field for the times. This was pre-Asia, but in fact this was the beginnings of that band and I went and rehearsed with Asia which is quite funny given the Steve Howe situation!"

While Trevor stuck out to do a solo album he found himself being dropped by Geffen and was about to sign a deal with RCA when he got a phone call from Chris Squire. "He said, 'Atlantic have sent me a tape. I'd love to meet you and have a play.' I think Richard Steinberg and Phil Carson had sent him the tape. Then me, Chris and Alan White got together for a play and it sounded terrible. It really sounded awful. But I realised that even though it sounded bad these were guys I'd like to play with in a band. With a bit of rehearsal and stuff something could happen. It was rough but there was potential. It was incredibly loud but not as loud as Motorhead! Yes had broken up at this stage and it was just going to be me, Chris and Alan doing the songs I'd written. Then Tony Kaye got involved and Trevor Horn came in as the producer. All the songs had been recorded when Jon came in right at the end."

As we have seen, the album was a marvellous mixture of old and new Yes, with the emphasis on the new. Says Trevor, "It was definitely fun to make. It was the first time we used a Fairlight Computer. Trevor Horn was great with all that. I'd had something like it on the original demos, but not exactly the same sounds.

"We just tuned in the sounds a lot better. Up until then there had been no samplers so nobody had heard sounds like we got on 'Owner Of A Lonely Heart'. We were very happy with what had been done. Then one day Chris played the tapes to Jon. Chris invited Jon to put a vocal down to one or two things and the results were amazing. After hearing Jon singing the songs we both felt that we wanted him involved, if he was interested. I must admit that until we met and worked together I was expecting a bit of a tyrant, but Jon is really easy to work with. It was about this time that we decided that with the distinctive sound of Jon's voice the band would be Yes!"

In 1984 Yes began a tour of America and Europe. Trevor admits he was none too keen on going out under the name of Yes when the concept of Cinema was dropped. "I wasn't enamoured about going out and playing like a Top Forty band and playing all the old stuff which I knew we'd have to do. I thought the music was different enough to be able to stand on its own feet. I also thought there would be a backlash from Yes fans who really embraced the old stuff and wouldn't accept anything new. It was obviously completely different. But after a lot of discussion everyone, including the record company, thought it was a good idea. I thought at least it would enable us to put on a bigger show and give us more creative freedom with the name Yes. I still maintain the album *90125* might have done just fine without the name – but who knows? We had a great tour and the album went to number one all over the place. We played in the States and Europe and we also did a beautiful tour of South America. Then we went off to Japan a little later."

There was another reason for not calling the band Cinema. As soon as the name was mentioned several previously unknown American groups called Cinema tried to sue. Says Rabin, "We discovered there were about three other bands also called Cinema. The minute word leaked out about what we were doing the other Cinemas all filed lawsuits claiming damages and loss of potential earnings. Funny how they never tried suing each other though! We even went so far as paying some of these people off just to get rid of them."

After having written all new material for *90125* Trevor then had to learn some traditional Yes material from the Seventies, much of it written or containing solo sequences by the previous incumbent of the lead guitar department.

Trevor: "Chris spoke to me about that. He said, 'Why don't we just choose a bunch of songs. The ones you really don't like, we won't do. The ones you find attractive we'll do.' Obviously there were songs like 'Roundabout' which I liked but I wanted to do them my way. The easy part was learning the songs. The hard part was trying to play something on them that wasn't just a facsimile. In fact the *90125* songs sounded better live than a lot of the older stuff. Although when we came to do our next album *Big Generator* the stuff did not sound as good live."

The band's American tour was delayed when Trevor suffered an accident in a swimming pool which led to an operation. Then in April 1984 they played several nights at the Los Angeles Forum to a total of 40,000 people. The shows featured a new set design and lighting and a state of the art sound system. The band played to sold out houses around the world. Jimmy Page even joined them on stage at Westfalenhalle, Dortmund, Germany, to jam on 'I'm Down', giving a taste of XYZ. The tour was captured on a home video release *9012Live* and there was a mini album called *9012Live-The Solos*, both released in 1985. The latter, recorded in Canada and Germany, featured solo segments from each member, together with concert versions of 'Hold On' and 'Changes'.

Although Yes had undoubtedly won a new lease of life there were still those in Britain and America who yearned for the band they had grown up with and found it hard to accept the new format. Says Yes sound man Roy Clair, "With Trevor Rabin it was different. I think he always felt

216

threatened by everybody who had been there before. If you toured with them like I had, then you liked that old band and still had allegiance to Steve Howe and Rick Wakeman. It was hard for you to change. So I think Trevor was definitely a little suspicious of all those who had been touring with them in the Seventies. So I think that's why Clair Brothers disappeared for that one tour. Maybe he thought we wouldn't give him the support we had given Steve. Then Trevor found out we weren't the way he thought we were! So he had us back."

Yes were back and enjoying huge success. *What could possibly go wrong – now!*

9

BIG GENERATOR – ABWH – UNION

After the enormous success of *90125* it seemed as if Yes might finally be free of the traumas, splits and bust-ups that had become the pattern of their lives since the end of the Seventies. In the event, it turned out to be just the start of yet more upset. The band was destined to experience more dramatic changes which would ultimately result in not just one but *two* versions of Yes.

The Eighties had begun with the upheaval caused by the departure of Rick Wakeman and Jon Anderson and their replacement by The Buggles. By the end of the decade Jon had left the group for a second time, only to be reunited with Rick Wakeman, Steve Howe and, unlikely as it may seem, original Yes drummer Bill Bruford, in a rival 'Yes' that called itself ABWH. Chris Squire, Alan White and Trevor Rabin were left as the sole remaining members of what we might as well call the 'official' Yes. Confusion and embarrassment reigned. Yet by 1991 the whole band was reunited in an act of atonement which led to an eight piece touring version of the group and a controversial album – which no one seems to admit to liking – called *Union*. It was enough to make a Yes fan freak. Nevertheless, the band hung on to its core fan base even though they kept coming back in different guises like actors in some Shakespearean comedy of errors.

It was certainly a trying time for Trevor Rabin, who with Chris Squire was faced with reconstructing the 'official' Yes. Trevor must have felt he was building a shiny new skyscraper, while a bunch of eco-warriors were trying to erect a pagoda Yes in the parking lot without planning permission.

Rabin headed up the band which reassembled in the studios in 1985 to begin work on an album it was fervently hoped would equal the success of *90125*. Studios in Italy and England were pressed into service with Trevor Horn brought back to assist with production. Then the whole caboodle headed for Los Angeles where production was taken over by Trevor Rabin and sound engineer Paul De Villiers. The result was *Big Generator*, released in September, 1987.

Remembers Alan White, "We started recording in Italy and did half the backing tracks. Then we came back to SARM studios in London with Trevor Horn and worked on the album there. The sessions produced 'Rhythm Of Love' which is one of the most played radio songs in America. After that album we kind of split apart for a while."

Trevor Horn encountered severe problems trying to produce the band. "I tried doing the next album *Big Generator* but I couldn't finish it because the circumstances were different," he says. "I did most of the backing tracks but it wasn't finishable from my point of view. They just couldn't agree. Jon would write one thing, Trevor would write another, Chris would write something else and they'd fight about it and I was in the middle. And I'm sorry to say it's down to one pile of shit being no different from another! In the end it's down to who can finish the song off and nobody could on that record for me and nobody ever did. It wasn't a case of being a committee. It was just warring factions trying to kill each other. When bands have been together for more than fifteen years they become completely money driven and it's whoever is paying the money, where it's coming from and what it's being paid for that determines what gets done recording-wise."

Given these circumstances it is no surprise that many who have worked with Yes come away with a jaundiced opinion of them. Trevor Horn denies this. "Oh! I don't have a jaundiced opinion of them. I quite miss them all and I had a lot of fun doing *90125*. Don't get me wrong. I'm not jaundiced about them at all. It's just that keeping any kind of musical enterprise like that going for as long as it has, with all the egos involved, isn't going to be easy. Just watch the movie *This Is Spinal Tap*. There are elements of Yes in that. Only, of course, Yes are a vastly superior band!"

Trevor Horn has not heard their albums since *Big Generator*. He hasn't listened to *Talk* or *Open Your Eyes* but he went back to see them play again on tour in the Nineties. "I think they should keep touring and keep playing concerts, like classical musicians do. Why not? It cheered me up when I saw Chris Squire play with Yes at Labatt's Apollo Hammersmith in 1998. I was right to think he was good. He always was! I like the stuff he plays with the songs. That's what's really clever, not the long bass solos. I've never heard anybody else do what he can with a song. The bass can be such an exciting instrument and yet in most people's hands it is really boring."

Chris Squire agrees it was difficult making *Big Generator*. "It took rather a long time," he admits. "We fiddled around trying to record it in Italy for tax purposes, but the studios didn't really work out, so we came back to London and for some reason Trevor Horn, who was going to produce it again, decided not to. *Big Generator* was a double platinum album but it lacked the lustre it started off with, although it had 'The Rhythm Of Love' which was number two most played track on the radio in 1987."

While most observers probably see Yes merely in terms of a series of albums released by alternating line-ups over a long period of time with varying degrees of commercial success, their career must also be viewed against a background of little-publicised personal experiences. Like everyone else, successful rock musicians have their ups and downs. Indeed, the uncertainties of life that we all experience, money problems, matters of health – mental and physical – and shifting personal relationships, tend to be magnified due to the unreality of the rock star lifestyle. Jon Anderson and his wife Jenny split up in the early Eighties, and midway through the decade Chris Squire divorced his first wife Nicki, who later became a singer and produced several records. All these events would naturally impinge on the progress of the band and their relationships.

Says Chris Squire, "By the time we were making *Big Generator* I had moved to Los Angeles. Because of the breakdown of my marriage I left England to try a fresh approach by living in America. I wanted to see how it would work out and of course it was pretty much a big party for a couple of years. Living in Hollywood, Los Angeles in those days, someone, somewhere was having a party every night. There'd be an opening of a club or some awards ceremony, so for a couple of years there was a lot of partying going on."

By all accounts Chris was burning the candle at both ends and there were fears for his health. "I met a lot of interesting people but by the time it got to 1989 I realised if I was going to carry on living in Hollywood I'd have to treat it less like a party town and get down to the job of normal living. I've never bought a place in the States, I have always rented a house, which was a very wise move to make because ever since I moved to America the prices have been going down and down, especially when an earthquake happens, which is another big blow to house prices! I've been a lot better off renting. One day we might buy a house and my new wife Melissa and I debate on where that will be all the time."

Certainly personal moods and circumstances can affect a musician's output and creative judgement, and business pressures also play a part in moulding the eventual outcome of a project. Says Trevor Rabin, "When we did *Big Generator* the stuff just didn't sound as good 'live'. I was quite happy with some of the album. It was a weird kind of stage for the band. We'd just had this huge album *90125*, the biggest Yes ever had, and no one had ever experienced the kind of success we were enjoying. And so it was, 'Okay, we'll do the next album.' Halfway through it the record company was saying to the world: 'This is going to be the next *Dark Side Of The Moon*! There was a lot of pressure and it obviously *wasn't* the next

Dark Side Of The Moon. There were just two or three good moments. It's quite funny. Billy Sherwood[22] has told me since that it is one of his favourite albums of all time. So some people liked it and it sold pretty well. It's platinum all over the place, although that's not the criteria of whether it's good or not. Trevor Horn started out producing it and although he and I have always got on really well, in the studio there were often heated arguments. But it was always for the right reasons. To our credit we are still close friends. I went to London a couple of years ago to be a session player on a Tina Turner album he was producing. So we've had our fun. I think he's one of the finest producers around but on *Big Generator* he wasn't too happy with working with Jon. That's my perception of why he stepped aside. It was a pity because he had a lot of valuable input. Tony Kaye also didn't respond to him creatively either and that led to a personal problem.

"A lot of people have ridiculed me for being a megalomaniac which couldn't be further from the truth. It's just because I played keyboards on the albums. And the reason I played keyboards was because Trevor Horn said, 'I don't want Tony Kaye playing keyboards.' So I've heard it said I'm a megalomaniac. It's not true. That's Jon's job! He proudly told me he used to be known as 'Napoleon' back in the early days. I said, 'Well hold that thought while I'm in the band!' "

Among the innovations Trevor introduced was a real brass section which many Yes fans didn't like. They claimed it was tampering with tradition. "If you don't try and develop new ideas and take some risks, you never grow," protests Trevor. A good example of new ideas employed during the recording was a bright yet strangely distant ambient sound – as if some of the instruments were being played in different rooms. "That's because they are! I had this weird idea while making *Big Generator* to do that. I had a friend with a studio in a castle on Lake Como near Caramati in Italy. The castle has these huge ballrooms. You could do drums in one room and guitars in another. I ended up mixing the album and co-producing it and I just went for shock value."

Among the shocks are Trevor's violent, off-the-stone-wall guitar breaks on the stomping 'Rhythm Of Love' which has to be one of the finest examples of Yes in dance mode. 'Big Generator' too has a grindingly powerful riff broken up by stabbing brass flares which push Jon's airy vocals into a pulsing metronomic groove; a thrusting performance by any band's standards. Alan's drums sound like they are breaking through the castle ramparts and enter into a battle with the guitar as Rabin and White lock together. More intergalactic guitar brings the piece to an abrupt

---

[22] Guitarist Billy Sherwood would join Yes in 1996.

cliffhanging conclusion. The ethereal quality of the slow paced 'Shoot High Aim Low' is enhanced by some of Trevor's most atmospheric extemporisation and Alan White's thunderous bass drum fills could conceivably cause CDs to shatter and crack.

"*Who says there's gotta be a reason, who says there's got to be an answer?*" demands Jon over the gradually fading chorus of 'Shoot High'. It's a masterful piece of production and a very clever arrangement on a piece that grows in stature with repeated plays. "That's one of my favourite tracks on the album. We did it live for about twelve shows and then we dropped it," says Trevor regretfully.

Alan White blasts away at high speed on 'Almost Like Love', a performance which is also the closest Jon has got to doing a rap record, although at this tempo he sounds closer to Sting than Ice T. The guitar goes berserk as White locks into some of the fiercest off beat drumming of his career. In view of all this good work it is surprising the two Trevors expressed doubts about *Big Generator*. This track alone is worth the price of the album. Strings pave the way for the familiar intro to 'Love Will Find A Way', clearly a classic Yes pop song. The snappy accents that underscore the vocals and Alan's rock steady beat are placed with precision timing. The ear catching line 'I eat at Chez Nous', which suddenly leaps out of the mix, is strangely intriguing. Why this sudden sophistication, one wonders? Don't rock musicians usually eat at McDonalds? Trevor Rabin conducted the strings on this track and says, "I hadn't written for strings for years and it was the first time I had actually conducted since leaving South Africa. I wrote the arrangement, did all the copying and did it in all the keys and clefs that the instruments were in. So those are all real strings on that song. No samples!"

There are many more fine performances on the album. 'Final Eyes' has a stirring acoustic ditty that harks back to the summery Seventies. It allows Jon Anderson to fully express his vocal character, which makes it all the more puzzling there should have been such dissent about his role in the band at this time. You can even hear what sounds like Tony Kaye's Hammond in the distance. A sudden blast of enhanced snare drum is enough to knock your head off, especially when playing this on headphones, so beware all those of a nervous disposition. Listening to this album is rather like scanning the heavens with the Hubble Telescope. Amidst the cosmos you find layer upon layer of stars, even in the darkest parts of the sky. Here too you find clouds of star stuff – a spiral nebula of creativity. The penultimate track, 'I'm Running', sounds astonishingly like early Yes, as if it were a souped up 'Time And A Word'. Alan's percussion provides a rich new seam of rhythmic impetus as he launches into a few choruses of Latin rhythm. The well placed Hammond organ tags are pure Yes '69 and the vocal harmonies swarm all over the surging rise in both tempo and temperature. Even Trevor Rabin's guitar breaks here sound for all the world like Peter Banks in full cry. It's exciting stuff. If the band of '69 had heard such production values they would surely have fainted clean away.

After this nostalgic burn-up, in which old and new are so skilfully blended, Jon Anderson has the last word with his bell-like vocals given free rein of expression on the brief but touching 'Holy Lamb (Song For Harmonic Convergence)'. Although there were rows in the studio, there was peace and harmony on the record.

Says Trevor Rabin, "I actually thought in a lot of ways it was the best album I did with the band – in part. There were some parts that I thought shouldn't have been there, like 'Holy Lamb' which I thought was pretty weak. What's a harmonic convergence? I don't know. Ask Jon. The album sold a couple of million but it certainly didn't do as well as *90125*. After that we kind of broke up for a short time and I did a solo album and tour. While I was doing that the ABWH thing started to happen."

★　★　★

Jon Anderson believed that his opinions about the attempt to make Yes a commercial hit machine with *Big Generator* had been vindicated. In any case he had become increasingly unhappy with his role in the band. "It was as though I'd been pigeonholed just to be happy to be the singer in the band. 'Get your cheque and don't make waves.' 'Okay, so you don't want to hear what I have to say. So what am I doing in the band?' "

And so Jon left the group for the second time after the completion of their 1987/88 world tour, thus concluding a stint with the eighth version of Yes which had run from June 1983 until September 1988. During that time he also released two solo albums *Three Ships* and *The City Of Angels*. Shortly after the news broke, Jon attempted to explain to puzzled Yes fans why he had quit once again. "It was purely down to not having fun, simple as that," he said. "I will never hang about just for the bread and I will never hang about for old time's sake. I do it purely for the music. If you're not true to yourself and true to your being, there's no point. That's not to say I would never work with them again. I have a respect for everybody that's been in the group."

Strangely enough Trevor Rabin says he didn't even know that Jon had actually left Yes after *Big Generator*. "I don't know if he *quit*. I wasn't aware of that until later. I was so busy doing an album I didn't even know it was kind of fizzling out. In fact I thought we were coming back together again in a year or so! We were having a break because making *Big Generator* had been such a traumatic experience."

Deep down inside his psyche what Jon Anderson really wanted was to locate and revive the old spirit of Yes, the spirit of the band he had taken to such critical and commercial acclaim in the early Seventies. So in 1988, ten years after his first bust-up with Yes, he picked up the phone and contacted old friends and inveigled them into forming a new, rival band which became known as Anderson, Bruford, Wakeman and Howe. It was a very worthy idea and one that should have helped restore the spirit of 1969, or at least 1972, or was it 1979? In a way it did. His initiative caused a huge row and even threats of legal action.

According to a report in *Billboard*, the US record trade magazine, on May 31, 1989, the version of Yes which included Tony Kaye, Trevor Rabin, Chris Squire and Alan White filed suit in the US District Court for the Central District of California to prevent the newly formed Anderson, Bruford, Wakeman & Howe from making any mention of Yes. The injunction they sought would prohibit ABWH from advertising and promoting their North American tour with references to Yes material or otherwise alluding to Yes music and intentionally 'creating confusion in the minds of the public over which group is the real Yes.' The suit also sought to prevent 'defendant' Anderson from discussing his former membership in Yes. ABWH were due to open their major US tour on Saturday July 29 at Mud Island, Memphis, Tennessee. The suit was based on a separation agreement dated May 22, 1984, which was entered into by all of the past and present Yes members which specified which musicians could continue to use the name Yes. The remaining musicians reserved the rights to use of the name and logo in promoting catalogue product. At the time Jon Anderson, who remained with the side continuing to use the Yes name, entered into a partnership agreement stipulating that a future 'withdrawing partner' from the group would no longer be allowed to use the Yes name or even refer to himself as a former Yes member after a specified date. When Yes signed with Atlantic, Jon Anderson contracted for only two albums and after their production undertook solo projects prior to forming ABWH in December 1988. The new band signed to Arista. The plaintiffs alleged that the new Anderson group had 'wrongfully converted' the Yes name in a *Los Angeles Times* advertisement describing an ABWH concert as 'an evening of Yes music plus . . .'

Other alleged instances of the defendants wrongful 'usurpation' of the Yes name included a promo pamphlet sent out by Arista containing allusions to Yes. A response was filed in court on June 5 which the defendants' attorney Elliot L. Hoffman of Beldock, Levine & Hoffman, called the Yes action, "An outrageous attempt by plaintiffs to stop the media and public from comparing ABWH's new recording with theirs – more specifically from saying that even under their new name ABWH, these defendants, all former members of Yes, are making much better music than the plaintiffs who are currently recording and performing as Yes. That's all this is about." Hoffman added that the allusions to Yes material in advertising were entirely consistent with the terms of the separation agreement.

Explains Jim Halley, "There was a problem with the name. When ABWH started to tour they billed it as 'An Evening of Yes Music'. The European promoters began splashing the name Yes all over the posters. It was in bolder type than Anderson, Bruford, Wakeman & Howe. There was a conflict about who owned the name and the logo but in the end they came to an accommodation."

Says Jon Anderson, "While we were doing ABWH we had Chris and Trevor and their management trying to sue us for applying the name Yes to who we were. It said, 'An Evening of Yes Music' but *we* never said we were Yes. It was the record company!"[23]

When the new group first assembled it wasn't entirely clear to all of them what the intentions were. In 1989 Bill Bruford found himself being asked if he'd do some new recordings with old colleague Jon Anderson. It seemed like a good idea but it turned out to be a less than pleasant experience, at least for the drummer. Recalls Bill ruefully, "Jon came round to see me and asked if I'd do some recording. I thought it was just going to be a session."

Jon told Bill somewhat casually, "We've done some tracks. Come and play on them." The drummer agreed. They chatted for a bit and then Bruford received an air ticket to Montserrat, island home of a famous recording studio, and also a rather large and threatening volcano. Fortunately, during ABWH's trip any eruptions were confined to the studio.

"Pretty much at the airport I realised Steve Howe and Rick Wakeman were there. I thought, 'Oh, oh, we're in trouble here'," recalls Bruford who was no less ascerbic in 1989 than he was when he quit Yes for King Crimson in 1972. "This obviously meant it was some sort of Yes project, although the name 'Yes' was not applicable because there was a new band called Yes in California. There was talk of Chris Squire joining the sessions. I said, 'No I can't do it with Chris. How about Tony Levin?' And that was fine.

"Off we went and recorded an LP which turned out to be by a band called Anderson, Bruford, Wakeman & Howe. I thought I was just going to put some drums on a Jon Anderson solo record. But I was always thrilled to play with Tony Levin. The music sounded pretty poky and I thought I could give it a run and see if anything came out of it. I think

---

[23] ABWH v. Yes was eventually settled out of court.

there were moments when it was genuinely very exciting, especially on tracks like 'Birthright' and 'Fist Of Fire'. There were big moments when Steve Howe was on acoustic guitar on top of Wakeman doing these wonderful Elgarian things on piano. For a second you'd think this was really good. This is *fresh*. This is where Yes should be. As a musician in a band you are always thinking, 'This is rubbish, I've heard this before, this is all imitative dross, but here is where it really sounds fresh. We should make more music like this.' "

When the band came to London and appeared at a press reception Bill came over to me and said rather mysteriously, "One step forward, two steps backward." I had little idea what he meant at the time. For a while Bill thought ABWH held out considerable promise and allowed himself to become quite excited about the prospect of doing more with the band. "Then came a big tour and there was very little time for rehearsal. So we just played the album on a tour. I thought maybe we could try a second shot at it and go into the studio to try round two. Again, some of the stuff we did as a trio – Tony Levin, Steve Howe and me – before Jon got in – sounded just terrific. But by this time the band was consuming so much money that the record company now felt obliged to dictate the songs. He who pays the piper calls the tune. So if you are a record company paying some kids millions of dollars to make a record you feel entitled to put in your six penn'orth. Trouble with that is you've then got record executives on the telephone every morning saying, 'Why don't you speed the bridge up? Why don't you take the tambourine away from the chorus?' Added to which Brian Lane, the manager, had perceived that on the American stadium circuit you can't really go round twice without some sort of a change. 'Anderson, Bruford, Wakeman & Howe' had done very well actually and sold three quarters of a million copies. The song 'Brother Of Mine' was all but a hit."

It seemed like ABWH was a viable project and certainly Yes fans welcomed the chance to see them. Although I never saw the band in concert, their appearance on a live video was very impressive. It was great to see Steve, Rick and Bill back together with Jon. But it couldn't last.

Says Bill, "The guys were trying to figure out how to improve on the first album. So we went to the South of France and a studio called Miraval for one of the worst, most unpleasant recording sessions I've ever had in my life. It was really dreadful. We started making a second ABWH album. After about a week it turned into a Yes album. The powers that be decided that in order to get sales higher than three quarters of a million it *had* to be a Yes album. The Californian Yessers would be kind of Sello-taped onto the album. The whole thing would become a huge mess. There would then be *eight* members of the band. This whole ghastly mishmash would be produced by a guy called Jonathan Elias and the album was going to be called *Union*. All this was going on while the musicians were kind of noodling and thinking what to play. The other Yessers included all the other lot – Rabin, White, Squire and anybody who wasn't in the European Yes! You see Jon and Chris had previously fallen out . . . one of a hundred and ten falling outs.

"So this record proceeded from something that was really quite promising, had not everybody got greedy. In my world everyone would have worked on ABWH and come up with fresh material. There was a plan and it could have continued. However Yes as ever is guided financially. Most of its musical movements now are motivated by sheer lack of money. In other words, because money needs to come in fast all the time, the shortest possible route to money is taken. It means the quickest delivery of the wrong album, the quickest booking of the wrong tour. Anything to help the next renegotiating of a publishing contract to keep the money coming in. So the group is always poorly financed and poorly structured which gives it no artistic freedom. So as soon as ABWH was about to flourish it was extinguished, either by businessmen being greedy or by the necessity of musicians to have more and more money. They were unable to make decisions in the studio and didn't know what they were recording. It was a horrible situation. Eventually a ghastly kind of lumpy album, automated to death with absolutely no feel, a sort of Yes compromise album called *Union* appeared, which then sold precisely the same number of copies as the ABWH album – 750,000."

Steve Howe was equally critical of *Union*. "It was a stupid, stupid waste of money and it wasn't even fun to make. It was fun when we started, when we were doing ABWH II and before it became Yes. To be honest I think both Brian Lane and Jon Anderson desperately wanted ABWH to be called Yes. Bill and I didn't want it to be called Yes because we wanted it to be a new band. But Yes at that point were behind and didn't have anything going so they kind of got moved over to Arista at great expense to us and then they stuck four tracks on the album which became a horrible hodge-podge. At first we thought it would hold water because of the quality of our music, let alone what they could come up with."

Before the *Union* armistice Chris Squire had been busy trying to keep the 'official' Yes together. "I guess we were going through that state of flux again, trying to re-invent Yes for the Nineties," he admits. In the absence of Jon Anderson as a working partner, Chris had begun working with American guitarist and songwriter Billy Sherwood. One of the best songs that came out of the Los Angeles camp was the Squire/Sherwood tune 'Love Conquers All' with lead vocals by Trevor Rabin, which later appeared on the 1991 *Yes Years* CD box set.

"Chris carried on making the next Yes album in Los Angeles with Trevor," explains Alan White, the only other long-standing member of the 'official' Yes. "At this time Billy Sherwood also started to get involved. Then the *Union* tour came about and everybody played on stage together. We were doing an album in LA while Anderson, Wakeman, Bruford and Howe were doing their own thing. We called them the Yes East while we were the Yes West."

The album *Union* was released in April 1991. Says Rick Wakeman, "I called the album *Onion* because it brought tears to my eyes every time I heard it! The *Union* album was the biggest pile of junk ever because when it was put together we weren't in the studio half the time. That's where technology really hurts because they did things like put stuff on computer and completely change it. It was an awful, disgraceful album. Because of the computers they had changed all my parts and I didn't recognise anything that I'd done. The producer got his mates in to play and the only person who didn't play on it was my dog."

Trevor Rabin laughed when I mentioned *Union* to him in 1998. "I'm happy to tell you I hated it! I thought one or two of the songs that Yes West did were okay like 'Lift Me Up' and 'Miracle Of Life'. Some of the stuff that ABWH had done was okay too, although it was nothing spectacular. The album was basically half of ABWH and half of the Yes I was in and when it was put together it was such a mishmash I just thought it was awful. It was a black mark on Yes I think. There are a couple of black marks actually. *Tormato* wasn't a particularly good album in my view."

★　★　★

The rights to the name 'Yes' were owned not just by Chris Squire (as the longest serving member) but by whoever was a member of Yes at the time. "It's not owned by Chris alone," says Steve. "The members of the band have a joint share, as I do when I'm a member. But if you leave technicalities have to be performed and certain eventualities are executed which are rules of the agreements. Basically it's 'goodbye'!"

To complete the Yes-like ambience of ABWH another old friend was roped in. Roger Dean had already been approached in the mid–Eighties to do some work for the group. Roger: "After *Big Generator* Phil Carson rang me and said they'd like to work with me again and could I design a new Yes logo? I did a square logo which I thought was great. But nothing came of it because Jon left the band and formed Anderson, Bruford, Wakeman & Howe which to me was like working with Yes. I enjoyed working with ABWH and that was good fun. Then later they did an album called *Union* and on that album I decided to put both logos!"

Jon, Rick and Steve were quite happy with ABWH but the drummer had become disenchanted after his experiences making their aborted second album. In a way it justified his decision to leave Yes for Robert Fripp's band back in the Seventies. "King Crimson, which has actually taken up more of my musical life than Yes, works in an entirely different mode," explains Bruford. "It takes full control of its own circumstances and makes music, any kind it wants, at any time it sees fit. It doesn't have to *kowtow* to a record company because it has a cash flow problem. So I get slightly irritated when King Crimson and Yes get muddled up together. They are entirely different working environments. One is in a permanent state of hysteria and the other is a relaxed situation where you can make some music if you want. They are as different as jazz is from rock. So the Anderson, Bruford, Wakeman and Howe thing ended rather sadly. *Union* was a very unhappy album which Rick didn't like and as far as I can make out . . . nobody liked. I thought the best things on there were Trevor Rabin's songs. Heaven knows who it was all credited to. There was a cast of thousands! It was a typical product of a record company's boardroom. The diseased thinking those people have will produce records like *Union* which are complete abortions."

If Bill sounds scathing in his present-day assessment of his old group, it is only because Yes once meant so much to him. "I feel sorry for Yes in a way, because this inability to control the finances has always meant they have lurched from one ill-considered decision to another. As a result their audience has been long-suffering in the extreme. I gave up ages ago as a fan of Yes. I lost it somewhere in the Eighties and didn't hear much of their music for a while."

From his office in Los Angeles, their old record company ally Phil Carson could see that the group (or groups – nobody was quite sure) was in trouble again. "[Manager] Tony Dimitriades phoned and asked me if I'd help out with Yes again as nothing was working. We reformed the band again and did the *Union* tour which was hugely successful."

Rick Wakeman found himself back in Yes for the third time when he was asked to take part in this 1989 tour. Says Rick, "The *Union* tour was a wonderful tour. Everybody was unhappy with the record – but the tour was fantastic." Rick could see problems from the start with the ABWH concept, however well intentioned. "That was desperately confusing for a lot of people because there were these guys who had written the music they were playing but apparently couldn't use the name of Yes. It was so bizarre. There were two bands at the same time and it was so ridiculous. But the *Union* tour was undoubtedly the most enjoyable Yes tour I ever did."

Jon Anderson loved it too. He found himself in the middle of the revolving stage watching the massed group of musicians go round and listening to the audiences cheer. "I felt like a bee buzzing around and pollinating everyone!" he says.

Bill Bruford, not surprisingly, was less impressed. "It was a ludicrous plan to marry the bands," he says. "I was on the *Union* tour which played 'in the round' and I didn't enjoy it very much. I was there to be well paid and I was also there for old time's sake and to spend a happy summer with some old acquaintances. This was not a time of creative music making. Alan I like a lot personally but I don't think we ever managed to co-operate in a musical sense. I kind of bolted myself on in a wholly unnecessary way. It was a bit like the cast of *Dallas* y'know? People bought tickets so they could see all these apparently feuding people standing on the same stage together smiling. I don't mind that. I was happy to do it for three months and then I really had to go back to work. It was a nightmare on stage with far too many people coming and going. 'Owner Of A Lonely Heart' got bogged down with at least five people playing ten instruments. It was sort of unnecessary. But then if you let the industry dictate to you, then you will get no less than you deserve. Yes has got no more and no less than it deserved – good, bad or indifferent. Personally I would have liked to see the band flourish and have a great creative output, but I think I sensed as far back as 1972 that that was unlikely. I don't think it has developed much. To be honest I never listened to *Topographic Oceans* but I thought 'Owner Of A Lonely Heart' was great. Maybe that could have gone further, but it was really Trevor's work!"

Steve Howe was part of the *Union* world tour which included spectacular dates at London's Wembley Arena in June, 1991, but he later left Yes again to tour as a solo performer. At the time he professed to be glad to be away from the pressures of a mega group situation. He confided later that at his wife Janet's suggestion he had brought a rowing machine before the tour in order to get fit for the physical ordeal of *Union*. "When the show came over to Europe from the States it got a bit messy on stage," he recalls. "There wasn't the keenness that the States brought about. However once we got back to London all the discipline came back. There was a kind of message that told us, 'You keep over to your side of the stage and do what you are supposed to do.' Everybody had a sense of duty and they weren't in it for scoring their own goals. England and the first leg of American touring was fine but the rest wasn't so balanced. With eight people and eight different possible directions it could be difficult."

Jon Anderson had often expressed the desire to get the original band back together again and this seemed to be the closest he could get to that idea. To this suggestion Bill responds, "Which original band? I'm not interested in that at all. I could only do a nostalgia tour once. Me – I'm still trying to get better on the drum set, which is what I've been doing for thirty years – and I'm beginning to make some headway!"

Jim Halley, who had been working with Asia during the Eighties, came back to Yes for the *Union* tour on which he worked specifically for Steve Howe. Steve travelled separately from the rest of the group during this period, not because he wished to appear to be standoffish – he just wanted to get on with the job. "He didn't particularly like hanging around in hotel rooms waiting for other band members or going to airports waiting for flights," says Jim. "He got himself a Mercedes station wagon and I drove him around the States and Canada for months on end. On the day of the gig we wouldn't travel more than 300 miles. If it was further than that, we'd leave after the previous night's gig and drive so far and then just find a motel. You don't go to sleep for two or three hours after a gig anyway, so we used that time for travelling and the next morning we'd complete the journey. It was fascinating to stop off somewhere in the dark and wake up in the morning and find yourself in the middle of a desert surrounded by red hills and fabulous scenery."

Scenery apart there was no doubt Steve Howe was also unsettled by the prospect of having Trevor Rabin on the same stage as him. He did his best to cope with the situation imposed by the 'Union' concept. Jim: "On stage during that tour Steve just did his thing and played the guitar. It was a bit strange having another guitarist around who had been playing Steve's part on previous tours on standard Yes tunes like 'Roundabout'. Suddenly there are two guitarists playing 'Roundabout'. It was like, 'Hang on a minute, he's playing my part! I don't want him to play that part. I want to play it because I recorded it and I don't want anybody else playing it. And I don't want to play Yes stuff that I didn't record!' Steve is very particular about his art. Wakeman must have felt the same about Tony Kaye and Bruford must have felt the same way about Alan White. Trevor and Steve did come to an arrangement but it was a little fraught at the beginning. An accommodation was made where they discussed it and came to a conclusion about who should play what. I tried my best to develop a rapport between the pair of them. It's not that they weren't speaking to each other. Steve just travelled separately from the rest of the band and they only ever met when they got on stage."

There was little socialising on the road between the band members, apart from Wakeman and Rabin. Bill says Chris used to stand on the other side of the stage from him and never exchanged a word. The only time most of the guys really came across each other was at a sound check for ten minutes. Says Jim, "They really didn't have a lot of communication going on. You'd hear that one person wasn't happy, so I'd suggest maybe they should talk to each other. I played a part in that because it hadn't really been discussed before, about who played what. I remember we arrived in Brussels in Belgium for the European dates of that tour and Trevor and Steve finally spoke to each other and worked out stuff. After all Trevor Rabin had been instrumental in keeping the Yes thing going for all those years without Steve Howe or Rick Wakeman involved."

Trevor Rabin's fondest memory of the *Union* tour was playing with Rick Wakeman. "Rick and I got on very well," he says. "I played guitar and he played keyboards and there was a song he played each night of the tour from *The Six Wives Of Henry VIII* that was particularly tricky. One night I jumped in on guitar and played with him. From then on we kind of bonded and have remained really good friends both musically and personally. While ABWH was going on, I was doing my solo tours and albums. Then the *Union* thing happened."

Trevor says the *Union* concept was done for "all the wrong reasons" but won't elaborate. "They all knew exactly what it was about. However I got on with everyone fine. When I say I got on well with Rick, it doesn't mean I didn't get on with Steve. I certainly got on with Bill. It's just that Rick and I established a musical and personal relationship. It was very strange doing the tour. I went in with major reservations. At the rehearsals I had squinty eyes, wondering what was going to happen! In fact the first couple of rehearsals were a bit of a nightmare. But it came together and melted into something okay. Some of the gigs were pretty good. It wasn't always possible to do the show 'in the round' in South America for example."

Up on stage for the *Union* tour were Jon Anderson, Chris Squire, Rick Wakeman, Tony Kaye, Steve Howe, Trevor Rabin, Bill Bruford and Alan White. "I was the main anchor," says Alan. "Bill played a lot of top kit stuff. I had been playing the songs for 18 years longer than he had! The band had grown used to playing them my way, so it was interesting that we had to turn it around a bit. But it really worked when we got going on the road. The whole band just got on with it. Quite frankly they were paying us well enough! In fact the band played quite well considering it was a big band with lots of doubled up instruments and complex arrangements."

Despite suspicions and reservations the *Union* tour was meant to be a healing process which tried to make amends for all the past upsets. Trevor Horn and Geoff Downes were not part of the process, but at least Steve, Rick and Tony Kaye were back on board and sharing a stage with Trevor Rabin, Bill and Alan. Jon was in the middle, rather like the sorcerers' apprentice, unleashing the powers of magic and conducting a spectacular show. Among their oldest fans sound man Roy Clair was delighted at this latest turn of events.

"They did great business on that tour. It was a long time since anyone had heard Rick Wakeman in America and a lot of the crowd came back to hear that old, nostalgic Yes. Tony Kaye had come back too but he wasn't the multiple keyboard wizard. He played the organ and refused to use the new synthesisers. When it was Trevor Rabin and Tony Kaye in the band in the Eighties, I missed Wakeman a lot. He had a special magic and I missed Steve too. But I had to get over that. I was supposed to be a professional and not care who's in the band and get on with doing the sound. But I did feel emotional because I was with them for so long and got so accustomed to hearing every note of every song played every night the same way. When it changed it didn't have the same feeling. The newer kids liked it. The band's new audiences liked the *90125* era and 'Owner Of A Lonely Heart' rejuvenated their career. The audiences got younger and it wasn't the old hippies anymore. The kids had never even heard of Yes and they heard the single and thought 'Let's go and hear this group' not knowing they had been around for 20 years before that."

Roy Clair observed that Yes had found a new audience to conquer and they succeeded. They also played to more people than ABWH. "When Jon did Anderson, Bruford, Wakeman and Howe it was mostly concerts in 'sheds' playing to crowds of around 5,000 a night," he says. "For some reason that group was big in Canada but without Rabin they lost a lot of those young kids who came to hear 'Owner Of A Lonely Heart'. In fact they did play the tune because Jon felt it was half his. But audiences grew suspicious. 'What's going on here?' Chris and Alan weren't in the group and Trevor Rabin wasn't in the group and they wanted to know why. In fact Yes with Chris, Alan and Trevor was in limbo."

According to eyewitness Clair everyone seemed to get along. Diplomacy helped. "They didn't all play at the same time," he says. "Some of them would walk off when it wasn't their song. Steve didn't play on the Trevor Rabin album material. He would walk off and then when he played, Trevor would walk off. A little jealousy? Just a little!"

Rick Wakeman's only regret after the *Union* tour is that he and Trevor Rabin were never together in a line-up of Yes that recorded an album. "The one line-up that is missing from the whole of Yes history is a studio album where Trevor Rabin and I play together. When I am a very old man, sitting by the fire reminiscing and I am asked if I have any regrets about Yes, my only regret would be there isn't a studio album with Trevor and me together. We would have had a wonderful time."

Trevor Rabin is a professional musician not given to great outbursts, but despite all the problems it seems he too enjoyed the *Union* tour. Shortly after the event, in 1991, he told me, "It was a unique experience because there was no telling what was going to happen! The funny thing was the way it evolved. First Jon Anderson called me and actually asked me to play on the Anderson, Bruford, Wakeman, Howe record, which I thought was a kind of strange request since there had been all these court battles between them. I was also pretty hard at work on something else and didn't want to do it anyway. That evolved into Jon calling me again, asking if I had any songs that might be appropriate for what they were doing. That seemed more logical so I sent some tapes. They said they liked 'em all and wanted to use them. I had a problem with that because there were some that I wanted to perform myself. But after a bit of haggling and talking we decided to put a whole comprehensive thing together. I was apprehensive and wondered if it was a legitimate thing to do, or a pure unadulterated sell-out! But once I had come to terms with the idea and realised we would do three songs I kinda liked, it seemed okay. Also I knew that when I came to do my next solo LP I would want new songs. Anyway, I was itching to get back on the road. The line-up seemed pretty interesting so I thought, well yeah, let's do it. I finished off the three songs and they landed up on the *Union* album."

Trevor found it a strange situation being in a kind of class reunion with people he hadn't met before. He had already been with Yes for nine years himself at this point and yet in the eyes of some of the veterans he was still 'the new boy'. "I'm the oldest rookie in the business!" he jokes. "I hadn't met Bill Bruford before the tour, although I had met Steve ten years earlier when I joined up with Chris Squire. I had been in Yes longer than some of the original members like Bill."

He found the revolving stage a moving experience. "It was actually very useful. We had a band of eight people who hadn't all played together before and with regard to Alan, Bill, Steve and myself with significantly different styles, we had to get the interplay going, so it was very useful being on a round stage. It was separate yet together. At first it was very weird because it didn't seem rock'n'roll. But once I got used to it, I kinda enjoyed it."

So after the *Union* experience did Yes end up as friends? "As friendly as people in Yes ever seem to get," says Trevor. "I don't think it is any secret that the band goes through periods of anguish and dissension and disagreement. That happens for some reason. It's still there and is part of the reason the band makes the kind of music it does. Relatively speaking the tour ended with us on pretty good terms."

There remained a difference in culture between the old and 'new' versions of Yes. Trevor Rabin was unable to detect any thread connecting the early Yes with the music played by the band with whom he was associated during the Eighties. "Was there a thread? I have to be honest and say – not really. The way the old Yes used to write and my way are quite different. They would get together and blindly go into things. I tend to get an idea and just finish it, then go ahead with the recording process. I didn't think *Union* was as good as *90125* or *Big Generator*. It was dissipated and two separate entities on one album. I don't think it was as cohesive as a band starting from scratch to do an album. But in the context of what was done and the reasons behind it . . . it kind of worked."

But Chris Squire was knocked out at the way the *Union* tour came together. "We had two of everything, two drummers, two guitar players, two keyboard players but there wasn't two of me and there wasn't two of Jon! Jon and I had spoken about doing this reunion for quite a few years. When it was finally suggested I was a bit reticent about the reunion. But I was surprised at how well it worked out. The funny thing was Rick Wakeman and Tony Kaye had never really met much before this tour. It turned out to be a nice way to celebrate our 23rd anniversary. And there never really was a problem with ABWH and Yes y'know. It all worked out in the end!"

Says Trevor, "The strange thing is the *Union* tour was quite fun once it started to get going. It was just the album. In fact I have never listened to it all the way through, I couldn't bring myself to do it. Who was in overall charge of it? Accountants mostly!"

When Yes had last played in England for their *90125* tour dates they had been disappointed by the audience reaction, which was not as loud or demonstrative as it had been in the States. But in 1991 they were very pleased with the warm welcome back home. During the year their *Yesshows* world tour included UK dates at Birmingham's NEC arena on June 25 and London's Wembley Arena on June 28 and 29. To coincide with the tour the four CD box set *Yes Years* (Atco) was released and it included a handsome booklet tracing the band's complex history. There was also a *Greatest Video Hits* which included many rarely seen promo videos, mainly from the early Eighties. The band didn't have much to do with the production of the box set as they were signed to Arista at the time. "Actually the record company put that together by themselves but we were consulted on which tapes and versions to use," says Trevor Rabin. "I thought it was done in a very tasteful way."

* * *

By 1992, the *Union* tour a fading memory, Rick Wakeman, Bill Bruford and Steve Howe were no longer members of Yes despite hopes in certain quarters that they would stay in situ. "I dreamed up a very plausible plan," said Steve, "where we would continue working as eight people. There are four guys who basically write the material and need to collaborate to get the arranging done. I suggested those four get together to get the music sorted. Arista were right behind this and said, 'Don't try to play together all the time. Bring in guests and just have fun with each other.' That was the idea I projected . . . and nobody liked it. Well the Los Angeles department didn't like it and then Jon said that the three of us weren't needed. He could see no way forward unless he got on with something, so Bill, Rick and I took a back seat.

"After 'Union' there was a time when there was eight people in the group and nobody knew who was permanently in the band and whether we were going to stay together. Then I got a call saying, 'Well, it's going to be *this* way.' It meant that Yes was going to carry on and do the *Talk* album without Rick, Bill and I. So I could see the sense in that. There was going to be big battles about who did what. But Roy Lott, who at the time was head of Arista along with Clive Davis, had a terrific idea. He said, 'Well guys, don't play together all the time! Do tracks that feature different people.' And that's what I wanted to do actually on the tour. I didn't want us to play together all the time and make the music go two places at once, but to try and feature two different line-ups. But that never happened because people like to be on stage and they didn't wanna leave. So you couldn't get anybody off the stage. Yes has had people join and leave in such a variety of fashions it's impossible to describe. But certainly they are curious and unusual. Rick, Bill and I were disappointed because we had sacrificed ABWH for Yes and at the end of it come out without Yes and without ABWH!

"So that's why I rejoined Asia as a special guest and in 1993/94 I went hell for leather on my solo career. I thought, 'What can I do completely alone?' That gave me a new lease of life because I discovered more of my own audience and my own music than I had ever thought possible. I suddenly freed up the idea of playing music in different settings. I had a whale of a time and went to Argentina, Japan and toured England three times and America twice. I did a lot of work in those two years."

In the end, after the dust had settled on the *Union* project and ABWH was also a distant memory, a new Yes album called *Talk* was produced by Trevor Rabin, featuring himself on guitar with Jon Anderson, Chris Squire, Tony Kaye and Alan White. It was released on the Victory label in 1994, and came during a period when the band was still under the aegis of Tony Dimitriades and East End Management. All the music and lyrics were written by Trevor Rabin and Jon Anderson. Tracks like 'The Calling' had a very powerful modern sound, with Trevor's angular lead guitar to the fore. The album was 'Dedicated To All Yes Fans' but was it really Yes music or just contemporary LA rock? It was an extraordinary example of the way the band was being tugged in different directions, swinging around like a magnetic compass during a period of sunspot activity. Even so, there were still elements of the traditional Yes sound, typified by the addition of Tony Kaye's Hammond organ, the occasional spurt of acoustic guitar and the vocal harmonies.

Alan White says that *Talk* was an album on which they spent a lot of time using new technology. "We had about 30 gigabytes of information and it was all done on a computer. A lot of the drums were played live but it was very experimental. It was also one of the most innovative albums the band has ever done with some great pieces of music. Trevor was at the helm a lot for that one. He was in the studio every day for 15 hours. We'd come in and out but it was basically his album. We toured with that in 1995."

Says Trevor, "At the end of the *Union* thing me, Chris and Alan decided we'd like to get back to the 'Yes West' line-up." The album he produced came out on Phil Carson's Victory label complete with a new logo on the cover designed by Peter Max. Although many Yes fans are disdainful of *Talk*, it does have character and power. On the opening number, 'The Calling', a huge drum sound is omnipresent and the socking back beat and raunchy guitar riff makes the band sound like The Rolling Stones. It's one of the rockiest and most natural tracks the band has done, despite the reputedly heavy use of technology.

"When we did *Talk* it was a journey into the unknown," says Trevor. "People get mislead. It wasn't done on computer, it was just done non-linear on hard drive which meant things could be manipulated in a different way. There were proper instruments – real guitars and drums and stuff – but no recording tape was used. Basically the entire album was done on four Macintoshes and I had a great time doing it and that really set me up to want to do film soundtracks. On tracks like 'I'm Waiting', I'd written that for Jon and he came in and re-wrote the lyrics and added some nice melodies and stuff. 'Real Love' was kind of eerie. When I started writing 'Endless Dream' which is the last track it seemed like an endless dream – it was such a long theme but I just had such fun while I was doing it. I'll never forget that when Jon came in to sing the backing track he had tears in his eyes. It was the first time I'd seen him with tears, other than when tours didn't do too well! When we went on the road I actually played the piano intro 'Silent Spring' live and there were a couple of times when I hiccuped."

'Endless Dream' is in three parts and there are some strange effects used, like elephants trumpeting. "It was actually the guitar," says Trevor. "That was one of the only extended pieces I did with Yes. The record company were very touchy about us doing singles and not doing pieces that were too long. When Chris, me, Alan and Tony Kaye first got together one of the first pieces we had was called 'Cinema' which was on *90125* but only in the first few minutes. However the original version of that song was over twenty minutes long. We had to cut it down to two minutes. We just used the beginning."

After *Talk* the Rabin connection seemed to be at an end. "What year did it stop for me? About 1989!" he says. "No . . . I haven't finished my association with Yes. Chris Squire called me at the end of their 1998 tour and we had a conversation." Trevor didn't see any of the band's *Open Your Eyes* tour dates and has yet to meet their most recent member, pianist Igor Khoroshev. "When I got out of Yes it was after 14 years and it was something I'd been thinking about for a while. I just thought I was stagnating and so was the band. I feel sure they are being more creative at this point. The funny thing is when I first joined the band people at a press conference asked me: 'Is this band going to last forever?' Who knows what the future will bring? I think after the *Talk* tour I was pretty much creatively done. What I wanted to do with the *Talk* album was write it and then tour for a couple of weeks so the band could rehearse and then record it live. Then I would put the vocals on. A lot of *90125* was really just the band playing live. It's much better to do it live than use click tracks. I'm not blaming anyone for the situation.

"When I left Yes the band was like a beached whale. Once it was in the ocean it swam magnificently. But to get it in there was a hefty job. I had wanted to tour under a different name in little clubs and just do a couple of weeks of playing, so we could learn the stuff properly and see how people responded to the music and then go and record *Talk*. But we never got around to that and because of the technology the album came across a little cold and it's a crunchy sounding record. Maybe somebody can remaster and warm it up a bit! We had a long tour on *Talk*, although it was the beginning of the end for me. I did actually suggest at one point that Billy Sherwood should come on the road with us. He had been doing some stuff with Chris and I thought it would be good to have him there to help out. But at the end of the tour I called Chris and said I wanted to move on."

After splitting with Yes at the end of the *Talk* tour Trevor Rabin concentrated on writing and recording film music and has since done around seven movie soundtracks. He was introduced to the scene by a friend who worked in a restaurant owned by martial arts movie actor Steven Seagal. He learned that Steven Seagal wanted to learn to play the Jimi Hendrix tune 'Red House' on guitar. "He asked if I would teach him and later I got a call from Steven asking if I could come over. I went over to his house, he played guitar and I taught him 'Red House'. He was really pleased and then said, 'I hear you wanna do movies. Do you wanna do mine?' So I did a Steven Seagal action movie called *Glimmer Man* and we became good friends."

Trevor has since done music for such movies as *Con Air* and *Home Grown*, a story about the pot growers of Northern California. He also did the music for the Bruce Willis blockbuster *Armageddon*, one of the biggest movies of 1998. His next project was *Enemy Of The State*, starring Will Smith and Gene Hackman. In 1999 he intends to release a new solo album and until Rick Wakeman fell ill there were also plans afoot for a collaboration between him and the former Yes keyboard player.

Although Trevor Rabin now has a secure future in both movies and his own solo work, he still has a high regard for the band to which he made such a big contribution during his many years at the helm. "The direction of Yes obviously changed once the five of us got together and after 14 years it's obviously time to go back. Up until the end of the 14 years I was the longest standing Yes guitarist. Chris Squire is the only one that's been there all the way through the band's history. I call him The Caretaker. The band sometimes hits on a formula and might want to move on but finds it hard to change either because of the record company or because the fans want things to stay the same. Most bands spend 15 years doing their first album and five minutes doing their second. They go on the road and play the second album and all everyone wants to hear is the first one! I'll never forget during the writing of *Talk* I spent some time with Jon and he had a whole load of equipment set up. He wrote this piece of music with some really low end equipment which he usually has around! I asked him what it was about and he said, 'It's what the day was like.' It was really attractive. He has a really creative imagination."

But Steve Howe, watching from the sidelines, remained unimpressed by *Talk*. "In 1995 *Talk* left a debris of un-Yes-ness! I know what our fans like and that album took the band to another level that was more remote from the fans. I had gone to Argentina just after Yes had been there with *Talk* and I heard all sorts of things about the show and about the ticket sales and about what happened in Florida. The whole thing was a disaster. They didn't even come to Europe because the shows were cancelled, so they had a lot of disappointments."

Yet again Yes appeared to be on the verge of collapsing from within. Yet again it was necessary to step back and reorganise in order to survive. And yet again, against all the odds and without Trevor Rabin, they would climb back from the brink of extinction with new management, a new label and new ideas . . . and some old faces.

10

OPEN YOUR EYES

Yes entered a strange period after completing their *Talk* album and tour. They seemed in danger of slipping back into an obscurity more dark and profound than at any time in their history. The band themselves may have had other ideas but the outside world had turned its attention away from the rock of ages past and was now concerned with far more exciting matters. From the start of the Nineties there was a whole new wave of bands and styles. Grunge co-existed with Rap while Heavy Metal became an increasingly diverse sub culture. Guns N'Roses, Megadeth, Metallica, Nirvana and Pearl Jam revitalised rock music with their tremendous power and commitment, and won the hearts and minds of a mass international audience. They also intrigued the critics.

Where could a band like Yes fit into this process? The answer was they couldn't. Rock critics were more likely to dissect the latest Goth phenomenon from Sweden than some Seventies supergroup. There were other problems for a band like Yes to face. Live music itself was beating a retreat in the face of the dance culture and its astonishing diversity of styles. If a promoter wanted a queue outside a club, or a crowd to pack out a festival, it was better to book a DJ than a live band. If this was tough for new young bands, it was even harder for veteran musicians now beginning to look their age, who could no longer hope to represent the cutting edge of anything. But that didn't mean they couldn't still function in a meaningful way and find their target audience. Astonishingly, despite all the changes in the topographic world spinning around them, Yes could find a way back to the people. By the end of the Nineties Yes could celebrate a thirtieth anniversary in style with a world tour and a revitalised line-up that mixed old and new talents.

Phil Carson, still a Yes loyalist, could see the problems that faced the group at the start of the decade and did his best to help out. "I was working with JVC when I set up the Victory label. I signed Yes and did what was probably one of the best albums they have ever done which was *Talk*. But of course it was totally at the wrong time. It sold around 300,000 around the world but nothing like what it should have done. I still think it was a bloody good album that Trevor produced. We did a pretty big tour and that was the end of it."

The album came out at a time when all the bands that Phil Carson had worked and grown up with had by now finished their 20-year careers. "They had been big from 1970 to 1990 so they'd had a good run," he says. "In the *Billboard* chart, even by the end of 1989 you would still see in the Top Twenty bands that had been around for 15 years or more. It was a unique period in the history of music when the parents and their teenage children were listening to the same groups! Led Zeppelin, Yes, Emerson, Lake & Palmer, Journey and Boston were still being played on radio. That couldn't last forever and that's when the musical revolution of grunge came along. It broke so quickly the radio formats fragmented overnight and there was nowhere for Yes to get played. It has affected everyone of that generation since. Jimmy Page and Robert Plant can't sell records. Their albums only just crawl up to gold level in the States. That kind of music is over as far as kids are concerned. Kids in the Fifties wouldn't have bought Glenn Miller records and that was only ten years before. Yet for *twenty* years the same kind of rock music was in vogue. At the start of the Nineties, all that genre of rock music virtually disappeared overnight. Artists who had sold ten million records found themselves selling two million and then zero."

If Yes were aware of these trends and this perceived wisdom, they cheerfully ignored it all, kept the faith and entered a surprisingly busy and productive era once they had recovered from the *Talk* period. The *Talk* album actually took 18 months to produce. After its release and the subsequent tour Trevor Rabin left the band and everything went very quiet until Jon and Chris discussed the idea of writing and performing together once again.

Says Jon, "The plan was very simple. I said to Chris and Alan that we really should work with Rick and Steve again and take Yes intact into the 21st century. The main point in getting back together was really to explore the classic line-up of the Seventies and find out how we would work together more than 18 years later."

After travelling the world Jon was now living in California, and he located an area where he thought the group – himself, Squire, Howe, Wakeman and White – could play and record. A series of three concerts was organised for March 1996 at the Freemont Theater in San Luis Obispo. Fans flocked to the shows after picking up the news about these performances on the Internet. The band performed brilliantly, their work captured on *Keys To Ascension*, the first of two albums recorded live during the San Luis Obispo concerts. The old firm were back, proving they still had their technical ability as well as their passion for playing those great

Yes arrangements. The album featured such classics as 'Roundabout', 'Starship Trooper', 'America', 'Awaken', 'Onward', 'Siberian Khatru' and 'The Revealing Science Of God'.

They also played two new studio pieces, 'That, That Is', a combination of four pieces, and 'Be The One', the first song that Anderson and Squire had written together in almost 20 years with contributions from Steve Howe and Alan White. With an attractive Roger Dean design the whole package should have been a big hit but it didn't quite work out that way.

Says Jon Anderson, "'Be The One' is about commitment and that's what we did. We made a commitment about being together again. You always believe what you are doing is right for the moment. So when we did the album *Keys To Ascension* we made sure it had all our greatest songs like 'Siberian Khatru', 'The Revealing Science Of God' and 'Starship Trooper'. We also had an hour and a half of new music on there. But because the record company that released it was not a big label there was no big money spent on promotion. Everywhere we went most people didn't even know about it. Only real Yes fanatics went out and bought it, yet I think it's a very valid piece of music for the end of the century. Pieces like 'That, That Is' are modern music and as valid as anything we have ever done.

"Unfortunately, after we recorded them Rick Wakeman decided he didn't want to tour anymore with the group so we had to let go of all that music that we had just recorded. It was an hour and a half of modern music that we wanted to take on the road. It took Rick a while to tell us he was frustrated with the business side. Who isn't? Hey . . . so get in the queue Rick. None of us are happy with the business and the way things are sometimes. None of us are happy with the way people who call themselves managers treat musicians. These are the terrible people we seem to fall in with. It's like the Mozart syndrome y'know? You've got to be on your deathbed doing your last piece of music with no money! Every which way I turn, somebody has ripped somebody off. Look at Billy Joel. He was screwed and screwed by people who he thought were his friends. Even Sting got screwed. People will always do things which aren't honest. When Rick decided to leave and didn't want to tour anymore, he was right in his own world. He felt uncomfortable so we just moved on."

Steve Howe was happy to be involved with a Yes that included Jon, Chris, Rick and Alan White. Early in 1995 Jon had called Steve and proposed getting back together with Rick and developing something more thoroughbred in the traditional Yes style. "I said, 'I'd love to do that!'" says Steve. "So in the summer Rick and I had a meeting with Jon in Los Angeles for a couple of days. Rick and I wanted to join the band. But Rick said right from the start he didn't want anything to do with the group's business affairs as it was all a terrible headache. There was a musical enthusiasm but for a year and a half we had management problems. We went from one lot to another and we got bogged down with the wrong people around us. During that time we did *Keys To Ascension* [Volumes One & Two]. In October 1995 we got together and rehearsed but without Rick who wasn't available. We did a mass of old material and it was a huge blackboard list of things to play. We started playing all this stuff and we found that 'yeah, we can do it!' The idea was to put a show together, do a video and make a live CD. It would include some new material as well and that was a bit of a hodge-podge I always thought – but there you are! This was commissioned by Castle Communications and we needed something like that to get going again. We got back together again with Rick in February 1996 and we did a more thorough rehearsal in order to get the show recorded."

The concerts that Steve refers to took place at the Freemont Theater, San Luis Obispo, California, on March 4, 5, and 6, 1996. The studio tracks were recorded during autumn 1995 and spring 1996 at their Yesworld Studio in San Luis Obispo, about three hour's drive north of Los Angeles.

Says Steve, "We did a show which was really poor. The scale and complexity was huge. We did everything from *Close To The Edge* to *Awaken* and *The Revealing Science Of God*. It was an *enormous* show with a wealth of material which was to come out on *Keys* 1 & 2. We did three concerts and it took a lot of juggling around to get the performances we wanted out of the three nights. There were things we did wrong but we won't go into that! We got some studio tracks recorded and mixed as well."

These were 'Be The One' and 'That', That Is which appeared on Volume One of the two CD set.

"After several months of preparation I went to San Luis Obispo and sat there for five weeks," continues Steve. "After four days I was supposed to go home. I was going to check through my vocals and update them. After a few days I called up my wife and said, 'Jan, I think I've got a mission. I'm needed here.' Five weeks later I was still there. There was nobody else in the studio from the band. Jon would pop in periodically but there was nobody from the band to help the studio guys put it together. I tried to make the 'live' material sound like I thought the guys would want. Obviously I didn't receive any income during this period and didn't get any appreciation for it either. But that's the kind of group it is . . . vague. I thought if I sit here long enough I'll make an impression! I could see how Trevor Rabin got left with *Talk* and in a way I got left with *Keys To Ascension*. I just helped bring in some continuity but after it was over I thought, 'Wow, never again.' Don't call me with a project like that. And suddenly *Keys To Ascension Volume Two* is needed! After discussions it was decided that Billy Sherwood would mix the live material. Then we did a remarkable thing. In November 1996, in five weeks, we recorded all the studio music for *Volume Two* which contained 45 minutes of new material called 'Mind Drive'. It has been said that 'Mind Drive' is the best thing we've done since the Seventies. Alan, Chris and Jon had done some demos and I came along and was able to interject some of my own riffs and themes. Jon then went away and Chris, Alan and I spiced it up a bit without changing the keys. We'd finished it in a record five weeks and didn't raise too many compromises. It was all very smooth and we worked like beavers. And then it wasn't put out straight away. The record label said, 'Well, if you're not going to tour, we're not going to put it out.' "

When it came to touring Yes faced two dilemmas – not only were they unsure of what kind of venues in which to perform but Rick Wakeman wasn't keen on touring regardless of where the concerts were held – and as a result the group was weighed down by indecision. Explains Steve Howe, "What happened was two ideas for touring had come up and Rick had said 'no' to both of them. My idea in 1995 was to go out and do a small theatre tour to get the flame going again . . . knock 'em out with a few nights. Everybody said 'yes' then everybody said 'no'. Rick said, 'I don't want to see Yes back doing theatres.' Then in 1996 one of our managers said, 'Okay, let's tour the amphitheatres.' So this tour was booked and we were going to go out and play in amphitheatres. But of course . . . there wasn't going to be anybody there. Nobody knew we were back together and we hadn't done anything. Nothing was happening and Rick then said 'no' to that one too. That was about it. Oh, and there was a third idea. Emerson, Lake & Palmer was going to tour with Yes. Jon didn't want to do that and Rick wasn't promoting the idea either. So we had tours passing us by and potential income . . . all going out the window."

Steve realised that what he considered to be the most crucial aspect of their lives – the opportunity to re-establish Yes as a professional, classic band – was also slipping away. "*Keys* was floating about but there wasn't anything going on. So a year went by and during 1997 we all sensed that we weren't going far with Rick. He got offered a whole new package by Left Bank Management, the deal we were about to do and the whole touring plan, and he turned it down. So we realised that Rick thought he could make more money on his own. So we got tired and kind of gave up on Rick and really everything opened up from then on. Billy Sherwood and Chris did some writing together and then these tapes started coming around. 'Would you like to play on this?' 'What do you think about that?' Meanwhile Jon and I were in different parts of the world. Whenever we spoke on the phone we said, 'Well, we're going to be writing sometime this year, let's try and mix it up with this stuff.' So months went by and I was finishing my own album *Quantum Guitar* together with my son Dylan. So while I was doing that album, Chris was writing with Billy and Jon was doing various projects.

"Eventually by the summer we got together with the new management and they designed a package where we could start work, do lots of touring and have an 18 month plan. Yes desperately needed a sense of organisation. So we all said, 'Yeah, we'll do it.' But when we came to finish the album which became *Open Your Eyes*, Jon and I had to compromise a great deal because we hadn't written or prepared backing tracks. So the tracks on *Open Your Eyes* were basically initiated and put together by Chris and Billy. It's not really Yes music. We had to grin and bear it and add a few bits and pieces. A couple were sort of intended for a Chris Squire solo album but then Billy got very keen to write something for Yes and the whole thing grew into a Yes album. So before you knew it we had the management saying, 'If you make this record quickly you can get on tour and we'll meet the autumn tour schedule.' So it was like a hurricane. At the same time Castle said, 'Oh, you're going to tour? Then we'll put out *Keys 2*.' They put it out just as we started touring America in October, 1997. We were going to release *Open Your Eyes* in early 1998, but when our management saw *Keys 2* coming out they wanted to get the new album out right away. So everything snowballed. But it's not a fan based record. It's a 'Get Yes on the radio' kind of record. Not that there's anything wrong with Yes changing its writing tack. After all, Jon and I had a good old fling in the Seventies. There has to be a balance. It's not a case of Jon and I only wanting to be in Yes if we can write all the material. It's about the group as an interactive, sharing concept. So we shared on *Open Your Eyes* but obviously I think there was far too much of that style of music in there. I couldn't explore enough to make a difference on the record. Anyway by October, 1997 we went on tour in America and first *Keys 2* came out and then *Open Your Eyes*, followed by Jon's solo album, *The More We Know*, and then my album *Quantum Guitar*."

There was certainly confusion about the amount of Yes product hitting the market in 1996/97. "*Open Your Eyes* was a commercial record and Yes shouldn't have done that because they had just done that with *Talk*," says Steve. "And in the middle comes *Keys To Ascension Volume Two* so it's a pretty confusing picture. The only thing that isn't confusing is Yes on stage. That's what started in October and what healed a lot of imbalances. Chris and Alan wanted Billy Sherwood to come into the band and Jon and I wanted Igor Khoroshev. That became the core of the band. Billy helped make this a great touring band and he brought in great writing skills as well. With Igor we had someone who didn't just replace Rick but superseded him. He's a fine player. Igor sent a tape to Jon saying he wanted to work with Yes. He put it away in a box and discovered it when we were looking for a keyboard player. We wanted someone to spend some time with us and really leap on the keyboards. We couldn't see Yes without a keyboard player. Jon played the tape to me in some gardens outside a hotel one day and said: 'What do you think of this guy?' We had been kicking names around and obviously Geoff Downes was in the frame. He'd even been asked if he'd like to join and he'd said yes he would. That was ticking over while Rick was deciding. I thought it was an interesting idea because I knew how well Geoff fitted in on *Drama* and of course we had worked together in Asia. I was strong on Geoff and the guys liked the idea. But when Billy became more involved with *Open Your Eyes* he hadn't given the keyboard player so much room so basically Geoff got on with Asia. Jon and I discussed other people like Eddie Jobson and Patrick Moraz. There was a huge chain of possibles. But we liked the idea of bringing in someone who was unknown and yet was so good. If there was any time when I've thought what a good band Yes was – it's now."

Rick Wakeman felt it was time to let Yes go. "In 1997 they asked me to do a tour with them but I was already working," he explains. "They had booked a lot of dates without telling me, so it was all a mess. I knew that I had the *Return To The Centre Of The Earth* coming up, a big project for EMI. I've got my TV programmes and I've got my own studio and label. I had to make some decisions in my life and I felt that Yes had gone as far as it could go. As individuals people can go elsewhere and do other things. If I personally had anything to do with it, Yes should not have done that last tour. Sure they should work with other people and find themselves again, then maybe every two years get together and do a few shows. Not a whole tour. But it's not for me to make these decisions. I could talk about all the difficulties with Yes I have been involved with over the years, but it is much more enjoyable for me to remember all the great times and positive things that came out. Nothing good ever comes out of backbiting and at the end of the day problems tend to sort themselves out. Out of all the rows, some really good music has emerged. I was going to say Yes have not been well managed, but the problem is Yes is unmanageable. Yes have got through more managers than Manchester City. I have to say that Brian Lane was the best manager the band ever had. He was the closest to having any control. But the band goes off and does things without prior thought, which sometimes works and sometimes doesn't. The amount of money that Yes has wasted over the years is beyond belief. But I hope very much that Yes gets remembered for the good things that it did and not for the periods of decline. So much good music came out of the band and at the end of the day, I hope that's what people remember."

There remains a strong bond between Jon Anderson and his charismatic keyboard virtuoso, and the singer much regretted that Rick had decided against going on the road again, evidently for good. "I've nothing but good memories of Rick and there is a great camaraderie amongst all the musicians who ever worked within Yes," says Jon. "We should stick to that. Like any kind of marriage there are ups and downs and we shouldn't go around saying things. There were times when we didn't agree but that's part of being in a team. Everyone has different emotions and that's what perpetuates the Yes style of music."

With Jon Anderson still of the opinion that Yes had more to achieve, the group was thus revived with yet another new line-up. The first of the new recruits was Billy Sherwood who would become the 13th member of Yes. Billy was born in Las Vegas, Nevada, on March 14, 1965, and although it wasn't until 1996 that he became a full member, he began his association with Yes in 1991. He co-wrote 'The More We Live – Let Go' and 'Love Conquers All' with Chris Squire for the *Union* album. As well as being co-producer on the *Union*, *Keys To Ascension* and *Keys To Ascension 2* albums, he became the writer and co-producer of the band's 1997 album *Open Your Eyes*, which began life as a Chris Squire solo project on which he was invited to collaborate. He also toured with Yes in 1994 as a sideman on the *Talk* tour.

Billy was a founder member of the band Lodgic with his brother Michael on keyboards. His other musical projects included World Trade and The Key and as a producer he had worked with such top artists as Buddy Guy, Jeff Beck and Steve Morse. Billy's own Los Angeles recording studio, The Office, is where Yes recorded studio tracks for *Keys 2*.

Says Billy, "I was a die-hard Yes fan and was pretty well versed in their history. Before I met Chris Squire I was working in my own band. My first band Lodgic was formed in 1984 and that band was produced by Toto after they had that big album *Toto 4*. That band broke up and then I formed World Trade in 1989 which was a bit more progressive. That was the album that introduced me to Yes because at the time Chris, Trevor, Alan and Tony Kaye were working in LA without Jon who was doing ABWH. I met the guys through Derek Schulman of our mutual record company. They liked World Trade and I was a Yes fan and one thing led to another.

"After the *Talk* tour the band split up and Yes returned to the classic line-up with Rick Wakeman, at which point I went back to producing some projects. Then I got a call from Chris asking if I'd like to mix *Keys To Ascension 1*. I went to the studio and mixed that and we had a good time working together. I worked with Steve Howe and the rest of the guys and they kind of suggested we make *Keys To Ascension 2* together and I jumped in on the production. We made the record at my studio with 45 minutes of studio tracks. After that Rick decided to split and he wasn't there anymore. I started doing some songwriting with Chris and before you know it we had the *Open Your Eyes* record. The tour was coming up and they said, 'Why don't you just join the band?' That's how it happened. It wasn't official until a week before the tour. After *Keys To Ascension* I was very inspired by working with those guys and I just started writing songs in that style. It was meant to be a Squire solo album."

Billy says by the time they had got close to finishing the album the label heard a song from Chris' solo project and said, "Why don't you guys do that one too. So we took 'Wish I Knew' and turned it into 'Open Your Eyes' but all the other material was all new and freshly written. I wrote most of it with Chris and everybody else jumped in after the process was already going. 'From The Balcony' came right at the very end. Steve and Jon came to the studio and wanted to do this song, so we put it down real quick."

In 'From The Balcony' Jon Anderson sings: *"Now I heard you singing, dreaming that you know me well, let me tell you far away, new state of mind."* It sounds like a pretty ballad when Jon sings it with Steve Howe playing acoustic guitar. But it has its darker origins and perhaps surprisingly it actually relates to how Yes were often in the firing line, when it came to past business negotiations. Jon explains what he was thinking about when he wrote it: "It was basically all about past managers who could be difficult sometimes. When I think about the history of this band and the history of rock musicians generally it makes me mad. As the song evolved though, it seemed to be more about the higher consciousness of the audience and it seemed like someone was looking down on us to make sure everything was okay."

Says Billy, "*Open Your Eyes* wasn't a number one smash but it got a lot of airplay on radio and the album sold about 200,000 copies and helped to heighten the awareness of Yes in the Nineties. I had been on the road with Yes before in 1994 when I was a sideman, but now I was in Yes as a full member. Being able to feel the power of the full band is very exciting. It is a great experience. On tour we stuck to the classics but I got to stretch out a bit on 'Owner Of A Lonely Heart' and 'Rhythm Of Love' and 'Open Your Eyes'. It was the first time Yes had two guitarists on stage at the same time apart from on the *Union* tour. I saw that tour. There were enough of 'em up there!"

Billy Sherwood likes many different styles of music apart from Yes. "But there was something about Yes that caught my ear early on which is just a challenging kind of approach to rock'n'roll. They have a different slant on how to do things which is always very appealing. They have great musicianship and they are just a very high quality band. In this day and age you'd be silly not to acknowledge that you have to have a balance between pop songs and rock on an album. At the same time you have to maintain the lengthy Yes style pieces. There are a lot of young people at our shows and for a lot of them it's the first time they've experienced a band like us. The looks on their faces show they are pleased and surprised and interested in the fact that 'live' musicians can actually play! It isn't just a thrash fest. Here is music that's expressive and interesting to listen to. Once you catch 'em they are hooked for life."

Rick Wakeman's replacement, Igor Khoroshev, the 14th man to join Yes and the second new recruit of 1997, is perhaps the most dynamic, outspoken and forceful character to become part of the family in many years. "He's very Russian!" says Steve Howe. But Steve, Jon and the rest of the band are very fond of Igor and are greatly impressed by his technique and the passion of his playing. Jon discovered Igor when he finally got around to playing a demo that he'd had in a bag of tapes for some time. Says Jon, "Igor is just wonderful. He's a real bright spark and a great character. He can play anything and he learned everything Yes ever recorded in the space of a month. He's quite remarkable. When he came to do an audition he played 'Revealing' all the way through. Then he played 'Heart Of The Sunrise'. When he started to play something else we said, 'Oh, shut up!' "

Igor Khoroshev was born in Moscow on July 14, 1965. He now lives with his wife and son in Boston, Massachusetts. He grew up listening to Yes music and says he knew their records "inside out" when he was asked to join the band.

Back in Russia in the Sixties, Igor's mother wanted him to be a piano player and he studied the instrument from the age of five, thus becoming yet another Yes man with formal musical training. "I hated piano all my life and I still do! I went to school and I wasn't a very good student because I am lazy by nature. I never liked to practise but I learnt in the last year or two that practise is actually good if it extends your abilities. So I feel much more comfortable playing now and being with Yes has been a great experience. I had an excellent childhood but I was always getting into trouble! I can't say there are many people like me, and I can't say that many do like me! But I seem to be successful. All my life I've been a happy guy. I had a lot of ambitions as a child and I still do. This is just a first step for me. Every waking hour I like to be doing something new."

As a teenager Igor played bass guitar in a heavy metal band in Moscow but most of his formative years were spent at various schools. He didn't leave college until he was 25, by which time he'd obtained a Master's degree in music. "After that I really didn't know what I was going to do. One day I thought it was a good time to just wake up, have a cup of coffee and maybe catch a plane and go to America." His plan was to visit friends. "I went to the United States and I never came back! I applied for political asylum and it was granted. So I am a refugee from the former Soviet Union. I came over in 1991 at the time of Gorbachev. I think I was one of the last people to be granted political asylum because there were so many changes in Russia – at least on paper – that they changed the laws in the US. So I was very lucky. Since I moved I got married, had a child and I've been all around the world. When I came to America I couldn't speak English and I didn't know any musicians. Then I met a few. I always played progressive rock and then I found out what I thought was progressive in the Seventies had become kind of regressive! Now I try to write music that nobody has done before. It's not commercial but it's unique. It's nothing like Yes might write. I am more into Prodigy and The Chemical Brothers. That's what I think is progressive music today."

Igor met one of his predecessors in Yes, during the second leg of the 1998 US tour. "I met Patrick Moraz. We got drunk and played in a hotel. It was like a concert that was absolutely spontaneous. After a Yes show we went back to the hotel where there was a grand piano and me and Patrick started to play. We just sat down and played for two hours. I wish that somebody recorded it because we played some beautiful music together. A lot of the Yes members were sitting and listening and it was such a great experience for me because Patrick is one of my favourite keyboard players. The name of the song we did was 'Fuck You I Can Play Faster Than You'. I'd love to meet Rick Wakeman. Maybe some day that will come. We'll all meet together in one great big happy Yes keyboard family! We could all do a record – five or six Yes keyboard players. I never met Tony Kaye. I liked his stuff at the very beginning but I fell in love with Yes music when Rick and Patrick were in the band. I find Tony Kaye a very interesting organ player. He's got those elbows made out of steel! And he knows how to use them. He can never get hurt when he bashes the organ with his elbows. That's the only way to play a Hammond B3. He inspired me to play the organ, because when I heard him, I thought, 'This guy is OUT there. This is the instrument I need.' Wakeman is into synthesisers and piano, but Tony Kaye is into organ, while Patrick Moraz can do it all. That was his problem really. He should try not to solo so much on top of tunes like 'Roundabout'. He plays like a non-stop machine! I love the guy but he's constantly soloing!"

Igor first began listening to Yes records in Russia when he was 17 after a friend introduced him to several British groups. He also listened to King Crimson, Genesis, Gentle Giant and Jethro Tull. "That's how I got turned onto that type of music and began to think I should try to create something of my own in that style. I played in a band with my friend. That's how I got into progressive rock, but I never got to see Yes in those days. I bought some tickets and they cancelled the show. It was only a year before I joined them. Jon Anderson found my tape somewhere. I never knew he had one. Actually I didn't send him the tape myself. I was trying to get a record deal for my own band at the time and working for the computer companies. I was creating Midi files which are music contents for the programs they use. It's a very good job. You just stay home and create the music you like and people buy it! Then Jon heard some of my piano works and he called me right away. He asked me if I'd do an album with him. Then a few weeks later he said, 'How would you like to join Yes on the road?' "

Igor thought it was a great idea but wondered how long he'd have to learn the material. With a nervous laugh Jon Anderson told him, "Three days." The next question was how much material Igor had to learn and the answer was, "Everything because we don't know what we are going to play". Igor then asked for a clue. Was it going to be Eighties or Seventies? When the reply came "Seventies" Igor said, "Oh my God!"

But he sat down and started to learn Rick Wakeman's parts on *Close To The Edge* and 'The Revealing Science Of God'. He tried to play the way it was done on the original records which even members of the band had forgotten over the years. After studying the records he had an audition before he could start to rehearse with the band. Once he passed the test they all had just ten days to get it together before the first show. Sometimes they practised the numbers in bits and pieces and then glued them all together on different days. "We would play a bit of 'Owner Of A Lonely Heart' and then take the rest of the day off," says Igor. "That gave me some time to sit down with the CDs and play them again and again."

After his initial contact with Jon Anderson, Igor got to know the rest of the guys at the intensive rehearsals. "They were very down to earth. Very funny, especially Chris Squire. Everyone has their own personalities and everyone is very nice. When I joined they still had a few songs left to put on their album, so there was a spot where I could play an organ solo. It was fun to work with Billy at his studio and to see the way they did things. I love the music of Patrick Moraz and Rick Wakeman. I am also into classical music. I put it all together and give it to the band on a plate. Yes must make music *together* and not be told what songs to sing and what sounds to make and where to play drums and where not to play drums. I don't know if that's how it worked before, but when I listen to the records like *90125* and *Big Generator* I assume that's the way it was. I don't feel much creativity coming out of anyone other than Trevor Rabin who I admire a lot. He prolonged

251

the life of Yes, but that wasn't the Yes that I fell in love with, the band that created so many moving experiences in music.

"I don't think the band now should be recycling itself. It is time to move on. Break the rules – just like they did in the Seventies and Eighties. Let's break it – one more time!"

Igor thoroughly enjoys his Yes tours. At first he thought Rick Wakeman fans might boo him off the stage. "It was scary. I went out on stage for the first time in Hartford, Connecticut, and it was the best show I ever did. But for the first few months I thought people didn't like me and they all wanted Rick back. Then I looked at a Web Site and read the fans' reviews and all the fans loved me! The people loved me! It encouraged me so much. I thought, 'Now I will play my heart out.' It was very important to me that the people who come to the shows liked it and gave me a chance."

Igor very nearly didn't get a chance to tour Europe. "All my paperwork was screwed up. The same thing happened to me in Japan! I made it in the end and I loved Japan. We had a very good response and I got to play some different solos. The music has got to be challenging to play and is got to be challenging to all those young musicians who are looking up and saying, 'What is Yes doing these days? Are they washed up or can they create something new?' I am positive we can do something new. Every member is so different in Yes. We all like different things and I am dying to hear how it will all work out now that Steve Howe and Jon Anderson are together again. Steve is an amazing guitar player. He is so musical I *love* him! Billy, too, comes up with grooves on guitar that are so modern, and Chris and Alan are such powerful players. I just sit there and come up with a little dramatic chord here and there to bring it all to some sort of conclusion. Everybody seems to be getting along together and doing great including Billy and Steve. Mind you, if they tried to bring in a second keyboard player I would quit!"

Igor tends to talk in jokey overstated terms but asked about the role of Yes and their place in music today he is quietly reflective. "I think Yes changed the way rock music is played today. Just think, they were much younger than I am now, when they were writing things like *Close To The Edge*. I admire them so much. If you look around you can count on the fingers of one hand the number of bands that have been around as long as they have, despite the fact they hardly had any hits. The Rolling Stones have been together longer but they play pop music and they do great. But Yes are still together and draw a crowd. I don't know another band that can do that. The people still love them and to be part of that big picture is a joy."

★ ★ ★

With the band back on the road life had some purpose and everyone seemed happy. Their album *Open Your Eyes* featured a bold and distinctive Roger Dean Yes logo in orange on a black cover. As the group geared up for a fresh onslaught other old friends rallied round the Yes camp. Their record company Eagle Rock asked Jim Halley if he would go on tour with Yes once again for the first time in many years to act as media and promotion consultant. He was also back as Steve Howe's personal manager. There was plenty of work to do.

The *Open Your Eyes* tour began in September 1997 and finished a year later with dates in Japan. They also visited America twice, and went to Europe and South America. During the 1998 tour Yes seemed more relaxed and together than it had been in years. As Jim Halley says, "It was their thirtieth anniversary. When people have known each other for thirty years, you can't love everybody you are thrown together with all the time. People have their personal and musical differences and sometimes that causes a problem. But I have never seen any blows being exchanged. I am sure they wouldn't have planned to gather in Vancouver in 1999 with producer Bruce Fairbairn to make another album if their past get-togethers hadn't been successful for them. Jon and Steve weren't really involved in the writing of the *Open Your Eyes* album. They only wrote a couple of tunes. I then suggested they should all get together and work like they did in the old days, which was when they developed their greatest music."

Reaction to the tour was very encouraging. Says Jim, "The audiences for their tour included young, old and in between. The *Daily Telegraph* in England showed a photograph of a very young kid with a Yes hat and tee shirt who couldn't have been more than ten years old. Jan Howe faxed it to her husband Steve at one of his hotels. That picture said it all. Thirty years after they started they were still appealing to people across the board, from sixty year olds who had followed them from the very beginning, to ten year olds just learning about the group. It gave them all great satisfaction. Outside the gigs there were lots of young kids waiting for them with CDs to sign. Their profile is very good again. *Open Your Eyes* wasn't the greatest Yes album but they played over 180 concerts to a lot of people."

Bill Bruford, too, is pleased that Yes still function but does not believe their music has progressed in recent years. "I personally think it stagnated somewhat. Trevor Rabin and Trevor Horn did that wonderful single 'Owner Of A Lonely Heart' which I loved. Yes gave their band to a smart producer to help revolutionise themselves, which Robert Fripp never would do. He won't give King Crimson to an equivalent Trevor Horn. In a way the Yes that had 'Owner Of A Lonely Heart' wasn't Yes. It was a different group and then of course that causes trouble. If a different group gets a hit record how does that equate with the band people know as Yes?

I saw the band when Jon Anderson left and Trevor Horn was singing. You never saw a more remarkable copy version or take off of Jon Anderson. It was unbelievably accurate. When you see Yes today I think what you probably see is a very good version of Yes playing at being Yes. They do it extremely well. But it is *not* the age of discovery."

Roger Dean is more charitable. "I went to see them play on their 1998 British tour in Brighton and I thoroughly enjoyed it. They used to play incredibly precisely but now they are playing better than ever because they know the music so well. If you have been in the music industry this long you are usually either lifeless or just about competent. But Yes are really good at playing their own stuff now and they are much more relaxed. I think they are better now than they ever were originally, and they were very good originally. There is familiarity and enjoyment now whereas before it was much more disciplined. Their performances seem more natural and easy. My ten-year-old young daughter saw them and was thrilled to bits. She thought they were brilliant. But having said that, when they kicked into a 15-minute piece from *Tales Of Topographic Oceans* they lost her there. I told her to hang in there, because they'd pick up again, which of course they did and she was really into it again. I think bands like Yes owe it to themselves to experiment in that way. If they don't experiment – then what's it all about? But I think running around trying to recruit a new audience doesn't really endear them to their old fans. They should now try to create the ultimate Yes album with the existing band with Steve Howe, Jon, Chris, Alan and ideally Rick. If they got really disciplined and wrote the album together and toured again I think within a couple of years they would be back where they were. With their core following they could be as big as Grateful Dead. The music industry is so fragmented now and there are so many different genres you can't be cool in every different nook and cranny. If there are already two million people who are really keen on what you do, it's a pointless battle to fight for new audiences."

Geoff Downes, survivor of the 1980 *Drama* period, remains a fan of the band. "I went to see them play in Cardiff in 1998 and they were still playing very well. Jon Anderson's voice had hardly changed at all and Chris Squire was still great on bass. In fact they were all playing well. They've consolidated their position and have their audience of die-hard fans who will turn up and see them. I noticed that they didn't play much in their set from the Trevor Rabin era. Albums like *Big Generator* and *Talk* didn't feature too heavily. I don't think Steve ever really considered Trevor to be a worthy replacement!"

Geoffrey still considers it a privilege to have played with Yes. "They are greater than the sum of their parts. If they have a leader at all I think it is

Chris Squire. You may not think so because he is always the quiet one in the background. The strange thing is there is always a kind of animosity towards past members. If you ever ask Anderson or Wakeman about my involvement they'd give you a big negative. For sure. There is a lot of malice around among the members of Yes. Not just towards me. Towards people in certain line-ups of the band. I don't know why, in what would seem to be a fairly innocuous, friendly English rock band, that people should get so uptight. When they did the *Union* tour Jon Anderson had this kind of percussion stand in the middle of the stage that he played. I don't think that went down too well. They used to refer to it as the bus stop. 'Someone take the bus stop away!' A lot of that goes on. There are terrible rows and you can just imagine what it was like on the *Union* tour. I don't think Steve Howe spoke to Trevor Rabin on the whole tour. They were communicating through interpreters – personal managers and the like. That's hardly what you would call band spirit."

Sixties' Yes veteran Peter Banks wasn't invited to join in the *Union* tour or even jam with the band, which he found most upsetting. In fact he was mortified as he was led to believe he had a chance of sitting in and was turned away at the last moment on the grounds that his appearance would be 'unsuitable'. Says Geoff, "That was a bit strange but when you start to understand what the band is about, it's hardly surprising. They're so individual that if anybody infringes on their space they become *persona non grata*. For a band with a positive, affirmative name like Yes it does seem strange there is a lot of backbiting and squabbling. There are these massive dramas. But they all get sorted out eventually. Then they'd flare up again! But I enjoyed my time playing with Yes."

The need to experiment and progress remains strong within the Yes ethos despite all the perceived mistakes and misjudgements of the past. Whatever they have done wrong in business or commercial terms, they have rarely failed artistically. Yet even today there are occasional rumbles of dissent. Sound man Roy Clair had reservations about the 1998 band. "The new keyboard player Igor was very good and a very nice guy but some of the kids wanted that original group, with Rick Wakeman," he says. "You know how kids are. You could tell them until you are blue in the face that the new keyboard player is as good as Rick and just as charismatic but they're not going to accept that. Nobody shouts abuse. They just don't show up. But a band with a substitute is better than no band at all. There are a lot of people who did enjoy their tour and the music. I think they were having fun and the audiences liked what they heard, so I guess all's well that ends well.

"For business to increase in the future they are going to have to come out with some new songs that the kids can identify with and that's hard to do these days. I think they'll maintain their core audience of around 55,000 people. It won't get bigger unless they come out with some music that's different or Wakeman comes back. I don't think *Open Your Eyes* was received very well. I don't think it made an impact. It was a good album but who knows what kids want these days? If I were a producer and knew that, I'd be a successful guy!"

In February 1998 Rick Wakeman's son Adam[24] was very nearly the next keyboard player in Yes. He was all ready to take over when it appeared as if new recruit Igor Khoroshev wasn't going to make it to England due to problems getting his visa. Rick refused to help out but his son was recommended for the gig and the band thought it was a great idea. It was a stressful but exciting experience for Adam. He had to learn the whole of the band's set practically overnight. He took it in his stride.

Adam is a fine musician and excellent keyboard player and singer. He has toured and recorded with his father and has also been to the US for Rick's religious music tours. He had his own band Geronimo Road which did a track on a Yes tribute album called *Tales From Yesterday*. Says Adam, "We did 'Starship Trooper' but the band folded when the singer went off to do a West End show and the drummer went off with The Seahorses."

Adam's most memorable moment came when he was expected to deputise for Igor, the man 'depping' for his dad! He might have been forgiven for feeling trepidation, having heard so many stories about Yes at home. "I can remember my dad saying after a tour, 'That's it. I'm never playing with them again!' So I was expecting it to be a complete nightmare. But after seeing the shows I went for a beer at the hotel with them and everyone seemed pretty cool. They were all very friendly towards each other and were very together. They were talking about the music and they were really enthusiastic about what they were doing and stuff which I thought was excellent."

Boston-based Igor did not have the right paperwork necessary to enter the UK and Yes faced being stuck without a keyboard player on their crucial homecoming gigs. Adam was put on standby. He had to sit down and listen to every record they had done. He laughs: "For a month afterwards I didn't want to see another bloody Yes album! But Jon and Chris said that if Igor didn't turn up I could do the rest of the tour. It was the most pressure I've ever been under." He had been out for the day with his girlfriend when he returned home to find 12 messages on his Answerphone from his dad, Jon Anderson and Chris Squire. Adam was stunned. "I thought, what's happening here! I never get that many messages! Then I

[24] Born on March 11, 1974.

was told that Igor had got stuck in America and I was being asked if I could do the gig. But I only had one Yes album and I hadn't really listened to the others. They thought I'd know them all. But I had only done 'Starship Trooper' before on stage with my dad. I used to have a Yes LP but I'd swapped with my brother Oliver for a football! But I thought if I had a week I could learn it all in time. They then said, 'We need you here at ten o'clock tomorrow morning!' So I bought seven Yes CDs. I had to learn a three-hour set. I stayed up *all* night listening and making notes. Then when I arrived at the rehearsal they said they wanted me to use Igor's keyboard licks as they didn't want to change the show around."

Adam went to the Manchester Apollo by train on Thursday, February 26 1998, and took a keyboard with him to work things out on the journey. But he found he'd left all the music and notes he'd written behind in the car that had taken him to the station. Adam's girlfriend then had to fax the notes to Manchester for when he arrived. But his problems hadn't ended there. The CD player he was using to play the Yes albums got knocked off the stage by a roadie and was smashed to pieces. "Everything that could go wrong, went wrong!" groans Adam. He stayed up the following night to study the set list but some of the songs were 28 minutes long. He gave up and went to sleep. Then came the latest message from the States. Igor had finally got his visa and passport and was on his way to play the concert. There were sighs of relief but there was also disappointment. The band asked Adam to stay on just in case there was a last minute problem. As a consolation prize for all his hard work Adam was invited to come on stage and play 'Starship Trooper', one of the songs he had spent so many hours trying to learn.

"Jon Anderson was really cool," says Adam. "He said, 'Igor's here but stay for the show.' Igor was really cool as well and he didn't mind that I got up and played the last number. I hadn't realised how precise the solos were. They have to be just like the original. It's a bit like a show really. I thought you could just play your own thing in a 24-bar keyboard solo, but at rehearsals Steve Howe would be the first person to pick it up and say it wasn't right. There's no room for improvising because people know the music so well. I suppose if I changed things it would make Steve sound different. Yeah, so it was a bit of a panic, but I got up and played 'Starship Trooper' and it was great! Jon Anderson took me up to the front of the stage and told the audience I had learned the entire set in a day and they gave me a round of applause. Everyone was cheering!"

Adam enjoyed hearing the band so much he went to see them play at their London shows at Labatt's Apollo in Hammersmith. "I wanted the chance to play 'Starship Trooper' again. Chris said there would be no problem at all. I didn't get there until late and when I got backstage I had a quick chat with the band and Igor said, 'Just walk on stage and do it.' Chris didn't mind but Steve and Jon weren't too keen. They wanted everything to be right because it was the London show. I think I would have played alright, but fair enough, it was their gig! Can you imagine if I had taken Igor's advice and just walked on? They would have said, 'What the hell are you doing here!' But I may get called back again one day."

The Yes revival picked up pace throughout 1998. Fans in the States and Europe were thrilled to see the old band back again and playing shows packed with Yes classics. A typical set would include 'Siberian Khatru', 'The Rhythm Of Love', 'America', 'Open Your Eyes', 'And You And I', 'Heart Of The Sunrise', 'Mood For A Day', 'Clap', 'From The Balcony', 'Wondrous Stories', 'Long Distance Runaround', 'The Fish', 'Owner Of A Lonely Heart', 'Revealing Science Of God', 'I've Seen All Good People', 'Roundabout' and 'Starship Trooper'. Few bands could assemble so much imaginative and stimulating stuff for a show and even this selection was only scratching the surface of all the Yes material 'in the book'. Needless to say the band received standing ovations at every gig as they played with the kind of fire and energy that Roger Dean noted at their Brighton performance.

On June 29, 1998, Eagle Records released the double Yes CD *Friends And Relatives* which featured a fascinating selection of Yes related material. The 19 tracks included a 1998 dance remake of 'Owner Of A Lonely Heart' by Jon Anderson as well as contributions from Rick Wakeman, Steve Howe, and Earthworks featuring Bill Bruford. Steve Howe played a version of 'Walk Don't Run' and was featured on excerpts from *Tales From Topographic Oceans*. Rick and Adam were billed as Wakeman With Wakeman on 'No Expense Spared' and 'Sync Or Swim', and there were full band versions of 'Close To The Edge' and 'America'.

Everything seemed to signal that Yes were at their happiest and on their best behaviour in many years, so it came as a big shock when news spread that their old friend Rick Wakeman had suffered a serious illness in the summer. At first attempts were made by his family to keep it a secret, as Wakeman was in the middle of organising his next big project, *Return To The Centre Of The Earth*. He had been commuting to America from his base in the Isle Of Man to co-ordinate recording sessions for the album that was due to be released on EMI Classics in January 1999, the 25th anniversary of the release of the original recording *Journey To The Centre Of The Earth*.

In August I went to meet Rick for an interview at Heathrow Airport, and there was no question he looked under stress and was clearly very tired. Then a few days later came the news that he had been taken to hospital suffering from pneumonia and pleurisy. Rick and his wife Nina were inundated with cards, flowers and messages from well-wishers around the world. It seemed that on the morning of August 13 Rick experienced breathing difficulties and chest pains after returning to the Isle Of Man from a trip to Glyndebourne in Sussex with Richard Lyttelton, the president of EMI Classics. His condition worsened and after a couple of days he collapsed unable to breathe and suffering chest and head pains. Nina phoned for a doctor who called an ambulance and in the early hours of Sunday August 16 Rick was taken to Nobles Hospital on the Isle Of Man. He was diagnosed as suffering from advanced pneumonia and pleurisy. To make matters worse he seemed to be displaying symptoms of Legionnaires disease. He was given intravenous antibiotic treatment and oxygen. He was finally discharged on August 24 and then underwent six weeks of rehabilitation as well as blood checks and X-rays. It was clear that although Rick had long ago given up drinking and smoking, his health was still in a perilous state and he could not hope to continue working at the same old punishing rate. Said Nina, "Rick has been told that his lifestyle has to change. Eighteen hour days are things of the past, as are long gruelling tours. In order to reduce strain on his body he has been ordered to reduce weight."

An Italian tour Rick had planned in November that year was immediately cancelled and recording sessions re-scheduled. "There is no doubt that this serious illness has placed many question marks over Rick's future and the reality of what he will be able to do in the future," says Nina. However once Rick had recovered he was back touring again with his band, although major shows with an orchestra were put on ice.

Most of the members of Yes were living or working abroad and they weren't aware that Rick was hospitalised until a week or so after the event, and they were shocked at the severity of his illness. But the band had to carry on with their own commitments. They still had to walk the treadmill of recording, touring and – once again – seeking the inspiration for new music to keep the spirit of the band alive.

At the end of the year they were off to Japan to rehearse for a month and then began work recording their new album for 1999. Said Chris Squire somewhat prosaically, "We want to make it as organically as possible. We'll just sort out the best bits . . . and put it on a CD!" Chris and Alan White now have a telepathic sense of communication after playing together for so long. "Yeah, and I can tell when he's gonna make a mistake too!" says Alan.

As a tribute to his old friend's towering command of the drum kit and loyal service to the band, Chris Squire now famously holds out his arms in supplication while Alan does his drum solo at the end of 'Long Distance Runaround'. "He got into holding out his hands when I play a solo," says Alan. "It's very funny. Depending on whether I'm playing well or not, I'll make it longer or shorter. And he's looking at me going, 'My arms are *aching*!'"

Jon Anderson looked ahead to the new album *The Ladder* which was eventually released in October, 1999. "We now wanted to make an album that would be the crowning glory of the thirty years of the band's history. We wanted everyone to say, 'We're so happy they stuck it out otherwise this album would never have materialised.' *Open Your Eyes* was a good album but unfortunately we were kind of playing a game of chance. We did an album of 12 songs and hoped maybe we'd get some radio play and even a hit record. That's what the management was pushing for. It sold a lot of records around the world but it didn't achieve the big breakthrough and the breakthrough might not be based on a hit single. It might be based on a hit album. Now we are going into the last year of the century and it's amazing that we are still going and it's amazing that we still have so much energy and are still very hungry to make it work."

In the second half of the Nineties Yes left their third manager Tony Dimitriades and his East End Management company and became managed by Left Bank with offices in London and Los Angeles. Despite the seemingly endless management problems that have dogged Yes' career since their earliest liaison with club owner Roy Flynn, the current arrangement seems to be working well, perhaps because Left Bank are responsible solely for 'career management' while 'business management' was handled elsewhere.

Old friend Michael Tait, who through Roy Flynn found himself driving the first line-up of Yes to and from their earliest gigs in the Ford Transit they called Big Red, has watched the latest Yes developments with fascination. He deeply regrets that the group has not always been given the credit it deserves. "Their early albums were absolutely brilliant," says Michael, "especially judged against their time. And yet *Rolling Stone* magazine, for example, did not even acknowledge that Yes exists. They never have done. Which is staggering if you are talking about the Seventies. They think that statistically all the albums of that period which we once called classics are now just rubbish. It just shows you – none of us really know anything. It's pretty scary! Yet to me the music of Yes was spellbinding . . . riveting stuff. (*Rolling Stone* have subsequently devoted a special tribute issue to Yes.) I think what has happened is that MTV has changed and ruined the music business totally. It gives a visual expectation that can never be achieved 'live' and it's just a terrible, terrible shame. Yet the band is happy and it is just wonderful to turn back the clock a bit and see them. Jon's voice is still pretty damn good. He's one of the few singers who can sing seven nights a week, which is an incredible gift."

Despite all the setbacks, the rows and splits, the recriminations and financial problems, Steve Howe remains optimistic about the future of Yes. "What creates a lot of excitement for audiences is the fact that this line-up works very well on stage," he says. "We had done nearly 140 shows by the summer of 1998. We had done a mass of shows, building the set, bringing in new material. We only did 'Open Your Eyes' from the new album and looked back at everything else. But when we were in England we were playing 'From The Balcony' which was Jon and I, and it was our only opportunity to get a piece of music that was totally the way we wanted it. There is something wonderful about simplicity. It brings out the best in artists. Doing a duet with Jon on that song was very exciting. It was almost like 'Madrigal' when Rick played the harpsichord on the *Tormato* album.

"I'm a great lover of touring and stage work is unpredictable but exciting. I love my wife Jan and my family so much that being on the road a lot can be an enormous problem. Only a strong and caring wife could put up with the sort of things that go on. It's crazy being in a band and we all have bills and mortgages to pay. Most people might think we all came out of the Seventies as millionaires, but we didn't and that was due to some extremely bad advice that we were given by management, account-ants and other professionals. We were used by those people. We were suckers. Musicians tend to find business as interesting as watching paint dry. 'I'll just go out and buy a new Aston Martin. Is that alright?' 'Yeah, you can do that.' 'Fine, oh by the way, pay my bills, file my tax and sign my cheques will you?' When you are living like that . . . no wonder it goes wrong! There have been eras in Yes history when we didn't come out with loads of money and yet it didn't make me that miserable. I think it made some people very miserable. I have been up and down like a yo-yo. In the Eighties Asia was immensely successful but it was short-lived and fell apart. Then came my time with GTR and after that was a very tough period before ABWH. It was a dicey period. The problem was the way GTR ended, which was really tricky."

Like most of the other musicians who have been a part of Yes Steve has faced his share of financial difficulties in recent years but has got on top of his own financial affairs in a way that rock stars often refuse to do. "I started to deal directly with the people who I used to keep at arms length," he says. Steve used to rely entirely on others to deal with record contracts but as a solo artist he had to learn how to make deals himself. On one occasion he was so surprised and pleased that he'd got the price he wanted for a solo album he put the phone down, lay on his back and wriggled his hands and legs in the air chortling with relief and delight. His children ran in somewhat worried. Was dad freaking out? "I hadn't ripped anybody off," says Steve. "I had just closed a deal, got the money and was very pleased. What I was most pleased about was keeping my family happy and secure. If that means doing a solo record or going on tour with Yes for a year, then I'll go to the ends of the earth to do that. I've done lots of things from Asia to GTR and my solo stuff but the best things seem to happen when I play with Yes. Touring is very productive and performing on stage with my guitar is as close as I can get to an art form.

"Yes haven't reached a peak yet," says Steve. "We're still striving for it. Sure we've made mistakes, like when the group releases the wrong records or doesn't tour in the right markets at the right level. We've toured when we didn't even have a record out. When those mistakes are made we have had to pay the price. We should just get back on the road creating really wonderful and intense music, new music that lives. We have our own sound. Chris plays a Rickenbacker and I play a Gibson. Jon has only got to open his mouth and you know it's Jon. But there are a lot of obstacles and the group has always had them. A good example is just finding somewhere to rehearse. 'Somewhere' could be anywhere in the world. Hawaii, Vancouver, London, Morocco! Then you have to argue about that. Alan lives in Seattle, Chris is in LA, Jon is sometimes in San Luis Obispo and I live in England. But Yes has been quite good at sorting out problems in the last couple of years and has better goals. We've not been foolhardy trying to get success we don't deserve. I just want Yes to have the success it deserves. That's the only way I'm interested. The more it tries to get there on the back of something else, then the more unimportant I think that is. We have got to break some new ground. I think we can carry new ideas. In the Seventies we'd do something like *Relayer* and then *Going For The One* and they are quite different albums. I can't describe what I want but I can feel it. The audiences are there. They are not pigeon-holed and nor are we. There are people coming to us out of the blue . . . young people hearing us for the first time, or the people who were raised on Yes music. In May, 1998 we played some concerts in Mexico, part of the dates we played in South America and they'd never seen us before. We had two nights with about 8,000 a night and these people went through the roof. That was something else."

Despite all their years on the road, in 1988 Yes were still finding new audiences and new places to play, like Poland, Hungary and Mexico. Says Jon Anderson, the inveterate traveller, "There are still so many places we want to play like Ireland. I've been wanting to go back there since the band started. We should go back to Cork – when we've got an audience! The fans who have followed the band for so many years deserve to see us live again. So we dream of that happening in the next few years and we want to make one album that really makes it viable. We are not making a comeback . . . we are moving forward. It's the right time and our music sounds better than it ever did."

Chris Squire is the only member of the band who has stayed all the way through. "Yes, I know. I am the one who has been stuck with all the bills too. I don't want to be looked upon as the leader of the band, but I have been here the whole time and in all fairness to Jon he was only *not* there for one album, the one with Trevor Horn. Alan feels like he's been there forever as well – because he has since 1972. The band has been going for thirty years and I had no idea we could possibly be in anything that would last this long. The only examples I really had when we formed Yes in 1968 was that The Beatles had been together since 'Love Me Do' came out in 1962. By 1969 they had broken up so that seemed like a long career to me. I thought if Yes could stay together for five or six years that would be amazing. Who knew it would end up being thirty? No one had any perception of that length of time in this kind of business."

Yes had several celebrations during 1998 including the Gold Albums award ceremonies at the Hard Rock Café in New York. But before that Chris Squire celebrated his fiftieth birthday. "It was on March 4 which was actually the day we played at Hammersmith at Labatts Apollo. So afterwards we had a get-together at the hotel and a celebration with all the kids and my mum and dad. That was a nice thing to happen. And of course Jon Anderson and I are getting on rather well. We've had our ups and downs – I'll tell you that. But we are too old to argue anymore. We usually used to argue about the musical direction of the band. They were professional arguments although they could get a little bit petty. To some extent it's not a bad thing to have some conflict, unless it festers and becomes nasty. We don't have that problem these days. The mood now is very good and everyone seems to be getting on very well."

It was a mood that would stay positive as the band faced the next phase of its career – into the New Millennium.

11

NO BOUNDARIES

As Yes approached the 21st century they embarked confidently on an intensive world tour that began in 1998 and would see them win new audiences around the world. It was also a great time for nostalgia, anniversaries and celebrations. However the band wanted to show they could produce a new album that was contemporary, relevant and would reflect Yes at its best. They had been through the lean years. Now they would restore Yes to its rightful stature with new music that was challenging, fresh and satisfying. Yet even as the countdown began for the New Millennium and plans were drawn up for their 31st album, fate had another shock in store for them.

The band gathered at Armoury Studios, Vancouver, Canada in November 1998 to rehearse new material. They planned to begin work on recording *The Ladder* in the spring of 1999, under the aegis of highly experienced independent producer Bruce Fairbairn. After spending a month or so preparing demos and selecting material the band reconvened in February to lay down tracks. Fairbairn's sensitive, disciplined production and Mike Plotnikoff's engineering brought a cohesion, clarity, structure and a strong live feel to the album. The songs retained their individual identity and yet seemed linked to a common cause. The band's enormous instrumental fire power was used sparingly, to enhance the songs rather than swamp them. Such discipline only enhanced their music and Yes grew to respect Fairbairn during their months in the studio together.

Bruce had begun working with Yes on the recommendation of Left Bank Management, who wanted to assist the band in their ambition to make their best possible CD. Fairbairn was intrigued by the string of ground breaking albums Yes had produced over the years and was particularly impressed when he realised that each member of Yes was a first class musician. It took a lot to impress him. The producer had spent years working with some of the hottest artists in the business. The walls of his studio were lined with the platinum albums he had produced for Aerosmith, Kiss, AC/DC and most recently The Cranberries.

Jon Anderson was especially keen on the liaison: "It was important that thirty years down the line we retained the classic Yes style and kept all the best ingredients of Yes music. Working with Bruce ensured we got the best performances out of everyone."

Indeed the 11 Fairbairn-produced tracks were intriguingly diverse and full of surprises, while retaining the celebrated Yes sound. Performances ranged from pop songs like 'It Will Be A Good Day' and the heartfelt ballad 'If Only You Knew' to a remarkable Afro-Caribbean section, which included the exuberant 'Lightning Strikes'. 'The Message' was a tribute to reggae star Bob Marley and nine minute long cuts 'Homeworld' and 'New Language' gave Billy Sherwood, Steve Howe and Igor Khoroshev welcome space for self expression. 'Face To Face' had some of the most joyful playing heard on a Yes album in many moons.

As work began on these splendid new songs, everything seemed to be going well at the Armoury. The band was happy and the music was coming good. Then just before final mixes were complete, the band was stunned by the sudden death of their new friend. Bruce Fairbairn, aged just 49, was found dead at his Vancouver home on May 17th, 1999. As word spread, the group found it difficult to comprehend the news.

During recording the band members had booked rooms in the same apartment building in Vancouver. Alan White says they were literally living on top of each other. "Steve Howe was on the sixth floor and others were on 19 or 20, so we were all on different floors. We all drove to the studio together each morning, as it was only a couple of miles away. We had recorded this way once before, when we did *Going For The One* in Switzerland. We could get away from family life for a bit, although Jon had his wife Jane with him. When the band are all together like that, you can concentrate on recording and things move along faster."

Alan recalls how well they got on with their new producer. "When we first went to Canada in November, 1998 we did a lot of writing together. Then Bruce Fairbairn came in and checked out the songs. He told us what needed changing. We went back in January and then cut the album. We had prepared the whole thing, before we even went in the studio. It was a combined effort, but Jon wrote a lot of the things and had plenty of ideas."

One of the most intriguing ideas involved a computer game. The first track on *The Ladder* is linked to a game called 'Homeworld' made by Sierra Games. Says White: "It's about a civilisation lost in space and looking for their home. We got involved with Sierra Studios and Relic Entertainment at an early point and Jon directed the lyrics towards that game. (*'Homeworld' is included on the soundtrack of the PC real-time strategy game.*) There were a lot of different kinds of song on the album. It's best to listen to the material a few times to get into the depth of the whole thing. I liked the wide variety of stuff we recorded and there was a mixture of old and new Yes, which was the way Jon wanted the album to go. It was like a late Nineties' version of the stuff we did in the Seventies."

Alan explains how Bruce helped them focus their efforts. "Bruce would say, 'I want you to play like you did on 'Roundabout'. We need something in that style here.' A lot of the songs lent themselves to good live performance and sound pretty good on stage. For the first three weeks of recording, the pressure was on Chris and myself to put all the basic tracks down. Everybody else can re-do their stuff if necessary, but we had to concentrate on getting the best drum and bass sound for the track and then go for a final take.

"It was good to have the rehearsal and writing period beforehand, because we knew which direction to go with the rhythms. There were three inter-related songs starting with 'Lightning Strikes' which went into 'Can I'. 'Face To Face' was another good song that Jon came up with. It is a very unusual piece and part of it is in 7/4 time, so we are still up to our tricks! Bruce had known the band for years, but we had never worked with him before. He'd been a fan and well into our music. It was really unfortunate what happened at the end and unbelievable when he died. Everybody had got to know him so well and we were one big happy team. I was at home in Seattle when it happened."

Alan reveals how Bruce's death impacted on the band. "As I was only living two hours from Vancouver. I got a call from the office to say there was an emergency and that I had to call Jon or Steve at the studio immediately. I couldn't raise anybody at the studio and finally got hold of Billy Sherwood who told me: 'Bruce died last night.' We had already mixed three tracks and that's how close we were to the end of the album. Jon Anderson found him in his apartment. Whenever he was working on an album, he didn't live in the same house as his family because of the hours he kept. Jon and Steve were in the studio waiting for him to come in at 1 p.m. He was always on time and he didn't smoke or drink that much and seemed a pretty healthy guy. So when he didn't turn up at the studio they thought it was odd. He was usually so efficient and would have called in."

Two and a half hours went by and the band were getting really worried, especially as there was no answer message left on Bruce's telephone. An engineer went round to his apartment and found the DAT tape he had left on the doorstep for Bruce the day before. It lay there untouched. Bruce's car was sitting on the drive. The engineer didn't want to go into the flat unaccompanied. He called up Jon and together they forced the front door open.

Alan: "Jon went upstairs and found Bruce lying next to his bed. He had just fallen over and died from a heart attack. It was a blow to all of us. Bruce had grown up in Vancouver and played in bands around the area. He'd had a great career and sold a lot of albums."

Bruce Fairbairn's funeral service was held on May 24, 1999 attended by his many friends from the music business. Steve Howe and Jon Anderson performed a version of 'Nine Voices' from *The Ladder* and the album was subsequently dedicated to Bruce's memory. After a respectful pause in the recording process Yes carried on with the project. They finished the work Bruce had begun with the assistance of engineer Mike Plotnikoff, who mixed the rest of the album.

Says Alan White: "It was strange making the album because we were looking for a new direction. Our last record wasn't really made with us all together as a writing team. This was more fun. Everybody sat around throwing in ideas and I like *The Ladder* because of that."

Jon Anderson felt he had the chance to express himself more fully, than he had in some years. "What came through was more openness in terms of musical ideas. It was not restricted to that kind of Los Angeles orientated music we had with Trevor Rabin. We got Steve Howe writing again and that started to re-kindle the Seventies style music. Funnily enough the first track 'Homeworld' nearly didn't get on the album. We had this series of pieces of music which I couldn't figure out how to fit together. We just went in there and I dreamed it up as a classic Yes piece of music. It was really all about getting people who had enjoyed Yes in the Seventies to come back. The band sounded great. Chris played great bass, Alan was really rockin' on the drums and everybody was performing well. There was a lot of light and shade. We had an hour of good music that we really wanted to perform on stage."

One of their most attractive songs 'If Only You Knew' was put together by Howe, Anderson and Igor and was dedicated to Jon's wife Jane. "She caught me when I was falling. I was really going through a tough time six years ago and when I met up with this beautiful lady, she really put me back on track. If you have someone who believes in who you are and what you do, it helps."

Jon was especially excited about the three linked tracks which include 'Lightning Strikes'. "It's just joyful Jump Up music with an Afro-Caribbean flavour. There's some brass used on it because Bruce used brass on every album he did. He had a bunch of friends who blasted away and provided a perfect backing. He also had his own band called Prism and they played a bit on 'Lightning Strikes'. 'Finally' is another great stage song. It's got that feeling . . . finally we actually made an album we all like!"

Strong narrative ideas were developed on 'The Messenger' which Jon devised with Billy Sherwood and Igor. Recalls Jon: "Bruce said, 'Write about SOMEBODY.' And I thought of Bob Marley. So it's a song about him. He was truly the messenger. It's strange, but just when we finished that track I walked out of the studio and MTV were showing a classic Bob Marley concert. So I thought, 'Gosh, that's a sign!' The penultimate song 'New Language' was all about getting the band to work out. Sometimes they got restricted by the click track we used in the studio. I said to Alan: 'I want to see you having a great time on drums, like you do on stage.' There's a great bit in the middle where Chris does a kind of 'Roundabout' bass line. There's a solo on top which is pure Yes. He dances beautifully on that! Igor was rocking on organ too. On 'Nine Voices (Longwalker)' Steve used his Portuguese guitar. We had just finished doing 'New Language' and Bruce asked what we were going to do next. So me and Steve went in and did a demo of this new song 'Nine Voices' which I thought was a good way to end the album. Bruce was always good at suggesting we did a song with a story about a real event."

Jon had become close friends with a medicine man called 'Long Walker' so named because he walked the length of America in 1977 in aid of native American rights. "In 1987 he got together with the Indigenous Council who are not part of the United Nations, because they are not land owners. They are high priests from Australia, Japan, Indonesia, Africa and the Romany folk who don't have any land. They have their tribes however and this is a song about the nine tribe members.

"They sing a special song to bring forgiveness into the world. These are the people who had been stripped of their land and their heritage. They created this song of forgiveness because they believe they are the caretakers while we, who think we are in charge, are actually out of the circle. They just want us to step back in. So that's the idea of the song. At the memorial service for Bruce Fairbairn, me and Steve did that song for him. It was one that he really liked and touched him. We had all fallen in love with Bruce because first and foremost he was a great guy. We were halfway through mixing when he died and Mike Plotnikoff just said, 'I wanna finish this album.' So we dedicated the album to Bruce. He had said to us, 'Just make the best Yes album you can. The rest will follow.' He told us to forget trends and fads. People would eventually recognise what we could do. I said, 'I'm with you!' "

Jon appreciated that Fairbairn was adept at telling people what to do – in the best possible way. "He'd say to me: 'Jon, please don't sing that lyric. We don't need that kind of lyric here. Come back tomorrow and write another chorus.' That's great. It was like a challenge. You started wanting to please him. If he smiled and said, 'That's great' you'd think, 'Thank God for that!' His studio had a beautiful lounge and it was filled with multi-platinum albums with ten million sales. I said to the guys, 'Look, there's the proof. The guy works miracles with musicians.' They realised that themselves. Our next step was to go on tour and bring happiness to all the people who came to see us. In fact we'd like to spend the next couple of years playing to more people and keeping the band rolling. Wherever we go we find a lot of people are still into the band and they are happy to see that we are still working."

Steve Howe was also pleased with *The Ladder* and felt it contained some of his best Yes work in years. He remembers how the initial approaches were made to find a new producer for the band. "Our management Left Bank were looking for a producer for us and they had worked with Bruce Fairbairn before on different projects. They mentioned Bruce and it all started while we were on tour in August, 1998. When we played Vancouver we took some time off to visit his studio there and we all took to him amazingly well. We prayed that he would say 'yes' to the idea of working with us. He was like putting out feelers. He told me just a week before he passed away that he had previously been working with a band who could hardly play. He said that we were all so talented, we could all do an album like this on our own. He said most bands only have one or two major talents. All of Yes were major talents! He was a very charming man and he invented a nickname for me. He used to call me Swami because of my potential for bringing spirituality to the music. He was a force to be reckoned with, but he didn't make any of us feel shy. He wasn't the sort of producer who would say: 'Well I know how to do that.' This was our record and he was producing it."

Bruce seemed to understand that Yes was a band that had come alive again. Says Steve: "All he had to do was make it even more 'alive'. He didn't want too much overdubbing and wanted to capture a lot of 'live' playing from everybody. The overdubs were treated carefully, so we didn't lose sight of who was playing what. I did all the lead guitar work on the record and Billy played a lot of rhythm guitar and a few of the breaks. His role was more in songwriting and structure. On 'Nine Voices' I used my Portuguese guitar over the keyboard and percussion. I felt it was better than the 'Open Your Eyes' era and there had been nothing like this from Yes for a long time. It was truer to the spirit of Yes we have consistently tried to find over the years, until we get sidetracked. We were all very excited about the album and although we are not saying it's the greatest thing since sliced bread, when you put it on, you can hear the group is alive and well!"

Howe thought *The Ladder* captured much more in the way of performance than had been the case for some years. Jon Anderson had been a great stimulus in this process. "We've all learnt our position in the band now. Jon can raise his hand or give a look and there is instant telepathy between us. Chris and Alan have an unspoken telepathy too. On songs like 'Lightning Strikes', 'Can I' and 'Face To Face' there is a feeling of surprise. Instead of leaning towards pop music, like we have done in the past, we tried different textures to create a colourful contrast. We got quite earthy on tracks like 'The Messenger' and 'If Only You Knew' has a strong English feel, as opposed to a kind of LA commercial sound. It's a really sweet song. Billy says it's the most commercial song he's ever heard Yes play."

The Ladder was undoubtedly a team effort and Bruce's death during the making of the album was a great blow to Steve. "It was a loss to us as well as to his family. It was tragic and so unexpected. He had taken us in hand and shown us so much. After his death we would not go back on anything Bruce had said. We put tremendous value on everything he'd done. This was a guy who only did one record a year and we were lucky enough to be with him for that last record. We had met a person who we thought was going to be the answer to our future as a band. We wanted to work with Bruce again and that's why I can't talk about *The Ladder* without thinking of him and expressing our great sense of loss."

Steve and the rest of the band appreciated what it was like to have a professional producer in charge. "He was a master at telling how it would all work. There would be no smoking in the studio. We'd work set hours, take specific breaks and he would call the tunes to work on. Occasionally he'd leave the studio for a couple of hours and say, 'When I come back I want to hear that sorted out.' We felt under pressure and yet we all respected him so much, what he said was adhered to, including punctuality and productivity. If something was supposed to take two hours, he'd say, 'That's it. A wrap.' He had all this scheduling in his mind and productivity could only be achieved by keeping to that schedule. We could have done more fiddling around and more overdubs, but he kept us on course. Jon was singing great and the harmonies were really refreshing because we kept away from big blocks of multi-tracking. You could actually hear people!"

Steve confirms that Yes benefited greatly from the Fairbairn regime. "When we started work in Vancouver the approach was that if somebody brought a song in, the band wouldn't play it. If they brought in elements of songs, then everybody would be free to marry them together. If the ideas were loose and not set in stone, the group could manipulate them. That's what we did and the album is an example of us returning to a more collaborative writing style."

It seems that Bruce even joined Yes for two weeks in the rehearsal room. Steve says he'd never worked with a producer who'd bothered to

270

come to rehearsals before. He picked out eight songs that he thought were noteworthy and said, 'Well, start playing them.' He also gave the band guidance on arranging and his input would clearly have been invaluable in the future. After recording proper started on February 1, 1999 Yes did all the songs as demos in the studio.

"After a week he said, 'Right, let's go back to the first song and let's cut it.' 'New Languages' was an important song and very demanding. There was so much collaboration and so many ideas from everybody. On 'Can I' for example Jon invented his own language which sounds like African. I came in occasionally and sang 'Ooh wop.' That was enough for me!"

Chris Squire was intrigued by the psychological effect making *The Ladder* had on the band. "Everyone was more happy at the end of making this album than any we'd done before. It was a great shame about Bruce Fairbairn, but he did a fantastic job. Although he is no longer with us, at least his last project proved to be a great one. We went to Vancouver with a completely open mind. All the gear was still in Japan from the gigs that we did the previous year, so we arranged to ship it to Vancouver ready for recording. We played a lot more things than ended up on the album but we made a pretty good choice. There was a bit of Seventies Yes but more importantly it has a Nineties feel. 'Lightning Strikes' was a great track because it didn't really sound like Yes. It is a combination of a South African and Caribbean feel in 7/4 which gives it that Yes twist. 'The Messenger' has a bass intro and I must admit there's a lot of loud bass on this album! I never said to anyone, 'Can you please make me louder, but for some reason they mixed the bass quite loud.

"Igor did a great job on the keyboards and he's such a good player you get a bit of Rick Wakeman and a bit of Tony Kaye combined. He's a bit of a combo! On this album everyone threw in their ideas. Billy played a supportive role to Steve but I think Bruce wanted it that way, to make Steve more of the lead guitar player. Billy also played a lot of interesting parts, which make a lot of the tracks move along. I also think *The Ladder* is one of our best albums. It has a landmark feel for us."

Igor Khoroshev was making his first appearance on a Yes album after briefly contributing to the previous *Open Your Eyes* CD. Enthuses Igor: "Every song on *The Ladder* has different textures and there is a wide spectrum of styles, so you don't get bored! That's what Bruce Fairbairn wanted. Many songs didn't make it onto the album for that reason."

Like his illustrious predecessors Igor used a real Hammond B3 organ on some of the tracks but he also used an organ simulator because the B3 might have 'bled' into the drum tracks. The simulator was put through a Leslie speaker cabinet to get an authentic Hammond organ sound. Igor was intrigued at the way Bruce Fairbairn went for a 'live' feel.

"Bruce used the rough 'live' keyboard tracks made while they were cutting the bass and drums. He said, 'I don't want to touch them.' I thought it would take a week to go back and re-cut all my parts with piano and organ and he just said, 'No, this sounds great. We're going to leave this in!' "

Igor says Fairbairn used the same approach with the rest of the band. "Jon had to go back and cut a few bits, but a lot of the record is 'live' with only a few overdubs. That's how Bruce Fairbairn worked. I found that just amazing. All the solos I played – stayed! I did a big church organ introduction to 'New Language' and that's all done on Yamaha keyboards. Maybe we should tell people it was recorded in a big cathedral somewhere. It used to be my dream. I'm recording with Yes so we must go to Paris and record with a cathedral organ. That didn't happen but it was performed 'live' in the studio. Bruce said, 'This is great, keep it. Don't touch it.' At first I thought this was all very weird. Then I looked at the walls and saw all the Platinum albums and saw how many records Bruce had sold and then I began to understand where he was coming from. He wanted to keep everything fresh. If there were little mistakes here and there he didn't care. He wanted to keep the human touch. I learned a lot from Bruce."

As the youngest member Igor was fascinated at the process of putting Yes arrangements together. " 'Homeworld' was originally called 'Climbing The Ladder' and that's an interesting piece of music. It wasn't actually picked by Bruce. Jon and Chris insisted we should check it out, to see how far it could go. One day we got together in the studio and we all started playing and listening to the demo tapes. Two months later we said, 'Let's try that piece of music again' even though the producer said it wasn't going to make it on the record. Billy came in with an intro and Jon wrote some lyrics on top and then Steve came up with the shuffle rhythm. Meanwhile Bruce told me to work on a solo piece for the cathedral organ to put into 'New Language'. When Steve started to play his part for 'Homeworld' I put part of my theme from 'New Language' on top so it became integrated. On 'Lightning Strikes' I also played a bit of organ. It was interesting how that came together."

While on tour in Japan Igor went into Jon's hotel room one night to drink some Sake and Jon played the new song for him. At that stage it had just three chords and Jon sang backed by a drum machine and acoustic guitar. However Igor could see the potential. 'Can I' was another song Igor liked. "Of course Bruce didn't know who had written what. He just picked the songs he thought were cool, so there were no politics involved in the picking process. He chose the best ones, so we didn't have to waste time working on songs that weren't so strong. I intended to use all kinds of different instruments like Harmonium and accordion and unfortunately I didn't get a chance to do that.

"There are a few pieces of music on the album that have these ethnic sounds like flutes. It's actually all played on a keyboard. The flutes at the beginning of 'Lightning Strikes' are Mellotron tape loops. The Mellotron was the first machine that used loops. You push one note and it will actually play the loop. In fact we used a CD which has a collection of hundreds of Mellotron sounds.

"I think this is one of the best albums Yes have released in the last ten years. Everybody contributed and that hadn't happened much in the past. This album is strong because all the musicians who had played together for thirty years got together in one room and wrote together. Yet it's bizarre there is such a happy feeling about the record, because it was raining the whole time we were writing, recording and mixing in Vancouver! It could have been dramatic and depressing music, but that didn't happen. *The Ladder* is a fun record!"

The Ladder was released in the UK on Eagle Records on October 1, 1999 complete with a special new cover painting by Roger Dean. An enhanced compact disc contained a demo of 'Homeworld' the PC game together with a screen saver and a Yes interview. A tour edition of *The Ladder* album was released on January 31, 2000 on Eagle Records. This two CD set featured *The Ladder* while the second disc contained three live tracks from the House Of Blues show in Los Angeles, including 'Homeworld', 'The Messenger' and 'All Good People' plus video footage of 'All Good People'. Eagle also released a special limited edition gate-fold double LP – pressed in heavy vinyl.

Once the album was completed the band set off to play the new material live on tour. On September 6, 1999 Yes began a series of hectic Latin American dates in Brazil, Argentina, Peru, Costa Rica, Venezuela and Mexico. The South American audiences were particularly vociferous and one ecstatic local critic wrote about Steve Howe: "After God and Mozart – He! Still, I get tearful eyes."

The set list changed on nearly every show, but numbers featured during the tour included 'Yours Is No Disgrace', 'New Language', 'Nine Voices', 'Perpetual Change', 'Lightning Strikes', 'Homeworld', 'It Will Be A Good Day', 'Hearts', 'Owner Of A Lonely Heart', 'If Only You Knew', 'Awaken', 'Roundabout', 'To Feel Alive', 'I've Seen All Good People', 'Long Distance Runaround', 'America', 'Clap', 'And You And I', 'Mood For A Day', 'Close To The Edge', 'Time And A Word', 'Ritual' and 'Sweet Dreams'.

A North American tour began on October 15 with a show at the House

Of Blues, Myrtle Beach, South Carolina. In November the tour continued to Toledo, Cincinnati, Rochester, Cleveland, New Brunswick and other East Coast venues before the band headed west to play three more House Of Blues dates in Los Angeles. Yes liked these club dates in a friendly, intimate environment that was conducive to good playing.

These club gigs were followed by shows in San Francisco, Seattle, Chicago and Detroit. In December Yes played two shows in Canada before heading to New York for three nights at the Bacon Theater. The tour ended with the last two gigs at the Tower Theater, Philadelphia (November 12, 13). These were the last Yes shows of the 20th century.

The year 2000 saw the band commence a full European tour in Ireland at the National Concert Hall, Dublin on February 6, followed by the Symphony Hall, Birmingham (February 8) and further shows in Sheffield, (10), Cardiff (11), Bournemouth (12), Manchester (13), Liverpool (14), Nottingham (16), Glasgow (17) and two shows at London's Royal Albert Hall (19, 20). The latter was an important homecoming to a prestigious venue where Yes started their career way back in November, 1968.

After the UK dates the band played shows in Portugal, Spain, France, Belgium, Holland, Italy, Switzerland and Germany during February and March. Most Yes fans were now familiar with the new material from *The Ladder* but when the group began their South American tour in September the previous year, it had been a different story as Steve Howe recalls: "They hadn't heard the album and when we started out quite bravely playing masses of new stuff it was a bit strange for them, especially in countries where we had never played before. So we only played a couple of tracks off the album. By the time we got to North America the audiences were kind of 'there' with the music and that helped a lot. We got a terrific response and people were saying *The Ladder* was the best album we'd made since the Seventies. But as the tour went on and we tried different songs, the feedback from fans was they would have preferred us to do more of the bigger, better known pieces. We had been going a bit heavy on the Afro-Caribbean stuff."

They started out doing 'Lightning Strikes' then found 'Face To Face' was becoming more popular and put both of them in the set. "We put out 'Lightning Strikes' as a single in America, thinking it was a catchy number," says Steve. "But singles are a kind of gamble. You hope you might get some airplay and give the album more legs. It was exciting when the album rushed into the charts. But then it kind of disappeared!"

They gave the record heavy promotion on tour but were mainly reaching a cult fan base rather than a mass pop audience. The fan base got wider as they played parts they had not reached before.

"The audiences in countries like Argentina were unbelievable," says

274

Steve. "South Americans in general have an intense relationship with their music. They sing along to Yes songs as if they were national anthems. Jon would be gently singing 'And You And I' and there would be a very large man in the audience singing along too! It was a kind of challenge. To be honest I was always rather fearful about going to South America. I had heard it was a place where you had to be careful. You mustn't wear any jewellery and should try and mingle rather than stand out! In some places the promoters said, 'Stay in the hotel. Don't go out.' There's no denying it can be dangerous on the streets. Rio de Janeiro in Brazil is quite spectacular but it is one of the most dangerous places of all. There was a huge scam on the beach while we were there. There was a police parade and all the thieves and low life ran along the beach hi-jacking tourists. So you can't be too careful.

"We didn't go to Chile because there was some unrest there with people burning the American flag. So we had to cancel our show there. Rick Wakeman warned us it was utter hell out there!"

Despite the perils of touring Yes continue to enjoy the fun of performing live and bringing their music to the fans. Says Steve: "We still love to play pieces like 'Awaken' and 'Close To The Edge'. I don't want to live in the past but I do like to play the older material and keep it authentic. I suppose I become hypersensitive about certain areas, but in a way that has enabled me to play guitar and fly around like I do. It was pretty breathtaking to be able to play at the Royal Albert Hall in London. We hadn't played there in donkey's years. It's a spectacular place and I remember playing there in 1968 at a show called The Pop Proms, with my group Bodast. We were on the same night as The Who and Chuck Berry. Bodast were actually Chuck Berry's support band. I remember Chuck coming in, looking at me and saying, 'We don't need you.' I said, 'Okay, I understand.' Then I took him aside and said, 'Look, I've got this great guitar. What do you think?' He picked it up, had a play and said, 'Fantastic guitar man, that's great.' So there were no hard feelings, even though he still didn't want me to play with him on stage! He only wanted the bass player and drummer. He guessed I wasn't going to contain myself and just play riffs. I wasn't upset. I was quite relieved because he tends to change numbers – midway through a song – and expects the band to follow. I did get to play the opening set with Bodast and so that was my first gig at the Royal Albert Hall."

Steve could take pleasure in the fact that his famous acoustic guitar solo 'Clap' proved one of the highlights of the Royal Albert Hall shows. He played it brilliantly well, breathing new life into his country pickin' favourite. On both nights fans packed the venerable old building to cheer an impressive selection of Yes songs old and new. On the last night the band's family members joined in the fun and Steve's son Virgil and Jon's Damian were seen dancing on stage during an exultant version of 'Roundabout.'

Earlier the audience had sat listening somewhat awestruck by the rich variety of music the band performed. Commented multi-instrumentalist and singer Willie Dowling, seated in the stalls during a mind-boggling version of 'Awakening': "This is symbolic music. It sure as hell ain't pop!" But there *were* elements of pure pop when the band stomped into the Caribbean flavoured 'Lightning Strikes' and 'Face To Face' which finally had the audience up on their feet and dancing. The latter proved one of the most popular numbers of the night.

The show was smooth and highly professional as befits such a well seasoned band. There were none of the technical hitches that used to bedevil Yes thirty years ago! Now computers, samples and the latest sound mixing technology ensure the group sounds as good on stage as it does on CD. Even the lighting and effects were more effective and subtle than the old days. There was no expensive scenery to shift around, but there was a light show, with a succession of Yes logos and Roger Dean's turbulent landscapes projected on screen, together with historic pictures of the group. It all added to the sense of occasion, highlighted by Jon singing a snatch from one of the oldest favourites in the Yes songbook 'Time And A Word'.

There were many facets and eras of the band on display. The pairing of Igor's piano and Jon's bell-like vocals, boded well for a proposed Igor-Jon album. Billy Sherwood's sturdy guitar fleshed out the arrangements and he was heavily featured on a stomping 'Owner Of A Lonely Heart'. Alan White's drums were either working overtime as a source of molten rock energy, or providing a dazzling array of subtle cross rhythms. On 'The Messenger' he managed to play a 6/8 rhythm on his ride cymbal while playing a reggae beat, no mean feat.

The Sunday night show kicked off with 'Yours Is No Disgrace' with Igor all in white rising above his skimpy array of keyboards like a Cossack and producing a huge range of sounds from Hammond organ to grand piano. When Jon Anderson wasn't singing with beautiful clarity or chatting casually to the audience, he was battering his percussion 'sound tree' or even playing a magical harp. 'Home World' from *The Ladder* gave Alan a chance to sock out a powerful backbeat and indeed his intros and fill-ins were a constant source of excitement. 'I've Seen All Good People' with its irresistible hook line and driving rhythm, brought the audience to their feet. Steve played steel guitar on 'And You And I' and there was even an unexpected touch of harmonica from Chris Squire.

Missing was Alan's drum solo and Chris' usual bass outing. Doubtless they felt they'd said it all solo-wise on the band's previous tour. More important was the band's exploration of some of their most fascinating pieces like 'Perpetual Change' (which does – all the time), and 'Awaken'. As the old dome rang with cheers Jon said: "This is an historic night for us. We started out here thirty years ago and thank you for staying with us."

After the Yes triumphs in Europe, there were no immediate plans to start recording a new Yes album, although Chris Squire and Billy Sherwood's album *Conspiracy* (Eagle EAAGCD126) was scheduled for release on February 28, 2000.

Steve Howe is amazed at the way Yes have survived and prospered. "Back in 1970 when I joined the group I wasn't even thinking about it lasting so long. I was probably thinking – would I still be alive – let alone the band! I had no idea that Yes would become such a huge chunk of rock history. We are all thrilled to be here. It is such an achievement to be around, unlike other bands like Genesis who aren't up and running anymore. We started in 1968 and here we are in the year 2000. Not many bands have done that. Over the course of the next year we will evaluate what we are doing. We want to see what we've achieved and where we are going.

"What will we do next? I guess we'll still be on the road. It gets tiring but I enjoy it tremendously and there is great joy in what we do. We're still crazy after all these years!"

Afterword

YES TODAY

Most of the characters from Yes and their associates who have contributed to *Close To The Edge* are scattered far and wide, but most are still actively involved in music making or at least retain an interest in what Andrew Loog Oldham once called 'The Industry Of Human Happiness'. So where are they now? In alphabetical order we present . . .

JON ANDERSON. Jon, the lead singer in Yes, helped write and record the band's 31st album *The Ladder* in Vancouver, Canada, with the late Bruce Fairbairn. Eternally nomadic, he has lived in France, the Caribbean, Los Angeles, and the mountains of Southern California and now lives with his wife Jane Luttenberger Anderson in San Luis Obispo, California. Jon released a solo album, *The More You Know*, in 1998, which was recorded in Surrey and France, with his wife Jane on backing vocals. He is working on another solo CD with Yes keyboard player Igor Khoroshev.

PETER BANKS. The first lead guitarist with Yes later led the bands Flash and Empire. Currently living in Barnet, Herts, England. He has recorded two solo albums including *Instinct* (HTD) in 1993 and *Self Contained* (One Way Records) in 1995. He also arranged the 1997 release of *Something's Coming* (NMC), the Yes album of radio broadcast material. His most recent CD is *Can I Play You Something?* (Blueprint) a 22-track compilation comprising recordings from 1964 to 1968 including pre-Yes material by Mabel Greer's Toyshop and Syn.

JACK BARRIE. The man who introduced Jon Anderson to Chris Squire and thus set Yes in motion was the manager of London's Marquee Club and an associate of the Marquee Organisation for 25 years from 1964 to 1989. He is presently acting as a consultant to the entertainment, catering and leisure industry. He lives in Wimbledon, London, with his wife Hilary and three sons Matthew, Daniel and Joe.

BILL BRUFORD. The original drummer with Yes lives in Surrey, England, with his wife Carolyn. He records and tours internationally with his own band Earthworks as well as King Crimson, and also runs Bill Bruford Productions Ltd.

PHIL CARSON. The former close ally of Yes and UK boss of Atlantic Records and Victory Records, now lives in Palm Springs, California. He is president of the music division of The Shooting Gallery film company based in Los Angeles. He has been involved in the creation of the stage play *The Benny Hill Story*. His son Jack Carson runs their artist management company whose clients include drummer Jason Bonham, son of the late John Bonham of Led Zeppelin.

ROY CLAIR. Yes' American sound engineer who introduced the band to sophisticated sound systems is now President of Clair Bros Audio Enterprises Inc. based in Lititz, Philadelphia.

ROGER DEAN. The celebrated Yes artist and designer is chairman of publishing and media company Magnetic Storm. He and his brother Martyn are developing ideas for films, games and books. Their début game *Secret Of The Black Onyx* was due out in Autumn 1999. A range of books on science fiction, music and art are scheduled for publication and they have several major architectural projects planned.

GEOFF DOWNES. The keyboard player with Yes during the *Drama* period is currently recording a new album with his band Asia at his own Loco Studios in Monmouthshire, South Wales.

ROY FLYNN. The first manager of Yes is now the proprietor of The Bull Inn, Charlbury, Oxfordshire, where he lives with wife Suzanne and son Alex. He was voted Host of the Year by Egon Ronay in 1997.

JIM HALLEY. Yes tour manager for many years lives with his family in Kings Langley, Bucks. He operates his own artist management company and manages Steve Howe as a solo artist.

TREVOR HORN. Yes' vocalist during the *Drama* period is, of course, now far better known as a successful record producer based at SARM studios in London, working with such artists as the singer Seal. Trevor owns SARM West and ZTT Records together with his wife Jill Sinclair. He has toured with Art Of Noise.

STEVE HOWE. The guitar virtuoso remains the lead guitarist with Yes. He lives with his wife Jan and family in Muswell Hill, London. Aside from working with Yes, he has recorded an album called *Portraits Of Bob Dylan*. His superb collection of guitars and other fretted instruments has been the subject of at least one coffee-table style book. His son Dylan has been playing drums with Ian Dury & The Blockheads and singer Gabrielle.

TONY KAYE. Yes' first organist is currently living in Los Angeles. Over the years he has worked as a session musician and touring artist and his more prestigious clients include David Bowie.

IGOR KHOROSHEV. The present keyboard player with Yes lives in Boston, Massachusetts, USA, with his wife and son. He also works for Cakewalk Software, and has contributed to a *Tribute To Emerson, Lake & Palmer* album as well as recording his own album *Piano Works*.

BRIAN LANE. The former manager of Yes, Asia and ABWH currently runs Bandanna management company based in London, England.

PATRICK MORAZ. The keyboard player who took over from Rick Wakeman in the mid-Seventies is currently working on solo projects from his recording base at Audio Playground Studio and Keyboard Museum in Winter Park, Florida. He has recorded ten solo albums since leaving Yes and has returned to the road for a series of solo piano concerts.

TREVOR RABIN. The South African born guitarist who injected new life into Yes in the Eighties is based in Los Angeles, and is busy working on film music scores and has produced a new solo album at his own studio.

BILLY SHERWOOD. The current guitarist alongside Steve Howe in Yes has his own studio in Los Angeles and has written and produced a solo album with Chris Squire.

CHRIS SQUIRE. The bass guitarist and founder member of Yes has a new solo album released in February, 2000, called *Conspiracy*, a CD with 14 tracks co-written with Billy Sherwood with contributions from Alan White.

MICHAEL TAIT. Yes' first roadie is President of Tait Towers, a stage construction company based in Lititz, Philadelphia.

ADAM WAKEMAN. Rick's son, who almost became the 15th member of Yes, is a keyboard player and singer and has recorded album tracks with Tracy Hunter, vocalist daughter of former Mott The Hoople frontman Ian Hunter.

RICK WAKEMAN. The best known Yes keyboard player who has lived on the Isle Of Man for some years with wife Nina, released *Return To The Centre Of The Earth*, a solo album in 1999 and was busy touring the UK in early 2000 and making regular TV appearances on shows like *Never Mind The Buzzcocks*.

ALAN WHITE. Yes' long-standing drummer and percussionist now lives with his wife Gigi in Seattle, USA. He teaches drums in his spare time when he's not busy touring the world with Yes and recording tracks for Chris Squire and Billy Sherwood.

Discography

YES

(At various times featuring Jon Anderson, Chris Squire, Peter Banks, Bill Bruford, Tony Kaye, Steve Howe, Rick Wakeman, Alan White, Patrick Moraz, Trevor Horn, Geoff Downes, Trevor Rabin, Billy Sherwood & Igor Khoroshev)

Standard US/UK releases excluding promo releases and Yes tracks appearing on Various Artists albums, unless otherwise noted.

7″ Singles

Sweetness/Something's Coming
UK Atlantic 584 280 June 1969

Sweetness (Edit)/Every Little Thing
US Atlantic 45-2709 January 1970

Time And A Word/The Prophet
UK Atlantic 584 323 March 1970

Sweet Dreams/Dear Father
UK Atlantic 2091 004 June 1970

Your Move/Clap
US Atlantic 45-2819 July 1971

Roundabout/Long Distance Runaround
US Atlantic 45-2854 January 1972

America/Total Mass Retain
US Atlantic 45-2899 July 1972
(reissued as Atlantic 3141, 1974)

And You And I – Part 1/And You And I – Part 2
US Atlantic 45-2920 October 1972

And You And I/Roundabout
UK Atlantic K 10407 January 1974

Soon/Sound Chaser
US Atlantic 45-3242 January 1975

America/Your Move
US Atlantic Oldies Series OS-13141 1976

Roundabout/Long Distance Runaround
US Atlantic Oldies Series OS-13140 1976 (and 1985)

Wondrous Stories/Parallels
UK Atlantic K 10999 August 1977

Wondrous Stories/Awaken
US Atlantic 45-3416 September 1977

Going For The One/Awaken – Part 1
UK Atlantic K 11047 November 1977

Don't Kill The Whale/Abilene
UK Atlantic K 11184 August 1978

Don't Kill The Whale/Release Release
US Atlantic 45-3534 November 1978

Into The Lens/Does It Really Happen
UK Atlantic K 11622 September 1980
US Atlantic 3767

Run Through the Light/White Car
US Atlantic 3810 January 1981

Roundabout/I've Seen All Good People
UK Atlantic SMA 141 December 1981 (issued free with *Classic Yes* album)
US Atlantic PR 415

It Can Happen (edit)/It Can Happen (live)
UK Atco B 9745 1983

Owner Of A Lonely Heart/Our Song
UK Atco B 9817 October 1983
US Atco B9187P (picture disc)
US Atco 7-99817 (alternative picture sleeve)

Owner Of A Lonely Heart/Leave It
US Atco 7-849999 November 1983

Leave It/Leave It (a cappella version)
UK Atco B 9787 February 1984

It Can Happen/It Can Happen (live)
UK Atco B 9745 April 1984
US Atco 7-99745

Love Will Find A Way (edit)/Holy Lamb (Song For Harmonic Convergence)
UK Atco A 9449 September 1987
99419 December 1987

Saving My Heart (album version)/Lift Me Up (edit)
UK Arista 114 553 July 1991

Owner Of A Lonely Heart/Make It Easy
UK Atco September 1991

Owner Of A Lonely Heart (original version)/Owner Of A Lonely Heart
(wondrous mix – edit)
UK Atco B 8713 September 1991

For Everyone (live from *The Sunday Show*, March 1, 1970)
New Millennium Communications February 1998 (single sided Italian release,
issued with the LP *Something's Coming*)

12″ Singles

Wonderous Stories/Parallels
UK Atlantic K 10999 September 1977 (limited edition, issued in both black vinyl
and blue vinyl)

Going For The One/Awaken (part 1)
UK Atlantic K 11047 November 1977

Owner Of A Lonely Heart (Red And Blue Remix Dance version) / Owner Of
A Lonely Heart
US Atco 0-96976 November 1983

Owner Of A Lonely Heart (Red and Blue Remix Dance version)/Owner Of A
Lonely Heart / Our Song (LP Version)
UK Atco B 9817T
US Atco 796 881-0 November 1983

Leave It (Hello/Goodbye mix)/Leave It (remix)/Leave It (a cappella)
UK Atco B 9787T/7 March 1984
US Atco 0-96964

Leave It (single version with edit)/City Of Love/Leave It (Hello/Goodbye
mix)/Leave It (acapella)
US Atco PR 587 May 1984

Love Will Find A Way (extended version)/Love Will Find A Way (Rise and Fall
Mix)/Holy Lamb (Song For Harmonic Convergence)
UK Atco A 9449T September 1987
US Atco 7-99449

Rhythm Of Love (Dance to the Rhythm Mix)/Rhythm Of Love (Move to the
Rhythm mix)/Rhythm Of Love (The Rhythm of Dub)/City Of Love (live edit)
US Atco 0-96722 December 1987

Owner Of A Lonely Heart (original version)/Owner Of A Lonely Heart (The Move Yourself mix)/Owner Of A Lonely Heart (2 Close To The Edge mix)/Owner Of A Lonely Heart (Not Fragile mix)
UK Atco 7567-96293-0 B 8713-T September 1991

Lift Me Up (Album Version)/Lift Me Up (Edit Version)/Take The Water To The Mountain
UK Arista 614 256 June 1991

Saving My Heart (Album Version)/America
UK Arista 614 553 July 1991

Cassette Singles

Twelve Inches On Tape
Leave It (Remix)/Owner Of A Lonely Heart (Red & Blue Mix)/Leave It (Hello/Goodbye Mix)/Owner Of A Lonely Heart
UK Atco B 9787 C March 1984
US Atco 90156-4

Rhythm Of Love (Dance To The Rhythm Mix)/Rhythm Of Love (Move To The Rhythm Mix)/Rhythm Of Love (The Rhythm Of Dub)/City Of Love (Live Edit)
US Atco 7-96722-4 January 1988

Lift Me Up/ America (1972)/Lift Me Up/ America (1972)
US Arista CAS-2218 June 1991

Make It Easy/Long Distance Runaround/Make It Easy/Long Distance Runaround
US Arista 74-98738 (US) August 1991

CD Singles

Leave It/Leave It
US Atco B9789 C March 1984

Love Will Find A Way (edit)/Rhythm Of Love
US Atco 7-94964 1987

Lift Me Up (edit)/Give And Take
US Arista AS-2218 June 1991

Saving My Heart/Lift Me Up/America
US Arista 664553 July 1991

I Would Have Waited For Ever (edit)/I Would Have Waited For Ever (album version)
US Arista ASCD-2344 1991

Owner Of A Lonely Heart (original version)/Owner Of A Lonely Heart
(Wondrous mix)/ Owner Of A Lonely Heart (2 Close To The Edge
mix)/Owner Of A Lonely Heart (Not Fragile mix)
UK Atco CDS 7567-96292-2 B 8713 September 1991

Owner Of A Lonely Heart (Move Yourself mix)/Owner Of A Lonely Heart
(album mix)/Owner Of A Lonely Heart (Wondrous mix/ Owner Of A Lonely
Heart (2 Close To The Edge mix)/Owner Of A Lonely Heart (Not Fragile mix)
UK Atco SAM 928 September 1991

Vinyl Albums

YES
Beyond And Before/I See You/Yesterday And Today/Looking Around/Harold
Land/Every Little Thing/Sweetness/Survival
Atlantic 588 190 August 1969
Reissued as Atlantic K40034 in 1972

TIME AND A WORD
No Opportunity Necessary, No Experience Needed/Then/Everydays/Sweet
Dreams/The Prophet/Clear Days/Astral Traveller/Time And A Word
Atlantic 2400 006 July 1970
Reissued as Atlantic K 40085 in 1972

THE YES ALBUM
Yours Is No Disgrace/The Clap/Starship Trooper: a. Life Seeker, b. Disillusion,
c. Würm/I've Seen All Good People: a. Your Move, b. All Good People/A
Venture/Perpetual Change
Atlantic 2400 101 July 1971
Reissued as Atlantic K 40106 in 1972

FRAGILE
Roundabout/Cans And Brahms/We Have Heaven/South Side Of The
Sky/Five Per Cent For Nothing/Long Distance Runaround/The Fish
(Schindleria Praematurus)/Mood For A Day/Heart Of The Sunrise
Atlantic 2401 019 September 1971

CLOSE TO THE EDGE
Close To The Edge: (i) The Solid Time Of Change, (ii) Total Mass Retain, (iii) I
Get Up, I Get Down, (iv) Seasons Of Man/And You And I: (i) Cord Of Life, (ii)
Eclipse, (iii) The Preacher The Teacher, (iv) The Apocalypse/Siberian Khatru
Atlantic K 50012 September 1972

YESSONGS
Opening (excerpt from Firebird Suite)/Siberian Khatru/Heart Of The Sunrise/
Perpetual Change/And You And I/Mood For A Day/Excerpts From The Six
Wives Of Henry V111/Roundabout/Your Move/I've Seen All Good
People/Long Distance Runaround/The Fish/Close To The Edge/Yours Is No
Disgrace/Starship Trooper
Atlantic K 60045 April 1973

TALES FROM TOPOGRAPHIC OCEANS
The Revealing Science Of God/The Remembering/The Ancient/Ritual
Atlantic K 80001 November 1973

RELAYER
The Gates Of Delirium/Sound Chaser/To Be Over
Atlantic K 50096 November 1974

YESTERDAYS
America (full length version)/Looking Around/Time And A Word/Sweet
Dreams/Then/Survival/Astral Traveller/Dear Father
Atlantic K 50048 March 1975
US SD18103 (Features full length America)

GOING FOR THE ONE
Going For The One/Turn Of The Century/Parallels/Wondrous Stories/Awaken
Atlantic K 50379 July 1977

TORMATO
Future Times/Rejoice/Don't Kill The Whale/Madrigal/Release Release/
Arriving UFO/Circus Of Heaven/Onward/On The Silent Wings Of Freedom
Atlantic K 50518 September 1978

YESSHOWS
Parallels/Time And A Word/Going For The One/The Gates Of
Delirium/Don't Kill The Whale/Ritual (Nous Sommes Du Soleil)/
Wondrous Stories
Atlantic K 60142 July 1979

DRAMA
Machine Messiah/White Car/Does It Really Happen?/Into The Lens/Run
Through The Light/Tempus Fugit
Atlantic K 50736 August 1980

CLASSIC YES
Heart Of The Sunrise/Wondrous Stories/Yours Is No Disgrace/Starship
Trooper: a. Life Seeker, b Disillusion, c.Würm/Long Distance Runaround/The
Fish (Schindleria Praematurus)/And You And I: a. Cord Of Life, b. Eclipse,
c. The Preacher The Teacher, d. The Apocalypse/Roundabout/ I've Seen All
Good People: a. Your Move, b. All Good People
Atlantic K 50842 December 1981

90125
Owner Of A Lonely Heart/Hold On/It Can Happen/Changes/Cinema/
Leave It/Our Song/City Of Love/Hearts
Atco 790125-1 1983

9012LIVE – THE SOLOS
Hold On/Si/Solly's Beard/Soon/Changes/Amazing Grace/Whitefish
Atco 90474 November 1985 (CD available in Japan only)

BIG GENERATOR
Rhythm Of Love/Big Generator/Shoot High Aim Low/Almost Like Love/
Love Will Find A Way/Final Eyes/I'm Running/Holy Lamb (Song For
Harmonic Convergence)
Atco WX 70 790 522-1 1987

THE LADDER
Homeworld (The Ladder)/It Will Be A Good Day (The River)/Lightning
Strikes/Can I?/Face To Face/If Only You Knew/To Be Alive (Hep Yadda)/
Finally/The Messenger/New Language/Nine Voices (Longwalker)
Eagle EDG 12088 January 2000
(Limited and numbered edition, double heavyweight vinyl LP. Gatefold sleeve
designed by Martyn Dean with painting, logos and lettering by Roger Dean.)

CDs

90125
Tracks as above
Atlantic 790 125-2 November 1983
Atco 7567-90125-2 (Digitally remastered) 1998

CLASSIC YES
Tracks as above
Atlantic 250842 2 December 1986
Atlantic 7567 82687-2 (Digitally remastered) 1998

CLOSE TO THE EDGE
Tracks as above
Atlantic 250 012 December 1986
Atlantic 7567-82666-2 (Digitally remastered) 1998

FRAGILE
Tracks as above
Atlantic 250 009 December 1986
Atlantic 7567-82667-2 (Digitally remastered) 1998

YESSONGS
Tracks as above
Atlantic 260 045 February 1987
Atlantic 7567-82682-2 (2 CD set) (Digitally remastered) 1998

THE YES ALBUM
Tracks as above
Atlantic K 240106 July 1987
Atlantic 7567–82665–2 (Digitally remastered) 1998

BIG GENERATOR
Tracks as above
Atlantic 790 522–2 August 1987
Atco 7567–90522–2 (Digitally remastered) 1998

GOING FOR THE ONE
Tracks as above
Atlantic K250 379 July 1988
Atlantic 7567–82670–2 (Digitally remastered) 1998

RELAYER
Tracks as above
Atlantic K 250 096 July 1988
Atlantic 7567–82664–2 (Digitally remastered) 1998

TALES FROM TOPOGRAPHIC OCEANS
Tracks as above
WEA 781325 September 1989
Atlantic 7567–82683–2 (2-CD set) (Digitally remastered) 1998

UNION
I Would Have Waited Forever/Shock To The System/Masquerade/Lift Me
Up/Without Hope You Cannot Start The Day/Saving My Heart/ Miracle Of
Life/Silent Talking/More We Live-Let Go/The Angkor Wat/Dangerous/
Holding On/Evensong/Take The Water To The Mountain/Give And Take
Arista 261558 April 1991

YES YEARS
Something's Coming/Survival/Every Little Thing/Then/Everydays/Sweet
Dreams/No Opportunity Necessary, No Experience Needed/Time And A
Word/Starship Trooper: a. Life Seeker, b. Disillusion, c. Würm)/Yours Is No
Disgrace/ I've Seen All Good People: a. Your Move, b. All Good People)/ Long
Distance Runaround/The Fish (Schindleria Praematurus)/ Roundabout/ Heart Of
The Sunrise/America/Close To The Edge: a. The Solid Time Of Change, b. Total
Mass Retain, c. I Get Up, I Get Down, d. Seasons Of Man/Ritual (Nous Sommes
Du Soleil)/Sound Chaser/Soon/Amazing Grace/Vevey (Part One)/Wondrous
Stories/Awaken/Montreux's Theme/Vevey (Part Two)/Going For The One/
Money/Abilene/Don't Kill The Whale/On The Silent Wings Of Freedom/Does
It Really Happen?/Tempus Fugit/Run With The Fox/I'm Down/Make It Easy/It
Can Happen/Owner Of A Lonely Heart/Hold On/Shoot High Aim Low/
Rhythm Of Love/Love Will Find A Way/Changes/And You And I: a. Cord Of
Life, b. Eclipse, c.The Preacher The Teacher, d. Apocalypse/Heart Of The
Sunrise/Love Conquers All
Atco 7567–91644–2 August 1991 (4 CD Box Set)

YESSTORY
Survival/No Opportunity Necessary, No Experience Needed/Time And A
Word/Starship Trooper/I've Seen All Good People/ Roundabout/Heart Of The
Sunrise/Close To The Edge/Ritual (Nous Sommes Du Soleil)/Soon/Wondrous
Stories/Going For The One/Don't Kill The Whale/Does It Really
Happen?/Make It Easy/Owner Of A Lonely Heart/Rhythm Of Love/Changes
(live version)
Atco 7567 91747-2 September 1991 (2 CD Set)
(Also released in Germany as double vinyl album)

HIGHLIGHTS – THE VERY BEST OF YES
Survival/Time And A Word/Starship Trooper a. Life Seeker b. Disillusion
c.Würm/I've Seen All Good People: a.Your Move, b. All Good
People/Roundabout/Long Distance Runaround/Soon/Wondrous Stories/Going
For The One/Owner Of A Lonely Heart/ Leave It/ Rhythm Of Love
Atlantic 7567-82517-2 1993

AFFIRMATIVE: THE YES SOLOS FAMILY ALBUM
Catherine Howard (Rick Wakeman)/Wind Of Change (Badger)/Nature Of The
Sea (Steve Howe)/Ram (Steve Howe)/Hold Out Your Hand (Chris
Squire)/Merlin The Magician (Rick Wakeman)/Ocean Song – Meeting – Sound
Of The Galleon (Jon Anderson)/Spring, Song Of Innocence (Alan
White)/Cachaca (Baiao) (Patrick Moraz)/Feels Good To me (Bill Bruford)/I Hear
You Now (Jon & Vangelis)/All In A Matter Of Time (Jon Anderson)/Etoile Noir
– Eyes Of Love (Trevor Rabin)/Dominating Factor (Peter Banks)
UK Coinnoisseur Collections Ltd VSOP CD190 1993

SYMPHONIC MUSIC OF YES
Roundabout/Close To the Edge/Wondrous Stories/I've Seen All Good
People/Mood For A Day/Owner Of A Lonely Heart/Survival/Heart Of The
Sunrise/Soon/Starship Trooper
US RCA/Victor 09026-61938-2 1993 (The London Philharmonic & The English
Chamber Orchestra with Anderson, Bruford and Howe)

TALK
The Calling I Am Waiting/Real Love/State Of Play/Walls/Where Will You
Be/Endless Dream a. Silent Spring b. Talk c. Endless Dream
Victory 828 489-2 1994
(Also released on vinyl in the UK; Japanese versions features The Calling
[extended] as bonus track)

KEYS TO ASCENSION VOL 1
Siberian Khatru/The Revealing Science Of God/America/ Onward/Awaken/
Roundabout/Starship Trooper/Be The One/That, That Is
Yes Records EDF CD-47
GAS 0000417 EDF 1996 (2 CD set)

KEYS TO ASCENSION VOL 2
I've Seen All Good People: a. Your Move b. All Good People/Going For The
One/Time And A Word/Close To The Edge: a. Solid Time Of Change b. Total
Mass Retain c. I Get Up, I Get Down c. Seasons Of Man/Turn Of The
Century/And You And I: a. Cord Of Life b. Eclipse c. The Preacher The Teacher
d. Apocalypse/Mind Drive/Foot Prints/Bring To The Power/Children Of The
Light: a. Children Of The Light b. Lifeline/Sign Language
Yes Records EDF CD457
GAS 0000475EDF 1997 (2 CD set)

OPEN YOUR EYES
New State Of Mind/Open Your Eyes/Universal Garden/No Way We Can
Lose/Fortune Seller/Man In The Moon/Wonder Love/From The Balcony/Love
Shine/Somehow . . . Someday/The Solution
Eagle Records EDL EAG 013-2 1997
Also released in the US as limited edition 'Surround Sound' album (BYCD3075)
1998

KEYS TO ASCENSION VOLS 1 & 2
(Same track listing as Keys 1 & 2)
ESF CD635
GAS 0000635ESP 1998 (Castle Communications)

YESSHOWS
Tracks as above
Atlantic 75567-82686-2 (Digitally remastered – Ritual now full length) 1998

YES
Tracks as above
Atlantic 7567-82680-2 (Digitally remastered) 1998

TIME AND A WORD
Tracks as above
Atlantic 7567-82681-2 (Digitally remastered) 1998

YESTERDAYS
Tracks as above
Atlantic 7567-82684-2 (Digitally remastered) 1998

GOING FOR THE ONE
Tracks as above
Atlantic 7567-82670-2 (Digitally remastered) 1998

TORMATO
Tracks as above
Atlantic 7567-82671-2 (Digitally remastered) 1998

DRAMA
Tracks as above
Atlantic 7567-82685-2 (Digitally remastered) 1998

YES – SOMETHING'S COMING: THE BBC RECORDINGS
1969-1970
Something's Coming/Everydays/Sweetness/Dear Father/Every Little
Thing/Looking Around/Sweet Dreams/Then/No Opportunity
Necessary,No Experience Needed/Astral Traveller/Then/Every Little
Thing/Everydays/For Everyone. *Bonus Tracks*: Sweetness/ Something's
Coming/Sweet Dreams/Beyond And Before
New Millennium Communications PILOT 25 (2 CD set) 1998
Released in the US as BEYOND AND BEFORE on Purple Pyramid
Records (CLP2462, 1998)
Also released in Italy by Getback Records on double vinyl album.

YES/ FRIENDS AND RELATIVES
Owner Of A Lonely Heart (98 Remake) (Jon Anderson)/Ice (Rick Wakeman)/
Red And White (Steve Howe)/Zone Of O (Esquire)/Up North (Earthworks &
Bill Bruford)/The Pyramids Of Egypt (Rick Wakeman)/Roundabout (Steve
Howe)/ Sync Or Swim (Wakeman With Wakeman)/Arthur (Rick
Wakeman)/Close To The Edge a. The Solid Time Of Change b. Total Mass
Retain c. I Get Up I Get Down d. Seasons Of Man (Yes)/No Expense Spared
(Wakeman With Wakeman)/Say (Jon Anderson)/Walk Don't Run (Steve
Howe)/Ron Thomi (Esquire)/10 Million (Jon Anderson)/Excerpt From Tales
From Topographic Ocean a. The Revealing Science Of God: Dance Of The
Dawn b. The Remembering: High The Memory c. The Ancient: Giants Under
The Sun d. Ritual (Steve Howe)/ The More You Know (Jon Anderson)/ Journey
(Rick Wakeman)/America (Yes)
Eagle Records EAG 091-2 (2 CD set) June 1998

THE LADDER
Homeworld (The Ladder)/It Will Be A Good Day (The River)/Lightning Strikes/
Can I?/Face To Face/If Only You Knew/To Be Alive (Hep Yadda)/Finally/The
Messenger/New Language/Nine Voices (Longwalker)
Eagle EDL EAG 254-2 September 1999

THE LADDER
Homeworld (The Ladder)/It Will Be A Good Day (The River)/Lightning Strikes/
Can I?/Face To Face/If Only You Knew/To Be Alive (Hep Yadda)/Finally/The
Messenger/New Language/Nine Voices (Longwalker)
Enhanced Bonus Disc: Homeworld (Live)/The Messenger (Live)/All Good
People (live video footage). Plus demo of Homeworld PCD Game, Screensaver
and Yes interview
Eagle EDL EAG 254-2 January 2000

CD ROM

YES ACTIVE
The Calling (CD version)/I Am Waiting (CD version)/I Am Waiting (live)/Real Love (CD version)/State Of Play (CD version)/State Of Play (demo version)/Walls (CD version)/Walls (live version)/Walls (instrumental version)/Where Will You Be (CD version)/Where Will You Be (instrumental)/Endless Dream (CD version)/Endless Dream (demo version)
US Compton's New Media 45445 06562 1995

ANDERSON, BRUFORD, WAKEMAN & HOWE
(Featuring Jon Anderson, Bill Bruford, Rick Wakeman and Steve Howe.)

7" Singles
Brother Of Mine (Edit)/Themes
UK Arista 112379 1989
(also UK picture disc)

Brother Of Mine/Themes
UK Arista 112444 June 1989

Order Of The Universe (Short Edit)/Fist Of Fire
UK Arista 112618 1990

10" Singles
Brother Of Mine (Edit)/Vultures (In The City)
UK Arista 260018 1989

12" Singles
Brother Of Mine/Themes: Sound/Second Attention/Soul Warrior/Vultures (In The City)
UK Arista 612 379 1989

Order Of The Universe (Long Edit)/Fist Of Fire/Order Of The Universe (Short Edit)
UK Arista 612618 November 1989

I'm Alive/Let's Pretend/Birthright (Live Version)
UK Arista 612770 1989

Cassette Singles
Brother Of Mine/Themes: Sound/Second Attention/Vultures (In The City)
US Arista CAS 9852 1989

Brother Of Mine/Themes: Sound/Second Attention/Vultures (In The City)
UK Arista 41007 1989

Quartet (I'm Alive) / Let's Pretend / Same
US Arista CAS 9898 1989

Order Of The Universe (Long Edit)/Fist Of Fire/Order Of The Universe
(Short Edit)
UK Arista 612618 November 1989

CD Singles

Brother Of Mine/Themes: Sound/ Second Attention/Soul Warrior/Vultures
(In The City)
UK Arista 662379 June 1989
US Arista 662379 (Picture disc)

Order Of The Universe (short edit)/Fist Of Fire
UK Arista 662693 October 1989

I'm Alive/Let's Pretend/Birthright (live)
UK Arista 662770 1989

Albums

ANDERSON, BRUFORD, WAKEMAN & HOWE
Themes/Sound/Second Attention/Soul Warrior/Fist Of Fire/Brother Of
Mine/The Big Dream/Nothing Can Come Between Us/Long Lost Brother
Of Mine/Birthright/The Meeting/Quartet/I Wanna Learn/She Gives Me
Love/Who Was The First/I'm Alive/Teakbois/ Order Of The
Universe/Order Theme/Rock Gives Courage/It's So Hard To Grow/ The
Universe/Let's Pretend
Arista 259970 June 1989
Reissued as Arista 262155 January 1992

ANDERSON, BRUFORD, WAKEMAN & HOWE: AN EVENING OF
YES MUSIC PLUS
Benjamin Britten's Young Persons Guide To The Orchestra/Time And A
Word/Teakbois/Owner Of A Lonely Heart/Clap/Mood For A Day/Gone
But Not Forgotten/Catherine Parr/Merlin The Magician/Long Distance
Runaround/Birthright/And You And I/Close To The Edge/Themes 1. Sound
2. Second Attention 3. Soul Warrior/ Brother Of Mine/Heart Of The
Sunrise/Order Of The Universe/Roundabout
Fragile Records CDFRL002 1993 (2 CD Set)